ART AND ARTIST

By Dr. Otto Rank

MODERN EDUCATION
A CRITIQUE OF ITS FUNDAMENTAL IDEAS

✽

Translated from the German by Mabel E. Moxon

HAVELOCK ELLIS *says: " Dr. Rank has a special claim to speak of education and psycho-analysis. For many years he was in the closest contact with Freud and has since taken a viewpoint of his own independent of the various schools. Moreover he posesses a remarkably wide culture and may be said to occupy today an international position. There must be many who will find his criticisms of this puzzling field of education as penetrating as I find them, and his suggestions as fruitful and worthy of meditation as they seem to me."*

AN AGATHON PRESS REPRINT

Art

AND ARTIST,

CREATIVE URGE AND
PERSONALITY DEVELOPMENT

by Otto Rank

with a preface by Ludwig Lewisohn
and a new foreword by Anaïs Nin

TRANSLATED FROM THE GERMAN BY
Charles Francis Atkinson

AGATHON PRESS
NEW YORK

Foreword © 1968 by Anaïs Nin
Used by permission of
The Journal of the Otto Rank Association

Reprinted 1968, 1975, with permission, by

AGATHON PRESS, INC.

15 East 26th Street
New York, NY 10010

Library of Congress Catalog Card Number: 68-16358 ✓
ISBN: 0-87586-010-9

Manufactured in the United States of America

FOREWORD

by Anaïs Nin

To fully recognize the relevance and contemporary quality of *Art and Artist*, a work written in the thirties and reprinted by Agathon Press, it is important to know the three vital impulses which directed thought towards the future through which he can be best understood today. First of all it was the work of a rebel, of a man who stood in a symbolic father-and-son relation to Freud, and who dared to diverge from his theories. Such a challenge of an already established and crystallized dogma is usually punished by repression, which is exactly what happened to Otto Rank. The disciples of Freud pursued a relentless excommunication which is only dying today with the man who practised it. He was erased from the history of psychoanalysis and from public evaluation of psychoanalytical movements. But his influence was strong, and expressed most directly through the Philadelphia School of Social Work.

The second vital factor was that Otto Rank was a poet, a novelist, a playwright, in short a literary man, so that when he examined the creative personality it was not only as a psychologist, but as an artist, and *Art and Artist* can be read both as an interpretation of the creative processes and an interpretation of art itself. These two aspects alone would suffice to gain him the appreciation of modern thinkers, but there was a third even more important to America's primary interest: Otto Rank was preoccupied with social problems, and felt individual therapy was not enough to solve its problems. He wanted it more widely and more generally applied and concentrated on its effectiveness through education and through the psychological training of social workers. He contributed to both. The Pennsylvania School of Social Work pioneered in this realm. Today The Otto Rank Association is responsible for disseminating his work actively and intelligently, and bringing about the reprinting of his books.

In *Art and Artist* Otto Rank treats of the relation between the artist and art. He states that "For the human urge to create does not find expression in works of art alone: it also produces religion and mythology and the social institutions corresponding to these." He defines the purpose of his book as one "going beyond the limits of the scientific absolutism that characterizes our modern psychology." In 1905 Rank had written, as a very young man, a short study of *The Artist* in which he tried to describe the psychology of a creative personality as psychologically intermediate between dreamer and neurotic. According to Rank, the two extremes of creativity, personal and collective, have been studied as separate rather than interrelated activities and it is his contention in *Art and Artist* that when examined more deeply the artist's work is related to the collective even if during his lifetime he seems to be running contrary to its course. In the chapter "Creative Urge and Personality" he underlines this distinction: "Religion springs from the collective belief in immortality; art from the personal consciousness of the individual."

He separates the artist from the neurotic: "The neurotic suffers fundamentally from the fact that he cannot or will not accept himself. The artist not only accepts his personality but goes far beyond it." Later on in the book he demonstrates how important this independence of the artist is for he has to remain separate and lucid in regard to the collective if he is to lead it, or illumine the way. Entering the intricate, subtle and complex art from the ideology conflicts, Rank brings us closer to present day problems. When the artist seems to be expressing a collective ideology he then makes the collective community feel its own immortality, he asserts the continuity of its life. If he seems to depart from this he is in a sense ostracized. Rank sees no such conflict between collective and individual art, only in those who do not grasp their interrelation: the critic. Rank demonstrates how art is born of a fear of loss and change. The problem lies in how to distinguish between the perishable, ephemeral forms meaningful only to the present and the eternal values. One of the most beautiful passages is in the opening of "Microcosm and Macrocosm":

> "The art work presents a unity, alike in its effect and in its creation, and this implies a spiritual unity between the artist and the recipient. Although temporary and symbolic only, this produces a satisfaction which suggests that it is more than a matter of passing identification of two individuals, that it is the potential restoration of a union with the cosmos which once existed and was then lost. The individual psychological root of this sense of unity I discovered (at the time of writing The Trauma of Birth) in the prenatal condition, which the individual in his yearning for immortality strives to restore. Already in that earliest stage of individualization, the child is not only factually one with the mother but, beyond all that, one with the world, with a cosmos, floating in mystic vapours in which present, past and future are dissolved. The individual urge to restore this lost unity is an essential factor in the production of human cultural values."

The last chapter of *Art and Artist* is devoted to "Success and Fame." In it Rank states:

There is always a distinct reaction of the artist not only against every kind of collectivization, but against the change of his own person, his work, and his ideology into an eternalization-symbol for a particular epoch. This resistance of the artist to his absorption into the community will show itself in more than his objection to success and fame; it will also influence his further activity so far as the assertion of his own individuality is concerned, and become a strong stimulus to further activity in general. Certainly this will be the case with the great artist who always tried to escape this collectivizing influence by deliberate new creations, whereas the weaker talent succumbs to a conscious concession to the masses or becomes mere raw material for the collective perpetuation instinct. These diverse outcomes of the struggle of the artist against success and fame, explain, too, how many of the greatest geniuses only attained fame after their own time, and, on the other hand, why mediocre gifts enjoy seemingly undeserved success."

This concept may be applied to Rank's own work and contribution, which were not in harmony with prevalent ideas of his time, which were original and a departure from dogmatism. This is the time for a just evaluation of his interpretation.

Anaïs Nin

"In the midst of the world," the creator said to Adam, "I have placed thee, so thou couldst look around so much easier, and see all that is in it. I created thee as a being neither celestial nor earthly, neither mortal nor immortal alone, so that thou shouldst be thy own free moulder and overcomer; thou canst degenerate to animal, and through thyself be reborn to godlike existence. Animals bring forth from the womb what they should have; the higher spirits, on the other hand, are from the beginning, or at least soon after, what they remain in all eternity. Thou alone hast power to develop and grow according to free will: in one word, thou hast the seeds of all-embracing life in thyself!"

PICO DELLA MIRANDOLA

PREFACE

by Ludwig Lewisohn

❧

Critics and historians of the arts must, at least in recent years, have become increasingly and uneasily aware of the fact that they were not in very close contact with their subject. Except in so far as they created independent and personal works of art by choosing as their subject-matter a work of art rather than an experience of life, they must in their heart of hearts have known that their statements could always be reduced to the formula: $A = A$. Henry James went abroad because he was not happy at home . . . Hawthorne wrote about a sense of guilt because he had a New England conscience . . . Shakspere and Michelangelo addressed their sonnets to youths because they had homo-erotic tendencies. . . . In all these statements and in a thousand far more complicated and apparently subtle ones the conjunction is meaningless. The statements are all reducible to $A = A$. And similarly all impressionistic critical statements, from the paragraph of the callowest reviewer to the stylistic exercitations of a Pater, a Jules Lemaître, or, if one likes, a Henry Mencken, could be reduced to the critic's assertion: I am I. . . .

From the days of Taine on, attempts have been made to remedy this state of affairs and to introduce into criticism a scientific element. But these attempts were foredoomed to failure. For they were all based upon the nineteenth-century notion of the universe as a machine. And this notion involved the supposition of the complete explicability of all phenomena. Yet it was observed that these mechanistic explanations always left Hamlet out of their play; that, in brief, like all merely mechanistic explanations, they left out the vital spark or soul or essence — the essential mark or quality or character that made the phenomenon what it was and differentiated it from others. Whatever well-formulated and even demonstrable " truth " these scientific explanations had, they had obviously no " reality " nor any profound relation to the living experience of any man in either the act of creation or that of appreciation. They told us many interesting superficial things. They never uttered the secret.

The Freudian psychology created the first revolution, the first radical change. Whatever its methodological limitations, to it belongs the undying credit of having revealed the structure of the human psyche, the character, at least, of the forces of which that psyche is the battle-field, and, finally and triumphantly, the identity of these forces with those in myth, in ritual; above all, in religion and in that whole congeries of qualities which differentiates man from the other primates and is at the root of the possibility of human culture. The limitation of the Freudian psychology was its general unwillingness to draw the ultimate conclusions inherent within itself. Like its great founder (cf. *The Future of an Illusion*) it was itself " sold " to nineteenth-century mechanistic doctrine; it, too, insisted on an unbroken chain of causality, of which all the links were to be the same in kind. It had the nineteenth-century passion for " reducing " all phenomena to a common denominator. And it had antecedently made up its mind as to the character of this denominator. Since man was " only " an animal by the general consent of a " scientific " age, it followed very smoothly that art should be " only " the sublimation of repressed sex-wishes. Hence the pure Freudian teaching gradually assumed a character of rigidity. Its brilliant beginnings were followed by no adequate developments. The Œdipus complex was used like an overdriven horse. If a man was an artist or a warrior or a neurotic or a tramp, he was convicted of having an Œdipus complex. But, as Dr. Rank admirably and convincingly points out, since all men have an Œdipus complex, since this relation and its difficulties are universal, the artist is still one who, by virtue of what he is in his own nature, reacts in a special way to this as to all other human experiences. And thus this so-called explanation leaves the mystery of genius exactly where it was before. Thus Freud and his original doctrine never quite transcended certain limitations of the century in which both were born.

It is the brilliant and memorable achievement of Dr. Otto Rank to have transcended these precise limitations. In a long series of works, culminating in recent years in *Wahrheit und Wirklichkeit* and, pre-eminently, in *Psychologie und Seelenglaube,* he has gradually and at last triumphantly brought the psychological interpretation of cultural phenomena from the nineteenth to the twentieth century. Precisely as the new physics, in its analysis of the atom, has come upon a dynamic element in a universe now no longer like a machine, so Dr. Rank, again like the physicists rejecting causality in its rigidly and hopelessly deterministic sense, has come upon a dynamic element in the human psyche and has reinstated in its proper place and function the psychology of the will. This revolutionary conclusion, derived from a quarter of a century of psycho-analytic practice, he has used in the interpretation of a vast mass of anthropological material and of material drawn from the history of the arts and of religion. He has descended to the centre from which all cultural phenomena radiate. He has intuitively grasped the realities of human processes by being at that centre and core of things. Much that he says is not either " demonstrated " or perhaps " demonstrable "; his arguments have no syllogistic structure. But anyone who has the creative experience will, like myself, read and ponder with a kind of awe the revelations concerning the character of that experience, especially in the opening and closing chapters of the work before us. The free creative and self-representative character of all art, its tendency of liberation from the biological, its self-justificatory and immortalizing urge, its need of and yet resistance to the collective culture of its age, the artist's conflict within the dualism of creativity and experience, his need of Muse and mate and the difficulty of combining the two, his resistance to his art itself, his desire for fame and his fear of being depersonalized by that essentially myth-making process — all these explanations and revelations made by Dr. Rank I cannot conscientiously call otherwise than literally epoch-making. They should and will open a new period in the study of the soul of the artist. They have, it is almost needless to say, this mark of all truths of the first order, that, once grasped, one can no longer imagine the landscape of the mind without them.

How, it may be asked, has Dr. Rank been able to arrive alone and uniquely — at least from the point of view of the English-speaking world — at this knowledge of the artist's soul and of the creative process? Because he has seen this process as a phase in that larger creative activity by which man, *being* man, has built up the totality of civilization. Thus, specifically, he has been able to interpret the development of creature to self-conscious creator in the course of the ages and, above all, the process whereby art gradually becomes differentiated from religion and tends finally to take religion's place. Thus he offers the first adequate explanation of that enormous preoccupation with art and with the artist which characterizes recent ages and, above all, the present age. He justifies and grounds both the artist's representative and his prophetic function, and will, I trust, free us, especially, again, in the English-speaking world, from that supremely silly and vicious notion that ranges art a little below flirting, a little — by courtesy — above baseball — among the pleasant ways of killing time. For he makes it abundantly and permanently clear that the emptiest-headed reader absorbed in an Edgar Wallace yarn is functioning in a manner basic to myth and religion, to all human psychology, to the entire civilizatory process.

In the natural and necessary course of his treatise, moreover, Dr. Rank solves a number of problems that have long vexed students of life and art and of the relations between them. Thus, for instance, he destroys the too facile notion of art as a by-

product of the sexual instinct, and points out the right and in-
extricable interrelations between these two urges. And thus, to
take an example from a different province, he solves the old
riddle of " imitation " in art, proving that the creative activity
is always a free and by intention a transcendent one, of which
" imitation " is but a cultural mood and method. I may finally
call the reader's attention to the extraordinary method of historical and psychological reasoning by which Dr. Rank reinter-
prets what the Romantics called " acceptance of the universe,"
and good and wise men of many ages " submission to the will of
God," as " volitional affirmation of the obligatory " and thus
shows us that the newest knowledge does but confirm the most
ancient wisdom of mankind.

This book does not need my commendation to psychologists.
Dr. Rank's reputation suffices. I am writing as one who has,
among other things, been engaged for many years in the art
and practice of criticism, who has seen all current methods
fail and all established techniques end in babble. As such I
would have this book gradually find its way into the hands of
all who " profess " literature, of all critics and reviewers and
students. It is calculated to create a revolution, to bring in a
time of deeper insight and of a more fruitful dealing with art
as an organic portion of that whole process and activity by
virtue of which man is human.

LUDWIG LEWISOHN

AUTHOR'S PREFACE

꙾

As this book treats of the *relation* between the artist and art, the field of its investigations is naturally a frontier strip. Consequently it requires not only an introduction to define its meaning and intention but, even before that, a negative delimitation for the purpose of excluding what is not, and is purposely not meant to be, included. Although it inevitably draws upon other subjects that are materially or intellectually relevant, it is neither a history of art nor a history of culture; neither an æsthetic of artistic effects nor a psychology of the artist in the narrower sense. At the same time, it is perhaps more than all these together, in that it attempts, first, to reveal the *human creative impulse,* broadly and genetically, and then to arrive at an understanding of its specifically artistic manifestations through their cultural development and spiritual significance. For the human urge to create does not find expression in works of art alone: it also produces religion and mythology and the social institutions corresponding to these. In a word, it produces the whole culture, of which the works of art in a particular style-epoch have to be regarded as one of the expression-forms. We shall therefore avoid, as far as may be, the attempt to " explain " completely any one of these expression-forms in terms of another one, and shall rather consider all the expression-forms of human culture, however various, first in relation to their origins in the creative impulse, and thereafter in respect of their *reciprocal action*. In this way we hope to avoid also a great deal of dry discussion of art, by resolving the material of debate in a higher synthesis, although in the course of this, new problems

will undoubtedly disclose themselves. For the difficulties arising out of conflicting opinions are, in many cases, only apparent, and due to the attempt of a biased individual to explain
things according to personal prejudices, such as, for instance,
the superiority of a particular culture or the preferableness of
a particular style or the eminence of a particular race over
all others.

In the course of our investigation we shall be able to show
how, in numerous disputed problems connected with the history of art and the psychology of artists, a method of treatment
that is founded on a sufficiently broad basis may reconcile all
the conflicting points of view; in particular, that to use the
social-psychological probe to penetrate into the individual,
while at the same time understanding the personal motive-
forces conditioning the collective ideologies, helps effectively
to co-ordinate all the individual branches of knowledge that
are necessary to the comprehension of so complex a structure as that presented by art. In any case, the previous attempts
to solve the problem of art one-sidedly — by cultural, ethnological, or stylistic standards — should warn us sufficiently
against drawing premature conclusions as to the specific characterization of artistic creativity. On the one hand, the individual urge to create is by no means the only specific quality of
the artist; equally, on the other hand, canons of style, evolved
from the collective consciousness, can by no means be regarded
as the true essence of artistic creation; the one individual factor represents merely the motive-power, while the other, collective, element provides the forms that are suited in the circumstances to its activity and utterance. Thus, also in the artist-type,
all that is characteristic is the specific *manner* in which he
reacts to the given individual and social phenomena — his ego
and the collective culture — the way, that is, in which he uses
the given *form,* inherent in the style, for the *artistic* expression
of his personal attitude. Correspondingly, in this presentation
we have on the one hand to put the collective cultural factor influencing the ideology of art on a far broader basis

than has heretofore been the case — that is, on the general human basis; and on the other hand we have to aim at a spiritual comprehension of these collective ideologies, which will only be made possible by going beyond the limits of the scientific absolutism that characterizes our modern psychology.

For even though the various human civilizations may each arise from the combination of a certain environment and a certain type of humanity, all human problems are, in the last resort, problems of the soul. By this we mean, not to say that the soul can be wholly explained in terms of modern psychology, as our mechanistic science would claim, but, on the contrary, to stress the autonomy of the spiritual, which not only works creatively in the religious, artistic, and social realms, but also determines the ideology which colours the psychology of the time. Such a borderline investigation of the various domains that surround the human creative impulse and its manifold forms of expression, it is therefore essential above all else to resist the temptation to accept any definite psychological theory as the principle of exegesis, remembering that the ruling psychological ideology itself appears to be as much in need of explanation as the other spiritual phenomena which it claims, either wholly or at least satisfactorily, to explain. For this satisfactory explanation, even if achieved, is often but a specious product resting on the ideological coincidence of the exegetical principle itself with the phenomenon to be explained. A fallacy of this sort can only be avoided if the various expression-forms of a cultural ideology are regarded primarily as parallel and equivalent phenomena of one and the same dynamic or organic process, which can only be comprehended through the whole process itself and are not explicable through one another. This being so, neither shall we expect that the artist's whole personality will be explained by his individual psychology. Rather do we hope, by a better understanding of the artist, as revealed by his artistic creativeness under the condition of the prevailing ideology, to throw some light on problems of personality development which the scientific method of psychology by its very nature must fail to solve.

In tracing the creative impulse, which manifests itself in such varied ways in the different ages and cultures, in its genetic development as to both individual and collective factors, we shall inevitably find that only a part of our material will be concerned with the actual artist-problem. Yet it seems to me not only unavoidable but positively essential to feel round the edges of the art-problem in this fashion, so that we may come to understand both the specifically artistic impulse to create and the moulding of its forms of creation as outgrowths of the contemporary culture and the individual dynamism underlying the artist-personality. A synthetic method of stating a problem, such as this, has of course disadvantages as well as advantages; but, in the present state of things, I consider it the only way in which understanding of the artist-problem can be promoted and attention drawn to various potential solutions that have hitherto been either unnoticed or inadequately recognised. Not that this book came into being through dissatisfaction with other art-theories and a desire to replace them by a better one: rather is it an organic growth rising out of an intensive struggle of many years' standing over a personal problem — a lived experience that ultimately took shape in the present work. The intention is, therefore, less to convince than to impress, the purpose in collecting this vast mass of material being solely that of giving an idea of the interlinkage and relationship of all the phenomena; but phenomena, as we know, may be interpreted in different ways, and it is only as *one* such interpretation of artistic creation that the book can be, or sets out to be, understood. This accounts, too, for the peculiar order of the problems and the consequent manner of their presentation.

Although this manner of presentation was the spontaneous result of the development of my own views, a glance at the existing state of research on art will show the crying need for

a comprehensive attempt to define the position.[1] For although
here and there a psychologist or a penetrating psychiatrist has
arrived at the conviction that the artist cannot be explained on
purely individual-psychological grounds, there have been art-
historians of high standing, particularly in the last quarter-
century, who have strained the — undoubtedly significant —
spiritual-historical aspect of art so far as almost to lose sight of
the creative artist himself in the process, reducing him indeed
to a mere tool of the *Zeitgeist*. In their laudable effort to present art as a part of the collective ideology, they have evolved
from the created work a psychology of the creative artist, with
the design not so much of elucidating the spiritual process of
production as of fitting in the artist somewhere or other. They
reserve a safe place, as one might say, for the creative personality in the general cultural milieu, for, after all, it cannot
be excluded entirely or wiped out of existence. Advanced
psychologists for their part will, on coming to the end of their
mechanistic wisdom, speak just as respectfully, though hardly
more understandingly, of the collective spirit of creative art
which they are apparently willing to acknowledge in some
way as a final irrational — and to them incomprehensible —
remainder of the art-problem. Between these two groups, the
spiritually and historically minded historians and the psychologically minded psychiatrists, there stand the modern æsthetes
whose interest lies in the psychological problems of art's boundaries. These come into close touch with first one, then the
other group, without finding the way out to a higher synthesis.
For just as the cultural-history outlook sees the artist only as
the vessel of a particular *Zeitgeist,* so the æsthetic studies him
primarily for his effect on the collective culture or its bearers,
the human beings belonging to it. But the psychologist again,
who prefers to study the creative process in the artist himself,
is too much inclined to underrate both his cultural dependence

[1] After completing my book, I came across an admirably clear and helpful statement of the presentday art problems in W. Passarge's *Philosophie der Kunstgeschichte
in der Gegenwart* (Berlin, 1930), which seems to make this need even more pressing.

and his æsthetic effectiveness, the factors that the other two modes of approach emphasize unduly.

But this one-sided and often polemical treatment of the subject from so many isolated view-points has at least had the effect, in recent years, of inspiring some attempt to bring these in line with one another, although no synthesis has yet emerged. The representatives of these respective interpretations regard each other with a certain respect — but get no further. Not only have they no common basis, such as might be found in that social psychology for which we are still waiting, but they also lack certain view-points which are fundamentally necessary in a cultural psychology of this order: the one, that of a cultural-genetic law of development, through which alone an understanding of the essential transformation of ideologies becomes possible; the other, a spiritual dynamism or dualism, which is not deterred by the finding of different and even opposing currents coexisting and equipotent within the same civilization or the same individual. Both ideas will be closely examined and explained in due course. For the present, however, we must continue our outlining of the general framework into which our investigation fits, no matter how unfamiliar our procedure may appear.

For if (as is here the case) one approaches the art-problem itself from a new aspect, it soon becomes clear that most of the related sciences, to which one would so gladly turn for information, fail one at the critical moments. To my mind, this very failure proves the ideological dependence, already alluded to, of the various competing sciences upon a dominating common culture. This ideological power, which appears to define, if not indeed to determine, the posing of problems (and even, to a certain extent, their solution) in all branches of scientific research within each particular cultural epoch, assumes, as is natural, different forms according to the world-outlook prevailing therein. But, consequently, an art-theory that is based on a particular philosophy or psychology, sociology or ethnology, has significance and usefulness only in so far as these sciences, themselves relative, are not altered by new discoveries or actually displaced by some radical change of outlook. This much indeed has been gained in recent years, that the kind of art-research which contented itself with applying a dictatorial scientific ideology to the problem of art has given way to a more profound conception: one which seeks to account for artistic creativity solely by its own inherent tendencies and feeling for norms. But, while admitting the superiority of the second method, both of these lines of thought seem to me to have been too extreme. If, for instance, the English sociologist Herbert Spencer and the French philosopher Taine stretched the evolutionary point in trying to explain all artistic creativity, equally the newer science of art and æsthetics in our own century stretches the norm-sense inherent in artistic creativity too far. How closely the spiritual-historical treatment of art, otherwise so alien to a psychologizing æsthetic, approaches it in this regard may be seen from a comparison of Dvořák's *Kunstgeschichte als Geistesgeschichte* (Munich, 1924) with Utitz's *Grundlegung der allgemeinen Kunstwissenschaft* (Stuttgart, 1914 and 1920). In Utitz the æsthetic, almost more even than in Dvořák the historian, we find stress laid on art as a world *sui generis,* objective in itself, and almost opposed by contrast to the artist. " Art determines the artist," says Utitz, " as science its disciples. In this regard the artist appears only as a creator of art. . . . It is our task to interpret the artist's character as such through the nature of art itself."

In opposition to this extreme standpoint we have the psychological efforts to grasp art through the problem of the individual artist. The two currents, that of the " natural " scientist's evolutionism and that of the " philosophical " scientist's psychology, which prevailed at the beginning of the nineteenth century are summed up by Wundt in his comprehensive *Völkerpsychologie* in an imposing thesis; but this also was doomed to sterility. With the ushering in of the new century psychoanalysis appeared which soon advanced from its original pathological sphere into the general human and cultural field. Psycho-analysts claimed to have contributed substantially to an understanding of the artist's psychology, and so to have opened up new paths in the study of art. But this hope, too, was stifled, after a promising beginning, by the dogmatism inherent in every mechanistic principle of interpretation, and no permanent contribution was made either to the science of art or to biography, although Freud himself gave valuable aid in the interpretation of a partial problem: that of æsthetic pleasure. In this he was definitely inspired by Theodor Lipps, the father of modern æsthetic, without whose subtle preparatory research Freud's own contributions to an understanding of æsthetic pleasure are unthinkable. But this remained an isolated contribution, which could not be developed either by art-historians sailing in the wake of philosophical science, or by æsthetes with psychological interests. For the former, they savoured too much of the psychology of the individual; for the latter, they were too specialized. The one group was too remote from psycho-analysis, the other too much opposed to it, to be able to make useful application of its ideas to the science of art.

I myself approached the problem of art from the individualist side of the artist's personality a good quarter of a century ago, after my first introduction to psycho-analysis. In 1905, when Freud's investigations stood at the zenith of pre-war materialism,[1] I wrote a short study on *The Artist,* in which I tried to produce a psychology of the creative personality; simultaneously, however, I developed a new theory of art up to a point which made it possible, quite recently, for the German art-historian E. von Sydow to say that I was "the only one who had produced a system of æsthetic within the framework of a

[1] It was in this year that Freud's basic work: *The Interpretation of Dreams* (1900) was followed by two supplementary studies on which I mainly relied in my youthful work of that period. These were his *Three Contributions to the Theory of Sex* and *Wit and its Relation to the Unconscious.* My own book appeared in 1907 with the title: *Der Künstler* and the sub-title: *Ansätze zu einer Sexualpsychologie* (an enlarged second and third edition appeared in 1918). *Der Künstler und andere Beiträge zur Psychoanalyse des dichterischen Schaffens* (fourth enlarged edition, 1925).

general cultural philosophy with psycho-analytical material." [1]
I only allude to this twenty-five-year-old work of my youth as
being the starting-point of my development; for although
written very much under the spell of the Freudian idea, it did
try to reach out beyond its mechanistic mentality to a genetic
cultural outlook founded on spiritual dynamism. And although my terminology was at that time essentially Freudian
— for I regarded the artist as psychologically intermediate between the dreamer and the neurotic — the actual problem of
the genesis of the artistic *personality* and the idea of attacking it from the spiritual-historical point of view were my own.
In the twenty-five years which have since elapsed, I have not,
at bottom, receded from this theme of my youth, although it
is only now that I return to it after a long but fruitful detour.
For in the mean time I have been chiefly occupied with two
borderland problems, which have brought me in many respects
closer to the understanding of our particular subject here, the
artist, but which are comprehensive enough for it to be unnecessary to excuse myself for the time spent on them. The one
theme is the individual-psychological development of personality which after an exhaustive study of this development in
thwarted neurotics, I was able finally to base on a dynamic will-
psychology. The second theme is that of collective creations,
as we meet them in primitive art, particularly in the myth
and its poetical offshoots, the fairy-tale, the saga, and the
epic.

In regarding these studies — which became steadily more
independent — as preliminaries to a deeper grasp of the artist-
problem, I should not omit to mention a certain negative

[1] In his book: *Primitive Kunst und Psychoanalyse* (1927), Sydow, who considered my
early theory of art too one-sided, as being suited only to one particular type—namely,
the Romantic—has in his own studies committed himself to an all too schematic "application" of the psycho-analytical theory—a danger which I had at least avoided,
although it was then a more threatening one than now, when psycho-analysis is
itself striving (though vainly) to overcome this schematism. Had Sydow also taken
my book: *The Trauma of Birth* (1924) into consideration, he would, besides obtaining
a more complete picture of my conception of art, have realized that the one genuinely
unforced application of psycho-analysis to the genesis of art is there anticipated in
reference to the genesis of architecture.

achievement: the fact that during all the years when I was constantly absorbed by problems, particularly those connected with poetry, I did not attempt a single biography (or pathography) of a famous artist. A sound instinct — for it was no deliberate purpose — seems always to have restrained me from this. For anything in the nature of psychographic material and view-points that I myself had to contribute invariably presented itself to me at once as something fitting into a larger frame, which, reaching out beyond the individual artist-personality, concerned either the study of motives, or the literary overhauling of traditional materials, or the social function of art.[1] In this book also, as in all my works on the psychology of art, I propose to follow the line of reaching out beyond what is individual in the artist-personality and to show, or at least suggest, the collective aspect, whether as material, inspiration, or ultimate aim. My intention is to point out the relation between these two tendencies, inherent in art and in creativity: the individual and the collective, the personal and the social, in their interaction, and correspondingly in their counteraction. For now, more than ever before, my feeling is insistent that artistic creativity, and indeed the human creative impulse generally, originate solely in the constructive harmonising of this fundamental dualism of all life. I arrived at this conception by a concentrated psychological study of the two human types which most clearly reveal success and failure in this struggle to overcome: the so-called neurotic type, and the creative.

Among my preliminary studies on the comprehension of art, *The Trauma of Birth* (1924) holds a unique position; for it represents the first attempt to free myself once and for all from the prevailing conception of art and also from

[1] *Das Inzest-Motiv in Dichtung und Sage. Grundzüge einer Psychologie des dichterischen Schaffens* (1912; second edition, 1926). *Die Lohengrinsage. Ein Beitrag zu ihrer Motivgestaltung und Deutung* (1911). *Der Sinn der Griselda-Fabel* (*Imago*, I, 1912). *Die Nacktheit in Sage und Dichtung* (ibid., II, 1913). *Der Doppelgänger* (ibid., III, 1914; separately, 1925). *Die Don Juan-Gestalt. Ein Beitrag zum Verständnis der sozialen Function der Dichtkunst* (ibid., VIII, 1922; separately, 1924). The last two essays are now available in a French translation under the title: *Don Juan. Une étude sur le Double* (Paris 1932).

the ideological constraint of Freudian psycho-analysis. In the chapter dealing with "artistic idealization" (pages 141 squ.) I tried to go beyond traditional artist-psychology and æsthetics for the origins of the two essential problems of all artistic creativity — the urge to create and the imparting of form — and to trace them to a basic spiritual principle of which the general form may be stated as the *gradual freeing of the individual from dependence.* And although this *self-creative development of personality* could in that particular context only be dealt with cursorily and also with a one-sided emphasis on biological dependence on the mother, there was already at least a hint of the essence of my conception of art in the view therein expressed that the form of a work of art not only is defined by the tendency of the creative impulse, but is already implicit in its very nature. "To draw attention to this law of form, determinative of content and biologically soundly based, and, here and there, to suggest, rather than solve, the problems cropping up behind it, are the main purpose of this book" (op. cit., page 4, Foreword). And whereas in my first book the sexual impulse (expanded to the libido-conception of Freud) and its repression had been taken to be the kernel of the creative impulse, in *The Trauma of Birth* I discerned the fact, which later I developed theoretically, that the creative impulse which leads to the liberation and forming of the individual personality — and likewise determines its artistic creativeness — has something positively antisexual in its yearning for independence of organic conditions. Correspondingly, my conception of repression differed from Freud's; for to him it is the result of *outward* frustration, while I trace it to an *inward* necessity, which is no less inherent in the dualistic individual than the satisfying of the impulse itself.

But in the course of this expansion of the biological repression-principle, on which my earliest view of the psychology of the artist-type was so one-sidedly built up (through the *creative will-principle,* the spirituality of which it is that predetermines the artistic urge to create), I have been forced into another conception of the part played by the collective element. That element, which undeniably exists in artistic creativity, I no longer reduced to the individual's biological self, but sought and found in his social environment, as also in the general ideology of the culture. It is, however, only through the individual efforts and cultural influences, of all sorts and all values, collaborating in it that the prevailing art-form, whatever it may be, becomes intelligible. This is why, in studying *primitive* art, as first set forth by Ernst Grosse (*Die Anfänge der Kunst;* Freiburg, 1894), we find chiefly the *social factor* figuring as the main element in artistic production,[1] the more so since we are debarred from any knowledge of the artists who practised in these periods. When, on the other hand, M. Hörnes (*Urgeschichte der bildenden Kunst in Europa;* 1898) sees in the practice of primitive artistic activity the satisfying of a purely individual need, or even a personal utility purpose, he is merely underlining that individual, motivation which is inherent in all productive art and may quite well have been stronger in the prehistoric period with which he deals than we find it in the "primitive" peoples who are historically known and whose ideology is definitely a collective one. This existence of an art which is (at least so far as we can tell) without artists has its paradoxical parallel on the individual-psychological side. For if the neurotic type, who fails to synthesize his dualistic conflict, be studied from the therapeutic angle, the impression received is that of individuals who (psychologically speaking) represent the artist-type without having ever produced a work of art.[2] It is to be observed that they do not produce inferior artistic specimens — either they do not produce at all or what they produce is not art. In short, it would seem that the creatively disposed and gifted type has to have something in addition

[1] Yrjö Hirn, in his book on the *Origins of Art* (1900), also ascribes primitive artistic activity to the social urge of enjoying or imparting pleasure. A similar intermediate standpoint between the individual and the social factors is adopted by Wundt in his *Völkerpsychologie* (Vol. III, second edition, 1908).

[2] With reference to productive forces in the neurotic type, see my *Analyse des Analytikers und seiner Rolle in der Gesamtsituation* (Vienna and Leipzig, 1931).

before it can become a really productive artist, while on the other hand the work of the productive individual must also be added to before it can rank as a genuine work of art.

Neither the cultural and scientific history of art nor the æsthetic psychology of the artist has so far provided a satisfactory answer to this central question of the whole problem of art: namely, what constitutes the correlation between the artist-type and the art-product; that is to say, the artistic creativeness and the art-form? And although it may seem evident that this common factor in the artist and the art-product must be a super-individual, collective element, so obvious a conclusion at once raises a series of questions, the mere meaning of which is enough to show that they but make the real problem more acute. The first among such questions is likely to be: what does this collective factor, both generally and particularly in the creative individual, mean? Following directly upon this comes the next question: what is the characteristic which distinguishes the specific *artistic* collectivity — subjective or objective — from others, such as religious, social, or national? In other words, why does the individual, endowed with this mysterious collective force, become now a popular leader, now the founder of a religion, and now an artist? For all such individuals appear to possess some super-individual source of power which makes them sure of influencing their contemporaries and those who come after them.[1] The sole explanation of this riddle — and the one which has had to serve us for close on two thousand years — is the assumption of a genius working within the artist; usually the genius is imagined as something divine, but this is only the religious formulation of a collective spirit. Even for so fine a psychologist as Lipps, who accounts for the æsthetic effect of a work of art by intuition (*Einfühlung*), this genius is a gift from heaven; and when Dessoir, in his *Æsthetics,* gives this mysterious something the designation of the unconscious — a dubious psychological conception in

[1] Compare with this what is said concerning the "leader" problem in my book *Modern Education,* chapter v. (New York: Alfred A. Knopf; 1932.)

any case — he has not elucidated any of its mysteriousness by so doing. For if one is not prepared to interpret the unconscious in the rationalistic sense of psycho-analysis as the repressed impulse, it remains but a pseudo-scientific metaphor for the inconceivable, the divine, just as the collectivity resolves itself according to Utitz into a social representation of the unconscious divinity.

Without wishing to forestall what will be said later on of the problem of genius and the divine spark in the artist, I must nevertheless allude here to yet another — and the last — of the preliminary studies in which I aimed at estimating the general significance and effectiveness of the universal spiritual principle which also, in a special form, is the source of artistic creativity. In the book referred to, *Seelenglaube und Psychologie* (1930), I made the first attempt to find, on social-psychological lines, a common spiritual root for the meaning and origin of collective ideologies. This root I conceived to be the belief in immortality, and this belief I regarded (if one can say so of any one belief) as *the* original ideology, out of which, as it became increasingly untenable, there arose various others, more securely anchored in reality, but always animated by the same immortalization tendency. In religion this is of course obvious, but in the social ideologies too, with their political form and their national content, the tendency towards a collective conception of immortality is easily recognizable.[1] In artistic creativity the same tendency is easy to detect, if one starts from the psychology of the individual artist and his inherent tendency to strive towards a goal. For whatever the artist achieves by his successful work is in actual fact immortality, a result from which we need only infer this intention in order to obtain an understanding of the individual will to art as a personal urge to immortality. In this sense, however, the feeling of immortality is not only the result of creating but actually the presupposition on which it rests. This

[1] Burke, for instance, in his famous *Reflections on the Revolution in France*, conceives of the state as a concretized immortality. Fichte, too, emphasized the immortality of national ideologies in his *Reden an die deutsche Nation*.

paradoxical relation of things gives us timely warning not to look upon the urge to personal immortalization as the sole source of the artistic creative impulse, but to seek out those special characteristics of the artist-type which lead him and enable him to satisfy this universal human craving in the particular æsthetic form provided by the style-laws of his cultural epoch.

And so we are thrown back from the artist's psychology on to style-psychology — and this is bound to happen frequently in the course of our investigations. We should, however, welcome it rather than resent it; for it is only through a synthetic comprehension of all the factors concerned with artistic production and achievement that we can make any progress in understanding the general problem of art as such and go beyond the narrowness of professional learning. Yet we ought not to forget withal that we owe to all these numerous separate investigations in the domains of style, folk-lore, and cultural history — one-sided though they may be in some respects — not only stimuli of many kinds, but even the very possibility of some synthetic integration of the whole. And here I should like to emphasize that I have tried to avoid giving undue weight to my own sphere of work, psychology, or giving it as an explanatory principle any exterritorial immunity. I take as illustrations those materials and view-points which seem to me to yield the most all-round picture of the art-problem. They come from the most varied scientific fields (including my own); and in this way I hope at least to bridge over those technical and scientific barriers which have up till now been rendered insurmountable by certain problems, in particular those of the borderland phenomena. For the rest, I leave it to the art-critics and the productive artists themselves to judge the extent to which my basic conception of the artistic creative impulse is helpful in their special domain or to the development of their own personalities.

Paris
December 1930

CONTENTS

❧

ILLUSTRATIONS

❦

ℜ Illustrations ℜ

Illustrations

INTRODUCTION

※

In art, as in everything living, there is no progress, but only varieties of one stimulus.

HEBBEL

INTRODUCTION

꧁꧂

If, on my returning after more than twenty-five years to my original artist-problem, I am able to put forward my conception of artistic creativity in a comprehensive form, I owe it not merely to the course of my own development, but also to the advances that have been made in the most varied departments of knowledge. For it was precisely in the period following the turn of the century, during which I struggled through to my own world-outlook, that the branches of knowledge bearing particularly on the study of art made such enormous progress as to necessitate a re-orientation of the whole art-problem. But without the asset of the experience I had gained in winning through to an independent outlook, I should, as a layman in the domain of art, hardly have been entitled to compete with the array of prominent specialists (above all, German) who, during that period, raised modern art-history to a level never before thought of. To me, however, the whole science of art seems to be permeated, as I have said before, with a far-reaching dualism, which not only comes out in differences of opinion among different scholars and the divergences of their schools, but reflects the dualism inherent in the problem of art itself. Now, my view of psychological problems included from the first the knowledge and acknowledgment of a dualism inherent in the individual and not dependent on any external opposition for its existence. It seems to me, therefore, that my whole conception of man should not only lead to a better understanding of the dualist nature of art, but also, to a great extent, help to overcome the contradictions arising from that dualism in the history of art-criticism.

The comparative method of treatment, which we have to use in studying the genesis of the creative impulse, may at the same time be used to clear up satisfactorily a number of contradictions, not intrinsically part of the problem of art itself, but brought into it from neighbouring spheres, and in the course of applying these to the understanding of art. If we reject those methods of psychological investigation which, from time immemorial, have assumed two types of artist and played off the one against the other, we are left with three important provinces of knowledge, all of which have disappointed expectations as to the value of their specialized advances to the science of art. These provinces are: *cultural history,* which, since the turn of the century, has opened up practically a new world of prehistory through archæology; then, in its wake, the study of *race* and the migration of peoples, the ethnological problems of which have been revived as determining the rise, decline, and supersession of the cultures; and, lastly, the *history of style,* the revision of which had become imperative since the materialistic conception of art that prevailed in the nineteenth century, culminating in Semper's " *Styl.*" In this last branch, thanks to Riegl, there was definitive progress in the attitude towards, and understanding of, art. But, considering the recent date of all these scientific achievements, we need not wonder that the historical treatment of the positively overwhelming mass of cultural and ethnological material provided by archæology in recent decades has not yet arrived at a uniform interpretation. Too much preliminary work had to be done by the specialized experts before they could arrive at any but provisional conclusions as to the significance of their excavations and discoveries.

Casual and most incomplete as are the data provided by the archæologists' recent discovery of prehistoric art when we try to survey them, in conjunction with the contemporary work of ethnologists on the practice of art by primitive peoples, we

see not only that an immense amount of work has been achieved
in a comparatively short time, but also that unsuspected problems have come up along with these results.[1] Conze, indeed,
had dealt with prehistory as early as 1871, but when we remember that it was not until 1879 that the Spaniard de Santuola
published his first report on the European cave-paintings of
the ice age, we realize the scope of the task which prehistoric
research has set the men of our own time. Moreover, if we
consider that the authenticity of this earliest report of the
incredible artistic skill of palæolithic man was at first disputed,
and that it took the discovery of the cave at La Mouthe, in
the south of France, to convince the prehistorians and lead
them to continue their researches, we shall realize how young
our knowledge of this hitherto unsuspected art-world is. It
was much the same with the art of the primitives: this was
really only included officially in the general scheme of art-
history in 1900, with K. Woermann's *Geschichte der Kunst
aller Zeiten und Völker,* after Ernst Grosse had written the
first comprehensive study of it in 1894.[2] Even the preliminary
monographs by Hildebrand (Eskimo, 1885), Hain (Dyaks,
1890), Stolpe (Hervey Islanders, 1892), von den Steinen (Bra-
zilians, 1894), Schurz (Indians, 1895), and Frobenius (Africans, 1895) appeared only just before the turn of the century,
although there have been innumerable publications since. The
same applies to the archæological discoveries in the prehistory
of civilized races. Take, for instance, Schliemann's excavations in Mycenæ in 1874, which were only brought to a successful conclusion after the turn of the century, by Dorpfeld at
Troy. It was only in 1895 that Sir Flinders Petrie started on
the excavations in Egypt which gave an entirely new picture
of its early times; it is the same with Crete, the quite recent

[1] While reading the proofs, I come across a very helpful survey of archæological
discoveries in the twentieth century by Friedrich von Oppeln-Bronikowski: Archäologische Entdeckungen im 20. Jahrhundert (Berlin, 1931).

[2] It is hardly necessary to refer to the very cursory treatment of primitive art,
written under the influence of Romanticism, by Franz Kugler in the first history of
art (1842).

archæological exploitation of which by Sir Arthur Evans is of incalculable significance for the history of art. (Excavation was begun there in 1899.) [1] Equally recent is the information that we have obtained about America's pre-Columbian art and particularly the magnificent Mayan monuments in the south. Once the late palæolithic wall-paintings of Spain had been discovered, in 1908, an incredibly large number of them were found in succession. The very similar cave-paintings of the South Africans, commonly called " Bushman art," have, again, only been revealed to us in the present century by the untiring research of Frobenius.

As we shall frequently have occasion to refer to the contributions made to art-history by these various discoveries and the research connected with them, in which leading prehistorians — Hörnes, Obermaier, Hauser, Klaatsch, and others — have also taken part, we turn for the moment, in this general survey, to the cultural-historical and ethnological problems on which some new light has been thrown by these glimpses into prehistory. In particular, prehistoric Europe has been elevated from its rôle of Cinderella by the abundant stone-age discoveries that have been made within its limits. For Europe has long been overshadowed by the ancient high cultures of the East, from which all the light which illuminated our old continent was supposed to come. And although, in the first joy of rediscovery, the new princess may have been acclaimed to excess, the fact remains that now any intelligent history of Europe that is not a mere relic of the school-books must be begun long before the great Migrations. So that, even after discounting the unnatural, but rather too subjective, nationalist enthusiasms of certain Germanic researchers for the newly discovered prehistory of Europe, we still have enough sure material to account for a Northern cultural circle with potentialities of influence similar to those of the better-known cultures of the South and particularly the East. As we shall have to deal with

---

[1] The third and last volume of Evans's great work on Crete appeared while the present book was being written, in the winter of 1930.

various special investigations of this description (such as Krause's *Trojaburgen,* 1893; Muchau's *Pfahlhausbau,* 1909; Scheltema's *Altnordische Kunst,* 1923) more thoroughly later, we will here refer to one only: namely, Carl Schuchhardt's *Alteuropa* — not only a basic work, but one of particular value for the cultural-historical aspect of art, in that it has kept fairly clear of the pitfall of national bias. The first edition (1918) bears the sub-title: " in its cultural and stylistic development "; the second edition, considerably altered and enlarged, appeared as: *A Prehistory of our Continent (Eine Vorgeschichte unseres Erdteils;* Berlin, 1926). The fact that Schuchhardt's conception of art is still the purely technical-mechanical Semperism of last century does not lessen the value of his observations on cultural- and folk-history, for there is only one of his opinions which essentially need concern us here: namely that, even in prehistoric times, he finds definite evidence of the same contrast between North and South which is found in the historical periods of artistic development, as, for instance, in the struggle between Gothic and Renaissance. And this dualism is not limited to Europe, at any rate as the term is understood in our present historical geography. Southern France, for instance, shows a stone age similar to that of North Africa, and, in the East, the radiation from the Southern cultural zone of the Mediterranean races did not stop short at the borders of Asia. If, for a start, we admit the distinctiveness and independence of the three culture-zones — Northern, South-western, and Eastern — as they are indicated by nature and established by archæological discoveries, we get a new picture of cultural development which will be full of significance for the understanding of the forms and styles of art as well.

These three great culture-zones, differentiated even in prehistoric times, were bound, sooner or later, to meet in the Mediterranean and create a mixed culture, which in its turn was quite distinctive and, as is not surprising, brought forth a human type of many and varied talents. The culture which we have recently come to know as the Cretan-Mycenæan leaves us in no doubt that historic Greece also was a result of these cultural mixings in " the Balkans," although at the same time we see something greater, too — the birth of a new and more harmonious type of human being which was at once the end-product and the conqueror of the old. Whether the now undeniable existence of Northern influence side by side with that of the South-west and the East is a justification of the theory of an Indo-Germanic penetration of Hellas is of little importance, compared with the fact that the influences of Northern and South-western cultural elements are now taking their rightful place along with those of the once un-challengeable East. All the same, it would be premature to throw the old formula *Ex oriente lux* overboard without more ado; rather does it seem that a new meaning can be given to it if we limit its application to a particular world-outlook which with good reason we may call the pre-scientific. For that which has undeniably enlightened our culture from the East is the intellectual penetration of phenomena with the tend-ency to bring them into a system, whether it be of a myth-ological, religious, or philosophical nature. In other words, it is intellectualism that we have taken from the East, while the North shows the opposite tendency towards the mystic, the nebulous, and the spiritual as against the intellectual. The South, again, shows a pretty definite leaning towards naturalism, which is alien to both the other cultures, in its direct association with nature; nay, more in the oneness of its human type with nature, which climatic reasons, not to mention others, cause the Northerner to reject, while the East is antipa-thetic to nature precisely on account of its hyper-intellectuality.

Be this as it may, there is one point on which almost all our scholars, writers of cultural history, and art-critics are agreed: that the North has produced an abstract, geometrical style of art, whereas the peculiar characteristic of the Southern style is natu-ralism. Only the East has proved difficult to " place"; for, from having been over-estimated as the prime source of all human culture, it is now denied any influence whatever. And so it comes about that we have Pan-Babylonians and Pan-Germanics opposing each other, each school trying to prove the superiority or independence of its own culture instead of taking trouble to analyse its specific characteristics. We shall presently be able to demonstrate, in connexion with a particular problem, not only how each of the three cultural zones excelled in the production of different art-forms, but how even today an intelligent comparison of the respective cultural materials may throw light on one and the same problem from different sides. For instance, in accounting for the widespread spiral ornament, we shall find the most and the best historical data in the North, while the South will contribute the nature myths necessary to its interpretation, and the East an explanation of it which borders on the scientific. While art- and culture-history are, quite rightly, interested in the succession in time of the phenomena and the different influences under which they come into being, we, on the other hand, regard it as our task to establish, not the spatial "whence" or the temporal "since when," but *the spiritual why*. This does not imply any intention of denying the effect of culture-drift or the importance of historical sequence; we merely think that the problem as to how the phenomenon in question arose at all — no matter when and where — is entitled to be considered at least as worthy of an attempt at solution.

We have discussed the cultural-historical aspects of the art-problem somewhat in detail here, because by implication they contain the style-problems within themselves. For if we identify the North with abstract and the South with naturalistic art, we present at the same time the psychological characterization of a corresponding human type who will produce just this kind of style. It is true that "North" and "South" are terms essentially referring to climate and the economic conditions dependent on climate; but these things do, after all, contribute definitely to the production of the human type concerned. And we must not forget that man is not *only* a product of his natural environment, since the essence of every culture is

determined by the greater or less degree of its domination of
nature and independence of her influences. In looking at art
from the ethnological or economic standpoint, we are apt to
overlook the fact that art is produced by man and not by Nature, although it is Nature that helps to form and educate man.
Here, again, the artist with his creative personality is almost
eliminated, as he is from the spiritual and scientific history of
art and the æsthetic which borders on psychology. Not only
does this apply to the prehistoric age, for which no report on
the individual man can reach us; it applies also to the artistic
development which works itself out in the full light of history.
When writers on art speak of a Gothic artist or an Impres-
sionist, they refer of course to the laws of style revealed in his
work. But the individual artist who employs this style as a
form of expression is something more than a mere representative of this tendency; and one often wonders what psychological significance such an æsthetic classification really has. To
put it in another way, does the Gothic artist stand for a particular type of man? And, supposing that he has found his
expression in the North, what is his spiritual structure, and
can it perhaps take root elsewhere than in Northern mother
earth — as was the case, we take it, with Michelangelo? And
will not a strong personality, like Michelangelo in the South,
or Goethe in the North, be inclined in any case to take over
the given art-forms, indeed, and even to develop them, but also
to break through, to overcome, these forms, to mix them with
others, to supplant them by others?

The fact that this not only is possible, but does actually occur
in the case of almost every great artist-personality, brings us
back to our *spiritual* dualism and to the experience that at any
rate the two tendencies — call them what one will — must be
potentially present in the artist, even though both do not always
find expression. In mentioning the following treatises on the
derivation of the creative impulse from this conflicting dualism,
I would remind my readers that even cool-eyed art-historians
are forced in the end to some such conception of the transmu-

tation of the laws of style. Two important critical studies on art which appeared in the same year (1923) arrive from totally different starting-points at the one conclusion: that the two opposing tendencies of style (which Scheltema in *Altnordische Kunst* calls "mechanical" and "organic," and Herbert Kühn in *Kunst der Primitiven* "imaginative" and "sensory") co-exist side by side and even develop one out of the other. Kühn starts from economic factors — wherein he had been antici-pated by Grosse and to some extent Hörnes — and connects naturalistic art with the nomadic hunter's existence, and the abstract art-form with that of the farmers and cattle-breeders who have settled on the soil. These simple parallels between economic forms and art-forms, which have been extended by others to the family organization (matriarchal = naturalistic; patriarchal = abstract), are applied by Kühn to a psychological opposition of consumption and production on the basis of the Marxian theory. He sees the hunter as leading an existence which mainly absorbs from outside and having in consequence a naturalistic conception of art-forms; whereas agrarian cul-ture is one of fruitfulness in creative art as in other respects. Kühn does not, indeed, as we have seen, accept any opposition of principle between the two tendencies, but deduces the one by a dialectical process from the other. But in one culture-zone it will be a development from the sensory to the imaginative, as in the South Seas or in Africa, where the natural model becomes geometricized; and another time — say, in the North — it will be the other way round, a development from the geometric style to the organic.

A similar process of development is recognized by Scheltema in his deep and subtle analysis of the style of specifically Northern art-forms. These he does not derive from economic forms, like Kühn, or technical-practical motives, like Schuch-hardt, but accounts for on a principle of spiritual development. While Scheltema, who has confined his special research to a strictly limited and definite field, sees the same development from abstract to organic repeated in every single phase of

xlv

development of Northern art, from the stone age to the bronze and iron ages, Kühn, with a wider scope, has managed to establish the recurrence of one law of development at different times and different places almost throughout the history of art. Thus in Crete a peak period of imaginative art was followed by frank sensorialism. "Altered in form, and yet quite similar, was the change which took place under the same laws, thousands of years afterwards, in America among the Aztecs and Incas, and again, centuries later, in Africa among the conquering races of Benin and Yoruba. In all these cultures the way leads unmistakably from imaginative to sensorial art, from collectivism to individualism, from the dualist outlook to the unitary, and from the strongly religious world to the practical everyday society." [1] The only exception to this rule that development leads from abstract to concrete appears to occur in the case of palæolithic man's naturalistic art. Scheltema excludes this art from his survey on the ground that no further artistic development from it is possible, and that the abstract art-form of the neolithic age is primary and intrinsic in the North. But I do not think the question can be disposed of so simply. For one thing, we cannot divide off the Northern neolithic so sharply from the Southern, for all their differences; and, for another, it remains doubtful whether the naturalism of the glacial age really represents the beginning of all artistic activity, whether, in fact, there are not more abstract art-forms, completely lost to us, which preceded it. It is risky to reconstruct the mentality of these people on no other evidences than the artistic remains of the glacial age which have been accidentally preserved. But it is nevertheless noteworthy that the sole explanation of the appearance of such highly developed drawing and pictorial art as this palæolithic has handed down to us comes from a physiologist, Max Verworn. In his book: *Zur Psychologie der primitiven Kunst* (1908) the scholar declares this art to be a " physioplastic " reproduction of nature which, in contrast to the later " ideoplastic " treat-

---

[1] Herbert Kühn: *Kunst der Primitiven*, p. 120.

ment, has a certain spontaneity, instinctiveness, and non-reflectiveness. It does not seem to me that this view does much more than give us a terminology that strikingly expresses the dualism which lies at the base of all artistic production, although it does at least imply an attempt at evaluation instead of a mere description. For even if we accept Verworn's terminology, we are still obliged to assume that glacial man, although in the main physioplastic in his rendering, must also have had ideo-plastic possibilities of no rudimentary order; otherwise he would not have been in a position to produce a work of art intuitively. All art, whether primarily naturalistic or primarily abstract, unites both elements within itself, and indeed itself arises (as we shall see) from a conflict between the two tendencies, of which first one, then the other, gains the upper hand. The decision does not, however, depend only on the culture and its economic environment, but equally upon the creative individual, in whom the same dualistic conflict exists, whether, as at a primitive stage, between life and death, or, at a later one, between body and soul, matter and spirit, individual and society.

Leaving aside, therefore, for the moment all attempts such as those above mentioned to assign values to the style-contrasts, and looking at the problem from its psychological aspect, we may say (following up an idea of Kühn's) that naturalistic art has always flourished where and when individualism was the order of the day or had obtained the mastery. This was not the case only in definite master-cultures with whose structure we are familiar, such as Crete, Mycenæ, Classical Greece, and the Renaissance; it applies also to primitive man — at least in the wider sense of the term. For even if this primitive man was no individualist in the sense in which those masterful natures were so — or even in the sense of our decadent psychologism — he was a lordly person relying upon his own strength before he became sedentary and united to collective bodies of men through agriculture. In any case, abstract art, in contrast to sensory or organic art, is usually collective, as is demonstrated by Northern and also primitive ornamentation as well as by religious Gothic. In these facts a paradoxical phenomenon discloses itself, which will not startle the psychologist and indeed will facilitate our approach to the understanding of the spiritual dynamism in artistic creativity. The autonomous individualism of primitive man, as well as that of the lordly masters appears to be more dependent on Nature in its artistic creativeness than is the sedentary collective type of man, who, though depending to a great extent on nature's moods and his own environment (of commerce), can yet rise to abstractions in art which are quite independent of reality. We shall see presently how this compensatory function of the art-form brings the development of personality and its dynamic need of equalization into unison. Here I would merely point out — in pursuance of an idea already put forward — that in neither of the two art-forms is it a question of an absolute style-principle, but only of a more or a less, while at the same time both style-forms alike possess the tendency to reproduce something absent, which in certain cases happens to be a natural object, while in others it pictures an idea. The obvious purpose in this tendency is domination, whether this takes the form of a naturalistic representation of an animal as a hunting spell or of the symbolic representation of a human abstraction. Behind both there is the creative will of the personality, which only now and then manifests itself directly, and at other times reacts to the compulsion of collective society and gives expression thereto. Undoubtedly this second art-form — here one agrees with Scheltema — is more capable of development, not only for stylistic and æsthetic, but for psychological reasons as well. For the abstraction at the base of this mechanical art represents even in itself a rising above nature, and it can be still further intensified and varied, whereas in naturalistic or organic art the objects within a given cultural environment are limited, so that the artistic effort to deal with them otherwise than in their natural setting does not find them very malleable. In a word, art consists in the latter case of arbitrary

xlviii

re-creation (not copying) of the given objects; in the other, of the new creation of ever changing ideas. Nevertheless, for both we must assume a creative force in the individual himself, which has to be studied in its various forms before we can arrive at a deeper understanding of the art-forms produced by it.

Chapter One

CREATIVE URGE AND PER- SONALITY DEVELOPMENT

❧

Socrates appears before us as one of those great plastic figures, all of a piece, such as we are accustomed to see at his period — a complete, classical work of art, which has risen of itself to that height. These figures are not made; they form themselves completely into what they are; they become that which they will to be, and to that they remain true. Thus Socrates, by his art and power of conscious will, formed himself for his own character and his life's task.

HEGEL

Chapter One

CREATIVE URGE AND PERSONALITY DEVELOPMENT

᠌

Since I originally approached the art-problem from the psychological side, and wish now, too, to study it'in relation to the development of personality, the historical method of presentation, which is usual in art-histories, is barred. Yet even for the psychological approach it is not the one side or the other that matters, but the fundamental dualism which appears as the basis of all cultural development in man. For if this dualism is as fundamental as we have assumed, it must make itself evident in the various stages of artistic creation as well as in the growth of personality, and will very likely reveal certain essential relations between the two. This, however, only becomes possible by taking a genetic view of the significances of the various ideologies from which both the style of a period and artistic creativeness in it are born. This comparative method, which we shall frequently adopt in all parts of this work, seeks, however, not so much to establish similarities or dependences as to establish a concatenation of meaning extending from the prehistoric cave-man to the individualistic artist-type of today with his " neurotic " psychology. If such a dualism really does exist in human nature, its existence must be just as demonstrable psychologically in the modern artist as it has been shown *æsthetically* in the history of style or *ethnically* in the history of culture. We use psychology, therefore, not as an exclusive principle of elucidation, but as an auxiliary that has been provided for us by the study of the modern artist-

3

type (not by his art); just as we use primitive art in order to understand the collective ideologies which condition creativity, and Oriental and Classical art in order to discover its intellectual interpretation. Our account may thus put readers off — the more that we ourselves shall often have to wrestle with certain cultural phenomena before we can apply the understanding thus won to the study of art.

Fortunately we have at least this much start, that a recent discovery has taken us up to the threshold of our own problems. I refer to the revolution in the understanding of artistic creativity which was set going by the Viennese art-historian Alois Riegl, and which since its first appearance in his *Stilfragen* (1893) has dominated all modern studies of art. Riegl posed it as a principle which illuminates the artistic creation of every age, that the peculiarities of style at various epochs are not to be explained by defective ability, but are only intelligible as the expression of a particular *will to form.* This view may seem self-evident to the psychologist, but it was unattainable either by psychology proper or by a psychologizing æsthetic. It could only come from viewing style, as Riegl does, as a manifestation of collective ideology. Unfortunately Riegl only lived long enough to illustrate his subtle and far-reaching theory in a single specialized department, that of Late Roman arts and crafts.[1] But the fact that so historically limited and artistically subordinate a domain should have given room for this form of description and presentation shows the brilliant achievement of Riegl in all its greatness. Rejecting the traditional mode of regarding art as a matter of objects and iconography, and understanding it as " form and colour in surface and in space," he ascribed to these crafts, even to the ornamentation prevailing in them, the same significance as vessels of the will to form as he did to sculpture, painting, and architecture — thus opening a wholly new chapter in art-history as well

[1] *Die spätrömische Kunstindustrie, nach den Funden in Österreich-Ungarn, im Zusammenhange mit der Gesamtentwicklung der bildenden Künste bei den Mittelmeervölkern* (Vienna, 1901).

as giving a wholly new method of approach. When we remember what an important part was played in prehistory by this form of art, hitherto a neglected stepchild, we may well admit that without Riegl's magnificent achievement the essence of primitive ornament and thus of abstract art in general would have remained unintelligible. Of course further work was necessary in order to give Riegl's idea the broad historical and æsthetic foundation which was far beyond the attainment of a single — and all too short — life.

It is therefore comprehensible that Riegl himself should not have been able to free himself entirely from the shackles of his own tradition and the æsthetic views of his age, and that in the application of his ideas he was restricted by academic prejudice. Though his account of the Classical art as an antithesis to Late Roman remains a permanent achievement of an almost spiritual attitude to art, he nevertheless succumbed to historicism in summarily declaring everything " Late Roman " which showed the same criteria of style, without thinking of the possibility of a psychological content in this conception. On the other hand he took the " denaturalization of the art-form," as it developed from the Classical to the decadent Late Roman civilization, as a law inherent in all artistic development, again without considering the possibilities of various other conjunctures influencing it. As Scheltema — who fully appreciates Riegl's main achievement — has shown, there are in the North similar abstract forms which have developed, not from any desiccation of natural forms, but in the reverse direction. The similarity of forms is explained by the similarity of the will, but this was not " Late Roman " in the North, nor " Nordic " in the South, but in both cases resulted from a collective ideology which characterized in the South the end, and in the North the beginning, of the development of a culture.

Thus, though this absolute art-will of Riegl remains the basis of all treatment of art, yet obviously a great deal, if not everything, depends on which manifestations of the culture as a whole we take for the study of the art-will of this particular period. Riegl did so on the craft-art, and thus at any rate remained within the sphere of art himself, which has obvious advantages, but (as we have seen from his mistakes) disadvantages as well. Other students also have discussed the collective ideology of particular periods, which decides its will to form also, in terms of its religious or philosophical tendencies, in order later to show these as taking effect in the art-forms. All these works of the Riegl school, which go more or less beyond their master's, are extremely valuable contributions to a new view of art, and will come to be regarded as such. But they all suffer from a certain one-sidedness, which is the more intelligible that the idea of Riegl's art-will, however collectively we may take it, yet contains in its very name a strong psychological element which absolutely demands the inclusion of the personality of the creative artist. Certainly we do not mean a psychological interpretation of the laws of style, by which their importance would be reduced to mere psychologizing; but we can only hope for a real step forward in our understanding of art if we can settle more definitely the part played by the creative individual in the collective work and then put the result into the great equation of all the factors which have any bearing, direct or indirect, on the creation of the art-forms.

Of course, for such an undertaking, which tackles the problem of art primarily from the psychological end, a different starting-point is required from that which is called for in a study of art from the stylistic or cultural-historical angle. Even if by art we understand, not the part played by the creator in the psychological sense, but the product, the work, or even the content of all art — at least for the particular period — we can for the time being sum up the relation of the artist to his art as follows: the artist, as a definite creative individual, uses the art-form that he finds ready to his hand in order to express a something personal; this personal must therefore be somehow connected with the prevailing artistic or cultural ideology, since otherwise he could not make use of them, but it must also differ, since otherwise he would not need to use them in order to produce something of his own. While this aspect brings us again to the dualism in the artist, there is, as we know already, a similar dualism at the bottom of the cultural ideology, as one of the manifestations of which the style of the age must be regarded. But the general ideology of the culture, which determines its religion, morals, and society as well as its art, is again only the expression of the human types of the age, and of this the artist and the creative personality generally are the most definite crystallization. The circular argument here is only apparent, for we may not disregard the creative process, which presents itself as an essential factor between the ideology of the art, the style, and the creative personality, the artist. We must admit, however, that we know almost nothing of this process in the artist, since here, more than anywhere, the hopes held out by modern psychology have proved delusive.

We shall quote later the authors who have been honest enough to admit the failure of scientific psychology to explain artistic creativity; but we would say at once here that this fact has been contributory to our own attempt to understand the problem of the artist purely in relation to that of art — the artist representing only one, the individual factor, while we have to regard art as the collective expression of their contemporary cultural ideology. The artist, as it were, takes not only his canvas, his colours, or his model in order to paint, but also the art that is given him formally, technically, and ideologically, within his own culture; this probably emerges most clearly in the case of the poet, whose material is drawn from the cultural possessions already circulating and is not dead matter, as is that used by the plastic arts. In any case we can say of all artistic creation that the artist not only creates his art, but also uses art in order to create. Withal, there remains still (quite apart from the cultural problem of the origin of style) the purely psychological problem as to what is the type, the individual, that for the creative expression of its personality takes this or that art-ideology in particular, what are the motives and processes which transform a creative impulse into art-achievements of high æsthetic value.

For the solution of this fundamental psychological question we have naturally to keep to the present, where we have a definite artistic type before us as a living phenomenon, and not merely his historical biography and completed work. But the prevalent psychology has already failed in the task of finding a satisfactory explanation for the birth of an individual work, even when the artist is historically known and his artistic personality has been studied biographically — where in fact the stages of growth can still be traced. Still less, then, is it likely that it could achieve an understanding of primitive collective art or the amazing achievements of the psychologically crude stone-age man. If any psychology is to explain this at all adequately, it will in any case have to be a new one and one that, while taking its bearings by primitive art, avoids, on the one hand, the predication of our own feelings in it and, on the other, the interpretation of our own æsthetic sensibility by reference to it.

The merit of developing Riegl's ideas to their logical issue and placing the æsthetic understanding of alien styles on a new basis goes in particular to a historian, Wilhelm Worringer; and his fundamental work: *Abstraktion und Einfühlung, ein Beitrag zur Stilspsychologie* (Munich, 1908; quoted according to the tenth edition, 1921), is doubly important for us as a starting-point because it also works out the psychological core of Riegl's attitude, at least as far as is necessary and possible in relation to the æsthetic problem. And if Worringer, as I should like to remark at once, was limited in his purely psychological penetration of the problem by the natural boundaries of his own interests, he did take æsthetic to the very verge beyond which it must give place to psychology.

For myself I became acquainted with Worringer's ideas when I had already settled my own interpretation of the prob-

lem of art; still I owe him many valuable suggestions, though
yet again I should have been unable to use these had I not of
myself gone beyond the traditional view of æsthetic, which
Worringer so splendidly criticizes and so fruitfully completes.
The idea of the will to form, when I came across it in the form
in which Riegl first expounded it and Worringer extended it,
sounded to me at once like something familiar. Not only had
I long ago come to the conclusion from my analysis of creative
artists that their productivity and the varying quality of their
work were not a matter of capacity; but I had got beyond
the individual psychology in my ideas about the creative personality and of the determining ideology, before I returned to
the problem of art. For me the problem of willing, in a philosophical sense of the word, had come to be the central problem of the whole question of personality, even of all psychology, and it only remained to apply it to the particular case of
the creative artist. Riegl's revolutionary treatment of art, in
the æsthetic and psychological form in which Worringer formulated it, gave me the courage to attempt an understanding
of the specific ideology of the artist — that is, his style — in a
similar sense to that which my psychology of the will had
opened up in dealing with other ideologies. The general principles and interpretation which are valid for the growth and
meaning of general ideologies must be applicable to the ideology of art, which we had recognized the peculiarities of
style to be. Further, the æsthetic laws deduced from the history of style must either coincide to a considerable extent with,
or at least be somehow related to, both the significance of the
whole cultural ideology and the manifestations of the creative
personality.

There was one point in particular in Worringer's work
which seemed to me to confirm my own notions of the origin
and significance of the general cultural ideology for the problem of artistic creation. In my *Seelenglaube und Psychologie*
I had, as mentioned above, sought to establish as the primary
ideology the belief in immortality which seemed to express

itself in artistic creation in the same ways as in religion and social institutions. The particular way in which this showed itself in style, however, remained, for the time being, beyond my grasp, until I had come to know Riegl's views of style and Worringer's æsthetic. For Riegl, it is true, who deals particularly with collective phenomena, the art-will is purely instinctive; according to the materialistic conception of Verworn, it is "physioplastic"; while for Worringer, who interprets it more philosophically, it is an almost "cosmic something" arising spontaneously from the abstract linear art which corresponds to crystalline form. So far, therefore, it has nothing to do with the individual will of the conscious artistic personality, though we might regard it as being in a Schopenhauerian sense its precursor. But the matter is not quite so simple that we could assume this instinctive art-impulse to have merely become individually conscious; for increasing individualization alters the whole cultural ideology and therefore art with it; and consequently abstract linear ornament is not now created consciously by the individual will of the artists as heretofore instinctively by the primitive impulse to abstraction, but replaced by new forms of expression.

For with this individualization the general art-form changes in its essence (some authorities think, in the direction of naturalism), but the creative personality also becomes other than it was. The question: How did the individual artist-type grow up at all in our Western culture if the artistic creation of earlier men and times was abstract and collective? is almost identical with the problem of the development of individuality and personality itself. But this is not a problem that can be solved by psychology alone; rather we may hope for a deeper knowledge of the development of personality from a better understanding of the development of art. As I have shown elsewhere, the immortality-belief in its various forms and cultural variations has certainly participated in it; and it is here, as already remarked, that I find the decisive point of contact with Worringer's æsthetic to which we may relate our study.

Its merit seems to me to be that it has shown this individual *urge to eternalization* of the personality, which motivates artistic production, to be a principle *inherent in the art-form itself,* in fact its essence. He says of primitive and also of Oriental cultures, whose style he is discussing: " The kind of satisfaction which they looked to obtain from art was not, as in Western art, that of sinking themselves in the external world, and finding enjoyment in it, but that of depriving the individual thing in the external world of its arbitrary and apparently haphazard character; that is to immortalize the object in giving it an abstract form and so finding a resting-place in the flight of phenomena. Their strongest impulse was to bring it close to its absolute value " (op. cit., p. 21).[1]

If, with this " instinctive urge to abstraction " as it appears very early in art, we compare the growth of other collective ideologies at a primitive level, we find to our surprise that, correspondingly, the other ideologies also become the more abstract the further we pursue them backwards. The most important as well as the best-authenticated instance of this is the development of religion, as I have tried to expound it in *Seelenglaube und Psychologie.* Primitive religion, as a belief in souls (as we know it), is originally so abstract that it has been called irreligious by comparison with higher religions, in which the gods have already assumed concrete form. But from a study of these abstract preliminary stages of religion, which are a matter of spirits and demons, we see also that the urge for abstraction in primitives is rooted in the soul-belief that, in the intellectualized form of the East, culminates in the absolute abstract of the soul. Compared with the idea of the soul or its primitive predecessors even the abstractest form of art is concrete, just as on the other hand the most

---

[1] We cannot at present enter upon the criticism of Worringer's exaggeration of his own principle of elucidation which in essence he seeks to exemplify by reference to the Gothic style. He appears therein to have succumbed to the same compulsion as Riegl, in that he calls everything "Gothic" that comes within the style-criteria of his own "Gothic" and thus reaches a "universal Gothic," which perhaps ought to be defined in terms of personality rather than in those of æsthetics.

definite naturalism in art is abstract when compared with nature.

If primitive art, then, is in its origins a concreted representation of an abstract idea of the soul and is at the same time the nucleus of what becomes at a later stage the figuration of God, we cannot possibly understand the change and growth of art-forms without following the change of the idea of the soul in human history. Here we may state, more definitely than we have as yet, that the main task of this book is to expound the *development and change in meaning of art-forms from similar changes in the idea of the soul,* which decides the development of personality, even as it is itself influenced thereby. Though we have later to give an account of the relation between the prevailing style in art and the contemporary belief in the soul, we can even now see how religion has always drawn art along in its wake from the earliest times to the present day.

The urge for abstraction, which owed its origin to a belief in immortality and created the notion of the soul, created also the art which served the same ends, but led beyond the purely abstract to the objectivizing and concretizing of the prevailing idea of the soul. Everything produced objectively in any period by the contemporary idea of the soul was beautiful, and the æsthetic history of the idea of the beautiful is probably no more than a reflection of the changes in the idea of the soul under the influence of increasing knowledge. The most illuminating demonstration that the source of the beauty-ideal lies in the contemporary ideal of the soul is found in the religious art of all times and peoples, but most conspicuously in the higher cultures, where the already unified idea of the soul was ideally embodied in the forms of their gods. Thus Anubis with his animal head was as much an ideal of beauty for the Egyptians as was Zeus with a leonine mane for the Greeks, or the tortured and martyred body of Jesus for the Christians. The concept of the beautiful, which inspires the works of art of a period, is derived, not from the abstract sig-

12

nificance of the soul-concept (in the way in which, for instance, the Romantics spoke of the " beautiful soul "), but from its concretization. That is, the religious art portrayed the idea of the soul in concrete form for the men of the time, in the shape of gods, and so, psychologically speaking, proved their existence. It is precisely the concreteness of art as compared with the idea of the soul that makes it convincing; for it creates something visible and permanent in contrast to something which was merely thought or felt, which was at first handed down from one generation to another only by means of mystic tradition and was only fixed in literature of religious form at a very late stage.

This close association, in fact fundamental identity, of art and religion, each of which strives in its own way to make the absolute eternal and the eternal absolute, can be already seen at the most primitive stages of religious development, where there are as yet neither representations of gods nor copies of nature. Almost all students of the art of primitive peoples get the unanimous impression that, as the first historian of primitive art, Franz Kugler, put it as early as 1842, " the intention of primitive art was far less towards the imitation of nature than towards the representation of particular ideas." More than fifty years later so great an authority as Leo Frobenius says the same of African art: " We cannot say that there was any direct extrovert effort at the attainment of some perfection of form.[1] All the objects of art come only out of the need to give plastic expression to ideas." We shall show later in detail how almost all these " ideas " turn more or less on the idea of the soul, which itself arises from the problem of death. Here we need only note that the redeeming power of art, that which entitles it to be regarded æsthetically as beautiful, resides in the way in which it lends concrete existence to abstract ideas of the soul. Art, then — at least in its beginning — was not the

---

[1] Following Ernst Vatter: *Die religiöse Plastik der Naturvölker* (Frankfurt, 1926). Vatter shows that the plastic of primitive peoples is unintelligible unless it is regarded as an expression of religious ideas.

satisfaction of the desire of the individual artist to attain immortality for himself in his work, but the confirmation of the collective immortality-idea in the work itself as a picture of the soul. Thus primitive art must be, like the primitive idea of the soul, collective in order to achieve its aim, the continuation of the individual existence in the species. And it follows, too, that primitive art must be abstract in order to reproduce this abstract idea of the soul as faithfully as may be.

Worringer was certainly right in denying that art began with the imitation of nature, or even had this object; but it was imitation all the same, though in a wider sense. The most definite representation possible of an idea *is* imitation, in the ideoplastic sense; and we might explain this very character of abstraction of primitive art by the fact that it faithfully represents an idea which is itself abstract. That is, the soul was depicted as abstractly as possible, in order that it might be like this abstract, and the further the divinizing of the soul in different personifications proceeded, the more concrete, or, as we should say, naturalistic, art became. If in this wise the obstinately defended theory of imitation (though not strictly in the sense of imitation of nature) is found to have a deeper significance in the soul, we may use the second disputed principle of the old æsthetic also to support our new structure. The accusation of aimlessness made against an art which exists only for beauty's sake cannot be sustained, either in respect of primitive art or in respect of the individual creative dynamism of the modern artist. Art unquestionably has an end, probably even serves a variety of ends — but the ends are not concrete and practical, they are abstract and spiritual. Primitive art above all has obviously some object, as Vatter points out (op. cit., p. 103), as deterrent, magic, charm; and it obtains it by making the supernatural ideology of primitive men tangible and comprehensible. In this is its value, its function, and hence comes the satisfaction it provides, which at later stages of æsthetic appreciation is deduced from the idea of beauty — an idea which originally, and even in Greek philosophy, was coincident with the idea of the good, the satisfying, and the useful.

The relations of art and religion, though so often discussed, would thus seem to call for a new treatment from our point of view; which we cannot give here, although in the course of a discussion centred on the development of personality we may be able to throw some light on hitherto unsuspected linkages. There is no doubt that even in the historical times of art religion used it as a means to represent, in objective and concrete form, the contemporary idea of the soul; but not, so to say, " illustratively," as if mankind were too immature to form abstract ideas of the soul. It *had* to be made concrete, pictorial, and real, so as to *prove* its existence, and had to be presented in matter to demonstrate its indestructibility. Not only, therefore, have we in the art-form (style) the expression of a will that varies from time to time under the influence of changes in the soul-idea, but the same principle holds even of the content of art — so far as it is religious — and, indeed, it is religious from the start, if we may give this name to the supersensible, even where it has not condensed into the idea of a god. It is therefore not a defective faculty of abstraction which drives to the concretization of the soul and its pictorial representation in the god, *but the will to objectify it and thus to impart to it existence and, what is more, eternity.*

Here we come to the interesting question to what extent the development of primitive art and its frank use by religion has itself contributed to the formation of a religion itself, and how far it was essential to it; in other words, whether the transition from animism to religion (that is, from the belief in the soul to the belief in God) was only possible through art, because in art lay the only mode of exhibiting the soul in objective form and giving personality to God.[1] It seems certain that art was at one time more abstract, since its purpose was to give existence to the non-existent by the truest possible copying. In the course

[1] We shall refer later to the apparent exception of the Jewish people, which condemned every representation of Deity as idolatrous, and consequently produced no art.

of development it merely became more concrete, a destiny which it shares with all other ideologies, as I have shown elsewhere, and with the development of human institutions out of these ideologies. Its culmination came in the individual art-creation of the Classical style as we have it in Greek work. There man himself — in his own full naturalness, yet in idealized beauty too — had become the vehicle of an immortal soul and was not, like the Oriental gods, a mere representative of the belief in the soul. *In this sense not only did the development of the soul begin with art, but the process of humanization of the soul completed itself in art and not in religion.* It was art, by its embodiment of man in lasting material, that finally gave him the courage to reassume the soul which, because of the transitoriness of its bodily form, he had abstracted into an absolute idea of the soul.

From a point of view such as this, art, though born from the same spirit as religion, appears not only as outlasting it, but actually as fulfilling it. If religion, as is hardly disputable, could only develop beyond soul-belief by the help of art, and if, moreover, as I would believe, the humanization of the soul, which implies the completion of religion, is accomplished by art, religion would almost sink to a transition stage of art. This is, of course, a matter of attitude — but it does seem certain that the development of art has always striven beyond religion, and that its highest individual achievements lie outside purely religious art, until in modern times it completely emancipates itself from that influence and even takes its place. But this tendency towards independence corresponds to an irreligiosity (or even an anti-religiosity) which is inherent and essential in all artistic creation, and which we must admit, in spite of its logically contradicting our own discussion, unless we are to sacrifice a decisive, and perhaps the most important, side of the creative impulse to a one-sided theory. Personal creativity is anti-religious in the sense that it is always subservient to the individual desire for immortality in the creative personality and not to the collective glorification of the creator of the world. The individual artist of course uses collective forms, among which the religious, in the widest sense, take first place, so as to overcome his personal dualism by a social compensation. But at the same time he tries to save his individuality from the collective mass by giving his work the stamp of his own personality. Hence it is quite rightly that Rudolf Kautzsch, in his brief but valuable paper *Die bildende Kunst und das Jenseits* (Jena, 1905), emphasizes the fact that on one side religion is a handicap on art; and we too have seen in our survey of prevalent theories of art that the periods of strong development of personality, or of constructive individualism like that predicated of the superman, have always been among the highest periods of artistic productivity.

Among these periods of floraison we have mentioned the prehistoric art of self-dependent palæolithic man, Classical Greek art, and the Renaissance. All these periods, which either are individualistic or are carried along by a definite cult of personality, show — in contrast to the abstract and rigid style of Egyptian, Christian, and to a certain extent even Gothic art — a vivid naturalism *which is certainly no imitation of nature, but rather an organic vitalization of fossilizing art-forms.* We have indicated in the Introduction the psychical significance of this antithesis and how it may be psychologically understood. Religion is the collective ideology *par excellence,* which can only spring from a powerful group-need and mass-consciousness, which itself springs from the need of the individual for dependence and implies his subjection to higher forces. Art also, which sprang originally from self-feeling, is then subordinated to religion, just as the creative personality is subordinated to the creator. *Religion springs from the collective belief in immortality; art from the personal consciousness of the individual.* The conflict between art and religion, which we can so easily trace in the individual artist, is thus ultimately a conflict between individuality and collectivity, the dualistic struggle within the creative artist of the two impulses of his own self. In this sense there is a reciprocal dependence between

17

art and religion, but, concurrent with it from the outset, an opposition between them. For, on the one hand, the artist has need of religion so as to make his own impulse towards immortality collective, while religion needs the artist in order to make concrete its abstract notion of the soul; on the other hand, the artist seeks to eternalize his individuality apart from the collective ideologies, while religion would deny the individual in favour of the community. Thus though art is in the last resort anti-collectivist — in spite of the fact that it makes use of the various communal ideologies, especially of contemporary religion and the style dependent on it — it yet needs these collective ideologies, even if only to overcome them from time to time by the force of personality. This fact may perhaps explain why the present age, with its strong individualism, has failed to produce any great art like other periods marked by strong personality and consequent alienation from religion. These other periods had strength in their religious and anti-religious currents, as well as other powerful collective ideologies, which our present-day society in its disruption lacks. Even if nowadays, with the decay of religious faith, the artist is immeasurably overvalued, this seems only a last effort at re-establishing a similarly decaying cult of the personality, of which we are just as incapable as we are of collective faith.

True, there was, probably, a time when the artist did play the part of the religious hero on earth, being the creative representative of a humanized god: the time, that is, when there arose content and concept of genius wherein dwelt the divine spark, the immortal soul. But if we want to understand the personality of the creative artist, we must turn for a while to the history of this idea of genius; for this idea has not always existed, though there were geniuses before it. The necessity for the birth of this idea, and its elaboration into a cult of personality, whose last stages only are known to us, seem to me to have arisen from the incessant conflict with, and final conquest of, these collective ideologies by a new type of humanity, which appeared first in Greece, but had to be reborn for western Europe in Italy. For Greece had, in spite of its extraordinary personality-culture, a strong national idea which defined the type, while in the Renaissance a new European personal consciousness arose which towered above religious and national boundaries and established a world-reign of humanism which could vie with collective Christianity.

The notion of genius as it grew up between the Renaissance and the eighteenth century was created by the artist as a new ideology, and henceforth it was as much a means towards production as had previously been the abstract idea of style derived from the collective belief in the soul. But this new " religion of genius," as Zilsel calls it,[1] centred on a type and no longer on a collectivity; it was indeed individual and even psychological, in its emphasis, based wholly on the artist and no longer on art, on style. At the Renaissance, out of which this genius was born, the Middle Ages were freed from the collective spirit of Christianity and fought through once more to personality. Now for the first time there appears the creative artist of the modern age, whose epigoni today produce their art without possessing either the collective ideology of earlier ages or the individual religion of genius which has produced the greatest of our great artists, a Michelangelo, a Shakspere, a Rembrandt, a Goethe. Such men as these, being tied to their age, stand in sharp opposition to a collective art such as had still ruled in the Gothic. They are alone and unique — in spite of their countless imitators — for they are individual; and not only in their personality and the works born from it, but their whole ideology is individual, since it springs from the notion of genius and is only possible through it. These men who are for us the representatives of the type " genius " embody the same process and achievement, on earth and individually, which in its religious form we saw beginning with the image of God. The idea of genius is, in its mythical origin, a *representation* of the

[1] Edgar Zilsel: *Die Geniereligion; ein kritischer Versuch über das moderne Persönlichkeitsideal* (Leipzig, 1918). See also, in connexion with what follows, the older work of Jacob Cahan: *Zur Kritik des Geniebegriffs* (diss., Berne, 1911).

immortal soul, that part of the personality which can beget (*gignere*) what is immortal, be it a child or a work.

The idea of the "Genius" comes originally from early Roman times, when it means the personal protecting spirit, of man, as opposed to woman, where it is called "Juno" and corresponds to the Egyptian "Ka" and Greek "daimon." Without discussing this notion of a psychical double of man, which is represented in different forms in the different doctrines of the soul, let us note here that the Roman Genius, in keeping with the cultural idea of Rome which was built up on the right of the father, acquired the literal meaning of "begetter." But Otto [1] is right in maintaining that the current explanation of Genius as a deified incarnation of masculine reproductive power does not fully explain the idea. Thus, Genius is also the god of one's birthday — and Otto concluded that the idea contains, as well as the notion of begetting, that of the descent also and indeed that of the continuity of all life. It is hard to see why philologists find this view so difficult, since it is precisely the stage of father-right that is characterized by the collectivizing of the personal reproductive impulse. And so the Roman idea of Genius contains from the beginning, in addition to the individual urge to reproduction, a collective element which points beyond the individual, in a way that is not true of the Egyptian Ka and the Greek daimon, both of which are purely personal.[2] For this reason it was specially fitted to become a social conception of genius that should include both individual and collective elements. Still the artist's concept of genius is more personal than collective and thus needs a new ideology. This could no longer be a personal peculiarity of style deduced from a collective idea of the soul, but had to become an *æsthetic of feeling* dependent on consciousness of personality.

[1] W. Otto: *Die Manen oder von den Urformen des Totenglaubens* (Berlin, 1923).

[2] E. Bickel shows brilliantly (*Homerischer Seelenglaube: geschichtliche Grundzüge menschlicher Seelenvorstellungen;* Berlin, 1925) how all these various soul ideas eventually, in the late period of Greece, passed into the new concept of psyche, which prepared the way for the Christian idea of the soul.

Thus the eighteenth century, which was completely sterile of any collective art and was distinguished only by a few dominant artistic individualities, produced an æsthetic as abstracted from the art-products of earlier ages. This was not, however, the universally valid " science of art " that it was for so long supposed to be, but was itself a new ideology of art, which was to replace the now decadent religious collective ideology by a psychological artistic ideology corresponding to the new genius-type. Æsthetic is thus the psychological ideology of art, born from the notion of the genius-type and not from the collective — and religious — notion of style. Our Classicist æsthetic in fact directs its gaze much more to the individual art-product of Classical artists, while the abstract style of which Worringer speaks appears much more as a collective product. When Worringer explains the incongruence of art-history and æsthetic by the fact that our æsthetic is nothing more than a psychology of the Classical way of feeling art, he is certainly right; but there will probably always be a similar incongruence between every ideology and its concretization, as indeed there actually is between our æsthetic and the corresponding intuitive (*einfühlende*) art, as also between the religious art of Egypt and mediæval Christianity and the works respectively produced by them.

In addition to this natural divergence between an ideology and its concretization, there is in artistic creation yet another decisive factor which æsthetic would have to neglect entirely if it sought to make its laws absolute, and this is the personality of the artist, with his own system of ideology, which perhaps runs largely parallel with the general, but by no means coincides with it. These problems of the boundaries between psychology and æsthetics we will postpone till a later chapter; here we need only state that even Worringer underestimates the influence of the creative personality when he is dealing with art- and style-forms from the standpoint of their æsthetic effects, however he may emphasize the importance of abstract art as well as intuitive.

True, in a summing-up which is perhaps the culminating
point of his magnificent argument, Worringer says that the
psychological victory over this æsthetic dualism is found in the
demand for self-renunciation which lies at the root of all
æsthetic experience and which is achieved now by intuition (*Einfühlung*), now by abstraction. But it is just these
ultimate psychological problems of art that will trip us up if
we have neglected or inadequately understood the creative
personality, an understanding that is an inherent necessity
in all æsthetic, however far it may advance into the domain of
psychology. For æsthetic, by its nature, can only deal with the
effect of a work of art, and it takes account of its creation by
an artist only by arguing theoretically back from the contemplator to the creator. But this conclusion, apart from its indirect
nature, is a fallacy; for as we (or at least as I, myself) have
been convinced by a study of the productive personality, there
is between that and the unproductive type not only a quantitative but a qualitative difference. The quantitative difference,
which is obvious, would be enough in itself to throw doubt on
the soundness of thus arguing back from the receptive to the
creative; and the qualitative demands a wholly new orientation
to the problem, which we shall attempt at least to suggest in
the chapter on the play-impulse and æsthetic pleasure. But
even at the outset it seems to me clear that the idea of intuition (*Einfühlung*) as fashioned by psychological æsthetic
has been attained as from a view-point of reception, while the
notion of abstraction which Worringer contrasts with it refers
rather to the spiritual attitude of the creative artist. In any case
there is here a vagueness of concepts, though it is not attributable to Worringer's unitary interpretation, but belongs to all
æsthetic. Ever since Aristotle's day this seems to me to have
begun with the tacit assumption that the artist intended to
present the effect he aimed at in its phenomenal form, and
that therefore there were involved in the creation, at least
potentially, the same psychological experiences and psychical

processes as are to be observed in the contemplator of the work and especially in the æsthetic critic.

Without disputing that in some cases the artist does aim at a definite idea effect in his work, it is certainly not the rule, especially with the individual work of the creative artist, since here the work of art is essentially an expression of his personality. Nor need we doubt that the artist occasionally does find pleasure and satisfaction in his creation, though the confessions of great artists themselves generally tell rather of the struggle and suffering of creating it. But the fundamental difference in essence between the creative and the receptive types, which are psychologically complementary, is not affected by such evidences. While æsthetic pleasure, whether in the creator or in the contemplator, is ultimately a renunciation of self, the essence of the creative impulse is the exactly opposite tendency towards assertion of self. Here again, however, we must be careful not to set up this opposition, in the form in which we have to state it, as if it were absolute. There may be periods in which a strong individualism or a particular development of personality expresses its tendency towards a self-assertion in creativity as opposed to other periods of collective subordination which involve rather a self-negation. In other words, the dualism of the individual and the community, which we showed to be the fundamental conflict, appears here also in a psychological form and in its relation to various forms of art. Even though we found religion with its collectivizing tendency to be ultimately restrictive of art, this really means only that under its influence another art grows and flourishes in which the individual art-expression, being alien, is thwarted and that this again reacts to force collective art into new paths. All the same, it seems psychologically indispensable to set an impulse of self-assertion against that of self-negation if we are to understand the creative personality as it develops out of the idea of genius.

Though this artistic type, as such, was only born with the

Renaissance and developed from the idea of genius, yet it must
have existed previously as a creative type in the sense of an urge
to self-assertion, since otherwise no art, and least of all the
strongly marked naturalistic art of prehistoric man, would
have been possible. Our psychological knowledge of the type
begins only with the Renaissance; and there already it denotes
— artistically, sociologically, and psychologically — something
different, which we can only conjecturally assume in the artists
of earlier epochs. *Psychologically* the notion of genius, of which
we see the last reflection in our modern artist-type, is the
apotheosis of man as a creative personality: the religious ideology (looking to the glory of God) being thus transferred to
man himself.[1] *Sociologically,* it meant the creation and recognition of " genius " as a type, as a culture-factor of highest value
to the community, since it takes over on earth the rôle of the
divine hero. *Artistically,* it implies the individual style, which
indeed still holds on to the exemplars that later appear in
æsthetic as formulated law, but which is already free and
autonomous in its divine creative power and is creating new
forms from out of itself. This artist, liberated from God, himself
become god, soon overleaps the collective forms of style and
their abstract formulation in æsthetic and constructs new forms
of an individual nature, which cannot, therefore, be subsumed
under laws. And so our Classicist æsthetic of the eighteenth
century appears as a final attempt to save the Classical forms
— if not wholly, at any rate in abstract formulæ — before they
were shattered by the individual *Sturm und Drang* effort of
the self-creative personality. Æsthetic appears here as the last
endeavour to find art's psychological justification in itself,
which corresponds exactly to the self-justification of the artist
in the psychological type of the genius.

Here begins the " art for art's sake " ideology, and here too is
the source of all artistic psychology, both of which began with

[1] See the extract prefixed to this book, from Pico della Mirandola's oration on
human dignity, which is described by Burckhardt (*Die Kultur der Renaissance in Italien*)
as "one of the noblest achievements of this cultural period."

the birth of the genius-notion. Psychology is, of course (at least as dealing with the problem of the personality), a young science, so that it will be best to start with its latest results that we may be clear as to what it has contributed to the elucidation of these problems and what still remains obscure. Now, the latest statements in this field show with astonishing frankness and unanimity that the psychology of personality has helped little or not at all to the understanding of genius or (as it is termed scientifically) the productive personality;[1] moreover, that it probably never will contribute anything, since ultimately we are dealing with dynamic factors which remain incomprehensible in their specific expression in the individual personality. This implies that they can be neither predetermined nor wholly explained even *ex post facto;* as, indeed, we cannot understand, in my view, personality at all, even man as such, by a purely individual psychology.[2] In any event, the notion of art had always proved too narrow to include under one aspect the varieties of productive personality or their manifold achievements; and on the other hand the psychological idea of the productive personality was far too wide to explain artistic production. For, psychologically speaking, there are productive personalities which never produce a work of art, or indeed anything creative at all; and, again, the poet may be so different from the plastic artist, the musician, or the scientifically productive type that it is impossible to bring them all under one head.

The study of a certain neurotic type, which I had already regarded as "*artiste manqué*" in my youthful work, gave me a new approach, on the basis of that analysis, to the problem of the creative personality. We have in such cases either individuals who, though they are really productive (since they

[1] E. Kretschmer: *Geniale Menschen* (Berlin, 1929; reprinted lectures of 1919); W. Lange-Eichbaum: *Genie-Irrsinn und Ruhm* (Munich, 1928); P. Plaut: *Psychologie der produktiven Persönlichkeit* (Stuttgart, 1929).

[2] One may be unable, for example, to arrive at an individual psychological explanation of homosexuality in the artist (Michelangelo, Shakspere) and yet understand why a particular artist-type is, and almost necessarily must be, homosexual (see pages 52 et seq.).

25

possess the productive force of dynamism), produce nothing, or else artistically productive men who feel themselves restricted in their possibilities of expression. Pure psycho-analysis of such types undertaken for the removal of inhibitions as indicated by Freud's therapy, did not help at all for the psychological understanding of the creative process, although it established a fair amount regarding their behaviour as individuals. The only tangible statement which Freud's theory could give us about the artistic process was that which asserted that the impulse to artistic productivity originated in the sex-impulse. But it is easy to see that this explanation (which I myself accepted in my first work on the psychology of artists) takes us no further in reality, being a pure paraphrase of the individual meaning already obvious in the very concept of genius (*gignere* = to beget). But psychology could not explain how from the sex-impulse there was produced, not the sex-act, but the art-work, and all the ideas called in to bridge this infinite gulf — " compensation," " sublimation," etc. — were only psychological transcriptions for the fact that we have here something different, higher and symbolical.

Dreams, too, which in the new interpretation of Freud seemed to promise so much for the elucidation of artistic creativity, proved, on a more careful comprehension of the problem, to be incapable of taking us beyond a superficial analogy.[1] The fact that we all dream and, in dreams, are all (in the fine comparison of Schopenhauer) poets of the stature of Dante or Shakspere is sufficient by itself to force to our notice the fact that we do not know what it is which allows a Dante or a Shakspere to do in waking life what we all, according to Schopenhauer, do in our sleep. They all (as I expressed it) superadd, to their equipment and their creative dream-fantasy, a particular ideology of art. And so we are back at our question, what individuals are driven and able to do this and what psychological presuppositions make it

[1] On the subject of dreams and art, see also Friedrich von Hausegger: *Das Jenseits des Künstlers*.

possible. If we approach the problem from the study of the productive neurotic type — that is, if we start with the artistic type living today — we arrive at the following condition for creative art. The neurotic, no matter whether productive or obstructed, suffers fundamentally from the fact that he cannot or will not accept himself, his own individuality, his own personality. On one hand he criticizes himself to excess, on the other he idealizes himself to excess, which means that he makes too great demands on himself and his completeness, so that failing to attain leads only to more self-criticism. If we take this thwarted type, as we may do for our purposes, and compare him to the artist, it is at once clear that the artist is in a sense the antithesis to the self-critical neurotic type. Not that the artist does not criticize himself, but by accepting his personality he not only fulfils that for which the neurotic is striving in vain, but goes far beyond it. The precondition, then, of the creative personality is not only its acceptance, but its actual glorification, of itself.

The religion of genius and the cult of personality thus begin, in the creative individual, with himself; he, so to say, appoints himself as an artist, though this is only possible if the society in which he lives has an ideology of genius, recognizes it, and values it. This leads straight to the realization that the productive personality, if it has once accomplished this self-appointment by the aid of his community's ideology of the artist, must justify this self-assertion under compulsion by its work and by ever higher achievement. And so the problem of the process of artistic creation, which is no more than a compulsory dynamic, shifts to its precondition, which is the glorification of the individual personality. At this point we have a fruitful parallel to the " absolute will to art " which Riegl talks of and Worringer defines as a lifting of the object out of nature and its eternalization in an abstract schematic form which reproduces the essential. We see that the very same process which at the primitive stage of the collective abstract style relates to the object takes place at the developed stage of individual art, in relation to the subject; in other words, the individual raises himself from out of the community by his inclusion in the genius-type in just the same way as the object is torn from its natural surroundings by its artistic stylization. The individual, as it were, abstracts himself in the style demanded by the genius-ideology and so concentrates the essence of his being, the reproductive urge, in the genius-concept. He says, more or less, that he needs only to create and not to beget.[1] The novelty of our present view lies, however, in this: that we have good reason for assuming that *this creativity begins with the individual himself — that is, with the self-making of the personality into the artist,* which we have described previously as his appointment to the genius-type. The creative artistic personality is thus the first work of the productive individual, and it remains fundamentally his chief work, since all his other works are partly the repeated expression of this primal creation, partly a justification by dynamism.

I regard it as the double advantage of this insight into artistic personality-development which is gained from a study of the modern type, not only that it is applicable to the understanding of all cultural genesis, but that, moreover (according to a theory of art which I only came across after the event), artistic personality appears to subsist already in the beginning of all artistic production. Certain modern art-historians assume that the origin of primitive art is to be found neither in the imitation of nature nor in the impulse to abstraction, but in bodily ornament. As far as I know, Ernst Grosse was the first, in the already cited book on the beginnings of art (1894), to insist on the priority of body-painting over ornamental decoration; and Adam van Scheltema particularly has tried to extend the idea even to prehistoric art (*Die altnordische Kunst;* 1923). It is sufficient here to refer the reader to a later exposition and to quote the (to the best of my belief) latest author who cham-

[1] Here, perhaps, there is a most suggestive link with Schulte-Vaerting's theory of the "sexual superman" (1928), which he regards as a biological throw-back phenomenon.

pions this view; according to which we should be justified in saying that the tendency towards self-creation which is brought to light in modern artist-psychology is one of the essential components of artistic creation even in primitive times. E. von Sydow (pp. 173 et seq. of his book quoted above) accepts the view that " the beginning of art lay in its application to the body." He does not, however, mention his predecessors, so that it is apparently psycho-analysis which led him to this idea. Yet, if this were so, the psycho-analysts interested in the problem of art would not have needed to wait for Sydow in order to introduce this principle of explanation into the history of art, and anyhow it would be a confirmation on their part of a view which is alien to them. For this view of art presupposes a voluntaristic psychology, which in my own case I was only able to reach after passing beyond the libido theory of Freud, and which takes Sydow also far beyond his sexualization of the artistic impulse.

Sydow, it is true, appeals to the deliberate interference with the natural form of the body in primitive tribes, which in some cases, although not always, is sexual in character: for instance, the deformation of the skull, the piercing of ears, lips, nose, etc. But even in the artificial painting of the body and the tattooing which is to be found all over the world, the sexual explanation fails completely; and so Sydow's generalization looks more like an instance of our self-conscious impulse to creation than a proof that art in particular has a sexual origin. " Art rose, not in any isolated and self-contained work, but by the moulding of the human body, to a formative plasticity, urged thereto by an idealized instinct of will to style. It is true, indeed, that even at this stage the art-form not only serves to give a close support to the human form, as it is found in nature, *but impresses and enforces a dominant form on the natural material of bone, flesh, and blood, as an assertion of its own independence;* so that art in this application of it to man himself achieves or seeks to achieve a truly *new creation.* It is only when the art of the body has been perfected that it separates itself from the body and becomes self-dependent in a permanent work" (op. cit.; italics mine). Yet again, to make this view sound, we must give a plausible explanation of why body-art passed over to ornament proper, a problem of which there have been some preliminary explanations, but which, if we assume the priority of "body-art," more than ever demands a clear psychological understanding of the development of personality — to which accordingly we must now pass.

Whatever the meaning of the much-disputed tattooing as the essential expression of body-art may be, it is at least certain that practical objects, such as hardening the skin or the attraction or repulsion of others, do not have a great bearing. The purely sensual interpretation of tattooing, as suggested by W. Joest,[1] has nowadays given place to the magic interpretation, as emphasized in Jane Harrison's well-known *Ancient Art and Ritual* and as has been admitted by W. D. Hambly in his most recent discussion of the subject.[2] But there is no sort of consensus of opinion as to the real point of this magical painting of the body. We shall have opportunity later to give our own view; here it is enough to state the general conclusion that an artistic achievement is also part of the business. It seems, too, worth mentioning in this connexion that certain linguists connect the German word "*malen*" (to paint) with the drawing-in of body-marks (*Mal*) or signs, just as the Tahitian word "*tatu*" is derived from "*ta*," which means mark or sign. Among the American Indians as well as the Australians and other peoples, a typical form of painting is, in fact, the sign of the tribe, which indicates membership of a particular totem, and is therefore in a sense a collective badge of the individual which robs him of his personality in order to include him in a community, and yet on the other hand does not merely label him, but enhances his individual significance by marking it off from certain others. Both would explain why tattooing follows on the puberty ceremonies at which the indi-

[1] *Tátowiren, Narbenzeichnen, und Körperbemalen* (Berlin, 1887).
[2] *The History of Tattooing and its Significance* (London, 1925).

FROM K. VON DEN STEINEN: DIE MARQUESANER UND IHRE KUNST (BERLIN, 1931)

vidual becomes both a personality and a member of a community. On the other hand, the belief held by the Fijians and
the Eskimos alike that to remain untattooed is to hazard one's
future happiness in the world beyond throws a light on the
religious significance of tattooing, a significance that inheres
also in membership of a particular totem-society. We have
thus along with the enhancement of (and even emphasis on)
the self its levelling-down by means of the collective symbol;
so that in fact we should find the fundamental dualism of art
even at the primary stage of human creative instinct. This discovery loses much of its strangeness and gains considerably
in probability when we remember that the same thing is found
in the mediæval guild uniforms, and still exists today in the
uniform of various professions, which marks out the individual
above his neighbours, but makes him, as beyond himself, a
member of a great professional group or class.

From this point of view, of course, we cannot admit it to be
mere chance that the "Bohemian" artist of modern times,
even as late as the close of last century, had a definite costume,
even a conventional mode of doing the hair and beard, which
were to mark him out as a "genius." The proper artist, who
had chosen art as his profession, had a special manner, almost
a special life, laid down for him; and in actual fact he had to
play a definite part determined by an ideology; so also, according to Dessoir, the actor nowadays represents this pristine type
of artist, where object and subject coincide, and the body
forms the material in which and through which the artist
creates. So, even at this last stage of the individual "artist's
art," we have the genius-type to which the artist tries to suit
himself even in costume and manner, serving as an ideology
for artistic creation; just as earlier æsthetic, and still earlier
religion, had provided the art-ideologies of their various times
and places. Yet, be it observed, these were ideologies of *art* —
that is, collective style-laws, as in religious art, or psychological
laws of feeling in æsthetes' art — but at this latest stage of
individual artist's art we are concerned no longer with an

ideology of *art,* whether abstract or emotional, but an ideology of the artist; and this means a justification of *art-creation* in the creative personality itself that struggles for eternalization, and not a justification of *art* by some abstract impulse of the soul, as in religion, or in æsthetic of sensation, as in psychology.

Now, though Worringer quite rightly opposes linear art, which develops from the impulse to abstraction, to the Classical art which is intuitive, this is obviously not enough, for we have here a third type of art, which is as different from the other two as the one is from the other. If we want a word to set in parallel with " abstraction " and " intuition " as expressing the spiritual attitude of modern art, based on an individual, we may talk of an art of " expression " — in fact the word, as " expressionism," has been taken as their slogan by a group of modern artists (according to Sydow, p. 117, called also " psychic vitalism "). But since we are ourselves living in the midst of this art, it is doubly difficult to pass from a purely æsthetic judgment to a psychological valuation. It is too tempting to look for a historical comparison and a cultural valuation of this " modern art "; Worringer, strangely enough, does not admit modern art to be the expression of any " will to form " of its own, but regards it rather as an expression of " inability," which he does, however, concede to the result of an excessive urge to equal — or to outdo — earlier epochs.[1]

We shall have to discuss in a later chapter the reasons for which our present-day Culture had to come out at the art that it has done. At the moment it is more important to notice in these art-forms only the exaggeration (or, if you like, the distortion) of a quality common to all creative art, which entitles such an art as this to its place with the rest in the development of forms; in the same way as we tried to understand abstract and naturalistic styles not only as art-forms but as psychical expressions. Then we shall see that we have here to deal not with a third type of art, nor indeed with a type of art or a style at all, but with spiritual needs which at one time are abstract,

[1] Wilhelm Worringer: *Künstlerische Zeitfragen* (Munich, 1921).

at another naturalistic, at a third individualistic. It is not our business to attempt an æsthetic judgment — least of all before we have studied the question how far the psychical basis of the modern artist can be traced up in the origins and development of Classical and abstract art. Yet it may be that the genesis of the creative personality, which is the problem that this book is seeking to unravel, will throw a new light on the form of art which is included under the æsthetic law of intuition (*Einfühlung*) and may even contribute to the elucidation of other, still obscure points in that abstract style of primitive art which so purely expresses the absolute will to form.

Chapter Two

LIFE AND CREATION

✵

> *What would live in song immortally*
> *Must in life first perish. . . .*
> SCHILLER

LIFE AND CREATION

ᘒᘖ

Before we trace the rise and significance of this "artist's art," if one may so call it, as it grows out of the primitive art-ideologies, it is perhaps desirable to characterize more clearly its essential precondition: namely, the creative personality itself. In spite of all "unconsciousness" in artistic production (a point to which we shall return later), there can be no doubt that the modern individualist type of artist is characterized by a higher degree of consciousness than his earlier prototype: the consciousness not only of his creative work and his artist's mission, but also of his own personality and its productiveness. If, as it should seem, the instinctive will-to-art (Riegl), which creates abstract forms, has in this last stage of artistic development become a conscious will-to-art in the artist, yet the actual process which leads a man to become an artist is usually one of which the individual is not conscious. In other words, the act which we have described as the artist's self-appointment as such is in itself a spontaneous expression of the creative impulse, of which the first manifestation is simply the forming of the personality itself. Needless to say, this purely internal process does not suffice to make an artist, let alone a genius, for, as Lange-Eichbaum has said, only the community, one's contemporaries, or posterity can do that. Yet the self-labelling and self-training of an artist is the indispensable basis of all creative work, and without it general recognition could never arise. The artist's lifelong work on his own productive personality appears to run through definite phases, and his art develops in proportion to the success of these phases. In the case of great artists the process is reflected in the fact that they had either a principal or a favourite work, at which they laboured all their lives (Goethe's *Faust*, Rodin's *Porte d'enfer*, Michelangelo's Tomb of Julius, and so on), or a favourite theme, which they never relinquished and which came to be a distinct representation of themselves (as, for example, Rembrandt's self-portraits).

On the other hand, this process of the artist's self-forming and self-training is closely bound up with his life and his experiences. In studying this fundamental problem of the relation between living and creating in an artist, we are therefore again aware of the reciprocal influence of these two spheres. All the psychography and pathography (with its primary concern to explain the one through the other) must remain unsatisfactory as long as the creative impulse, which finds expression equally in experience and in productiveness, is not recognized as the basis of both. For, as I already showed in my essay on Schiller (written in 1905), creativeness lies equally at the root of artistic production and of life experience.[1] That is to say, lived experience can only be understood as the expression of volitional creative impulse, and in this the two spheres of artistic production and actual experience meet and overlap. Then, too, the creative impulse itself is manifested first and chiefly in the personality, which, being thus perpetually made over, produces art-work and experience in the same way. To draw the distinction quite drastically between this new standpoint and earlier ones, one might put it that the artist does not create from his own experience (as Goethe, for instance, so definitely appears to do), but almost in spite of it. For the creative impulse in the artist, springing from the tendency to immortalize himself, is so powerful that he is always seeking to protect himself against the transient experience, which eats up his ego. The artist takes refuge, with all *his own* experience only from the life of *actuality*, which for him spells mortality and decay,

[1] *Das Inzest-Motiv in Dichtung und Sage* (chapters III and XVI). I found the same conception later in Simmel's *Goethe* (Berlin, 1913).

whereas the experience to which he has given shape imposes itself on him as a creation, which he in fact seeks to turn into a work. And although the whole artist-psychology may seem to be centred on the "experience," this itself can be explained only through the creative impulse — which attempts to turn ephemeral life into personal immortality. In creation the artist tries to immortalize his mortal life. He desires to transform death into life, as it were, though actually he transforms life into death. For not only does the created work not go on living; it is, in a sense, dead; both as regards the material, which renders it almost inorganic, and also spiritually and psychologically, in that it no longer has any significance for its creator, once he has produced it. He therefore again takes refuge in life, and again forms experiences, which for their part represent only mortality — and it is precisely because they are mortal that he wishes to immortalize them in his work.

The first step towards understanding this mutual relation between life and work in the artist is to gain a clear idea of the psychological significance of the two phenomena. This is only possible, however, on the basis of a constructive psychology of personality, reaching beyond the psycho-analytical conception, which is a therapeutic ideology resting on the biological sex-impulse. We have come to see that another factor must be reckoned with besides the original biological duality of impulse and inhibition in man; this is the psychological factor *par excellence,* the individual will, which manifests itself both negatively as a controlling element, and positively as the urge to create. This creator-impulse is not, therefore, sexuality, as Freud assumed, but expresses the antisexual tendency in human beings, which we may describe as the deliberate control of the impulsive life. To put it more precisely, I see the creator-impulse as the life impulse made to serve the individual will. When psycho-analysis speaks of a sublimated sexual impulse in creative art, meaning thereby the impulse diverted from its purely biological function and directed towards higher ends, the question as to what diverted and what directed is just being dismissed with an allusion to repression. But repression is a negative factor, which might divert, but never direct. And so the further question remains to be answered: what, originally led to such repression? As we know, the answer to this question was outward deprivation; but that again suggests a merely negative check, and I, for my part, am of opinion that (at any rate from a certain definite point of individual development) positively willed control takes the place of negative inhibition, and that it is the masterful use of the sexual impulse in the service of this individual will which produces the sublimation.

But even more important for us than these psychological distinctions is the basic problem of why this inhibition occurs at all, and what the deliberate control of the vital impulse means to the individual. Here, again, in opposition to the Freudian conception of an external threat as the cause of the inhibition, I suggest that the internal threatening of the individual through the sexual impulse of the species is at the root of all conflict. Side by side with this self-imposed internal check, which is taken to be what prevents or lessens the development of fear, there stands the will as a positive factor. The various controls which it exercises enable the impulses to work themselves out partially without the individual's falling completely under their influence or having to check them completely by too drastic repression. Thus in the fully developed individual we have to reckon with the triad Impulse-Fear-Will, and it is the dynamic relationship between these factors that determines either the attitude at a given moment or — when equilibrium is established — the type. Unsatisfactory as it may be to express these dynamic processes in terms like "type," it remains the only method of carrying an intelligible idea of them — always assuming that the inevitable simplification in this is not lost sight of. If we compare the neurotic with the productive type, it is evident that the former suffers from an excessive check on his impulsive life, and, according to whether this neurotic checking of the instincts is effected through fear or through will, the picture presented is one of fear-neurosis or compulsion-neurosis. With the productive type the will dominates, and exercises a far-reaching control over (but not check upon) the instincts, which are pressed into service to bring about creatively a social relief of fear. Finally, the instincts appear relatively unchecked in the so-called psychopathic subject, in whom the will affirms the impulse instead of controlling it. In this type — to which the criminal belongs — we have, contrary to appearances, to do with *weak*-willed people, people who are subjected to their instinctive impulses; the neurotic, on the other hand, is generally regarded as the weak-willed type, but wrongly so, for his strong will is exercised upon himself and, indeed, in the main repressively so it does not show itself.

And here we reach the essential point of difference between the productive type who creates and the thwarted neurotic; what is more, it is also the point from which we get back to our individual artist-type. Both are distinguished fundamentally from the average type, who accepts himself as he is, by their tendency to exercise their volition in reshaping themselves. There is, however, this difference: that the neurotic, in this voluntary remaking of his ego, does not get beyond the destructive preliminary work and is therefore unable to detach the whole creative process from his own person and transfer it to an ideological abstraction. The productive artist also begins (as a satisfactory psychological understanding of the " will-to-style " has obliged us to conclude) with that re-creation of himself which results in an ideologically constructed ego; this ego is then in a position to shift the creative will-power from his own person to ideological representations of that person and thus to render it objective. It must be admitted that this process is in a measure limited to within the individual himself, and that not only in its constructive, but also in its destructive, aspects. This explains why hardly any productive work [1] gets through without morbid crises of a " neurotic " nature; it

[1] This applies, not only to most artists, but also, as Wilhelm Ostwald for one has convincingly proved, to the scientific creative type (*Grosse Männer;* Leipzig, 1909).

also explains why the relation between productivity and illness has so far been unrecognized or misinterpreted, as, for instance, in Lombroso's theory of the insanity of genius. Today this theory appears to us as the precipitate left by the old endeavours to explain genius on rational-psychological lines, which treated such features as depart from the normal as "pathological." However much in the Italian psychiatrist's theory is an exaggeration of the materialism of nineteenth-century science, yet undeniably it had a startling success, and this I attribute to the fact that genius itself, in its endeavour to differentiate itself from the average, has probably dramatized its pathological features also. But the psychologist should beware of deducing from this apparent factor any conclusions as to the production or total personality, without taking into account the feeling of guilt arising from the creative process itself; for this is capable of engendering a feeling of inferiority as a secondary result, even though the primary result may be a conviction of superiority. As I have said elsewhere, the fundamental problem is *individual difference,* which the ego is inclined to interpret as inferiority unless it can be proved by achievement to be superiority.

Even psycho-analysis in its turn did not succeed in surmounting Lombroso's materialist theory of insanity or supplementing his rational explanation by a spiritual one. All it did was to substitute· neurosis for insanity· (which was at bottom Lombroso's own meaning), thus tending either to identify the artist with the neurotic — this is particularly the case in Sadger's and Stekel's arguments — or to explain the artist on the basis of an inferiority feeling. (Alfred Adler and his school took the latter view.) [1] It is characteristic that during the last few years the psychiatrists (such as Lange-Eichbaum, Kretschmer, Plaut) who have contributed most towards clearing up the

[1] A characteristic instance of how, in avoiding the Scylla of Lombroso, one may fall a victim to the Charybdis of analytical psychology is afforded by Victor Jonesco's book: *La Personnalité du génie artiste* (Paris, 1930), which I read only after the completion of my own work. A praiseworthy exception is Bernard Grasset's original essay: *Psychologie de l'immortalité* (Paris, 1929).

position of genius are precisely those who have managed to keep clear of the one-sidedness of these psycho-analytical schools. And if these researches have not made any important contribution to the understanding of the process of creating, psycho-analysis, even in its exaggerations, must at least be credited with having discovered that experience, in so far as it is the anthithesis of production, embraces not only the relations of love and friendship, but also those morbid reactions of a psychic and bodily nature which are known as " neurotic." A real understanding of these neurotic illnesses could not, however, be satisfactorily obtained as long as we tried to account for them in the Freudian sense by thwarted sexuality. What was wanted in addition was a grasp of the general problem of fear and of the will-psychology going therewith which should allow for the exercise of the will, both constructively and destructively, affecting the ego and the work equally. Only through the will-to-self-immortalization, which rises from the fear of life, can we understand the interdependence of production and suffering and the definite influence of this on positive experience. This does not preclude production being a creative development of a neurosis in objective form; and, on the other hand, a neurotic collapse may follow as a reaction after production, owing either to a sort of exhaustion or to a sense of guilt arising from the power of creative masterfulness as something arrogant.[1]

Reverting now from the production-process to experience, it does not take long to perceive that experience is the expression of the impulse-ego, production of the will-ego. The external difficulties in an artist's experience appear, in this sense, but as manifestations of this internal dualism of impulse and will, and in the creative type it is the latter which eventually gains the upper hand. Instinct presses in the direction of experience and, in the limit, to consequent exhaustion — in fact,

---

[1] How this feeling of guilt can hinder or, on the other hand, further productivity I have shown in my book: *Wahrheit und Wirklichkeit* (1929) in the section on the sense of guilt in creation.

death — while will drives to creation and thus to immortalization. On the other hand, the productive type also pays toll to
life by his work and to death by bodily and spiritual sufferings
of a " neurotic " order; and conversely in many cases the
product of a type that is at bottom neurotic may be his sole
propitiatory offering to Life. It is with reason, therefore, that
from the beginning two basic types of artist have been
distinguished; these have been called at one time Dionysian
and Apollonian, and at another Classical and Romantic.[1] In
terms of our present dynamic treatment, the one approximates
to the psychopathic-impulsive type, the other to the compulsion-
neurotic volitional type. The one creates more from fullness
of powers and sublimation, the other more from exhaustion
and compensation. The work of the one is entire in every
single expression, that of the other is partial even in its totality,
for the one lives itself out, positively, in the work, while the
other pays with the work — pays, not to society (for both do
that), but to life itself, from which the one strives to win freedom by self-willed creation whereas for the other the thing
created is the expression of life itself.

This duality within one and the same type is of outstanding
significance in the psychology of the productive type and in the
work it produces. For, while in the two classes of neurotics
(frustrated by fear and by the will respectively) the form
of the neurosis is of minor matter compared with the fact of
breaking down the inhibition itself, by the curative process of
dynamic equilibration, in the productive type the dynamism
itself determines not only the kind but the form of his art. But
this highly complicated problem is only mentioned here with
a view to discussion later, and we will turn from the two artist-
types, which Müller-Freienfels, in his *Psychologie der Kunst*
(Vol. II, pp. 100 et seq.) characterizes as " expressive artists "
and " formative artists," back to the problem of experience
which is common to both. This problem, as was pointed out

[1] E. von Sydow distinguishes these polar opposites, from the standpoint of æsthetic,
as "eros-dominated" and "eros-dominating" (op. cit., p. 164).

at the beginning of this chapter, only becomes intelligible through the conception of immortality. There appears to be a common impulse in all creative types to replace collective immortality — as it is represented biologically in sexual propagation — by the individual immortality of deliberate self-perpetuation. This is, however, a relatively late stage of development in the conception of immortality, after it has already become individualized — a stage preceded by attempts to create conceptions of collective immortality, of which the most important is religion. I have tried in another connexion [1] to show how, within religious development itself, the idea of the collective soul was gradually transformed into the idea of the individual god, whose heir the artist later became. In the foregoing pages likewise I have indicated that the initial conception of an individual god, subsequently to be humanized in the genius, had itself been helped on, and perhaps even only rendered possible, by art. But there was an early stage of artistic development, which was at the same time the climax of religious development, in which the individual artist played no part because creative power was still the prerogative of the god.

The individual artist, whose growth from the creative conception of a god has been sketched out, no longer uses the collective ideology of religion to perpetuate himself, but the personal religion of genius, which is the precondition of any productions by the individual artist-type. And so we have *primitive art,* the expression of a collective ideology, perpetuated by abstraction which has found its *religious* expression in the idea of the soul; *Classical art,* based on a *social* art-concept, perpetuated by *idealization,* which has found its purest expression in the conception of beauty; and, lastly, *modern art,* based on the concept of individual genius and perpetuated by *concretization,* which has found its clearest expression in the personality-cult of the artistic individuality itself. Here, then, in contrast to the primitive stage, it is the artist and not art that

[1] *Seelenglaube und Psychologie* (1930).

matters, and naturally therefore the experience of the individual takes on the significance characteristic of the romantic artist-type.[1] Here, obviously, not only do we see the tendency — in our view the basic tendency — of the artist-type to put oneself and one's life into one's creative work; but we see also how, in the eyes of this type, the problem of the relation between experience and creation[2] has become an artistic (æsthetic) one; whereas it is really only a psychological one, which discloses, indeed, important points of contact with art (considered as an ideological conception), but differs from it in essence.

For the romantic dualism of life and production, which manifests itself as a mixture of both spheres, has, as a typical conflict within the modern individual, nothing to do with art, although obliged like art to express itself creatively. This romantic dualism of life and creation, which corresponds to our psychological dualism of impulse and will, is, in the last resort, the conflict between collective and individual immortality, in which we have all suffered so acutely since the decay of religion and the decline of art. The romantic type, flung hither and thither between the urge to perpetuate his own life by creating and the compulsion to turn himself and life into a work of art, thus appears as the last representative of an art-ideology which, like the religious collective-ideology, is in process of dying out. This does not prevent this final attempt to rescue the semi-collective " religion of genius " by taking it into modern individualism from bringing forth outstanding and permanently valuable works of art; perhaps, indeed (as Nietzsche himself, the ultra-Romantic, recognized), it requires that it should. On the other hand, it is just the appearance of this decadent type of artist which marks the beginning of a new development of personality, since the tendency to self-

[1] What interests us today in Byron, for instance, is his romantic life, and not his out-of-date poetry.

[2] See W. Dilthey's book *Erlebnis und Dichtung*. The artist-personalities examined there in relation to this problem are, as is natural, chiefly romantic types (Lessing, Goethe, Novalis, Hölderlin).

perpetuation is in the end transferred to the ego from which it originally sprang. (See later the chapter: " The Artist's Struggle.")

On this issue the romantic becomes identical, as a psychological type, with the neurotic — this is not a valuation, but merely a statement of fact — and for that matter the comparison may even be reversed, since the neurotic likewise has creative, or, at least, self-creative, forces at command. We can thus understand the experience-problem of the individualist type of artist also only by studying the nature of neurosis, just as the therapy of the neurotic requires an understanding of the creative type.[1] Now, the neurotic represents the individual who aims at self-preservation by restricting his experience, thus showing his adherence to the naïve faith in immortality of the primitive, though without the collective soul-ideology which supports that faith. The productivity of the individual, or of the thing created, replaces — for the artist as for the community — the originally religious ideology by a social value; that is, the work of art not only immortalizes the artist ideologically instead of personally, but also secures to the community a future life in the collective elements of the work. Even at this last stage of individual art-creativity there function ideologies (whether given or chosen) of an æsthetic, a social, or a psychological nature as collective justifications of the artist's art, in which the personal factor makes itself more and more felt and appreciated.

If the impulse to create productively is explicable only by the conception of immortality, the question of the experience-problem of the neurotic has its source in failure of the impulse to perpetuate, which results in fear, but is also probably conditioned by it. There is (as I have shown) a double sort of fear: on the one hand the fear of life which aims at avoidance or postponement of death, and on the other the fear of death which underlies the desire for immortality. According to the

[1] This is a point of view which I endeavoured to present in my last technical work: *Die Analyse des Analytikers und seine Rolle in der Gesamtsituation* (1931).

compromise which men make between these two poles of fear, and the predominance of one or the other form, there will be various dynamic solutions of this conflict, which hardly permit of description by type-labelling. For, in practice, both in the neurotic and in the productive type — the freely producing and the thwarted — all the forces are brought into play, though with varying accentuation and periodical balancing of values. In general, a strong preponderance of the fear of life will lead rather to neurotic repression, and the fear of death to production — that is, perpetuation in the work produced. But the fear of life, from which we all suffer, conditions the problem of experience in the productive type as in other people, just as the fear of death whips up the neurotic's constructive powers. The individual whose life is braked is led thereby to flee from experience, because he fears that he will become completely absorbed in it — which would mean death — and so is bound up with fear. Unlike the productive type, who strives to be deathless through his work, the neurotic does not seek immortality in any clearly defined sense, but in primitive fashion as a naïve saving or accumulation of actual life. But even the individualist artist-type must sacrifice both life and experience to make art out of them. Thus we see that what the artist needs for true creative art in addition to his technique and a definite ideology is life in one form or another; and the two artist-types differ essentially in the source from which they take this life that is so essential to production. The Classical type, who is possibly poorer within, but nearer to life, and himself more vital, takes it from without: that is, he creates immortal work from mortal life without necessarily having first transformed it into personal experience as is the case with the Romantic. For, to the Romantic, experience of his own appears to be an essential preliminary to productivity, although he does not use this experience for the enrichment of his own personality, but to economize the personal experiences, the burden of which he would fain escape. Thus the one artist-type constantly makes use of other life than his own — in fact, nature — for the purpose of creating, while the other can create only by perpetually sacrificing his own life. This essential difference of attitude to the fundamental problem of life throws a psychological light on the contrast in styles of various periods in art. Whatever æsthetic designation may be applied to this contrast, from the spiritual point of view the work of the Classicist, more or less naturalistic, artist is essentially *partial,* and the work of the Romantic, produced from within, *total.*[1] This totality-type spends itself perpetually in creative work without absorbing very much of life, while the partial type has continually to absorb life so that he may throw it off again in his work. It is an egoistical artist-type of this order that Ibsen has described in so masterly a fashion. He needs, as it were, for each work that he builds, a sacrifice which is buried alive to ensure a permanent existence to the structure, but also to save the artist from having to give himself. The frequent occasions when a great work of art has been created in the reaction following upon the death of a close relation seem to me to realize those favourable cases for this type of artist in which he can dispense with the killing of the building's victim because that victim has died a natural death and has subsequently, to all appearances, had a monument piously erected to him.[2]

The mistake in all modern psychological biography lies in its attempt to "explain" the artist's work by his experience, whereas creation can only be made understandable through the inner dynamism and its central problems. Then, too, the

[1] These types, evolved from a study of psychological dynamics (see my *Die Analyse des Analytikers*), are, as I have since discovered, accepted as the essential key-concepts of all polar contrasts of style by P. Frankl in his *Entwicklungsphasen der neueren Baukunst.* True, Frankl's work is not merely limited to architecture, but more narrowly still to the contrast in style between Renaissance and Baroque. We shall presently see, however ("*Schönheit und Wahrheit*"), that this contrast between totality and partiality is a general spiritual distinction between the Classical-naturalistic and the primitive-abstract styles.

[2] Shakspere's *Hamlet* and Mozart's *Don Juan* are familiar examples of the reaction after a father's death, while Wagner's *Lohengrin* followed on the death of the composer's mother. These works are supreme examples of artists negotiating with the problem of the Beyond. To these instances may be added Ibsen's epilogue *When We Dead Awake;* here the death is that of the artist himself.

real artist regards his work as more important than the whole of life and experience, which are but a means to production — almost, indeed, a by-product of it. This refers, however, to the Classical type only, for to the Romantic type his personal ego and his experience are more important than, or as important as, his work; sometimes, indeed, production may be simply a means to life, just as to the other type experience is but a means to production. This is why Romantic art is far more subjective, far more closely bound up with experience, than Classical, which is more objective and linked to life. In no case, however, will the individual become an artist through any *one* experience, least of all through the experiences of childhood (which seem pretty universal). The becoming of the artist has a particular genesis, one of the manifestations of which may be some special experience. For the artistic impulse to create is a dynamic factor apart from the content of experience, a will-problem which the artist solves in a particular way. That is, he is capable of forming the given art-ideology — whether of the collective kind (style) or the personal (genius-idea) — into the substance of his creative will. He employs, so to say, personal will-power to give form or life to an ideology, which must have not only social qualities like other ideologies, but purely artistic ones, which will be more closely specified from the point of view of æsthetics.

The subjective character of modern art, which is based on the ideology of a personal type of artist, imposes also a special outlook in the artist towards his own creative power and his work. The more production is an essential means to life (and not just a particular ideological expression of it), the more will the work itself be required to justify the personality — instead of expressing it — and the more will this subjective artist-type need individuals to justify his production. From this point of view as well as others it is easy to see that experience, in its particular form of love-experience, takes on a peculiar significance for the Romantic artist, whose art is based on the personality-cult of the genius-concept. The primitive artist-type finds his justification in the work itself; the Classical justifies the work by his life, but the Romantic must justify both life and experience by his work and, further, must have a witness of his life to justify his production. The fundamental problem of the Romantic artist is thus the self-justification of the individual raised above the crowd, while the Classical artist-type expresses himself in his work — which receives a social justification by way of general recognition. But the Romantic needs, further, whether as contrast or as supplement to this social approval, a personal approbation of his own, because his feeling of the guilt of creation can no longer be allayed by a collective ideology any more than he can work effectively in the service of such an ideology. In this sense his artistic work is rather a forcible liberation from inward pressure than the voluntary expression of a fundamentally strong personality that is capable of paralysing the subjective element to a great extent by making collective symbolism his own. The artist who approximates more nearly to the Classical type excels less, therefore, in the creating of new forms than in perfecting them. Further, he will make much more frequent use of old traditional material, full of a powerful collective resonance, as the content of his work, while the Romantic seeks new forms and contents in order to be able to express his personal self more completely.

Thus, as the artist-type becomes more and more individualized, he appears on the one hand to need a more individual ideology — the genius-concept — for his art, while on the other his work is more subjective and more personal, until finally he requires for the justification of his production an individual " public " also: a single person for whom ostensibly he creates. This goes so far in a certain type of artist, which we call the Romantic, that actual production is only possible with the aid of a concrete Muse through whom or for whom the work is produced. The " experience " which arises in this manner is not, like other sorts of experience, an external phenomenon set over against creative work, but is a part of it and even identical with it, always providing that the Muse — in practice, usually a real woman — is suited to this rôle or at least makes no objection to it, and so long as the artist can maintain such a relation on the ideological plane without confusing it with real life. It is this case, in which the conflict between life and creation reaches extreme intensity, that we so often see actualized in the modern type of artist. Here the woman is expected to be Muse and mistress at once, which means that she must justify equally the artistic ego, with its creativeness, and the real self, with its life; and this she seldom (and in any case only temporarily) succeeds in doing. We see the artist of this type working off on the woman his inward struggle between life and production or, psychologically speaking, between impulse and will. It is a tragic fate that he shares with the neurotic, who suffers from the same inner conflict. Another way out of the struggle is to divide its elements between two persons, of whom one belongs to the ideological creative sphere, and the other to the sphere of actual life. But this solution also presents difficulties of a psychological as well as a social order, because this type of artist has a fundamental craving for totality, in life as in work, and the inner conflict, though it may be temporarily eased by being objectivized in such an outward division of rôles, is as a whole only intensified thereby.

The same applies to another solution of this ego-conflict which the artist has in common with the neurotic, and one which shows more clearly even than the complicated love-conflict that it is at bottom a question not of sexual but of creative problems. From the study of a certain class of neurotic we have found that in many cases of apparent homosexual conflicts it is less a sexual perversion than an ego-problem that underlies them, a problem with which the individual can only deal by personifying a portion of his own ego in another individual. The same applies, it is true, to heterosexual love-relations, from which the homosexual differs only in that the selfward part of this relation is stronger, or at any rate more distinct. If the poet values his

Muse the more highly in proportion as it can be identified with his artistic personality and its ideology, then self-evidently he will find his truest ideal in an even greater degree in his own sex, which is in any case physically and intellectually closer to him. Paradoxical as it may sound, the apparently homosexual tendencies or actual relationships of certain artists fulfil the craving for a Muse which will stimulate and justify creative work in a higher degree than (for a man) a woman can do. It is only as the result of the artist's urge for completion, and his desire to find everything united in one person, that it is mostly a woman that is taken as, or made into, a Muse, although instances of homosexual relations between artists are by no means rare.

Greece, in particular, with its high development of purely intellectual ideologies in art and philosophy, was of course the classical country of boy-love; and there is nothing contradictory in this, particularly if we understand the boy-friendship in the Greek spirit.[1] For it was in the main, or at least collaterally, a high spiritual relation which had as its basis and object a " pedagogic " training for the boy. The master — whether philosopher or sculptor, or, in other words, artist in living or in shaping — was not content to teach his pupil or protégé his doctrines or his knowledge: he had the true artistic impulse to transform him into his own image, to create. And this, by the way, was the form of personal immortality characteristic of Greek culture at its height, which not only found expression in works of art or spiritual teaching, but sought fulfilment in a personal, concrete successor. This successor was no longer (or not yet, if we think of Rome) the physical son, but the like-minded pupil. This is why the spiritual relation of pupil-and-master — which Christianity was to set up again as the centre of its doctrine of life — has remained a more important thing to the creative artist than the juridical father-and-son relation which psycho-analysis seeks to regard as fundamental,

[1] See my account in *Modern Education* (New York: Alfred A. Knopf; 1932), pp. 24–6.

whereas it is spiritually of a secondary order. And in Greece, therefore, the state of being a pupil did not mean the mere acquiring of a certain discipline and the mastery of a certain material knowledge, as in the civilization of father-right, but the forming of a personality — which begins by identification with the master and is then "artistically" developed and perfected on the pupil's own lines. In this sense the Greek was creative before he arrived at creating works of art, or, indeed, without ever shaping anything but himself and his pupil. Socrates is the best known of many examples of this.

This educative ideology of the artistic Greek nation, which is manifested also in boy-love in all its aspects, brings up the question: did that Greek art, which may seem to us today the main achievement of the Greek civilization, perhaps represent to the Greek a mere by-product thereof, an auxiliary, in fact, to the education of the men, who as the real vessels of the culture were thus enabled *inter alia* to practise art for its own sake? This brings us to another question: was not every great art, whether of primitive or cultivated peoples, bound up with some such cultured task, which lies beyond the bounds of æsthetics, but also beyond all individual artist-psychology? In any case, there are numerous literary proofs of the high degree to which the Greeks were conscious of this national importance of their art. They said that men should learn from works of art and try themselves to become as beautiful and perfect as the statues around them. This gives us an insight into the characteristic way in which the Greeks extended their own creation of individual personalities to include a whole nation, which was not content to produce works of art for their own sake but strove to create an artistic human type who would also be able to produce fine works of art. Seen in this light, boy-love, which, as Plato tells us, aimed perpetually at the improvement and perfection of the beloved youth, appears definitely as the Classical counterpart of the primitive body-art on a spiritualized plane. In the primitive stage it is a matter of physical self-enhancement; in the civilized stage, a spiritual perfecting in the other person, who becomes transferred into the worthy successor of oneself here on earth; and that, not on the basis of the biological procreation of one's body, but in the sense of the spiritual immortality-symbolism in the pupil, the younger.

Christianity took over this ideal of personal character-formation in the symbol of the Exemplar-Master, but, in proportion as it became a world-wide religion of the masses, it was unable to carry it out at the personal level. The collective immortality-dogma, which became symbolized in Christ, relieved the individual of this task of personal self-creation; Christ instead was no longer a model, but became a victim who took upon himself voluntarily the development of everyone's personality. Correspondingly, Christian art remained stationary in the abstract collective style of the religious ideology, until in the Renaissance it was freed by the emergence of a new type of personality. It was not mere imitation of Classical Greece, but the expression of a similar ideology of personality that led the artists of the Renaissance to try to re-experience the Greek ideal of boy-love. We see, for instance, two of the really great artists, of entirely different social environment, expressing the identical spiritual ideology, with such far-reaching similarity that the notion that the mere accident of a personal experience produced both cases must be dismissed. They both, Michelangelo and Shakspere, found almost identical words in their famous sonnets for the noble love which each of them felt for a beautiful youth who was his friend. Michelangelo's case is the simpler in that we at least think we know to whom his sonnets were addressed, although it might equally well be the short-lived Ceccino Bracchi or Tommaso de Cavalieri, the object of a lifelong adoration. It is not even clear in some of his later sonnets whether his " idol " refers to his young friend or to Vittoria Colonna, whose platonic friendship came later. The content of Shakspere's sonnets is a far more complicated matter. His ideal has been sought among the widely differing persons among the aristocracy of his day. His adoring friendship for the youth in question was not, as with Michelangelo, followed by a soothing maternal friendship, but was broken in upon by a young and beautiful woman. Here, as in his dramas also, woman figures as an evil, disturbing dæmon that the Elizabethan dramatist never succeeded in transforming into a helpful Muse, but always felt to be an obstacle to creative work; whereas in his young friend he found the ideal which spurred him on and aided him. But whatever the decision reached by zealous scholars concerning the identity of the person addressed in his immortal sonnets, this " biographical " fact seems to me unimportant as compared with the psychological evidence that this glorification of a friend is, fundamentally, self-glorification just as was the Greek boy-love. In this sense, not only are the sonnets in fact self-dedicated — as is creative work of every description — but they reveal that peculiar attitude of the creative instinct towards the creative ego which seeks to glorify it by artistic idealization and at the same time to overcome its mortality by eternalizing it in art.

The fact that an idealized self-glorification in the person of another can take on physical forms, as in the Greek boy-love, has actually nothing to do with the sex of the beloved, but is concerned only with the struggle to develop a personality and the impulse to create which arises from it. This impulse is at bottom directed to the creator's own rebirth in the closest possible likeness, which is naturally more readily found in his own sex; the other sex is felt to be biologically a disturbing element except where it can be idealized as a Muse. But the likeness to himself will not only be found in the bodily form of his own sex, but also be built up with regard to the spiritual affinity, and in this regard the youthfulness of the beloved stands for the bodily symbol of immortality. In this manner does the mature man, whose impulse to perpetuate himself drives him away from the biological sex-life, live his own life over again in his youthful love; not only seeking to transform him into his intellectual counterpart, but making him his spiritual ideal, the symbol of his vanishing youth. The sonnets of both the

Renaissance artists are full of such laments over the vanishing youth of the beloved, whose glorious picture it is the duty of the poem to preserve to all eternity. Just as we know, from the psychology of the creative genius, that his impulse to create arises from precisely this tendency to immortalize himself in his work, so we can be in no doubt as to whose transitoriness it is that the poet deplores with almost monotonous reiteration. In these sonnets there is so complete a revelation of the meaning and content of the whole output of their authors, and indeed of the nature of the artist's creative instinct in general, that their high valuation and, no less, their intriguing ambiguity become comprehensible. Yet they are easy to understand if we regard them as the subjective completion of their author's objective creations, for in their naïve self-projection they admit their own transitoriness to be the reason for their own perpetuation in poetry.

From this point of view, then, the biographical presentation, even when it can be done with certainty, seems to us inessential. We are by no means cast down when this method fails, for we can understand that beyond a certain point failure is unavoidable, since the creation of a work of art cannot be explained even by the reconstruction of an inspirer. Thus the factual and concrete biography of Michelangelo or Shakspere does not enable us to understand their work the better; rather we are left more amazed than before at their coincidence. Vasari, anyhow, declares that the one and only portrait by Michelangelo which was true to nature was that of his young friend Tommaso Cavalieri, " for he detested copying the actual appearance of anyone who was not completely beautiful." The same ideal fashion in which he immortalizes the beloved in poetry corresponds exactly with Shakspere's attitude to *his* ideal. For the English poet also has the conscious intention of immortalizing his friend's beauty at least in his verse, if time is bound to destroy his bodiliness. This is the constantly reiterated theme in the Shakspere sonnets, and Michelangelo had the same feeling in the presence of the beloved youth: that his beauty should be incorporated into eternity. Not only is it evident from this self-immortalization in the work that the matter is at bottom one of self-immortalization expressed in another (in the ideal), but both these artists have expressed with great clearness, and to the point of monotony, the idea of oneness with the friend. Shakspere says:

"What can mine own praise to mine own self bring?
And what is't but mine own when I praise thee?"

(Sonnet XXXIX); and Michelangelo in one of his sonnets not only says that a lover "transforms himself" into the beloved, but in a letter presses this transformation of the beloved into his own image, so far as to call his friend Tommaso "a genius who is a stranger in this world." [1]

This psychological solution of the much-disputed sonnet-problem shows how experience, and still more the whole attitude towards life, grows out of the struggle to create and so reduces the problem of experience to the problem of creativity. For the extent to which the artist succeeds in actualizing his love-ideal, in the service of his own self-immortalization, is of minor importance compared with the basic attitude that his work discloses — namely, one originating in dissatisfaction with artistic creation and so urging the creator in some form or other towards life — that is, towards the actual experiencing of his fundamental self. In any case his impulse to form man in his own image or in the image of his ideal inevitably brings him into conflict with real life and its conditions. These conditions are not artistic, but social, conditions, in which one individual has to respect another and is not permitted to remake him. Now, a certain measure of conflict is, of course, necessary to creative work, and this conflict is, in fact, one of the fields in which an artist displays his greatness, or, psychologically speaking, the strength of his creative will-power. By means of it he is able to work off a certain measure of his inner con-

---

[1] The references are taken from Emil Lucka's book on Michelangelo (1930).

flict in his art without entirely sacrificing the realities of life or coming into factual conflict with them. In any case, the destructive results of this ensemble of realities upon the neurotic, as we are able to observe them in his neurosis, show that what distinguishes him from the artist is that the latter constructively applies his will-power in the service of *ideological* creation. A certain type of artist, for whom Goethe may stand as the model, will learn to deal with his experiences and conflicts economically and in the end wisely, while another type exhausts his strength in chasing after stimulating experiences so that his conflict does not come out in production. For the artist himself the fact *that* he creates is more immediately important than *what* he produces, although we are inclined to make his classification as a particular type depend upon the result, his art-work. Here again we find ourselves at a point where art as the result of production must be sharply differentiated from the artist as a creative individual. There is, in fact, no norm for the artist as a type, although we are constantly tempted to set up more or less precisely formulated norms both for art and for the individual work of art. Production is a vital process which happens within the individual and is independent at the outset from the ideology manifested in the created work. On the other hand, the work can show an equal independence towards the artist who has created it, and can in favourable instances be compared with other works within the categories of art; but it can never be compared with its author or with the artist as a psychological type. Between the two — artist and art — there stands Life, now dividing, now uniting, now checking, now promoting.

Here we must return once more to the relation of the artist to woman (or to the opposite sex). In the life of many an artist this is a disturbing factor, one of the deepest sources of conflict, indeed, when it tends to force or beguile him into closer touch with life than is necessary or even advantageous to his production. To make a woman his Muse, or to name her as such, therefore, often amounts to transforming a hindrance into a helper — a compromise which is usually in the interest of productiveness, but renders no service to life. Here, again, everything naturally depends on the artist's dynamic type and his specific conflict over life and production. There are artists for whom even a feminine Muse represents nothing but a potential homosexual relation; for they see in her not so much the woman as a comrade of like outlook and like aims, who could equally well — and possibly better — be replaced by a male friendship. On the other hand, there is an artist-type which is totally unable to produce at all without the biological complement of the other sex and indeed depends directly on the sexual life for its stimulus. For the type which is creative in and by means of sexual abstinence has its opposite in another type which, strange to say, is not only not exhausted by the sexual act but is definitely stimulated to create thereby. Schulte-Vaerting has described this type as the "sexual superman," but it seems to me rather that here too some hidden mechanism of fleeing from life is involved, which impels the artist from biological mortality to individual immortality in production after he has paid his tribute to sexuality.

This leads us to the profoundest source of the artistic impulse to create, which I can only satisfactorily explain to myself as the struggle of the individual against an inherent striving after totality, which forces him equally in the direction of a complete surrender to life and a complete giving of himself in production. He has to save himself from this totality by fleeing, now from the Scylla of life, now from the Charybdis of creation, and his escape is naturally accomplished only at the cost of continual conflict, both between these two spheres and within each of them separately. How this conflict and the triumph over it is manifested in creative working we shall seek to show in the chapter on "The Artist's Fight with Art." For the moment we are dealing only with manifestations and attempted solutions within the sphere of life, irrespective of whether these are concerned with persons of the same or of the opposite sex. In every case the artist's relation to woman has more of an ideological than of a sexual significance, as Emil Lenk has demonstrated in a study on creative personalities (*Das Liebesleben des Genies*; Dresden, 1926). Usually, however, he needs two women, or several, for the different parts of his conflict, and accordingly he falls into psychological dilemmas, even if he evades the social difficulties. He undoubtedly loves both these persons in different ways, but is usually not clear as to the part they play, even if — as would appear to be the rule — he does not actually confuse them one with the other. Because the Muse means more to him artistically, he thinks he loves her the more. This is seldom the case in fact, and moreover it is psychologically impossible. For the other woman, whom, from purely human or other motives, he perhaps loves more, he often enough cannot set up as his Muse for this very reason: that she would thereby become in a sense de-feminized and, as it were, made into an object (in the egocentric sense) of friendship. To the Muse for whom he creates (or thinks he creates), the artist seldom gives himself; he pays with his work, and this the truly womanly woman often refuses to accept. But if his relation takes a homosexual form, this giving is still more obviously a giving to himself; that is, the artistic form of giving through production instead of surrendering the personal ego.

True, from the standpoint of the ego, the homosexual relation is an idealizing of oneself in the person of another, but at the same time it is felt as a humiliation; and this is not so much the cause as the actual expression of internal conflicts. For, in the dynamism which leads him to create, the artist suffers from a struggle between his higher and his lower self which manifests itself equally in all the spheres and utterances of his life and also characterizes his attitude to woman. She can be for him at once the symbol of the highest and the lowest, of the mortal and the immortal soul, of life or of death. The same applies too, as we shall see, to the work itself or to creation, for which the artist is prepared to sacrifice everything, but which, in the hour of disappointment and dejection, he

frequently damns and curses. There is in the artist that fundamental dualism from which we all suffer, intensified in him
to a point which drives him with dynamic compulsion from
creative work to life, and from life back to new and other creativity. According to the artist's personal structure and spiritual
ideology, this conflict will take the form of a struggle between
good and evil, beauty and truth, or, in a more neurotic way,
between the higher and the lower self. It is a struggle which,
as we shall presently see, determines the cultural-genetic start
and development of the creative instinct itself. In the personal
conflicts of the individual artist the fundamental dualism which
originally led to cultural development and artistic creation
persists in all its old strength. It cannot, however, be reconstructed and understood as a matter of individual psychology
from an analysis of the artist's personal past, because the modern
individual not only comes into the world with humanity's
fundamental dualism, but is also potentially charged with all
the attempts to solve it, so that his personal development no
longer provides any parallels with the development of the race.

For if we inquire into the relation between work and production in the artist, we must bear in mind that there are two
kinds of experience, just as there are at least two ways of artistic
production. Whereas in pre-analytical biography it was chiefly
the artist's later and proportionately more active experience
that was brought into relation with his creativeness, psycho-
analysis, with its emphasis on the decisive importance of
infantile impressions, brought this more passive stage of experience into the foreground. This conception got no further, however, than the banal statement that even the artist was not
immune from those typical experiences of childhood which
one had come up against in analysing the adult. Just as Freud
saw the cause of neurosis in these typical childhood experiences
themselves and not in the individual's particular reaction to
them, so did his school claim to see in those same childhood
impressions the experiences which led to artistic creativity,
though without being able to explain the difference between

one outcome of them and another. An inexplicable " remainder " had therefore to be admitted, but this remainder embraced no more and no less than the whole problem of artistic creativity. Beyond this statement analytical psychography has to this day not progressed, as the latest comprehensive publication in this province shows.[1] And although the Œdipus complex, and the sexual problem of the child that is bound up with it, still forms the centre, this is rather the sign of a fatal stoppage than a proof of the superlative importance of this family problem. The whole of analytical pathography has battened for more than a quarter of a century on the Œdipus problem, which was first applied to artistic creation by Freud (in his *Interpretation of Dreams*), without, however, reaching even the point at which I came out when I published my book: *Das Inzest-Motiv in Dichtung und Sage* (1912, planned in 1905), to which I gave the sub-title: *Grundzüge einer Psychologie des dichterischen Schaffens.*

In this book, as already mentioned, the Œdipus problem is treated mainly as a motive and only in a minor degree as an individual complex; hence its ideological significance was considered as well as its psychological. Although, under the spell of the Freudian idea, I gave pride of place to the individual as against the collective psychology (which I have since learned to appreciate as " ideology," [2]) yet with respect to the latter, too, I certainly did not steer clear of psychological premises in dealing with this collective motive which we find in myth and saga before the poets made a theme of it. But, be this as it may, the book has even now not been superseded; indeed, analytical art-criticism has not yet put itself in face of its problems — to which I must at this point return. That the poets struggled so intensely with the Œdipus complex was regarded at the time as a proof of its ubiquity, and so it actually was so far as concerned

[1] *Die psychoanalytische Bewegung*, II, No. 4, July–August 1930 (also contains a bibliography of pyscho-analytical biography). In his introduction Dr. E. Hitschmann describes my book on the Incest-Motiv as fundamental for the analytical survey of art and the understanding of artistic creativity.

[2] *Seelenglaube und Psychologie* (1930).

individual psychology. But from the standpoint of the psychology of artistic production, the poets' wrestling with the Œdipus experience seems to me to mean something essentially different: namely, that the artist reacts more strongly than, and certainly in a different way from, the normal person to this unavoidable average experience of the parental relation. This is not, however, because of the experience, but because of his peculiar reactivity, which in the case of artistic expression we call " creative." Now, from the comparison that I drew in my generalized formulation of " the artist " (also in 1905) between artist and neurotic, it results that the latter also reacts differently from the average person to these and similar experiences. Only, this distinctive reaction does not, with him, lead to production, but to inhibition or to fixation. The artistic reaction is thus distinguishable from the neurotic by an *overcoming of the trauma* or of the potentiality of inhibition resulting therefrom, no matter whether this is achieved by a single effort or is spread over the whole life-work. This overcoming, however (so far as my researches have taken me), is only possible — or at any rate only psychologically explicable — in one way, and this, as we have learned from the therapy which helps to overcome these development-inhibitions, is through volitional affirmation of the obligatory, which in every case not only works usefully, but is also definitely creative. Applied to the special case of the Œdipus conflict, it appears to me today that it is the willed affirmation of the inhibitive family ties that is the creative and at the same time liberating factor. But this affirmation of the given, which in relation to family symbols manifests itself as erotic desire (towards mother and sister) and thirst for battle (with father or brother), corresponds on the one hand to creative appropriation and on the other to a constructive victory over it.

And with this we are back again at the fundamental process of artistic production, which consists in just this deliberate appropriation of that which happens and is given (including passive experiences) in the form of individual new creation.

The Œdipus complex forms one of the cultural symbols of this conflict because it synthesizes the biological, psychological, and characterological sides of it. But, even so, it only symbolizes — even in the case of a child, for whom the Œdipus complex is already the expression of an inner experience and not merely adaptation to an outward destiny. It even seems to me as if the Œdipus myth itself, if taken in the Greek spirit,[1] were an experience of this same striving for independence in human development: namely, the deliberate affirmation of the existence forced on us by fate. That which is dimly but unequivocally preordained for the hero by his birth, in the mythical account, he deliberately makes his own by embodying it in action and experience. This experience is a creative experience, for it serves to create the myth itself, and the sagas, poems, and tragedies based on it, whose various representations of the one theme are determined by the collective ideological outlook of the moment and the interpretation appropriate thereto. But the life of the individual hero himself will inevitably be destroyed, whether this human destiny be interpreted in terms of heroism, fatalism, or tragedy.

[1] See my explanations in *Die analytische Reaktion* (1929), pp. 68 et seq., and also in *Modern Education*, chapter vii.

Chapter Three

ART-FORM AND IDEOLOGY

> *What am I myself? What have I done? All that I have seen, heard, noted I have collected and used. My works are reverenced by a thousand different individuals. . . . Often I have reaped the harvest that others have sown. My work is that of a collective being and it bears Goethe's name.*
>
> GOETHE

Chapter Three
ART-FORM AND IDEOLOGY

ॐ

As soon as we interpret the Œdipus material as the collective symbol of a development-process which permeates both the single individual and humanity, and which the creative individuality overcomes in its artistic expression — as the creative Greek nation overcame it in myth — we have revealed to us one of the deepest laws of all artistic productivity: the fact that, in works of art, form and content not only constitute an inseparable unity, but actually express one and the same thing in two different ways. We have seen likewise that the process which goes on in the creative personality during the artistic shaping of this content finds its symbol in the content of the Œdipus myth. Only, the various art-styles differ as to the manner in which an artist achieves both the unity which constitutes a work of art and harmonious combination of the current ideology with his personal one. *Primitive creative art,* which is based on the collective soul-ideology, achieves unity through abstraction in style; that is, by neglecting everything incidental, temporal, and individual; *Classical art,* which is based on the æsthetic ideology of beauty, achieves unity through conformity between and sheer identity of the specific ideology of art and the general ideology of the people, the one unrepeatable example of which is the Greek culture. Finally, *modern Romantic art,* which is based on the psychological ideology of the artist-type, achieves this unity in art through his *reaction* to the discrepancies existing both within the artist himself and between his personal ideology and the prevailing collective ideology. The first of these unities, therefore — that of primitive art, attained through abstraction — is *static;* the second — that of Classical art, based on projection — is *harmonious;* and the third — that of Romantic art, as the outcome of victorious conflict — is *dynamic.* Thus the first is predominantly one of flat drawing (ornamental); the second, predominantly plastic and figuring (vital); and the third, essentially poetical and musical (rhythmical). These classifications are, of course, to be taken in a very general sense and, like all attempts to set up a historical, critical, or other hierarchy in the fine arts, must always remain unsatisfactory. It may be, indeed, that the real giants in art are just those who somehow exceed the limits of their art's proper sphere. For instance, Rembrandt stands out from the ranks of painters by reason of a dynamism which really is characteristic of literature and music; Homer was lauded, even by the ancients, as the greatest of painters; Dante, in words, is distinguished by a genius for rhythmical presentation, which is one of the features of pictorial art, and in this he has near rivals in Shakspere the dramatist and Wagner the musician, while the sculptor Michelangelo was at bottom an architect who built with human bodies, and his modern successor, Rodin, discloses very strong painter-qualities such as the Florentine despised.

Taking everything into account, however, the course taken by art-history forces us to regard primitive art as flat and linear, Classical art as essentially plastic and figuring, and modern art as verbal and rhythmical; and the fact that in each of these epochs great things were also produced in other spheres of art is to be ascribed to just such overleapings of frontiers by outstanding artist-personalities, who are to be found at all stages of development, but particularly of artistic development — where they step out of the frame of the prevailing art-ideology and achieve incomparable masterpieces, not only in their own domain, but in the realm of art generally. For although they made use of a given ideology, they rose so high above themselves that the result was a work of art which fell into no category and yet was more than personal, a super-individual achievement which thereupon its imitators invested with an ideological significance corresponding to the general recognition accorded to it. If, however, we look at the three kinds of art — graphic, plastic, and rhythmic — from the viewpoint of the artist and his psychological dynamism, we discover other categories, bearing on the problem of artistic creativity, which extend beyond the individual artist and are linked with the great general problems of cultural history.

Whereas primitive art is perpetuated through abstraction, and Classical art achieves immortality through idealization, Romantic art rounds off this immense transformation-process of spiritual development in making vivification its chosen mode of overcoming that fear of death from which the immortality-idea and urge to eternalization first sprang. Primitive art looks beyond individual, mortal life towards an ever-lasting life of the soul. And the essence of Classical art lies in the fact that it renders life itself everlasting — that is, tries to conserve the actual man as he is and lives — the very thing that the primitive Egyptian sought to do by mummification, save that in Greek art the conservation was achieved symbolically by the æsthetic idealization of the human body in a permanent material such as marble. But modern art, with its dynamic of expression, differs from both these style-forms; neither starts from an abstract of the living nor aims at an ideal conservation of it, but its style-form consists in a vivification of the essence of the actual. This can, however, only be achieved at the cost of real life.

The three art-ideologies, as we thus differentiate them — the abstract, the æsthetic, and the realistic — are based therefore on varying attitudes to life itself, and these attitudes, although determined by the prevailing collective ideology, will still be found to vary in the different individuals of the same epoch. Now, it is my belief that a non-contemporary outlook on vital problems is always essential to the artist, an outlook which deviates more or less from the prevailing ideology and its art-style. In other words, I believe that the artist's personality, however strongly it may express the spirit of the age, must nevertheless bring him into conflict with that age and with his contemporaries; and this again explains why he is obliged, in his work, to convert the collective ideology into one of his own.[1] In this sense not only does a work of art represent unity of form and content, but it achieves also a unification of personal and collective ideologies of immortality. The artist is, after all, primarily an individual who is unable or unwilling to adopt the dominant immortality-ideology of his age — whether religious, social, or other — and that, not because it differs ideologically from his own, but because it is collective, whereas what he aspires to is an individual immortality. In fact, art sets out to secure this individual immortality by collective methods, while the neurotic clings to the naïve immortality of the individual, which leads to fear of life and terror of death. But the artist obtains his individual immortality by using the collective ideology for his personal creativity and, in this way, not only re-creates it as his own but presents it to humanity as a new collective ideology on an individual basis. Thus he himself becomes immortal along with his work.

According to whether immortality is sought collectively, socially, or individually, the various culture-ideologies differ among themselves as also do their religious and artistic forms. The primitive artist overcomes individual mortality both by the abstract art-form which is man's spiritual proxy and by his collective soul-ideology. In contrast to this the modern artist has, as we have pointed out, actually to sacrifice life to make his work live, and this sacrifice involves both his own life and that of others. In the modern work of art, therefore, the personality of the artist or of his model really lives on dynamically, again an effect which can be achieved only at the cost of real

[1] The different aspects of this problem are further dealt with in the sections "Beauty and Truth," "The Artist's Fight with Art," and "Success and Fame."

life. But in the primitive work of art it is not the whole being that lives on as an individual, but only his abstraction — corresponding to the collective idea of the soul, which does not vivify that being dynamically, but abstracts him into a timeless form.

If, then, on the one hand, the artist's ideology is in complete harmony with the collective ideology of his time — is, indeed, the most complete expression of it — it is possible that the essential factor of his creative dynamism arises from a personal conflict between the individual death-problem and the collective immortality-idea of the particular cultural period. Yet, as we have already remarked, the primitive artist too — of whom we know nothing — would seem to have broken away, as an individual, from the collective soul-ideology, to the extent of finding the pure abstraction of the soul-idea (or its psychic representative) inadequate and being driven to concrete expression, even though it were of an abstract order. The Classical artist, also, as seen at the height of the Greek culture, was not content merely to accept the national or political immortality-ideology of Hellenism, but stayed it, so to speak, with its religious genesis, in that his sculpture lifted the human being out of the social and replaced him in the spiritual-religious domain. And, lastly, the modern artist, into whose individuality we can gain an insight (not only on the basis of historical data, but also because it expresses itself in its creative work), falls, as an artist-type to itself, outside the social, technical, and scientific ideology which characterizes our contemporary collectivism. He conserves, in his own type, the type rationalized by the conception of genius, the *art*-ideologies of past ages, just as the Classical and the primitive artists preserved the immortality-concepts of culture-epochs which were either dead or decaying. Thus, the unity of form and content, which must be regarded as the essence of creative work, comes into question even at this, the most general level of treatment: art preserves even dead or dying cultures, the epochs of human development and not only the single creative individual and his limited period; it also vitalizes them — that is, renders them immortal in the particular art-form.[1]

Having reached this level, it is perhaps worth while looking downwards on to the plains of purely technical problems, although these, again, can only be artificially detached from the general problem. Material is an essential factor of art-form, and to material in its turn belong the technical means of handling it and the capacity of the craftsman. The fact that, in German, the word "art (*Kunst*)" is allied with "can (*können*)" does not, as we now know, prove that even in practice art was primarily the being able to do a thing. The root relationship is perhaps characteristic rather of German mentality than of art. Be that as it may, for all the emphasis we lay on the will-to-art as against technical ability, we must admit that the material and its treatment represent an essential factor of artistic creativity and the work produced. The Greek sculptures are unthinkable without the supernatural splendour of the marble and equally so without its durability, and this is meant not only in the material sense, but in the ideal sense of the collective immortality-ideology. In the same way, not only are Rembrandt's dynamic portraits unthinkable without the high stage of development that had been reached in oil-painting; but in his "Anatomy," as in Leonardo's anatomical studies, there is evidence of some medical knowledge of the body, living and dead.[2]

[1] In this connexion it is important to note what Hermann Bahr (*Sendung des Künstlers;* Leipzig, 1923; p. 137) says, in support of his views, that actually in all the arts of all the nations of all times it is the same work of art which is created over and over again. "Not all of Greece is autochthonous: its art is a renaissance of Egypt, just as Rome is a renaissance of Athens, and the history of the Christian West nothing more than a renaissance of Rome." With reference to Goethe, too, he writes: "Thus he lived in art as if in the memory of the true art: his writing became an aid to memory and to the understanding of former art-periods long since expired." Very appropriate, too, is his mention of Nietzsche's deep-rooted condemnation in *Human, All-too-human* of the "revolution in poetry," for in poetry's break with tradition he sees the end of art.

[2] The dissection of corpses was first permitted by the ecclesiastical authorities in the Renaissance, and then only occasionally in the case of executed criminals. It was not until the middle of the sixteenth century that Vesalius (1514–65) introduced the thorough anatomical study of the human body, although information has recently

℘ Art-Form and Ideology ℘

The lyrical power of expression of a Goethe, a Hölderlin, or a Stefan George is only possible on the basis of a highly developed and refined cultural language, which has not only technical, but human aspects. (See chapter on " The Formation and the Creation of Speech.") We are justified, however, in asking how far these technical advances in the use and treatment of the material are not also themselves attributable to a genuine will-to-art, which previously — or simultaneously — creates the medium which the will-to-form needs for its execution. In oil-painting this relation to material is clearly visible in the experiments of Leonardo, Rembrandt, and other painters; but in principle we can draw the same psychological conclusion with regard to sculpture, poetry, and music — even without a close acquaintance with the history of the material — namely, that the actual individual art-will is manifested primarily and essentially in the choice and treatment of the material, while the content of what is presented has more relation to the collective ideologies — although these of course are in a high degree individualized in the work of art produced.

---

reached us of the astonishing anatomical knowledge possessed by the ancients. (See chapters: "Microcosm and Macrocosm" and "The Formation and the Creation of Speech.")

The rise of the science of anatomy probably influenced Renaissance art and undoubtedly had a definite effect upon its ideology. Apart from Leonardo's personal anatomical studies, which are an outgrowth of his whole scientific ideology, it seems to me probable that Rembrandt was also reacting to the new science of the human body when, in 1632, at the age of twenty-six, he painted his "Anatomy." I have the feeling that this young artist, who in his earlier youthful works had shown more "Rembrandtesqueness," was making a concession to the materialistic and realist ideology of his day in painting this " Anatomy Lecture of Professor Nicolaes Pietersz Tulp." It is as if he wished to show that he, too, knew something about anatomy, and that it was pure choice that made him forgo this "imitative art" in favour of dynamic expression. As we know, Rembrandt's whole life and work were torn by a conflict between the two, which brought him into serious disfavour with his patrons, who were paying for portraits true to nature and not for studies in light- and colour-effects. The second anatomical picture, "Doctor Joan Deyman's Anatomy Class" (1656), of which, unfortunately, only a fragment is preserved, in the Rijksmuseum, is more of a "real" Rembrandt as Karl Scheffler in his book: *Holland* (Leipzig, 1930; English translation, New York, 1932) regards it too.

However that may be, Rembrandt's "Anatomy" is an illustration of the ideal case in which the picture not only represents anatomy but actually *is* the anatomy, ideologically expressed, to which the artist demonstrates his attitude by painting it in his own manner.

These reflections bring us once more to the question of the hierarchy of the arts in respect of their historical and æsthetic valuation. In stating that the essence of modern art lies in its living dynamism, we did not forget that the primitive expressions of art known to us are likewise based on live rhythm (as are also dancing, song, and music), nor that ornament, with its recurring motive, shows a distinctly rhythmic character although, by contrast, the rhythm itself is as it were frozen, abstract, or dead. Yet this, again, is but a contradiction in logic that is inherent in our conception of artistic development; for, psychologically considered, it merely proves the oft-quoted relationship between modern and primitive art, in spite of the fact that their ideologies are basically different and indeed almost diametrically opposed. For primitive art is still entirely at one with life, forming, indeed, with regard to dance and ritual (singing and music) an essential component of the collective communal life, out of which there develops only gradually the productive artist and the onlooker-community in a passive rôle as two separate spheres.[1] Modern art, on the other hand, even in its most vivid dynamic expression, stands *opposed* to life. It is in the position, so to say, of having taken refuge in art-form rather than, like primitive art, having found in it the expression of life.

The primitive-art ideology is the religious belief in the soul, which leads, on the one hand, to a symbolic abstraction of the forms of life in linear-ornamental art and, on the other, to a concrete presentation of that abstraction. The tendency to concretize arises out of the individual-immortality concept, while the craving for abstraction corresponds to the *collective-*immortality concept. Modern art on the other hand is based on no such consoling idea of immortality, whether of a collective or individual nature. Its compelling motive is *fear of life and experience,* and this motive it carries over into the creative sphere, in the course of which process the individual will binds the biological driving force in the art-form in order to conserve

[1] See Jane Harrison: *Ancient Art and Ritual.*

76

it. It must be confessed that not only is the unity of the modern work of art (which it shares with art in general) the result of a reaction on emerging victorious from a struggle, but its dynamic vitality is also a reaction to the fear of life characteristic of the modern individual; for since the decay of our collective ideologies relative to religion and state, we suffer from this fear more than any previous generation has done.

Not only is primitive art at one with life as an essential part of it, but the artist is, if not wholly in harmony with the collective ideology, yet far more so than is the case, or even can be, in our modern society. Beginning with the Classic art of the Greek floraison, through the links that join it to our modern art-developments, and right into the latter, we find in increasing measure that it is just the very highest work that the productive artist achieves in response to pressure from the most diverse influences, so that this work, though certainly the typical expression of his individuality and epoch, is, over and above this, that of other cultures and alien ideologies. It is this fact that raises it to the timeless sphere of pure art. Classical Greece itself, though definitely influenced by Egypt, Crete, and the North, still seems to us today to be the pure product of the Hellenic spirit, in contrast to the art-development of mediæval Europe, where the ideologies are clearly a mixed product with Italian Renaissance and Northern Gothic as the two chief ingredients. Yet the great artists who were born of this epoch experienced in themselves and reproduced in their works the struggle of these different cultural ingredients, in both its constructive and its destructive aspects. Into this category come Shakspere's mixture of imported Renaissancism and the rising spirit of the Reformation in England; Dürer's Italian and Leonardo's French experiences; Goethe's flight from the *Sturm und Drang* ideology of Gothic to the more harmonious sphere of Southern Mediterranean art; also Nietzsche's struggle on the one hand with Hellenism and on the other with the Christian in him; Hölderlin, ruined by diversity of ideologies, and Kleist's inability to win through from Romantic unsteadiness to the

Classical ideal.[1] These, and many other great modern examples, might be quoted as proofs of the disunity of the artist with himself and with his environment which differentiates the modern artist from the primitive and, in a sense, from the Classical. But these problems cannot be discussed without including questions of mixed races, the influence of the country, and other biological, social, and economic conditions.[2]

We now return from the problem of the creative artist's mixing of ideologies to the fact of the occurrence of various art-forms within one and the same cultural epoch. From the creative artist's point of view this is naturally no problem, for the matter is one of specially favourable conditions for production characterizing a particular period of development, or even of some vital necessity providing the stimulus for creative work in great variety during that period. Neither is it a problem from the ideological standpoint — at least not an insistent enigma — that different art-forms should come into existence and actually mature simultaneously. For here problems arise only as the result of the co-operation at any given time of the creative urge and the ideologies that are at its disposal. The artist creates essentially by reason of an inward urge which we may describe as the individual will-to-form, and whether he objectifies this in a picture, a statue, or a symphony is rather a technical and formal matter than an individual problem. This is particularly the case with the great artist whose poem is plastic, whose portrait is poetical, and whose

[1] Arthur Burkhard, professor of literature at Harvard University, has in a preliminary study (*German Quarterly*, Vol. II, No. 4, November 1929) described this conflict between two opposed elements—in the artist and his work—as the hall-mark of *German* art, which he formulates as, in the last analysis, a conflict between expression and form. In my opinion, however, this is the characteristic of modern art in general, and in so far as art today is still national—in France or Italy, for instance—it is derived from Classical ideologies.

[2] Of basic importance is Reibmayr's *Die Entwicklungsgeschichte des Talents und Genies* (Munich, 1908). Kretschmer has also a very good summary in the two chapters: "*Die Züchtung der Begabung*" and "*Genie und Rasse*" of his *Geniale Menschen* (Berlin, 1929). See also the general survey in Paul Schultze-Naumburg's *Kunst und Rasse* (Munich, 1928) and, for German literature in particular, Josef Nadler's *Literaturgeschichte der deutschen Stämme und Landschaften* (3 vols., Regensburg, 1914-18).

music is architectonic in effect.[1] Nevertheless it may be said that drawing was characteristic of primitive art, while sculpture is the Classical expression-medium, and the rhythmic arts (poetry and music) the modern. Poetry in particular can be historically proved to be of relatively recent date — relatively not only to the vast spaces of time which separate us from the prehistoric cave-paintings, but even to those covered by historical evidence within our reach. Moreover, poetry as a species of art is bound up with writing, as its material, and this particular immortality-technique was a very late discovery, which reached sure fulfilment only with the printing of books. The form in which the art of poetry existed before its fixation through writing can only be conjectured from a few traditional magic formulæ and the prayer-like songs which were performed chiefly in honour of some godhead or hero. With such primitive peoples as we are still able to observe, singing appears to play an inferior rôle as against dancing and instrumental music, possibly because they are too fearful of pronouncing the " word " that is still identical with the thing that it designates. This magical effect of the spoken word, which here asserts itself as a dread of the evoking call, may on the other hand be *salutary,* as when it forms the basis of songs and hymns — in which we recognize the oldest form of prayer and which we must also regard as the original form of the art of poetry.[2]

---

[1] The Innsbruck archæologist Heinrich Sitte has demonstrated in his synthetic essay on Bach's *Chromatic Fantasia and Fugue* (No. V of the manuscript series, *Preussische Jahrbücher*, Berlin, 1921) that "its thematic content contains the Parthenon frieze, Giotto's frescoes in the Scrovegni Chapel, Dante's *Divine Comedy*, Beethoven's *Ninth Symphony*, and Goethe's *Faust*. All these works, therefore, although uttered in different languages, are really all the time one and the same composition" (Bahr, op. cit., p. 137). Sitte's discovery that Bach set his own family name to music in this fugue is another striking example of the inseparable unity of the form and content of a work of art. The fugue is not only by Bach: it *is* Bach, the whole Bach, as man and as triumphant artist. "Out of the double cry of anguish: B [flat]—A—C—H [= B natural]," continues Sitte, "there grew an uninterrupted cry of higher and higher triumph: A—B—H—C. And this motive, so unique in origin, he made . . . without any trickery into the boldest fugue which he ever wrote, and which comprises his whole human existence, in joy and in sorrow, as if it were his portrait."

[2] In a preliminary introduction to a history of American literature Ludwig Lewisohn very rightly lays stress on the "sacred" origin and character of literature (*This Quarter*, summer 1929). The book has appeared since (*Expression in America*).

For the rest, the earliest poetical products of the primitives, as of civilized peoples, are *epic* in character; either they are mythical stories of gods which are reminders of men's lost immortality, or they are human stories of heroes which bewail the tragic mortality of the living being.[1] But these productions have an unambiguously collective character and, in this respect, are definitely not out of keeping with the primitive art-ideology. Nor do we know the individual writers of these myths and epics, and this is not merely for lack of historical data, but because oral tradition admits of no such individual authorship. And whether the man who, later, wrote down any such song — even with additions and embellishments of his own — can really be described as its author, even if we could trace him, is a question which the Greeks tried in vain to solve in their research on Homer.[2] Today we are certainly too ready to regard offhand the recorder of ideas as their author — a technical way of looking at it which has already gone far beyond the pure idea of creativity.

But the question as to wherein the collective element of mythic and epic poetry consists has become a central problem in scientific literary criticism ever since the Romantic period. It is probable that various individuals — even, perhaps, races and nations — participated in the beginning and particularly in the oral handing-down of these poems. And equally we may suppose that this collective genesis also corresponds to a collective *content* of that which was transmitted. A race or a nation appears as the victorious hero of the story, mostly in the figure of an individual champion as representative and carrier of the race's interests.[3] In every case the hero and his fate are the main thing, and not the poet, in whom we should take little interest if we did know him. For the motive of his song

[1] See, further, the chapter "*Traum und Wirklichkeit*" in my book: *Seelenglaube und Psychologie* (1930), and later expositions in the following chapters of the present work: "Myth and Metaphor" and "The Poetic Art."

[2] Cf. my preliminary studies on the folk-epic in *Imago*, V (1917).

[3] This point of view is emphasized in the *Psychoanalyse de l'art* (Paris, 1929) by Professor Charles Baudouin of Geneva.

and saga was, at this stage, certainly not individual, but collective or, as we should call it today, " national." The individual author of modern times differs from the collective creators of folk-epic, not only through the personal nature of his theme, but also because he himself, his individual ego, is the real hero of his story. In lyric poetry, with its reflection of fleeting moods, this is plainly and admittedly the case, but it also applies to a great extent to novels and even to dramas. It is as if the personal artist-ideology, which we have taken as the foundation of modern art, comes in the individual poet to consciousness of itself. Hence the favoured position, the high cultural significance indeed, of the author as censor of morals, philosopher of life, and educator of mankind in our world of today. In attaining this position of general responsibility he has, however, left the sphere of pure creativity, which, from now on, he represents only in his ideology. He is now himself the work of art, but as such he can represent either a good or a bad one, according to whether and how he succeeds in shaping his life. Goethe remains, in this regard also, the unparalleled model of a universal genius of the modern age; for he was able to balance the destructive elements in him creatively, by absorbing them into his poetry and his various other constructive activities, and thus to shape his life as an artistic-constructive whole. Other great writers have failed to achieve so complete a harmony, either ruining the artistic build of their lives by Romanticism or leading a philistine existence in order to have enough vitality left over for creation.

This fact confronts us again when we come to deal with the problem of the individual artist-personality as expressed in the relation between experience and creativity. No single causal relation appears to exist between the two phenomena —certainly not the one favoured by psychography, which purports to explain creativity by experience in general or by special experiences. It seems likely that the reverse is more possible, since the creative will which underlies them both manifests itself more clearly in the created work than in experience. On the other hand, creativity itself is, of course, a special form of experience and one peculiar to the artist, and all depends in the last resort upon whether the individual is capable of restoring harmony, or at least a temporary balance, between the two forms of experience — artistic and vital — and to what extent he succeeds. This does not by any means signify that the person who better adapts himself to, or succeeds in, life must needs be the better artist. In this respect Goethe forms a signal exception in the whole long line of really great men whose lives have been swallowed whole by their work. Croce maintains that this was the case even with Goethe, but in reality the *man* Goethe has come to be more important to us than his work, which we are inclined to regard as more interesting from a psycho-biographical than from a purely artistic standpoint. Goethe himself looked upon his works as " fragments of one great confession," as " life's traces," and it looks as if this had been more or less consciously the artist's general attitude towards his work. His work is not only his particular expression of life: it both serves him and helps him to live, and his worth as an artist comes second — or even plays no special part at all. A mediocre work, acceptable only to a small circle, may yet satisfy the artist more and mean more to him than the undying world-fame of a poem that has grown into a folk-song, the author of which most people are quite at a loss to name.

Again, we must admit that the psychology of a productive personality gives no clue to the understanding and appreciation of art. The Romantic who, having adopted the attitude that I once called " artist-mania " and now call art-ideology, neglects or sacrifices or even destroys his life has often achieved more in art than the genius who allows the human being in him to come to fruition also. What makes Goethe the highest type of artist in our eyes is not really his work, any more than it is his civic life — which served rather to protect him from his own genius than to enhance it. Where he is great is in his attitude to art and life, his conception of their relation to each other, which he only bought — and dearly enough — after long wrestling. As Bahr so excellently puts it, his achievement lay in having "put down the revolution by which he had risen" and "in recognizing that art's freedom lay in its submission to the law." This explains his aversion from all Romanticism, which meant, at bottom, from the Romantic within himself; for the Romantic stands at the other end of the scale of artistic development as the pioneer and earliest specimen of the individual artist-type, whose art-ideology is the cult of personality with its idea of liberty. Not only is he an individual-revolutionary in creation, but he confuses life with art: he *is* dramatic or lyrical, he acts the piece instead of objectifying it, or rather he is obliged to act it as well as merely objectify it. His art is as chaotic as his life, whereas the pure art-ideology is based on order, law, and form — in fact, on traditional and therefore collective ideologies. Now, Goethe wished to re-establish this pure art epistemologically, and therein lies his greatness as an *artist-type*. First, however, he had to curb the individual Romantic in himself, and this he succeeded in doing, though only at the expense of his productive power, which exhausted itself in the conscious and deliberate transformation of the Romantic type represented by him into a Classical artist-type, and which nevertheless he never completely achieved in his work.

If Goethe's importance lies rather in his representing the purely Classical ideal, as against the personal artist-ideology of Romanticism, than in his actual creative work, he is perhaps the first example — and at the same time the highest possible type — of the poet who becomes a universal genius. Also, in our own day, such a type could express himself as an essayist, a cultural critic, or a first-class journalist. As we have already pointed out, our modern author has become conscious of the personal art-ideology that is within him; but the first result of the process has been to project this intuitively recognized artist-ideology on to the history of art and to misinterpret the whole of its development in the light of its latest phase. We have seen how the establishment of a will-to-form (originally impersonal) as the real creative element had an essentially progressive and deepening effect on the study of art as a problem, and we shall find that the extended application of this theory to the genius's personal, and the modern artist's conscious, will-to-art has thrown new light on the whole question of art and artist. At the end of our first section we left it an open question whether an understanding of the individual artist-type with its personal will-ideology — working itself out primarily in the artist's ego — might not clear up certain methodological ambiguities in Worringer's æsthetics. However abstract we imagine the primitive will-to-art that is supposed to produce simple art-forms of crystalline structure, it still retains a tinge of anthropomorphism — even in Schopenhauer's philosophical interpretation of it. For the will is a human phenomenon, and we cannot assume offhand that Nature and all her creatures possess it, even in the form of " unconscious willing." Certainly, in our view, the individual will is a derivative of the biological life-impulse, but it is a purely human derivative, though, again, it is in a prime mover of Nature that we find the biological premiss; this differentiation between life-impulse and expression of will, which psycho-analysis has ignored, seems to me to be the basic human problem *par excellence* since it comprises both the dualism of ego and species, of mortality and immortality, that is inherent in the individual, and all those creative tendencies which go beyond the mere function of propagation. In any case we fail to see how the sex-urge, which is designed primarily to preserve the race, should produce even the most primitive ornamentation, still less a higher art-form. The attempt made by psycho-analysis to find such a solution is today recognized to have been a failure, and only left the real problem more acute than before. Not even in cases where the *content* of the representation has a more or less definite relation to the sexual function or its organs — as in the case of certain primitive art-symbols — can we find an intelligible path from the direct to the symbolic or sublimated expression of the sexual instinct unless we build the bridge of the individual will which converts the propagation of the species into a perpetuation of the ego. Even with animals, to whom we cannot ascribe this individuality-consciousness (or at least not in the same degree), the development and variation of species do not appear to be the achievement of a sexual instinct that is focused on reproduction and repetition, but (as first Lamarck was bold enough to postulate) the result of an individual condition of suitability, and it is only a judgment by results — namely, the better adaptation of the individual — that leads us to predicate some sort of deliberate intention in it.

Be that as it may, once we recognize that the modern artist has of himself arrived at a consciousness of the individualness of the creative will that he formerly attributed to his god, we are bound to assume that a similar will-tendency existed in the artist of former epochs, even though he may not, as an individual, have always been conscious of it. One might think, then, that this volitional creative urge came nearer to the sexual instinct in proportion as it was more unconscious — that is, in proportion as we come nearer to primitive art. But this hasty conclusion as to the predominantly sexual character of primitive art has been refuted by objective observation [1] and cannot be used to support the thesis of the sexual character of creative art, just as we may not, on the other hand, refer the self-consciousness of the modern artist back to the genesis of artistic development. For despite this closer relationship of the unconscious will to the instinctive, never, at even the lowest stage of any creative production, do the two come together. The will, conscious or unconscious, will always be the expression of the individual, the indivisible single being, while sexuality represents something shared, something generic which is harmonious with the individually-willed only in the human love-experience [2] and is otherwise in perpetual conflict

[1] See, for instance, Emil Stephan's important work on art in the South Sea Islands (*Südsee Kunst. Beiträge zur Kunst des Bismarck-Archipels und zur Urgeschicht der Kunst überhaupt;* Berlin, 1907).   [2] See my *Technik*, II, p. 77.

with it. In art this conflict is won in a different way; though
closely akin to the individual conquest in love and the collective conquest in religion, it is differentiated from both by a
specific element which we may broadly call the æsthetic. We
shall deal with the peculiar qualities which this consists of in
our next section. In closing this chapter we need only say, without particularizing, that the artistic solution of this original
dualism is not merely psychological, but appears, as regards
its evolutionary history, to lie between the religious and the
erotic solutions. The religious solution is at bottom collective;
that is, the individual is delivered from his isolation and becomes part of a greater and higher whole — not in the bio-
logical-generic sense, but through his spiritual ideology, by becoming one with God. In the love-experience, which becomes
possible only at a stage of fully developed individualism, we
see this spiritual process objectified: God, as representing the
idealized self, is found in the beloved, and, with the sense of
union, the individuality seems to be exalted and intensified,
lost, and yet enriched. Finally, in art, which has developed out
of the collective consolation-ideology of religion and at whose
further limit we find the Romantic artist striving after the
complete love-experience, the individuality-conflict is solved
in that the ego, seeking at once isolation and union, creates, as
it were, a private religion for itself, which not only expresses
the collective spirit of the epoch, but produces a new ideology
— the artistic — which for the bulk of them takes the place of
religion. True, this happens only at the summit of individual
" artist's art," where there is deification of the genius-concept
and an adoration of works of art which is comparable only
to the worship of statues of gods, though they already represent
mere men. Before this, art is still — particularly in its Classical
period — an individual working-out of the forces of which
religions are made. These forces then become concentrated in
the single creative individual, whereas before they animated a
whole community. The works of these peak periods of artistic
production manifest in their development the individualized

religion-forming forces which finally return, by way of Romantic love-experience, to their origin, which is the personal craving for immortality of the ego. All three ideologies, however — the collective-religious, the social-artistic, and the individual-erotic — lift the individual above the biological life-plane of reality — in which only the sexual immortality of propagation counteracts the individual isolation — on a higher, super-natural, super-real, or super-individual sphere wherein reigns an ideal collectivity that is created by individual intention and may at any time be altered at will.

Chapter Four

THE PLAY-IMPULSE
AND ÆSTHETIC PLEASURE

All fine imaginative work is self-conscious and deliberate. No poet sings because he must sing. At least, no great poet does. It is so now, and it has always been so. . . . There is no fine art without self-consciousness.

OSCAR WILDE
(The Critic as Artist)

Chapter Four

THE PLAY-IMPULSE
AND ÆSTHETIC PLEASURE

꙳

A long and intricate path leads from the individual's creative will-to-art, through all the preliminary stages of creation and the artistic creative act itself, to the finished work which, released from its creator, produces in the recipient that which is called æsthetic pleasure. Along this path lie, on the one hand, all the complex problems of the psychology of creative personality, and, on the other, the artistic choice of material which, through sketches and studies, struggles to find the ideologically adequate expression. There is also, however, the question of æsthetic effect as well as that of the critic's appreciation of the work. And, finally, there is the general valuation of it by contemporaries and posterity, which we summarize in the term "fame." Now that we have gained some insight into the artist's personality and have fully recognized the mixture of individual and collective ideologies which is characteristic of the art-form, we may turn to the purely psychological aspect of the problems of art. In so doing we have, as has been pointed out, to avoid studying the psychological problem one-sidedly on the strength of its æsthetic effect and so neglecting the primary urge for expression in the creator. The dualism for which we have here to account by presenting both aspects at once is thus one of dynamic expression and æsthetic enjoyment, the one being manifested in the psychology of the creator, and the other in that of the recipient.

Worringer has very rightly objected that art has up to now

91

been studied far too much from the standpoint of the æsthetic effect of the finished product, in the case of the Classical above all. The catchword of this method of criticism was "intuition (*Einfühlung*)," a word minted by Theodor Lipps, which, according to Worringer, stops short at the psychology of Classical art. To this intuitive æsthetic of Classical art he opposes the abstraction-character of primitive art, which produces pure style-forms where the craving for "feeling oneself into" leads to naturalism. But valuable as this critical demarcation of the Classical art-feeling may be, Worringer's application of his psychology of style to the problem has not enabled him to grasp the spiritual part played in the forming of style by the individual's urge to artistic creativity.[1] He takes a step in that direction by regarding a kind of fear in primitive man, which he characterizes as "space-fear (*Raumangst*)," as the psychological motive for abstraction, but this theory seems to me on various accounts to require questioning and supplementing. That abstract form is evolved, psychologically, under the influence of a fear that drives men to seek safety in the eternal (and, I might add, in the self-willed) seems to me correct. But to regard this as being also the beginning of all artistic creativity is, I feel, an unjustified and also unnecessary piece of "historization," quite apart from the fact that it ascribes to the primitive a "prime fear" which I should take to belong rather to our own psychology than to his world-outlook. But of this more later. In any case the earliest art-form of which we have so far heard — the "naturalism" of palæolithic man — is not abstract; neither does it appear to spring from any primitive fear, but rather from a naïve feeling of superiority at being able to control nature. Worringer's æsthetic development of the Riegl theory, therefore, in making clear its central point, has brought out its weakness also. In the first place, we see no ethnological or psychological justification for the actual fear ascribed to the primitive, whose psychology is here based on a timeless

[1] Karl Schultze-Jahde warns us of the necessity of separating style as regards object from style as regards modes of expression (*Ausdruckswerk und Stilbegriff*; Berlin, 1930).

abstraction-style. The collective ideology underlying abstract art-forms is undoubtedly based on a sense of fear; but the first product of this is a belief in the soul — in fact, religion — and not, at that stage, artistic creativity, which appears to arise only out of an individual self-assertion against that fear. It is this individual need for expression that is overlooked by all æsthetic, including Worringer's.[1] Yet this exists in the individual of every age just as definitely as does the frightened feeling of dependence which leads to collective immortality-ideologies, whereas art, how much it may employ collective style-forms, is derived from the personal urge to immortalization. Only, at certain times and in certain situations this feeling of terrified dependence gains the upper hand and urges the creative individual to make use, like the rest, of the collective forms produced by the religious and social ideologies of such periods as a means to express his personal urge to immortalization. On the other hand, periods of superlative self-confidence produce a naturalistic art-form as a manifestation of command over nature. And even if both style-forms are based, as Worringer maintains, on the need for self-renunciation, yet we must not overlook the equally strong tendency to self-affirmation which may express itself, at one time directly as supremacy over nature, and at another indirectly as an ideological freeing from her dependence. In naturalistic art, which is born, not of fear, but of man's sense of superiority (whether imaginary or justified), man rises to an imitative command of his world-around; on the contrary, in abstract art, which is born of a sense of dependence, he appears as *self-creative*.

But this creative self-affirmation is as little the specific essence

---

[1] For this reason the one attempt (unique, so far as I am aware) to construct a general æsthetic on the fear of the ego (in Worringer's sense) was bound to be unconvincing on the main issue, although many hitherto neglected points were usefully emphasized. I allude to Erich Major's *Versuch einer neuen Aesthetik* (1913). The author assumes "the sources of artistic creativity" to lie in the "will to immortalize," which he derives from the fear of external dangers. It is a pity that he places his theory of fear in essential opposition to the psycho-analytical erotization of artistic creativity and does not advance beyond this controversy to the creative will-power which is already beyond sex and fear (see also above).

of artistic creativity as self-renunciation is that of æsthetic experience. For, as Worringer himself suggests, abstraction and
intuition are not specifically characteristic of artistic experience, but are general psychological attitudes towards the
world, and they also manifest themselves in correspondingly
varied art-forms and artistic expressions. What, then, is this
art-form-in-itself, which the will creates, now by abstraction,
now by naturalistic introjection, and now again by self-
projection into nature? To answer this question we must
turn again from the æsthetic criticism of style to psychology
on the one hand and to philosophy and the genetics of Culture
on the other; for only so shall we understand the need for
self-renunciation or self-assertion in one form or another.
Riegl's assumption of an absolute will-to-form, though it has
been of such immense value to the science of art, does not,
psychologically, solve this spiritual problem, but rather obscures
it. For this absolute will-to-art is regarded even by Worringer
as corresponding to a universal creative instinct in nature,
which can produce mineral crystals and primitive ornament
alike. And yet between these there is precisely the difference
that exists between nature and spirit. And this is no æsthetic
difference, for an elaborate crystal structure may arouse precisely as much admiration as a perfect picture. It is an essential
difference, consisting in the fact that the crystal has *grown* and
is a part of nature, while the work of art produced by human
hands belongs to a second, super-real world, which is just what
we instinctively feel art in its higher stages to be.

In spite of — or perhaps because of — his nearness to nature,
the primitive spends a far greater portion of his total life than we
do on a super-real plane, to which he is elevated by his magical
conception of the world. We know now that not only his art
but his whole attitude towards life is abstract, based as it is on
a naïve belief in the soul. With the primitive, therefore, art
cannot be detached from his supernatural conception of the
world, for it remains — as, for that matter, even in highly developed communities — an essential and inseparable part of

the collective life as a whole. It is only not so for us, whose whole world-picture is realistic and becomes from day to day more concrete, and for whom art (side by side with the scanty shreds of religious feeling that remain to us) is only a last remnant of that super-real world which it formerly objectified and of which it was a part. In this magical world-picture, to which art also belonged, the need for self-renunciation, as we understand it, had no place; for it only appears when there is a dualism of two worlds to promote a desire to flee from one into the other. This urge of ours to the renunciation of self, which finds its æsthetic satisfaction in art, we have already contrasted with the religious and the erotic renunciations of self which are achieved respectively through collective and through individualistic ideologies. The æsthetic self-renunciation, similarly, is founded on what we may call a "social" ideology, since the work of art, for all its personal dynamic expression, always strives to make an effect on others, whether it adopts more or less collective style-forms for the purpose.

But the central question of all æsthetic is: how does the artist achieve this effect, that enables so many others to identify themselves with his work? The older æsthetic answered this by referring it to nature-imitation. The creative artist, one was told, identified himself so extensively with nature that he was able to imitate it, and this human imitation of nature, again, made it possible for the non-productive person to identify himself at least with this imitated nature. But the explanation is so unsatisfactory and presumes so many psychological improbabilities that it could not survive the critical analysis of modern æsthetics, and already it is considered as definitely refuted. Once it had been established, however, that art had nothing to do with imitating nature, a new theory of its aims became necessary. For to the nature-imitation theorists art must have seemed an aimless pastime, an ideal vision — as the Classicist æsthetic tried to define it — soaring above all utilitarian criteria. Today we know, for instance, that the aims of primitive art were, though definite, not directly practical; they began by being ideal aims and only thereafter, through religious ritual and wonder-working magic, decisively influenced man and his destiny. The first formula that we found for primitive art followed from our view of it as a concrete presentation of the abstraction underlying the magical world-outlook, of which the essence is the soul-concept. Here art still coincides almost completely with religion, but this means, not that it is identical with the transcendent, but that — now as later — it is the objectification thereof. If belief in the soul may be taken as religion, or at any rate as the preliminary stage of it, we must admit that art was at first, and for a long time to come, the handmaid of religion. Its "aim" was to prove the existence of the soul by concretizing it, and it achieved this by presenting the abstract in abstract form — that is, by imitating as faithfully as possible, not reality, but unreality. Thus we can detect both the imitative instinct of artistic creativity and the practical aimlessness of art even in these primitive stages. The imitation, however, concerns the unreal, which later becomes steadily more naturalized and humanized, while the aimlessness concerns reality — a fact which æsthetics has, strangely enough, inverted by looking for imitativeness, *vis-à-vis* reality, in which domain it has no purpose — and so being led to deny that art has any aim except that of æsthetic gratification.

This error must mean something, as does every error, including these views of mine, should they prove to be such. For even an error contains a possibility of thought, and every possibility of thought contains a possibility of being. There may be people today who feel themselves so scientifically enlightened that they can regard the whole of religion as one monstrous "error" of mankind, one of its most dangerous illusions. Yet this error has greater significance, even today, than their "truth," if it were truth. The most probable and also the most consoling explanation of this contradiction would be a historical one. It seems to us certain now that primitive art was no imita-

tion of nature, but something serving quite definite ideal purposes; this would not, however, exclude the possibility that it
took its pleasure later in a purposeless imitation of nature, and
for proofs of this we might point to periods of extreme realism.
Yet even if these are not to be regarded as the expression of an
individualist art-ideology, as we have suggested, there would
still be another way of accounting for them. Could we not say
that, actually, art never did in fact set out to imitate nature aim-
lessly, but that the men of a certain epoch interpreted it as doing
so when they described this imitation historically as art's origin
and ideologically as its mission? This explanation, be it remarked, would suit all alternatives, whether art was really this
or only appeared to be so to the eyes of the æsthetic. It is at least a
possible interpretation and is also certainly a possible ideology
of art, apart from the fact that we know exactly what an immense influence this Classicist æsthetic had on the artistic
creativity of the eighteenth and nineteenth centuries.

In other words, the problem is: how could such an obviously
false ideology of art arise at all in connexion with primitive
art? And why was it accepted by the artists of a certain epoch
with apparently overmuch eagerness? Fundamentally this
seems to me a question for cultural philosophy, the true answer
to which must be deferred until we have disposed of some of
the problems of individual psychology more relevant to the
title of this section. For we can only approach the æsthetic
element characteristic of art, which is predominantly a psychological problem, by analysis of the individual as we have opportunity to study him today.[1] We must of course bear in mind
the sources of error which are found in every individual
psychological investigation, and especially in one undertaken
with the object of understanding historical phenomena. But
no other course is open to us, and we can only hope in the first
place to probe deeply enough into the individual to be able

---

[1] And, after all, does not the prevailing theory of æsthetic come from a *psychologist*
(Lipps)? His *Einfühlung*, translated here "intuition," means really "feeling oneself into."

to grasp certain general human elements, the value of which as aids to an understanding of artistic creativity and pleasure we can then put to the test. In any case we may expect to glean something about the modern artist-type in the process, which may possibly throw light (or fresh light) on the æsthetic problems of Classical and even primitive art. We may well take warning, however, by the exaggerations of the Classicist æsthetics which sought to reduce all artistic creation to the formula of a particular epoch, even though we are of opinion that art must contain essential elements that are common to all the ideologies of the various generations and epochs.

Now, there is one æsthetic theory, which comes from one of the greatest Classical artists of all time — namely, Schiller — that makes a bold bid to solve simultaneously the problem of artistic creativity and that of æsthetic gratification. This derivation of the problem of art from the *play-instinct* seems to me, even at the present day, to be a safe starting-point for a psychological voyage of discovery into the dark realm of æsthetic. In his famous letters: *Über die ästhetische Erziehung des Menschen,* Schiller places the individual between the two worlds of the senses (reality) and the will (moral), to which he ascribes, on the one hand, the material-instinct, and, on the other, the form-instinct. The play-instinct gives expression and life to both in harmonious union, and the result is beauty. From this height of æsthetic-philosophic contemplation it only remains to flash a light into spiritual abysses, as did Nietzsche in his *Birth of Tragedy,* or to descend oneself into the depths of psycho-biological processes, after the manner of the psychoanalytical treatment of art. But today what even Classical antiquity, which produced so many masters, says to us about art is meaningless, be it Socrates' moral identification of the beautiful or Aristotle's conceptual separation of these categories, wherein he asserts an absence of will in the beautiful, but ascribes to it a direct pleasurable effect; or, yet again, other views such as those of Plato or Plotinus which, like the utterances of the Delphic priestess, sound mystical and profound, but only reveal their profundity if one can interpret them aright — or, indeed, interpret them at all. Least of all shall we glean anything from the intellectual æsthetic of Baumgarten, the spiritual father of the imitation theory, to say nothing of the philosophical speculations of Romanticism.

The newer art-theories, with their anthropological orientation, assign — particularly since Spencer's acceptance of the Schiller view — a special rôle to the variously interpreted play-instinct, although insisting at the same time upon the imitative instinct and on a "preservative instinct," which obviously corresponds to our immortalization-tendency. But the play-instinct itself, which Schiller had so incomparably described as a harmonious phenomenon binding the two human worlds, presently became the object of anthropological, sociological, biological, and psychological analysis, without, however, becoming much more intelligible from the æsthetic standpoint. Spencer himself regards play as the outlet for superfluous energy; Lazarus, as recuperation after the fatigue of real life; Groos, as exercise preparatory to these; and, lastly, Wundt emphasizes the "unconscious or conscious imitation of purposeful actions" as well as the "pleasing effect" of play, and the "re-formation of the original aims in imaginary ones." If we applied this to art, therefore, we should find ourselves back at the theory of aimless imitation, whereas the unsoundness of that theory (however undeniable its right to exist) was the very starting-point of our discussion. It only shows, once more, that all our anthropology, sociology, biology — yes, and psychology — do not at bottom get beyond reality as the ultimate explanatory principle and can only understand even a make-believe action (Spencer), such as play presents, as an imitation of a real activity.

Neither does psycho-analysis, with its medical-anthropological attitude, take us any further in this, as we see from the isolated example of Pfeifer's crude application of the infantile-erotic complexes to the existing theories of play (*Imago,* V, 1917). The little that Freud himself has said about art does not go beyond a comparison of poetic imagination and play,[1] while, later, he defines play as a "motoric hallucination" (*Totem und Tabu*, 1913). This definition, which requires a definition of hallucination itself if it is to be intelligible, probably amounts to no more than the theory of wish-fulfilment. But this theory stops short at the problem of will, and the particular character of wish-fulfilment which distinguishes hallucination from dreams, play, art, and, indeed, religion is left unexplained by psycho-analysis. We are, therefore, at once driven back on will-psychology, at least for our starting-point towards a deeper insight into the general problem of the play-instinct and æsthetic gratification. Now, I have already, in another connexion, starting from the psychology of the neurotic and discussing psychotherapeutic possibilities of curing him,[2] emphasized the therapeutic and indeed absolutely vital character of illusions in contrast to Freud, who regards them (even from a historical point of view) merely as infantile wish-fulfilments which we have to outgrow.[3] I believe, however, that everything that is consoling in life — that is, everything therapeutical in the broader sense — can only be illusional, and even the therapeutic effect of analysis I have tried to explain in my latest "technical" work by the unreality of the analytical situation.[4] To understand the work of art in its specific import, then, we have not only to advance, in our search for an explanation of creative imagination, from the wish-fufilment theory to will-psychology, but also to get hold of the negative aspect of the immortality-ideology in the fear-problem of the neurotic. Now, I have always regarded the neurotic as a failed artist. In other words, to the eternalizing tendency of the individual will (as manifested collectively in religion and personally in the love-experience) there must be superadded a particular kind of overcoming of fear; and this we can certainly study better in the

[1] *Der Dichter und das Phantasieren* (1908).   [2] *Wahrheit und Wirklichkeit* (1929).
[3] For in Freud's *The Future of an Illusion* art still offers "substitute satisfactions" for the oldest cultural abnegations (in imagination).
[4] *Die Analyse des Analytikers und seiner Rolle in der analytischen Situation*, 1930 (*Technik*, III).

failed neurotic with his thwarted productivity than in the creative artist. For the artist overcomes this isolating fear socially,
by getting society's sanction for his personal immortality-
symbolism, whereas the neurotic fails to overcome his mortal
fear because he has nothing to compensate it, either individually
(in love), collectively (in religion), or, least of all, socially.
Now, the study of neurotic fear has led to the conclusion that
the general problem of fear, in whatever form we encounter
it, cannot be handled and explained as a problem of reality, but
at bottom represents an irrational phenomenon. Herein, incidentally, lies the very pardonable error of the Worringer concept of fear, which is far too realist to explain the abstract urge
to art. For external fear no more leads to compensatory artistic
activity than real sex-impulse does so. This unreality of fear is
also confirmed by the better comprehension that we now have
of the primitive world-attitude, for the primitive's fear relates to
the irrational and not to the real; we believe that we can fairly
say, therefore, that this immortality-ideology of his on which
the religious, artistic, and social creations are founded has been
determined, not by actual fear — fear of external dangers —
but by inward fear of the unreal, and precisely because of its
intangibility.[1] Fear is, in contrast to fright, not a real phenomenon: it cannot be traced to and explained (as psycho-analysis
has attempted to explain it) by any real danger, even such an
internal danger as one might postulate, for example, in the
individual's own insistent impulses (Freud). For every adequate cause of fear that we find, without or within, merely
gives it the impress of fright, without touching the prime
phenomenon of human fear of the unreal and irrational.
Indeed, the linking of this prime fear even with the notion of
death — unreal as this must be to our ignorance, and peculiarly
close as it stands to the prime fear — seems a sort of tacking-on
by way of afterthought. The prime phenomenon itself I characterized in another connexion (*Technik*, III) as " life-fear,"
because seemingly it is something given along with the life-

[1] See: *Seelenglaube und Psychologie* (1930).

process itself and working against the individual's fear of losing himself in life.

In so far, therefore, as the negative-inhibitive fear of life, as well as the positive will to perpetuation, acts in the creation of ideologies (including artistic ideologies), we have to deal with a second *unreal* factor. To put it in another way, the fear that urges towards perpetuity is precisely as unreal — or, shall we say, illusory or fantastic — as the positive will-to-art that builds up for itself a second reality next above, parallel with, or inside the first. But neither of these two tendencies alone is capable of constructing an ideology, be it of a religious, an artistic, or a social character; it requires the two together, co-operating according to the needs of the moment, to do that. Yet they are not one, they are not causally connected in such a way that the fear of death leads to the will to eternalization, or the complete achievement of the will to eternalization leads to the fear of life. This may seem to happen, or actually happen, even at a later stage in that which I have called the creative sense of guilt; but also it may only emerge from the attempt to overcome this fundamental dualism in the individual. Originally the positive will to eternalization seems to have led by itself only to actions of a predominantly magical order which, in the course of ritual development, became pre-artistic expressions of a " practical " sort (dance, and eventually instrumental music and song), while the restraining fear led solely to magical hush-ceremonies which we meet later in religious (like neurotic) ceremonial. Only a combination of the two — in other words, a volitional grip on, and conquest of, the fear-phenomenon — leads to the creation of ideologies in which the will to eternalization satisfies itself (in the first instance) collectively, and individual fear is suspended or at least temporarily mitigated. Yet not only is the unreal character of these ideologies obvious, but (after what has been said) their unreal origin also: that is, the unreal motivation which they have in the individual.

Thus, at the very commencement of human development —

then, indeed, in far greater measure than subsequently — we have the unreal element as the decisive factor which led to expression in art. But if religion is originally unreal, and the (psychologically speaking) equivalent love-experience at the other end of the scale is predominantly real, art stands in the middle, realizing the unreal and rendering it concrete. In so doing, it merely follows a universal law of development which I have formulated in my *Seelenglaube und Psychologie:* namely, that human development consists in a continuously progressive concretization of phenomena that were originally purely ideal or spiritual. In this sense the whole of cultural development is an artistic, or at least artificial, attempt to objectify human ideologies. Nevertheless, art does stand out from the general line of development by the fact that it retains a substantial element of the original unreal character. Indeed, in certain artistic tendencies, and, for that matter, in its general development, it even emphasizes the unreal and spiritual element in contrast to this universal concretization-tendency and tries to protect itself against being pulled down to the levels of actual use. Herein, we may fairly say, lies one of the motives for the æsthetic theory of the " purposelessness " of art: art in fact should represent this unreal ideality in an increasingly concretized world; while, on the other hand, the imitative principle (as we shall see) appears as a reaction of the creative sense of guilt, driving the individual out of his unreal world and back to nature.

Throughout the steady concretization-process of the super-real ideologies — which become ever more earthly and end by actually humanizing the creative god in the artist — art conserves the irrational principle which finds expression in the individual creative will on the one hand and the æsthetic immortality-concept on the other. It refuses to conserve the human being by imitating nature and man; neither does it console by offering substitutes for what is unattainable or has been renounced, in reality: what it seeks is to prove by objectification the emotional reality of what has never been real and can never be made real. This psychic actuality is not, however (as analysis would have it), a precipitate of the real, but an idealism *a priori* anchored beyond all reality, which the will to eternalize objectifies in the artistic immortality-concept. This specifically artistic immortality-ideology renders its creator immortal along with his work, by putting, on a work which expresses the prevailing collective ideology, the stamp of the individual artist-personality. This intermediate character of the work of art, which links the world of subjective unreality with that of objective reality — harmoniously fusing the edges of each without confusing them — has been superbly turned to account by the play-instinct, as Schiller æsthetically conceived it. The only question is whether the æsthetic play-instinct, which transfers a conception taken from play to art and artistic productivity, really produces the latter or merely accounts for its pleasurable *effect*. For play, after all, differs not only conceptually, but factually, from art. It has in common with art the combination of the real and the apparent; yet it is not merely fancy objectivized, but fancy translated into reality, acted and lived. It shares with art the double consciousness of appearance and reality, yet it has more of reality, while art is content with the appearance. Here we are reminded of Plato's definition, or, rather, poetic description, of art — which is really but the reflection of his whole picture of life; for does he not explain daily life as the shadow of an actual reality, which he calls the Idea, and does not art therefore naturally represent for him only a shadow of that shadow, a copy of a copy? Had he meant that this artificial image of our shadow reality might have caught something of the original idea underlying it in the process, his conception would be so far removed from his ascription of an imitative character to art that we should be able to accept that conception. It would not appear to be so, however. For art to him is imitation ($\mu\iota\mu\eta\sigma\iota\varsigma$), and play, which for the Greeks was such an outstanding cultural factor, he seems to have regarded, quite generally, as just such a copy of real life.

But as we shall discuss in a later section the origin and significance of human play, as a problem of folk-psychology which is allied to, but by no means identical with, artistic creativity, we will now return to the pleasure-giving character that is common, as it seems, to art and play. It seems to us that Schiller in his treatise contributed more to this purely æsthetic problem of satisfaction or pleasure than to the problem of artistic creativity proper — particularly in that he was able to regard the notion of the beautiful, which so greatly exercised æsthetic, as the result of the harmonization between the material-instinct and the form-instinct. But the *contemplation* of the beautiful aroused pleasure, satisfaction, or liking, and the central problem of scientific æsthetic is to find out why and how this happens. This, however, takes it for granted that the artist creates the beautiful that thereupon arouses pleasure in the enjoyer, a conclusion which seems an arbitrary assumption based on the effect of the work of art upon us. In other words, it is assumed in æsthetic that the artist desires to create the beautiful and, in so doing, enjoys a pleasure corresponding to that of the spectator or listener. Yet that is just what we do not know, so that we can only say that we call a work beautiful when *we* get some pleasure-value or other out of it. Herein perhaps is to be found the origin of Socrates' ranking of the beautiful on a level with the good and the useful, and of Plato's identification of it with the true — in the sense of his doctrine of Ideas, which leads him to interpret the soul's intuition of a self-beauty (αὐτὸ καλόν) as the recollection of its prenatal existence. And so we find the link with our previously outlined explanation of the beauty-concept as a derivative of the soul-concept, and also the relation with the immortality-concept, by bringing the prenatal — that is, a supernatural — state into the account.[1]

At this point we can consider also the psychological

---

[1] I have already in my *Trauma of Birth* (1924) tried to work out the psychological significance of this prenatal condition to artistic creativity and particularly to Greek art. See the section on "Artistic Sublimation."

significance of æsthetic pleasure in the beautiful, whether felt by
the artist himself or put into the work by the enjoyer. In spite of
the difference between art and play, there is this element common to both, that they operate on a *plane of illusion,* which
has its setting and its pattern in our own soul-life. Analysis of
the modern human type, moreover, has taught us to understand the emotional life (*Gefühlsleben*) as such an inner plane
of illusion on which all experience is played out more or less
potentially, without actual happening (*Technik,* III).[1] This
provides us in principle with an internal phantom existence
without actualized experience, but one in which the individual
does not necessarily become conscious of its illusory nature.
It is only by looking at the matter thus that we can understand dream-life as an artificial phantom life on the illusionist
plane of the emotions ("life is a dream"). In play and in art
the individual is able, by the aid of a collective or social ideology, to find such an illusory plane, whereon he can live
potentially or symbolically without doing so in reality. The
pleasure that he finds in this phantom life on an illusory plane
lies in the fact that it enables one to avoid the expenditure of
real life, which is, basically, in the escape that it provides from
life itself and, behind all, from the fear that is inseparable from
real life and experience.

Freud was the first to recognize the saving of energy as
essential to the pleasure derived from wit and, eventually, to
all æsthetic pleasure,[2] but his view of energy as libidinous prevented him from extending this conception to the nature of
pleasure generally, the purest form of which is, from a philosophic point of view, æsthetic pleasure. But if, as Schopenhauer

[1] I should like to refer my readers here to an older interpretation in a book to which
I have not been able to gain access: Alexander Bain's *The Emotions and the Will*. The
special nature of artistic emotion is there discussed in a chapter on "The Æsthetic
Emotions."
[2] *Wit and its Relation to the Unconscious* (1905; English translation, 1916). As I
understand it, Freud in his *Theory of Sex* (written at the same time) takes the partial
character of pleasure into account in his notion of "pre-pleasure"; in this case the
final pleasure, in our sense, would correspond to the sum of one's satisfaction in successful partializing *and* the output economized.

was perhaps the first to recognize, pleasure is not only nourished from positive sources but may even be just a condition characterized by the absence of fear or guilt, then the belief in the sexual origin of all pleasure, commonly assumed with the scientific support of psycho-analysis, becomes at least questionable. Actually I have already dealt with the problem of pleasure and non-pleasure in its relation to the time factor in my *Wahrheit und Wirklichkeit* (1929, p. 102), where I suggested that the essence of pleasure lay in a certain brevity, and that of non-pleasure in the prolongation of any state, even one that was at first pleasurable. If we combine this factor of temporariness with the quantitative principle of economy, it would seem that pleasure is not only relatively short, but also relatively small — in fact, *partial*. From this view of æsthetic pleasure we should thus arrive at the general formula: pleasure is the result of a *successful* " partialization," in which avoidance of fear, which element would necessarily be present in a totality of experience, acts to enhance pleasurable emotions. Every pleasurable feeling would therefore include, besides positive satisfaction (successful partialization), a being-spared (from fear, totality, life, and so on). And this again brings us to the view that æsthetic pleasure is not sexual,[1] but that, on the other hand, sexual pleasure may also be termed " æsthetic " in so far as it is momentary and partial — the two qualities which seem to us to sum up every pleasurable emotional experience. The greater the economy, the greater the pleasure — provided always that this saving can be made in a relatively short space of time, for the neurotic, too, goes cautiously with life and seeks to conserve vital strength, only he is always saving and his mere hoarding gives him no pleasure. Æsthetic pleasure is the highest or purest form of pleasure just because it supposes reception and gain, but not giving. But this clearly applies only to the one who enjoys the work of art and not to the creative artist. For him, therefore, a different psychology from the

[1] Cf. Arthur Kronfeld's *Sexualität und aesthetisches Empfinden in ihrem genetischen Zusammenhange* (second edition, Strassburg, 1906), though his work has now been superseded.

æsthetic must be found. For the artist is also sparing of life in that he substitutes creation; but then, again, he also wastes as he creates and this brings him new conflicts, from which again he seeks to escape by living. In this sense all doing and feeling which fall within the province of sublimation, from the purely æsthetic to the simple emotional, would not be substitutes for real life and experience imposed from without — no consequence of deprivation, that is — but the deliberate creation of a plane of illusion, on which there is the possibility of a seeming life, entailing less expenditure and therefore less fear, and therefore again a surplus of pleasure. Here the theory of the draining-off of superfluous energy in play is inverted: since now it is the play — that is, the attitude of make-believe — that releases forces which are set free by the saving of life.

With this we have found the key to a fundamental problem of life, to understand which is of far-reaching importance also for the psychological and ideological significance of artist and art. I have discussed this problem of partial and total experience in another connexion (*Technik*, III): namely, in relation to the hindrance of fear which thwarts the neurotic equally in his life and his work. The productive aspects of this conflict I was only able to touch upon briefly, but in any case the neurotic presented itself to me as a type predisposed to total experience and hindered only by fear — which in him is also total — from productively and constructively following up this tendency. The result is, not only that he checks all manifestations of life because their totality would let loose fear (that is, fear of death), but that the check is excessive (because total), and he only creates more fear, which manifests itself as fear of life. His only thought, one may say, is to save life and life-force, but this saving brings him no æsthetic pleasure, but neurotic dissatisfaction, because it dreads every sort of spending, even spending on a plane of illusion. From the therapy of such cases it has emerged that the neurotic must first learn to live playfully, illusorily, unreally, on some plane of illusion — first of all on the inner emotional plane. This is a gift which the artist, as an allied type, seems to possess from the outset, and in an even higher degree than the average person possesses it. For the artist too is a totalist type that, unlike the average, cannot live in perpetual " partialization," but is forced to totalize every act of life. And on the artistic plane of illusion, in the act of creating — which is at once appearance and reality, a part and a whole — he finds it possible to conquer creatively this fundamental human dualism and to derive pleasure therefrom.

For when he creates, the artist uses the whole of himself without being in danger of losing that self therein, for it is certain that the work itself, from his point of view, represents only a part of his ego, although it does in fact represent the whole artist and his personality. It is just, like every good symbol, a *pars pro toto* solution, in which, however, the artist does not go charily with his life, like the neurotic, but positively spends it as he creates. This again he does not actually, but essentially — that is, he puts into it his being, his " soul," as we say — and this then stands for the whole living ego, just as the abstract soul in primitive and later immortality-beliefs represents not only the whole individual, but even more than that: his essence, and with it the essence of man and of humanness in general. Once more we find art expressing the same thing as the abstract-soul concept, only in an objectified form, which we call beautiful precisely in so far as it is unreal, " more than earthly." For this very essence of a man, his soul, which the artist puts into his work and which is represented by it, is found again in the work by the enjoyer, just as the believer finds his soul in religion or in God, with whom he feels himself to be one. It is on this *identity* of the spiritual, which underlies the concept of collective religion, and not on a psychological identification with the artist, that the pleasurable effect of the work of art ultimately depends, and the effect is, in this sense, one of deliverance. The self-renunciation which the artist feels when creating is relieved when he finds himself again in his accomplished work, and the self-renunciation which raises the enjoyer above the limitations of his individuality becomes, through, not identification, but the *feeling of oneness* with the soul living in the work of art, a greater and higher entity. Thus the will-to-form of the artist gives objective expression, in his work, to the soul's tendency to self-eternalization, while the æsthetic pleasure of the enjoyer is enabled, by his oneness with it, to participate in this objectivization of immortality. But both of them, in the simultaneous dissolution of their individuality in a greater whole, enjoy, as high pleasure, the personal enrichment of that individuality through this feeling of oneness. They have yielded up their mortal ego for a moment, fearlessly and even joyfully, to receive it back in the next, the richer for this universal feeling.

Chapter Five

MICROCOSM AND MACROCOSM

This Atman (human being) that I have in my heart is smaller than a grain of rice, smaller than an oat, smaller than a mustard-seed. . . .

This Atman that I have in my heart is greater than the globe, greater than the expanse of the air, greater than the heavens, greater than all spaces of the universes. In it are all deeds, all scents, all tastes contained; it embraces all, it speaks not and cares for naught.

This Atman that I have in my heart, it is this Brahman. With it I become One when I depart this life. He who has attained to this knowledge, for him verily there is no more doubt.

Upanishads

Chapter Five

MICROCOSM AND
MACROCOSM

ༀༀ

The art-work, then, as we have seen from our inquiry into the nature of æsthetic pleasure, presents a unity, alike in its effect and in its creation, and this implies a spiritual unity between the artist and the recipient. Although certainly temporary and symbolic only, this produces a satisfaction which suggests that it is more than a matter of the passing identification of two individuals, that it is the potential *restoration* of a union with the Cosmos, which once existed and was then lost. The individual psychological root of this sense of unity I discovered (at the time of writing *The Trauma of Birth*, 1924) in the prenatal condition, which the individual in his yearning for immortality strives to restore. Already, in that earliest stage of individualization, the child is not only factually one with the mother but, beyond all that, one with the world, with a Cosmos floating in mystic vapours in which present, past, and future are dissolved. The individual urge to restore this lost unity is (as I have formerly pointed out) an essential factor in the production of human cultural values. In discussing its effects on cultural, religious, and artistic creations I could naturally, even then, scarcely help drawing attention to the collective and indeed cosmic aspects of this problem, especially as I had been interested in the theme "Microcosm and Macrocosm" since 1907 (see *Trauma of Birth*, pp. 73, 167).

In connexion with our present study of art it now becomes necessary to examine this human striving towards a super-individual unity and its spiritual premisses from the standpoint of those collective world-outlooks in which it has found more or less definite expression. It is in the world-picture of the ancient East that the clearest expression — systematic, even if not strictly scientific — of this fundamental unity of the individual with the universe is found. But this must only be taken in the sense that the Eastern culture-peoples systematized in their micro-macro-cosmic structure a general human feeling which we find in a more primitive form in all nature-peoples. And although there is no sign with the primitives of a developed system of human-astral relations, corresponding to that of culture-peoples, the world-outlook of the uncivilized is founded on the same identity with the universe, which goes beyond even the specifically astral parallelism of the heavenly picture and the earthly life. It will become still clearer in the course of our investigations that the old Oriental world-picture does merely represent an ideological formulation of the primitive identity-with-the-universe on a cultural plane which we can best describe as intellectual (or pre-scientific); it was only a question of a particular *ordering principle* of life, founded on astronomical observation. The primitives' working-out of the principle was rather terrestrial, whereas the progress of culture seems to be characterized by a " celestializing " of pure human egocentricity. And as the world-picture of the ancient East, with its pre-scientific ideology, lies somehow nearer to us than does the magic world-unity of the primitives, we prefer to start from the developed macro-micro-cosmic system of the Babylonians, as revealed to us by the antiquarian research of the last quarter-century. The rise of this world-system, in which all earthly being, becoming, and perishing are to be read in the heavens, has been placed by Hugo Winckler, the rediscoverer of the ancient Oriental world-picture,[1] in the fifth to sixth

[1] See Hugo Winckler: *Geschichte Israels*, Part II (1900), pp. 275 et seq. Also his *Himmels- und Weltenbild der Babylonier als Grundlage der Weltanschauung und Mythologie aller Völker* (*Der alte Orient*, III, 2, 3; Leipzig, 1901); *Die babylonische Geisteskultur* (Leipzig, 1907), the last-named a popular presentation. This conception of Winckler's has definitely influenced the whole present-day study of Oriental mythology, as is seen in

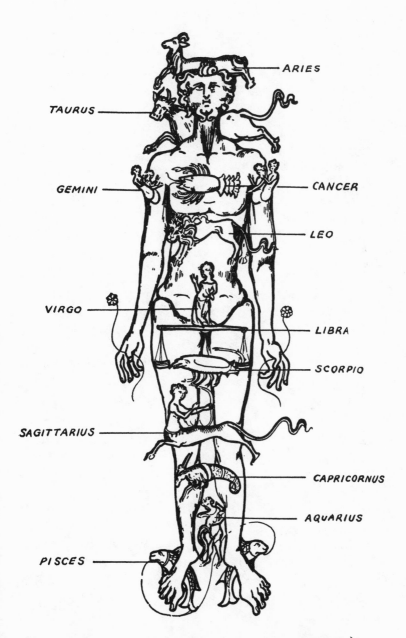

ARIES

TAURUS

GEMINI

CANCER

LEO

VIRGO

LIBRA

SCORPIO

SAGITTARIUS

CAPRICORNUS

AQUARIUS

PISCES

DANZEL: MAGIC ANATOMY (EUROPE)

millennia B.C.[1] Its home is Babylonia, whence this astral world-doctrine and astrological religion is said to have travelled over the whole earth. Although we are not able here to go into the vexed technical questions of the origin, age, and spread of this doctrine, its indisputable importance may be summed up, for the moment, in Winckler's popular description: "The whole universe is the great world, the macrocosm; its parts are small universes in themselves, microcosms. Such a *microcosm* is man, who is in himself an image of the universe and a perfect being. But the great universe is likewise a man, and as it is 'God,' God has human form. '*In his own image,*' therefore, was man created. This was still the belief of mediæval medicine, which we know to have had (chiefly for the purpose of bleeding) a method of dividing up the human body according to the twelve signs of the zodiac (head, ram; neck, bull; arms, twins; and so on). On this the 'scientific' treatment of a patient was based. . . ."

Winckler immediately adds a remark which with one sweep lays bare the whole psychological problem — the problem, namely, of how this theory of parallelism arose and what, in the last resort, it signifies. This is a question which received

---

the astral-mythological school headed by E. Stucken (*Astralmythen;* Leipzig, 1907), and of ancient Oriental religions, the leader in which field, Alfred Jeremias, has recently sought to show that the non-Semitic Sumerians were the real inventors of the celestial system (*Die Weltanschauung der Sumerer;* Leipzig, 1929).

[1] Widespread discussion has arisen over the dating of the Babylonian astronomy, which, according to Winckler, forms the basis of the ancient Oriental world-picture. His chief opponent is F. X. Kugler, who, in a learned two-volume work (*Sternkunde und Sterndienst in Babel;* Münster, 1907–9), seeks to prove that it was only in the last seven centuries before Christ that a real astronomy developed. The far-reaching conclusions which he draws from this late dating of astronomical knowledge are given in his essay: "*Auf den Trümmern des Panbabylonismus*" (*Anthropos,* IV, 1909). Boll goes even further, for he describes the astral-mythological system as a modern fantasy (*Neues Jahrbuch für das Klassische Altertum;* 1908). On the other hand, A. Jeremias, in *Das Alter der babylonischen Astronomie* (Leipzig, 1908), places that age in the third millennium B.C. It suffices for our purpose, however, to know that there is, independently of scientific astronomic evidence, abundant proof of parallelism between celestial (macrocosmic) and terrestrial (microcosmic) phenomena in the ancient Eastern culture; and there is the affirmation of P. W. Schmidt, important for our later investigations, that the astronomical-mythological system is not found among the nature-races ("*Panbabylonische und ethnologische Elementargedanken,*" *Mitteilungen der Anthropologischen Gesellschaft* of Vienna, Vol. XXXVIII, No. 2, pp. 73 et seq.).

most unsatisfactory replies both from Winckler and from the religious and mythological experts of his school, who when they assume that the Oriental culture-peoples "read off" their cult myths from the heavens, are really getting little beyond the facts premissed in the world-outlook itself, and leaving the problem of how the myths got up there unsolved. But even the purely psychological explanation, according to which they would be projections of human observation and processes on to the heavens, indicates no more than the need to anthropomorphize, and leaves it an open question why it was the heavenly bodies and happenings in particular that became so humanized, on the one hand, and supposedly so able to influence men so decisively on the other. A clear example of this mixing of terrestrial and celestial factors is provided by the Babylonian time-reckoning, of which Winckler says—in continuation of the remarks quoted above—"In the Babylonian mathematical tables the number 12,960,000 is treated over and over again in all its parts and possible combinations in relation to the sexagesimal system. . . . The significance of this number has been explained to us by Plato, who took it over from the Pythagoreans. According to him, this number was the arithmetical expression for the law controlling the universe. . . . The explanation given . . . is based essentially on the fact that the number of days required to make a human being (in the womb) is 260. . . . The year, reckoned at 360 days, makes 12,960,000 days = 36,000 years, or one hundred times as many days as years. And this, according to Babylonian calculation, is the number of years in a world-age. Plato reckons the duration of a human life at one hundred years (= 36,000 days), so that one day of a man's life corresponds to one year of the universal world-year. Thus the two numbers of man and the universe (and therewith the godhead) are brought into an inward relation: they are *mirror-images* of one another."

But we, too, do not get beyond this mirror-image explanation if we merely seize upon the obvious suggestion that these

speculations started from human phenomena (birth, duration
of pregnancy, etc.) and were subsequently brought into line
with celestial time-measurement. For the real question concerns, not the starting-point — whether it was celestial or terrestrial — but the motive for bringing the two groups of phenomena into relation at all. And, though it may be that Plato's
explanation of the Babylonian estimate of a world-age was a
matter of later, Pythagorean, arithmetic, there still remains
the remarkable fact that the old Mexican theory of the world-
ages contains the same "subjective factors" of human periodicity — in particular, the relations of planetary time-reckoning
to the duration of pregnancy. Thus Danzel thinks that "the
260-day period of the "Tonal-anatl," which plays a special part
in the Mexican calendar, may have been based on the duration of pregnancy as well as on astronomical spaces of time.[1]
For a general explanation of the subjective factor in time-
reckoning and calendar-making — designed originally to fix
good and bad days for certain undertakings and for the curing
of sicknesses — Danzel refers us to the periodicity of certain
human processes which has been established recently by Kam-
merer, Fliess, and Swoboda; in particular, the congruence of
female menstruation with the phases of the moon, which no
doubt was already familiar to ancient folk-lore, may be regarded, perhaps, as a substantiation of the micro-macro-
cosmic parallelism.

"The calendar symbols," says Danzel (*Mexiko,* I, p. 25),
"which considered determination for a given period, are signs
for dæmonic forces that in turn are regarded as the controlling factors of organs and parts of the body, and therefore as
having originally a subjective co-significance." This relating
of microcosmic and macrocosmic positions forms the basis of
what Danzel calls the "magic anatomy" intended for practical
purposes and for augury. The soothsayer, who was also, as a

[1] T. W. Danzel: *Mexiko,* II, p. 25. Ernest Fuhrmann (*Mexiko,* III, p. 21) has added
more weight to this supposition in that he bases the Mexican year on the prenatal
age of man and refers the new chronology (which is not based on the sun's course)
to this embryo year.

rule, a conjuror of illnesses and healer of the sick, found in the system which correlated parts of the body and signs of the day a means of ascertaining the dæmon-worked causes of sicknesses and determining the day which, as controlled by favourable dæmons, would prove suitable for a cure. Such ideas are not confined to Mexico, however. They are found as far away as New Zealand, India, and China and stretch from the description of " metaphysical prime man " in the cabbalistic books almost down to the present day.[1] We shall easily see, however, in following up the development which a similar macrocosmizing of the people took in Babylon, that it is only when these purely subjective factors have been overcome, and their hold on men shaken off, that a higher cultural development became possible. For this reason our modern psychological explanation of the macrocosmic system as an anthropomorphous projection on to nature remains inadequate — quite apart from the fact that these collective cultural images do not appear to square with our individual-psychological postulates. And if I nevertheless begin by drawing attention to them, this is because, for one thing, these subjective factors are as a rule not taken into account or are even denied by the archæologists; and, for another, in order that their inadequacy for the explanation of these cultural-ideological phenomena shall be obvious.

Thus Danzel himself refers us, for an explanation of the mythological projection on to natural objects — which are thereby made into gods — to the investigations of L. Staudenmaier, who was able to produce something similar when experimenting on himself. According to him, there are special dispositions in the psyche for imaginative " personifications "

---

[1] Abundant material for this interesting medicinal aspect of the ancient culture-picture will be found in a two-volume work by Hovorka and Kronfeld: *Vergleichende Volksmedizin* (Stuttgart, 1908). The chapter on "Bleeding," in particular, deals with the relation of the signs of the zodiac to the various parts of the body. There is an overwhelming mass of material also in Stephan Steinlein's two volumes: *Astrologie, Sexualkrankheiten und Aberglaube in ihrem innern Zusammenhange* (Munich, 1915). Lastly there is A. Warburg's *Heidnisch-antike Weissagung in Wort und Bild zu Luther's Zeiten* (Heidelberg, 1920).

which stand in a definite relation to certain physical organs.[1]
Herbert Silberer, although in reviewing Staudenmaier's book
(*Imago*, II, 1913) he finds in it no more than the material for a
psycho-analysis of the author, has yet himself established the
existence of the same phenomenon from another point of view
— namely, the purely psychological — as Staudenmaier has not
failed to point out (second edition, p. 81). Because for Silberer
too it is a matter of what he calls " auto-symbolic " happenings,
such as he himself observed when abstract ideas reached presentation under concrete pictorial forms; he has indeed used the
psychological explanation of such auto-symbolic happenings —
which on occasion may perfectly well be personifications — to
reinforce his psycho-analytical explanation of dream-pictures.[2]
The pictorial symbolism of dreams was already recognized in
ancient Greece through Artemidorus of Daldis,[3] and the great
physician Hippocrates, too, had adopted the point of view that
in dreams there is a transformation of internal sensations into
symbolical pictures. In *Das Leben des Traumes* (Berlin, 1861),
R. A. Scherner has made the first attempt in modern times to
demonstrate this idea scientifically. He puts forward a whole
system of body-symbolism, which Volkelt then made the basis
of his book: *Die Traumphantasie* (Stuttgart, 1875), and finally
Freud thoroughly sexualized it in his *Interpretation of Dreams*
(Vienna, 1900). Scherner demonstrated the part played by *all*
parts of the body in the building-up of the symbolism and,
at the same time, worked out more particularly the symbolism
of the house — to which we shall come later. For Freud it was
merely the sexual elements which were of interest in this, but
(as Scherner and Volkelt have aptly remarked) the house is
not the only sphere used for the symbolization of bodiliness in
dreams; and then, again, as Freud rightly adds, this tendency

[1] L. Staudenmaier: *Die Magie als experimentelle Naturwissenschaft* (Leipzig, 1912;
second, augmented edition, 1922).
[2] H. Silberer's work was published in the *Jahrbuch für psychoanalytische . . . Forschungen* (1909–14) and the *Zentralblatt für Psychoanalyse* (1911–14).
[3] *Symbolism of Dreams*. Annotated translation by Friedrich S. Krauss (Vienna, 1881).
The sexual portions were translated by Hans Licht for Krauss's *Anthropophyteia*, Vol. IX.

to symbolize one's own body is by no means peculiar to the
dream, but belongs to the activity of the imagination generally
— a fact already discovered by Volkelt, for that matter. Thus
this subjective "explanation" of mythical phenomena by
psycho-biological happenings leads us out again to the very
problem that it was fetched in to solve: namely, to that of the
particular nature of that type of human thought and imagination which, in contrast to our logical process of thought, is
called "unconscious" by Freud, "autistic" by Bleuler, "symbolic" by Jung, "prelogical" by Lévy-Bruhl, and "mythical"
by Cassierer. All these names, variously as they may be interpreted, are at bottom only modes of emphasizing, as against
the older views, the fact that this "primitive" thought of
ours — so opposed to our logical and scientific scheme of connecting and concluding — is not purely arbitrary, but obeys
"a law of its own peculiar sort and cast." [1] But whereas modern
research, particularly after the lead given by Lévy-Bruhl, has
endeavoured to determine the mode of alogical combination
practised in this primitive thinking, I should like here to tackle
the problem from another angle, with particular regard to
Cassierer's theories. It seems to me, in fact, that the linking-up
of heterogeneous conceptions in the primitive world-picture,
which seems to correspond to our mental process of causal
association, rests primarily on a special articulation of the universe which alone renders these strange linkages intelligible.
This articulation of the universe is done primarily from a
purely egocentric point of view which classifies things of the
outer world, psychologically speaking, into those belonging to
the ego, and therefore forming a part of it, and those not belonging to the ego, which are therefore foreign or hostile to it.

In this division of the world into good and bad, to which
the ego and non-ego naïvely correspond, experience of useful
and harmful things appear to play a part, if not a decisive one.
Otherwise it would be impossible to understand how the Australian or Indian, whose totemistic world-idea is based on some

[1] Ernst Cassierer: *Die Begriffsform im mythischen Denken* (Leipzig, 1922).

world-classification of this kind, regards a particular tree as belonging to his ego, and a certain other as hostile to it. Supposing, then, as I for my part believe, that to every good thing there must correspond some bad thing, we are brought back to the more important question, what does such a partitioning of the world mean at all? To my mind, it is the same necessity as that which has led us to the causal world-view: that is, the desire to reach the good and avoid the evil by *predetermination*. The extent to which our intellectual-scientific causality takes account of this necessity is clear enough. But in the primitive, experience, which for want of a scheme of causal connexions he cannot have, is replaced by a naïve pre-classification which enables him to characterize one group of things as good and clean, and another as unclean, forbidden, or tabu. By avoiding all contact with this second group the primitive expects to avoid all evil, and should evil befall him nevertheless, he takes this as a proof that he has, consciously or unconsciously, violated the scheme of division. We cannot here describe in detail the experiences, or, better, spiritual ideas, on which this primitive division of the universe is based. All that concerns us at this point is to make clear the difference between the primitive and the civilized world-pictures. In the first the notion of *dividing* appears to me to be what lies at the root of the whole world-outlook; and in the second the principle of *uniting*. The latter is not, indeed, absent from the primitive world-picture, but it is only a result of the avoidance of certain things dangerous to the ego, while in the civilized world-picture causal linkage stands in the foreground, with avoidance as its result.

In any case, since the appearance of Durkheim's great work [1] we have no excuse for regarding the totemism of the primitives as a mere principle of the social structure, but must see in it a universal principle of world-partition. "Actually the

[1] Émile Durkheim: *Les Formes élémentaires de la vie religieuse* (Paris, 1912). The same "universal totemism" has been shown to exist among the Marind-Anim in Dutch New Guinea. See P. Wirz: *Die religiösen Vorstellungen und Mythen der Marind-Anim und die Herausbildung der totemistisch-sozialen Gruppierungen* (Hamburg, 1922).

differentiation of the various clans according to their totems is
not confined to the narrow social circle that it primarily concerns, but extends more and more widely till it embraces finally
every sphere of existence, natural and spiritual. Not only the
members of the clan, but the whole universe, with all that it contains, is articulated, by the totemistic form of thought, in groups
which either belong together or are separated from each other
according to definite kin-relationships. All things, animate
or inanimate, are eventually swept into this structure in some
way or other " (E. Cassierer, op. cit., p. 17). Yet Cassierer himself remarks that Durkheim's explanation of this division of
the world according to the divisions of human society is unsatisfactory (op. cit., p. 24). The truth is, we cannot arbi-
trarily pick out any one section from this universal classification
of the world for the purpose of explaining the rest by it until
we have realized the significance of the system as such.
Whether, like Durkheim, we select the social class-system as
our starting-point and apply it to the universe, or, like Freud,
take exogamy or animal tabu, we shall always come to in-
sufficient or false conclusions with regard to the whole; in
doing so we should be postulating the applicability of a scale
of world-values that is not adequate for the primitive system
and seems rather to be an importation into it from our own.

If we take as our basis the broadest possible principle of
division, which we find in the totemistic world-picture of the
primitives — namely, that into objects hostile or friendly to the
" I " — and if we take into consideration not only the practical
experience of the primitive but his spiritual foundations also,
we shall arrive at *one* fundamental difference between his
thought and ours. This is the notion, arising from the naïve
immortality-belief that death can be avoided, provided that
one knows and avoids the forces threatening the " I " and, at
the same time, knows how to use the helpful and strengthening
forces to one's advantage. The essential means to this end is
the individual will, which must either be strong enough to
fight and control the evil that threatens in the world or good

enough to evade or ward off the bad influences. This world-outlook, which perhaps finds not only its finest but also its clearest expression in the Germanic Baldur myth,[1] can best be described as " magic," because it presupposes that natural happenings can be influenced by human forces of will and does not merely aspire thereto, as is the case in our practical-technical world-scheme. The magic world-classification would thus, at bottom, rest on a distinction (not experimental, but volitional) between death-bringing and life-furthering objects, with the consequent tendency to avoid the former and keep the latter favourably disposed. We shall have to show, later, how this anti-causalistic assumption in the primitive world-picture was bound to regard certain facts, such as sexuality, as hostile to the " I " and therefore to life; on the other hand it could endow man, in situations which would seem to us excessively dangerous, with a blind confidence in his powers provided that he felt himself to be at one with the forces friendly to his ego.

So much already seems clear, however — that the astral world-picture of the Babylonians, with its relation between the celestial and the terrestrial, aimed at seeing good or evil events in advance, with the intention of avoiding those which were destructive and death-bringing, and bringing about those which brought healing and happiness. So also with the pre-Babylonian Sumerians: they originally used astronomical observation, not for calendar-making, but for its bearing on their personal fate, seeking to foresee its peril so as to forestall it. This attitude, which even today dominates our scientific ideology and is the foundation of the primitive's magic world-picture, manifested itself in the ancient Oriental civilization in a form which we are now in a position to regard as the transition from the magic to our scientific world-outlook. For it becomes ever clearer that the practical-technical aims attained by astronomy,

[1] Baldur could not be slain by his brother, Hödur, because all things in nature were bound to him in friendship — one may say, were at one with him. Only the mistletoe had contrived to be excluded from the universal oath of unity, and thus became his undoing. As in all myths in which the hero is vulnerable in one spot only, death inevitably breaks through despite all precautions.

physics, and chemistry as they grew out of astrology, meta-physics (cosmogonies), and alchemy, were not implicit in the original intention in man, but asserted themselves as gradual results of the increasing cognition and recognition of his de-pendent relation to nature. In the beginning, then, man did not observe the stars for the purpose of an objective chronology,[1] but had greater problems and higher aims in mind. What in-terested him was life and death, life's span and death's dan-gers, and the origin which he hoped might disclose possibilities of rebirth to defeat his transience. What he finally found, however, was a measurement, as exact as possible, of the pri-mary clock presented by the rotation of the heavenly bodies. What he sought was a means of influencing the duration of time in the sense of the desire for immortality, and he did not find it.

Here we recognize a driving motive for the projection — or, better, the relating — of human and heavenly (cosmic) phenomena: the individual is thereby lifted out of his uncer-tain everyday life and above his mere primitive identity with the All and becomes identified with the regularly recurring and consequently imperishable stars. Amongst these stars, as we now know for certain, it was the moon that played the chief, or at least the original, rôle — and naturally, since this heavenly body is differentiated from all the rest by its gradual waxing and waning, which positively invite comparison with organic growth and decay. Here, then, was another mode of ensuring rebirth after extinction, to assimilate one's life on earth to the moon's phases (which we know to have been laid down in the oldest chronologies and calendars) and so by magic identification to make oneself like her. According to the scanty remains of this primitive moon-cult — which at a later stage of development was driven out almost everywhere by the sun-

---

[1] See also Ernst Zinner: *Die Geschichte der Sternkunde von den ersten Anfängen bis zur Gegenwart* (Berlin, 1930); also Franz Boll: *Die Lebensalter* (Leipzig, 1913), and the same author's comprehensive exposition: *Sternglaube und Sterndeutung* (Leipzig, second edi-tion, 1919). More generally, see: Franz Strunz: *Astrologie, Alchemie, Mystik. Ein Beitrag zur Geschichte der Naturwissenschaften* (Munich, 1928).

cult, which belonged to a different ideology — it seems certain
that it was originally of female nature and that the moon-god
only appeared as a supplementary counterpart to the moon-
goddess, as her son or brother (later: son, brother, and hus-
band). These mythological traditions of all civilized and most
primitive races have their sociological counterpart in the fact
that the remains of the moon-cult also point to primitive conceptions of society, in which the woman still played a greater
part than that which we find allotted to her in the patriarchal
organization of high cultures with their sun-cult.[1]

The reconstruction of the old Oriental world-picture, though
it has made our present outlook on human cultural development much broader by compelling us to recognize the spiritual
as well as the material factors, has in particular cases rendered it difficult to decide where the starting-point for this
relating of earthly and heavenly is to be placed. The only
certainty seems to be that *cultural* development has advanced
by way of the cosmic, and that in particular the artistic
working-out of a culture remains inexplicable unless we posit
a macrocosmization of the earthly. In any case, we should
beware of naïvely projecting our own practical-technical mentality into the so-called primitive culture, which was in
a sense more spiritual than the present civilization. Whatever may have been projected into heaven from earth, it is
more important for the understanding of a culture that (as
has now been proved) certain celestial processes had to be
imitated in cult-form on earth in order that man's cosmic identity, and with it his immortality, might be assured. For choice,

[1] Bachofen was the first to point out this connexion in the ancient primitive cultures in his *Mutterrecht* (1861), but it has since received widespread corroboration from
later researchers, in particular Frobenius, who discovered traces of a matriarchal
culture in prehistoric Africa (*Das unbekannte Afrika*, Munich, 1923). Whether the
duration of the female period and pregnancy (which in any case varies as between
individuals) should not be regarded as the attempt at a macrocosmic assimilation of
woman to the moon may be left an open question. Certainly we find no allusion to
this astonishing parallel in the oldest traditions, whereas even now we can observe
any day how easily these biological processes may be influenced, and their timing
altered, by psychic factors.

the actors in these celestial dramas were the king and his family. The original kingship — traces of which are preserved even in the few surviving and constitutional monarchies of to-day — was a divine kingship: that is, the ruler's whole mode of life was prescribed, down to the smallest details, by the cosmic laws which it was the very business of the astral doctrine of the time to establish. This order of things clearly survived in the Incas of Peru, in the mikado of Japan, and in many other instances of which traces are seen in the pre-Aryan Dravidian culture of India, the pre-Babylonian Sumerian empire, and the related South African culture.[1] Without the knowledge of this " cosmic " idea of the state, which obliged the king to be a living proof of the immortality-principle for his subjects, we should still be unable to comprehend how and why the original exercise of art was, in these " celestial " cultures, devoted almost exclusively to the religious service of myth-cults connected with the disposal of the dead. It would appear, from the discoveries of archæology, that only the king, as vessel of the immortality-principle, was buried according to a prescribed cult-ritual; even so, the assistance of art would be still more necessary on that occasion to produce the desired cosmic identity than for his service during his " artificial " life-course.

Enough has been said, without entering at present into the detail of tomb-art, to show once again the fundamental meaning of artistic creativity — the art, that is, of rendering concrete by pictorial representation that which is thought and is spiritually real — in fact, to prove its existence. This pictorial representation of something thought, whatever its objective content or its style, must necessarily be in the nature of creation, because in it man is macrocosmizing himself and thereby rising above his nature. And if there is, in artistic creativity as such, a tendency towards cosmic perpetuation (which has only become individualized in modern art), we may go a step further and regard the belief in the soul which led to artistic creation

[1] For India, see Frazer: *The Golden Bough;* for Sumeria, Woolley's works on Ur; and for Africa, L. Frobenius: *Erythräa* (Berlin, 1930).

as man's first creative achievement. For the original idea of immortality, before it had anything spiritual about it, was a primitive transformation-belief — though no doubt the germ of the later belief in the soul was latent in it — a belief in certain individuals 'that they possessed an active power of returning to life, of (in a way) reproducing themselves by self-creation. In the earliest *culture*-stratum to which we have had access, only the king, whose life-course, even so early, had to be "cosmic," was believed to have this immortality of the "soul"; and it may well be, as Woolley suggests, that the human sacrifices buried with the royal corpse were selected from those who were found worthy to share the king's immortality, to which as ordinary "mortals" they would have no claim.

This cosmic rôle of the king as vessel of immortality seems to me to explain also the strange institution of the ritual murder of kings, traces of which were found by Frobenius in Eritrea after Frazer had produced abundant material (from southern India in particular), and Zimmern had found further traces in Babylon. The sacrifice of the king is — like the human sacrifices in Mexico — his privilege. As representing the immortality-idea he may not die a natural death; on the other hand this very fact made his death by violence a necessity, and accordingly he was slain by his successors, who were assisted by the youngest of the royal wives (Frobenius). The sacrifice of the king is thus only the logical conclusion of his whole supernatural existence, the passing ordained for him because of his rôle in this earliest human drama. The supernatural, divine character with which the myths of later historical times invested his birth [1] attaches in older times to his death. From this fate he was spared later, in certain cultures, by the substitution of a criminal or a slave.[2] But this mitigation

[1] As early as *c.* 2800 B.C. the first Semitic ruler of the Sumerians, Sargon of Akkad, describes himself as the virgin son of the Mother of the Gods, and so proclaims himself the saviour of the Sumerian people.

[2] H. Zimmern describes a Babylonian New Year's festival which bears a close resemblance to the Christ myth — belonging, indeed, to the same range of ideas, since Christ, as carrier of the immortality-idea, would not be capable of dying a natural death.

only means that the original double meaning of the king's murder — the bestowing of immortality as his privilege, and the taking away of it — was distributed between two persons. And, for that matter, the funeral rites, in spite of the extreme contradictions in the traditions (Frobenius), leave us no doubt that it was sought to make the murdered king's return easier and at the same time impossible.[1]

Much light is thrown on the most primitive idea of the soul by a custom observed at the burial of chiefs throughout Oceania and also in Africa and South America. It is founded on the belief that the soul — that is, the power of rebirth — resides in the liquid portions of the human body. These, of course, are the first to decompose. Not only are the corruptible parts scrupulously collected, therefore, but the putrefying liquid is pressed out of the corpse itself until it is left quite dry and withered. Such, at any rate, is said to be the underlying idea, for it has not been really established, in spite of the abundant material collected (by Frobenius in particular). To me the reason for this custom seems to lie in the ambiguity already alluded to: namely, hesitation between facilitating the return and preventing it. For sometimes the products of decay, so carefully gathered into a vessel, are preserved until new life shows itself in them, while at other times they are thrown into the bush. Whether this is done with the intention of doing away with them or of incorporating them with the general cycle of nature remains an open question. In any case the dried (as it were, mummified) body is walled up in the rocks, ostensibly because it is " definitively " dead; yet in practice this skin-and-bone skeleton is preserved in many graves to this day. Instead of seeking a uniform solution, therefore, we propose to assume an inherent double significance in funerary custom [2] (which no

---

[1] Certain African traditions (Frobenius: *Erythräa*) lead to the assumption that the *emphasizing* of one or another of the inherent tendencies of the ritual was influenced by the character of the slain king, who in one case may have been feared and in another wanted back again.

[2] A similar ambiguity exists with regard to prehistoric "crouching" graves, with their bound corpses, which, on the one hand, were designed to prevent the dreaded return of the dead and, on the other, to facilitate the return of the released soul to

doubt reflects the justifiable doubt in immortality) and to examine only the *one* side of this belief that seems to have led
to the development of the soul-idea.

We allude to the conception of the " soul-worm," which is
known to the tribes of Madagascar as the *Fanany* myth. This
is obviously founded on observation of the worms appearing
on a corpse, which do undeniably denote new life. From this
purely corporal notion of a transformation a path leads to the
first conception of the soul by way of substituting for the worm
some other animal, also at first small and creeping, such as a
snake, a lizard, or other live creature living in the ground, the
rocks, or the water.[1] The Fanany myth, mentioned below, of
the Betsileo in Madagascar shows already a certain progress
from the primitive worm to the soul-animal.[2] The Betsileo
squeeze the putrefying liquid out of the bodies of the dead at
the feet and catch it in a small jar. After two or three months
a worm appears in it and is regarded as the spirit of the dead.
This jar is then placed in the grave, where the corpse is laid
only after the appearance of the Fanany. A bamboo rod connects the jar with the fresh air (corresponding to the " soul-
holes " of Northern stone graves). After six to eight months
(corresponding possibly to the embryonic period) the Fanany
(so the Betsileo believe) then appears in daylight in the form
of a lizard. The relatives of the dead receive it with great cele-
brations and then push it back down the rod in the hope that
this ancestral ghost will prosper exceedingly down below and

---

the deserted body (possibly aided by the resemblance of the corpse's attitude to the
embryonic position). Compare the discussion on these two theories, which again
appear only to reflect the double significance of the custom, in H. Klaatsch's *Die
Anfänge von Kunst und Religion in der Urmenschheit* (Leipzig, 1913; pp. 39 et seq.).

[1] "Once we admit the worm to be the vessel of the soul, the transition to the snake
in general is a natural consequence, as the latter appears to a naïve intelligence as
merely an enlarged edition of the former" (Erich Küster, in his learned work: *Die
Schlange in der griechischen Kunst und Religion;* Giessen, 1913; p. 64, foot-note 1).

[2] From Sibree's *Madagascar*, pp. 309 et seq., quoted by Frobenius in *Der Seelenwurm*
(1895) and reprinted in *Erlebte Erdteile*, I (Frankfurt, 1925), a treatise which deals
principally with the "vase-cult" arising out of the storing of decayed remains in
jars (see our later remarks on the vase in general).

become the powerful protector of the family and, for that matter, the whole village.

In this valuable tradition not only do we clearly perceive the transition from the primitive worm-transformation to the idea of certain soul-animals that have nothing actually to do with the decomposing-process itself, but also the transition to totemism. For the soul-animal, unlike the soul-worm, is addressed as a collective spirit, by which the whole community benefits, and the sending-back of the lizard to its underground residence is not carried out in the interest of the particular dead person and his revitalization, but in the interest of the community, which, indeed, may sacrifice the individual (see the "building-sacrifice" later) in order to thrive the better as a whole. Later totemism — the idea of descent from a definite animal species [1] — seems to emerge only from a secondary interpretation of the soul-worm idea or the soul-animal idea in accordance with a "law of inversion" (Frobenius) peculiar to mythical thought; just as the myth of the Creation as the projection backwards in time of the myth of the end of the world is in itself only a formal expression of the principle of rebirth. This adaption of the soul-worm idea to the totemistic derivation of man from the maggot is set forth clearly in the creation-sagas of the Samoans and Tonga Islanders, especially in those collected by Schirren (*Die Wanderzüge der Neu-Seeländer und der Naui-Mythus;* Riga, 1856). Tangaroa sent down his daughter Tuli in the guise of a snipe to people the naked rocks. A creeper, thus brought into being, withered. Out of the leaves and stems of the rotting plant there arose worms. Tuli chipped them with her beak and made men out of them. Another

---

[1] The idea that it was originally a question of small animals has recently been proved by a valuable piece of research on Indian myths by Ida Lublinski: "*Eine weitere mythische Urschicht vor dem Mythus,*" *Zeitschrift für Völkerpsychologie*, VI (1930). In explanation of the preference for small animals as bearers in mythical action, the author refers us, if not expressly, yet I think unmistakably, to the observation of the phenomena of decay in the dead body. On the significance of small animals, see also what is said in *The Trauma of Birth* (1924; pp. 16–19), and further in *Seelenglaube und Psychologie* (1930; p. 25).

EGYPTIAN GRAVE STELE, 3200 B.C.
(*Bird and snake*)

widespread idea is also here: namely, that of the soul-bird,[1] which, on the analogy of the worms, may be assumed to have originated from the carrion-eating birds. Here too, therefore, the creature figures in the beginning as the representative (abductor) of the soul and only later became its "bringer."

But the significance for art of these early ideas of the soul is not only one of the history of motives as this is set forth by Frobenius, Weicker, and Küster — to name only the most important writers — who have shown us respectively the "Kawok"- (lizard-) jars, and the representations of birds and of snakes which are found right on into the Classical age. These soul-concepts convey to us also the immense part played by the animal in general in the history of religion and art of all times and peoples. (A comprehensive work on this subject has recently been written by Fuhrmann: *Das Tier in der Religion;* Munich, 1922.) Light has also been thrown by African tradition on the transference of the soul-concept from the original small creeping creatures to certain species of larger mammals. According to Lublinski, the conviction still exists among a great many African tribes that dead chiefs transform themselves from the worm-stage into snakes, leopards, or other animals.[2] The Barundi, for instance, believe that the dead king becomes a snake. "He is sewed up in skins and slowly roasted before a fire. The first worm that creeps out of the corpse is placed in a pot with milk and is fed until, one night, it leaves the pot. It seems to be assumed, therefore, that the snake develops out of this worm. Other tribes often believe that this worm grows into a leopard" (op. cit., p. 53). I am inclined to think, however, that this substitution of large animals,

[1] See the reference to the veneration of the vulture which devours human carcasses in my *Don Juan-Gestalt* (1922); also H. Klaatsch, op. cit., pp. 36, 42. The whole subject is comprehensively treated by Georg Weicker in *Der Seelenvogel in der alten Literatur und Kunst* (Leipzig, 1902).

[2] According to Ratzel (*Völkerkunde*, second edition, I, p. 284), the northern Madagascans believe that the spirits of the chiefs go into crocodiles, and certain rajahs in Timor pride themselves on their descent from the crocodile. The South African tribes recently studied by Frobenius (*Erythräa*) imagine the souls of their dead kings to be lions (Mondoro) and fear them accordingly.

particularly beasts of prey, for the worm does not point merely to the honouring and glorification of the chief, but that more complicated emotions find expression therein. Above all, the character of a beast of prey assigned to the chief's soul displays it once more in its dangerous aspect; we may also take into consideration another motive, which I have already emphasized in *The Trauma of Birth,* when contrasting the small and large animals, and this motive has quite a special significance in the development of art, inasmuch as it concerns religious art in the sense of grave- and tomb-decoration.

The motive in question is that of being swallowed by a large animal, which, in contrast to the gradual and partial devouring by worms, suited the symbolic representation of rebirth through the mother (the conception of the womb as an animal). The traditions relating to this stretch through the whole of Classical culture to far on into the Christian symbolism of rebirth and can therefore receive only brief mention here, although they play a great part as motives in artistic representation. Certainly the idea of the womb as an animal has been widespread among different races of all ages, and it furnishes an explanation of (for instance) the second burial custom discovered by Frobenius along with the Fanany burial in South Africa. This consisted in placing the dead king's body in an artificially emptied bull's skin in such a manner that the appearance of life was achieved. This bull-rite was undoubtedly connected with the moon-cult (compare our "mooncalf," even today) and belongs therefore to the above-mentioned maternal culture-stage, at which the rebirth idea also made use of maternal animal-symbols, the larger mammals being chosen.[1] Yet we must not overlook the fact that this "mother's womb symbolism" denotes more than the mere repetition of a person's own birth: it stands for the overcoming of human mortality by assimilation to the moon's immortality. This sewing-up of the dead in

[1] Frobenius suggests—and the suggestion is supported by other cultural evidence—that cattle at this stage of culture were kept for ritual purposes only and not for breeding. The cultic origin of farming and breeding was first brought out by Eduard Hehn: *Die Entstehung der Pflugkultur* (Heidelberg, 1909).

the animal skin has its mythical counterpart in the swallowing
of the living by a dangerous animal, out of which he escapes
by a miracle. Following an ancient microcosmic symbolism,
Anaximander compared the mother's womb with the shark.
This conception we meet later in its religious form as the Jonah
myth, and it also appears in a cosmological adaptation in the
whale myths collected in Oceania by Frobenius.[1] Hence, also,
the frequent suggestion that the seat of the soul after death
(macrocosmic underworld) is in the belly of an animal (fish,
dragon). The fact that in these traditions the animals are always those dangerous to man indicates that the animal womb
is regarded not only as the scene of a potential rebirth but also
as that of a dreaded mortality, and it is this which led to all
the cosmic assimilations to the immortal stars.

Thus we perceive a development of the belief in the soul,
ranging from the denial of maternal origin (as a symbol of
mortality) to the assumption of divine descent from the imperishable stars, with the king (or chief) at first as earthly
representative thereof. This development, which has left a
precipitate in art-history also, goes, however, beyond the animal,
and the final result of the whole process, in the early Oriental
world-picture, is the transfer of the animal to heaven. But to
understand the detail of this development, which eventuated
in the curious signs of the zodiac, we must remind ourselves
that the very earliest conception of this animal was that of the
soul-worm and similar reptiles or amphibians, and that these,
living, as they did, half underground and half in the water,
stood nearer to the macrocosmic womb-symbolism than did
the larger mammals or the birds of the air, venerated by a later
cult. Again, the idea of the soul-worm as emerging from the
soft parts of the human body bears a close relationship to the
idea of the animal's interior (the mother's womb) as the origin
of life — later, as the seat of the soul — although even at the

---

[1] L. Frobenius: *Im Zeitalter des Sonnengottes* (Berlin, 1904); on Classical tradition,
Hans Schmidt: *Jona. Eine Untersuchung zur vergl. Religionsgeschichte* (1907). For a general
survey, see the chapter: "Myth and Metaphor" of this book.

primitive worm-stage we can see a hint of parthenogenesis —
in other words, a self-creative tendency of the soul-concept.[1]
This tendency becomes still clearer in the celestial assimilation
of man, and of other large mammals living on the earth, to
the stars, which constantly renew themselves; and in the end
it finds the purest creative expression in the spiritual conception of the soul, released from all matter, which first began to
take shape in Greece.

What makes the evolution of the soul-concept, therefore, so
important in an analysis of the art-problems is the fact that
not only does it form the hypothesis and incentive for all creative work, but this evolution is seen to be in parallel with the
origin and expression of the creative urge itself. Whereas in
the beginning the soul-concept was concerned only with the
keeping of something given — that is, with the conservation
of life — the essence of creativity lies first in the ability to *re-
generate* something lost and eventually in the triumph of *new-
creating* something that had never existed. On the basis of this
formulation it is easy to fix the point at which the sexual
ideology became important to man, attaining a significance
which it had never before possessed and was subsequently to
lose. After all, it can neither be used to preserve man's own
life (being, on the contrary, regarded as hostile to the ego),
nor can it make possible the new creation of that which never
existed; its sole use lies in the re-generation of what has been
lost; and therefore, at a particular stage of development that
has not yet reached real creativity, it becomes a symbol of
human — namely, of reproductive — power. Those theories
which have made out that artistic creativity is the expression
of the sexual impulse have only made use of a transition phase
of man as creature to secularize the conception of man as
creator. Indeed, this latter conception itself, as manifested in
the idea of God, amounts to nothing less than an objectifica-

---

[1] There is a biological parallel to this conception in the modern view of "epi-
genesis," according to which new elements become effective in the new organism
born from the bisexual parent cells which had no previous existence in those cells.

tion of a creative urge that is no longer satisfied with self-reproduction, but must proceed to create an entire cosmos as the setting of that self.

In man's relation to the animal also, which has helped him out of his subterranean mortal origin into his heavenly immortality, we can trace the same transformation from man as creature to man as creator — in other words, from religion to art. In the ancient Oriental world-outlook, at its climax in the Babylonian culture, we find, side by side with the well-developed masrocosmos-system (with man on a level with the universe), a primitive technique of soothsaying which made use of the entrails of freshly killed sacrificial animals. From the number (and possibly the position) of the intestinal coils the priest deducted favourable or unfavourable portents of the fate of the land, particularly with regard to undertakings that the king had in contemplation. This hieromancy, also, rests on the belief in some spiritual power, originally localized in the lower body; man questions this spirit as to the future because, being no longer willing to wait and see what that future will be, nor able as yet to shape it creatively himself, he wants to know in advance. Here we have a reaching-out beyond even cosmic assimilation, which certainly promised immortality, but also fatalistic, preordained uniformity without the possibility of creative development. Now, although this reading of entrails (which is considered by scholars to be of high antiquity) may have survived as the echo of a primitive custom (perhaps the Fanany burial), the form and date of its appearance in the Babylonian culture show it definitely to be a reversion of macrocosmized man to his animalistic chthonian nature on which he still feels his earthly existence to depend. In other words, in this mantic, man's destiny was looked for again where it had lain of old — in his own interior,[1] such as the

[1] Whether we have here also the earliest beginning of a psychological outlook, a sort of introversion, such as the Greeks, in taking over from the ancient East, crystallized in a spiritual form, must for the present remain a pure speculation. It is at least a striking coincidence that the first attempts to systematize human gestures as the evidences of inward processes are found among the Babylonians. This commencement

Babylonians practised with their birth-omens, which must be regarded as the forerunners of our astrology.[1]

In any case, with the Babylonians primitive hieromancy very soon acquired a form which denotes the broad outlook of a high stage of culture: this was the *inspection of the liver* and was based above all on differentiated anatomical knowledge, but on a better-founded conception of the soul as well. For whereas the idea of the entrails as the seat of animal life still bears traces of its derivation from existence in the womb, the liver mantic transferred the seat of the soul to a vital organ of the individual himself, and for this reason the liver came to be regarded by the Greeks and Romans as the seat of thinking-power and also of instincts and desires.[2] According to Jastrow, who has gone most closely into the subject,[3] it is already mentioned on inscriptions of 2600 B.C.; and it is probably much older. He takes divination from the liver of the sacrificial animal (particularly the sheep) as primary, and its application to the prophetic reading of the heavens as secondary; Jeremias, however, regards the liver mantic as a reading of the heavens transferred to the slaughter-house. Here again is undoubtedly a case of the reciprocal play of earthly (human) and heavenly (cosmic) processes. As the liver mantic, like all others, was brought into use originally to discover the fate of the country (which depended upon the king), it was bound to have super-individual aspects, which readily took on macrocosmic

of a psychology of expression has been preserved for us in the neo-Babylonian "twitching-books," one of which has been published by B. Meissner in the *Sitzungs-bericht der Preussischen Akademie* (1921).

[1] Morris Jastrow: *Babylonian-Assyrian Omens* (1914); Dennefeld: *Babylonisch-Assyrische Geburtsomina* (Leipzig, 1914); Ungnad: "*Das Alter der Geburtsomina*" (*Orientalist. Literaturzeitung*, 1917); see also Fischer in the *Gynäkologische Rundschau*, 1916.

[2] See the article: "*Leber* (Liver)" in M. Höfler's *Die volksmedizinische Organotherapie und ihr Verhältnis zum Kultopfer* (Stuttgart, n.d.).

[3] M. Jastrow: *Religion der Babylonier und Assyrier*, II, pp. 213 et seq., and 273 et seq.; also: *The Liver in Antiquity and the Beginnings of Anatomy* (University of Pennsylvania, Medical Bulletin 20, No. 1, January 1908). The soul of the living is called in Babylonian: *kabittu* (= liver) or *libbu* (= heart). The Babylonian soothsayer, called in Latin *haruspex*, is said to have taken his name from the Sumerian *har* (= liver) (see Boissier: *Note sur un document babylonien;* Geneva, 1901; and, by way of comparison, Jeremias: *Handbuch der altorientalischen Geisteskultur*, second edition, 1929, p. 261, foot-note 1).

ANCIENT CLAY LIVER WITH MAGICAL SIGNS

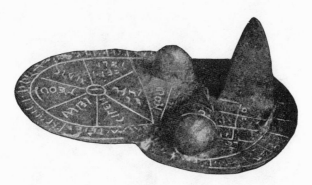

THE ETRUSCAN BRONZE LIVER FROM PIACENZA

forms. A proof of this is its "artistic" imitation in clay, which, as shown by a discovery, may be traced back to 2000 B.C. (Jastrow).

The liver as the seat of life counted as a small-scale cosmos — in other words, as a copy of the whole man — just as the soul was still his essence. This is why, in explanatory texts, certain parts of the liver which had been studied individually were given names such as fissure, mouth, finger. On the other hand, the mountain, street, palace, and gate of the liver are also spoken of, and this indicates a macrocosmic interpretation. (A certain part of the liver still carries on a trace of its cosmic significance in the modern anatomical nomenclature: *processus pyramidalis*.) The Etruscan bronze liver of Piacenza, discovered in 1877, which Jastrow calls "a microcosm reflecting the macrocosm," shows this significance developed in detail,[1] but shows also that the Etruscans combined with the liver mantic, adopted presumably from the Babylonians, another cult of horrible human sacrifice that was quite foreign to the old Oriental cultural sphere. The macrocosmic interpretation of the liver as the image of the cosmos is, after all, only the counterpart of the microcosmization of heaven, into which all imaginable earthly things and, above all, animals were transported (signs of the zodiac).

This microcosmization of the cosmos is seen in another symbol of the ancient world, which likewise found its most defi-

[1] The very division of the edge of the Etruscan bronze liver into sixteen regions, corresponding to the sixteen heavenly regions, gives it an external resemblance to the cosmos. The top side of the liver represents heaven, and the flat side the earth, and every separate part is linked with a particular activity of the god of the world. See Körte: "*Die Bronzeleber von Piacenza*" (*Mitteilungen des Kais. Arch. Inst. Römische Abt.*, Vol. XX, p. 362). The whole subject has been comprehensively dealt with by W. Bartels in *Die etruskische Bronzeleber von Piacenza* (Berlin, 1910–12). The difficult work of deciphering the Etruscan inscriptions we owe to Albert Grünwedel (Tusca, Leipzig, 1922). His interpretation of the texts is, however, so full of expressions of his personal abhorrence of the Etruscan mentality that one more than distrusts the objectivity of interpretations which are in themselves sufficiently doubtful. According to Jeremias, the Etruscans took over from the Babylonians not only the liver mantic, but the art of town-planning, which was later adopted by the Romans, as was bird-augury (*Allgemeine Religionsgeschichte*, second edition, Munich, 1924, pp. 226 et seq.).

nite formulation in Babylon. We allude to the conception of
the earth's navel (to which we shall return when dealing with
the development of architecture) at this point because it is
bound up in many traditions with those of the liver. This is
obviously because, in both cases, it is the symbolization of something essential and central that is in question: in one case, in
the interior of the body; in the other, on its exterior.[1] This
conception of the navel as the earth's centre does not, as the Pan-
Babylonians would have it, appear to have arisen in the
East and from there to have travelled over the whole of the
earth; for Roscher's thoroughgoing research on the subject [2]
has proved that it existed in many different places, mostly
totally unconnected, among, for example, the Peruvians, the
inhabitants of Celebes, the Arabians, Persians, Phœnicians in
Cyprus, and others. Fuhrmann even claims to have found the
temple ornament of the Delphic navel again in South Sea
ornament.[3]

As the world-navel also counted as the entrance to the earth's
belly — the underworld — it was at the same time regarded as
the starting-point of the world's creation, in conformity with
its microcosmic parallel. "The whole of antiquity seems to
have thought that the organic life of the embryo developed
from the navel as the *centre* of the body — an idea which must
almost involuntarily have led to the notion that the navel of
the earth was also the starting-point of the world's creation"

[1] For the combination of navel and liver, see F. Hommel: "*Ein neues Bindeglied zwischen Etrurien und Kleinasien*" (*Memnon*, I, 86). The so-called templum or navel of the world from Troy, as depicted, for instance, by A. Jeremias in: *Das alte Testament im Lichte des alten Orients* (second edition, Leipzig, 1906; illustr. 21), resembles the liver used for divination purposes, by the Babylonians and the Etruscans.

[2] W. Roscher: *Omphalos. Archäologische volkskundliche Abhandlung über die Vorstellungen der Griechen und anderer Völker vom "Nabel der Erde"* (Leipzig, 1913); also: *Neue Omphalosstudien. Ein archäologischer Beitrag zur vergleichenden Religionswissenschaft* (Leipzig, 1915); and: *Der Omphalosgedanke bei verschiedenen Völkern, besonders bei den Semitischen* (Leipzig, 1918) (quoted as "Roscher I, II, or III" respectively).

[3] The further application of this idea to the dome-shaped tomb and church cupola generally is shown by Fuhrmann in his *Grabbau* (Munich, 1923). "Starting from the beautiful navel-symbol of Delphi, we may safely assume that all ornamentation which consists in the tying up of separate balloon-shapes stands for the exceedingly important mother- or woman-symbol that signifies rebirth in the flesh" (p. 57).

(Roscher III, 16). We shall show, in our next chapter, how the navel attained to such importance, and here we need only point out that the basic idea of chthonian creation, in that it is based on an animal analogy, is older than the supernatural, heavenly creation. In conformity with this development of man from biological creature to creative and self-creative spirit, the earth's interior (corresponding to the female abdomen) was looked upon as the centre of creation and consequently was conceived of as the belly of an animal. Later the whole body came to be the (earthly) underworld, and the head (consciousness, will, spirit) became heaven, which eventually became identified with man, just as the earth had been with woman (mother).[1]

This development, which we infer on psychological grounds, receives definite confirmation from an interesting study by Eberhard Hommel,[2] who, in continuation of Fritz Hommel's (his father's) "Symbolism of the Parts of the Body" in the astronomical alphabet, points out that in various languages — Greek, Slavonic, Syrian, Arabian — the palate, which arches itself over the throat like a vault of heaven within the mouth-cavity, bears the designation "heaven." The study in question is devoted mainly to proving in detail that the double meaning, heaven-palate, still existed in Latin (*palatum*) and Etruscan (*faladum*), so that this symbolism is preserved not only in the "magic" anatomy of mediæval astrologists, but partially to this very day in medical nomenclature. And this macrocosmization has quite possibly influenced the formation of language itself as well as the nomenclature; for (quite apart from these investigations, apparently) Ernst Fuhrmann has "demonstrated for the first time in *Schwedische Felsbilder* (1923) how the valuation of these (Nordic) consonants came about in the most natural way: namely, by the identification of events in the sun's course with the positions of the mouth in which

[1] See A. Dieterich: *Mutter Erde. Ein Versuch über Volksreligion* (Leipzig, 1905).

[2] "Etruscan *fala*(n)*dum* — Latin *palatum*, and an old name for the god of heaven" (*Orientalistische Studien, Fritz Hommel zum 60. Geburtstag*, Vol. I, Leipzig, 1917; pp. 233 et seq.).

consonants were produced" (quoted from *Afrika,* p. 7).[1] But Hommel's excellent work discloses yet another relation of art-historical importance between the upper portion of the human body (head) and the upper part of the world (heaven). The part in question is the neck, or, rather, the vertebræ of the neck, which form the connexion between the rest of the body (lower body) with the head. The *seven* vertebræ with their step- or tower-formation became the pattern of the seven steps leading to heaven and even of the "seven heavens." "Atlas," the topmost vertebra of the neck, bears the heavenly vault on his *shoulders* according to ancient belief, and Hommel notes that: "Seven-tiered towers were indeed frequent in ancient *architecture* as cosmic symbols of the seven planet spheres. And highest of all there was the vaulted sphere of the skull, which corresponded to the upper heaven of the fixed stars."

The relation to the art of building — that is, architecture as distinguished from simple domestic building — which now confronts us is of fundamental importance to the whole problem of artistic development. For whereas house-building is generally agreed to have been in the first instance a matter of the protective cave,[2] which is clearly recognizable as the chthonian womb-symbol, architecture begins, like all "higher" development, with elevation above the ground, but also with the remaking of the house from a mere covering (the mother's body) into the symbol of the whole man himself — and, what is more, of the creative ego and no longer of the protective

[1] It is noteworthy that while E. Hommel claims to trace the old Etruscan god of heaven to pre-Hellenic Greece, Krause, on the other hand, traces it to the German north (*Die Trojaburgen Nordeuropas;* Glogau, 1893).

[2] Fuhrmann believes that building was still thought of as essentially subterranean, even when the structure rose high above the ground as in mausoleum or cathedral architecture (*Der Grabbau*). For the whole subject see also H. Muchau in *Pfahlhausbau und Griechentempel* (Jena, 1909). It is worth noting that psycho-analysis has done more towards elucidating the genesis of building (though not of architecture) than it has towards helping me to explain art, particularly since I traced the so-called "womb-symbolism" to the urge to restore the actual womb-situation in my *Trauma of Birth* (1924). For later literature, see: Sterba: "*Zur Analyse der Gotik*" in *Imago*, X (1924); Kuhnen: "*Psychoanalyse und Baukunst*" (ibid.); Sydow: *Primitive Kunst und Psychoanalyse* (1927); Löwitsch: "*Raumempfinden und moderne Baukunst,*" in *Imago*, XIV (1928).

mother. We see, then, at work in the development of a single branch of art (which assuredly belongs to man's earliest creations) the selfsame principle that psychologically we have had to take as the basis of every artistic creation: namely, the creative self-representation by means of which the individual frees himself from his dependence on a biological mortality in order to immortalize himself in durable material.

Now, if the macrocosmization of man, which reached its summit in the ancient Oriental culture, leads to religion and particularly to star-worship, it is, on the contrary, the microcosmization of the cosmos, which finds its highest expression in the Greek style, that underlies art and artistic creation. Before we are able to demonstrate this by the development of Classical architecture, we must, after describing the cosmic system, trace this process of microcosmizing the universe, which probably has its roots in the Babylonian world-picture, even though it first flowered in the Cretan culture and only reached maturity in Classical Greece. If, as I think, we have in Babylonia the critical point of transition of this development-process which converts the animalistic-chthonian world-picture into the spiritual, heavenly one, it becomes extremely important to be able to refer to some tradition in which a fragment of the link between these two worlds appears to have been preserved. It was Peiser who (in a lecture delivered at the general meeting of the Vorderasiatische Gesellschaft in 1912) first drew attention to Babylonian representations of the labyrinth, which has so marked a resemblance to the famous Cretan labyrinths and the Nordic labyrinth spirals, the so-called " Trojaburgen." The meaning and aim of these drawings remained quite unsolved, however, until a new archæological find came to light. Koldewey made a photographic copy of a tablet discovered during the excavations of the Deutsche Orient Gesellschaft in Babylon and dating, as far as can be told, from 1000 B.C.[1] Deciphering the annotations on this tablet, Weidner at last succeeded — in his own words — in finding "the solution of

[1] Robert Koldewey: *Das wiedererstehende Babylon*, p. 239.

the riddle that the evidence itself suggests in any case." [1] The term used there for the labyrinth figure is well known from Babylonian literature on the subject of the entrail mantic. Literally translated, it is the "palace of the entrails," by which is no doubt meant the entrails as a whole. Naturally, Weidner does not fail to point out that the designation "palace" is "not without its significance in connecting these drawings of entrails with the labyrinths of the Ægean culture." In any case he claims to have produced the proof that in these spiral drawings —of which usually a whole row is found ornament-wise on a tablet—"we have before us representations of the entrails (intestines) of sacrificial animals from which prophecies were made."

But just as the suggestion evoked by the evidence failed to reveal the solution of the riddle to researchers before Weidner, so it took another learned treatise by E. Hommel—already known to us as a brilliant interpreter of the cosmic anatomy— to point out the obvious in establishing the womb-significance of these intestinal spirals (representing the body's interior) beyond a doubt. In his work: *Zur Geschichte des Labyrinths* [2] there will be found abundant material for the widespread conception of the womb as an animal interior out of which the hero, by his own strength and mostly by the destruction of his perilous prison, finds the way back to life. Although we must defer to the chapter "Myth and Metaphor" the discussion of the creative aspect of these traditions, already mentioned (whale myths; Perseus type), we may just mention here the rebirth significance of this set of mythological ideas which culminates, not in a wish to return to the mother, but, on the contrary, in overcoming this mortal origin by assimilation to the sun's course (see Frobenius: *Im Zeitalter des Sonnengottes*). In this sense, the "palace of the entrails" stands not only for the animalistic housing of the soul, but also for the macro-

[1] F. Weidner: "*Zur babylonischen Eingeweideschau. Zugleich ein Beitrag zur Geschichte des Labyrinths*" (*Orientalistische Studien. Fritz Hommel zum 60. Geburtstag*, Vol. I (Leipzig 1917).

[2] *Orientalist. Literaturzeitung*, 22nd year, 1919.

cosmic world-structure on which the earthly palace was modelled.

The development of the soul-concept, therefore, as it has been determined by the collective ideology (including artistic creativity) of the nations, presents itself to us as the perpetual association and rivalry of two groups of ideas: the one is the notion of a life after death in the same form as that familiar to the living; the other, the idea of return in a new form, which varies with the cultural development. The first idea of a simple extension of life in another locality, but in the same form, is undoubtedly the earlier and more primitive conception, which sees death only as a migration to another region. Corresponding with this is the conception of the dead soul, generally regarded today as the most primitive of ideas on soul;[1] here the soul only appears with death; the living man has no " soul " — needs none, so to say — for the soul at this stage is only an expression for the altered life extended into the beyond, this being originally imagined as under the earth, in the grave. The grave thus becomes the house of the soul — that is, that of a human being who is living on elsewhere — and for this reason house and tomb are inseparably linked (as we shall show in the following chapter) and only intelligible through each other. We shall also have to show the connexion which leads from the idea of the grave as the house of the soul (as which the dead person now figures) to the conception of the human body itself as the " housing " of the soul, because this connexion is of extraordinary importance for an understanding, not only of architecture, but also of the whole development of art. For the moment it is sufficient to formulate

[1] See the following important new works in which recent ethnological material on the primitive races has been produced in rectification of Erwin Rohde's (*Psyche*) animistic conception: W. Otto: *Die Manen oder von den Urformen des Totenglaubens* (Berlin, 1923); Ernst Bickel: *Homerischer Seelenglaube. Geschichtliche Grundzüge menschlicher Seelenvorstellungen* (Berlin, 1925); and J. Böhme: *Die Seele und das Ich im Homerischen Epos. Mit einem Anhang: Vergleich mit dem Glauben der Primitiven* (Leipzig, 1929). The first, so far as I know, to uphold the pre-animistic materialism (which comes very close to our materialistic science) is Rudolf Kleinpaul (*Die Lebendigen und die Toten in Volksglauben, Religion, und Sage;* 1898) and the next, Hans Naumann (*Primitive Gemeinschaftskultur;* 1922).

this process on these lines: originally, man *became soul* at his death, while later, living man *has a soul* which only parts from the body at death.

Now, while this side of the immortality-belief — with its idea of the continuation of man's life as soul, in a locality other than the earthly — led to the development of the religious belief in the beyond, and so to a culmination in the idea of the immortal soul, it would seem that it was the belief in *transformation* that proved of greater importance for the development of art. This belief was, even at the lowest stage — for such we believe the Fanany myth to be — connected with the animal, which from materialistic totemism right into spiritual Christianity remained the connecting symbol of the return to earthly life. Only, the conception of the soul-worm (and crawling animals related to it) shows the transformation of man into the animal (in the sense of the later doctrine of the transmigration of the soul), while the idea of animal burial (animal casing) presupposes on the contrary the rebirth of man out of the animal (the mortal womb). In most religious customs and traditions, as well as in the corresponding artistic representations, we find the two immortality-ideologies side by side, as if man sought to ensure himself doubly against any doubt of the possibility of a continuation of existence. Still (as we have already observed) the varying attitude of man towards the animal at different culture-stages serves as one of our most enlightening fossil guides to the reconstruction of the *history of man's rise from creature to creator — which means, from religion to art.*

To give a broad idea of our meaning and by way of regaining touch with our original theme of the entrail-labyrinth, we would remind our readers of the development of the Classical age of religion and art as it lies before us, stretching from Egypt to Christendom. In Egypt we have, side by side with a quite materially understood life-extension of the dead (in his double, *Ka*), whose body was protected from decay by mummification, the idea of animal rebirth in the strict " super-totemistic " ani-

mal cult, and, finally, the first dawning of a spiritual rebirth of man himself in the Osiris myths, with their incestuous
immortality-symbolism.[1]

Egypt therefore became, in art as well, the classical land of
human-animal hybrids, such as we see in its animal-headed
gods and its sphinx-pyramid, which represent a mixture of
animal-belly and earth-belly. It was the Greeks who first succeeded in freeing the human being from the animalistic (as I
have shown in my *Trauma of Birth*); either they caused the
animal monsters to be slain by divine heroes (for example,
Œdipus' killing of the Sphinx) or — which comes to the
same thing — they banished them to the underworld. This
underworld then became the model for the Christian hell,
with all its monsters and the beast-like ruler at their head —
only, the Christian conception of hell became moralized beyond the Greek idea of the underworld, just as the Christian
conception of the soul spiritualized the purely human soul of
the Greeks and thus in a sense macrocosmized it afresh.

For whereas originally the earth's interior was regarded
as equivalent to the human interior (abdomen), from which
all life springs and to which it appears to return, in Christianity
the earth itself became the underworld, while heaven became
that upper world which, to the Greeks, was still an earthly life

[1] The brother-and-sister relation, indicated in the Osiris myth, is neither a feebler
form of the mother-incest nor a disguise of union with a sister, but, as the traditions
of primitive peoples teach us, a deliberate replacement of mother and wife by the
sister — as one who has neither borne the brother himself nor bears him children. In
the African burial rites it is often the sister who brings the dead king back to life,
precisely because she had nothing to do with his birth or that of his children. With
the introduction of the sister as awakener of others to life, mortal rebirth is eliminated
and recourse is had to the creative power of the soul itself. In Egypt as in Peru, which
is culturally akin, the king, considered as God, took his sister to wife and had as his
successor the son of this marriage; but the motive for this was ritual and not sexual
and is accordingly always symbolized macrocosmically (moon and sun). The king
marries his sister because he, as God (star) wandering on earth, is immortal and may
therefore not propagate himself in the children of a strange woman—any more than
he is allowed to die a natural death.

Cultural-historical and mythological material concerning this will be found in
my book: *Das Inzest-Motiv in Dichtung und Sage*, second edition, 1926, chapters xii,
xiii. For incest as a symbol of rebirth, see Jung: *Wandlungen und Symbole der Libido*
(1912), and, for the spiritual significance of the same, my *Seelenglaube und Psychologie*
(1930; pp. 127 et seq.).

within this world. In this respect, as also in the reinstatement
of the great mother of the gods, Christianity stands nearer to
the ancient East, and particularly to Egypt, than to Greece.
Egypt was a land of the dead, not only ideologically (in its
religion), but even in its earthly life, which was regarded as
a preparation for life beyond in the underworld. The Greeks
were the first, and perhaps the only, people to live really on
earth and in the light of the sun — hence their sharp dividing-
line between the upper world and the under, in which the
dead led a bloodless, soulless existence. But it was not in the
vague Beyond that the Greek looked for the immortality that
his earthly life, for all its charm, denied him, but in a spiritual
and yet still human upper world wherein the Classical art and
the Classical philosophy found an imperishable expression.
While the Egyptian lived below the earth, and the Christian
above it, the Greek, with all his spiritual requirements, stood
firmly planted upon it; and yet for him the culture-forming
link with the under and the upper world did not petrify into
mere formalism. In the case of Rome, with its exclusively
worldly orientation, it did so. Roman civilization sought immortality neither in other-worldly nor in intellectual ideologies,
but, like the Jewish race, in a purely national ideology, which,
however, did concretize into a world-dominion never before
paralleled — to be transformed again in due course by the
Church into a theocracy.

This transference of the plane of human life which manifests itself in the changing ideology — religious, artistic, and
political — found individual expression at the same time in
the microcosmic development from lower (body) culture to
the upper (head) culture. This came about by shifting the
localization of the soul from the lower to the upper region —
macrocosmically from the underworld to heaven, microcosmically from the lower part of the body to the head [1] — and the

---

[1] The story of the birth of Pallas Athene out of the head of Zeus seems to me to
be the first Hellenic forerunner of the Christian Logos-ideology. E. Hommel (loc.
cit., p. 249) interprets it as a cosmological outcome of Greek anatomy and physiology.

agent is the macrocosmic body-symbolism, of which we see the two poles in the entrail-liver auspices on the one hand and the stellar religion with its astrological application on the other. The decisive turning-point in this development from the animalistic idea of rebirth to the spiritual principle of immortality we take to be the ancient Oriental world-outlook, which travelled, for many thousands of years and by the difficult and roundabout route of animal-worship and animal-cult, from Babylon through Egypt and Greece to cosmopolitan Christianity. But we saw also that it was the soul, or, rather, the varying conceptions and localizations of the soul, that formed the bridge from the lower animal world to the divine upper world. The decisive point in the *religious* process of elevation above the animal was, as we have seen, in Babylonia, where hieromancy was steadily evicted by the worship of the stars, while the animals out of which astronomy was to grow were gradually removed to places in heaven as constellations. The decisive point in the *artistic* development from the chthonian-animalistic principle to the spiritual-creative is to be found, we think, in the Cretan-Mycenæan culture, which formed the link beween Egypt, Greece, and the European culture-zone, and to which we shall now turn to investigate the labyrinth symbol.

In this we start from the similarity between the Babylonian mantic of entrails and the labyrinths of the Ægean culture-zone — a connexion supported additionally by Weidner's epigraphic evidence. According to the Minotaur saga, localized in Crete, the bull-headed monster inhabits the labyrinthine palace. Here Theseus succeeds in overcoming him and ending

---

He gives the following very ingenious account of this microcosmic origin of the Greek cosmology: From the head of Zeus, representing heaven (that is, the skull), there emerges through the hole in the back Pallas Athene (that is, the seven-storeyed neck, symbol of the plant heaven). The part of midwife is played by the old smith- and heaven-god, who has to open the head and so receives his allotted place in anatomical symbolism as Atlas-Faland in close proximity to this opening. Further, there springs from this opening of the Zeus-heaven the Æon (Greek αἰών, spinal marrow) and out of this again, according to the Classical physiology of humours, the seed from which the human race is formed (cf. Plato:*Timæus*).

the Athenian tribute of human sacrifices, but is himself only able to find his way out of the tortuous maze by the help of the thread given to him by Ariadne. This labyrinth was traditionally supposed to have been at Knossos, the royal seat of Minos, and had been built by Dædalus to serve as a dwelling-place for this monster, born of a union between Queen Pasiphaë and the Poseidon-bull. Thus in this traditional story we find already all the elements that we have just discussed, united in a mythical narrative which bears the mark of Greek mentality. It is clear that in making this bull-headed creature, the Minotaur, a monster the Cretans were expressing their detestation of the Egyptian animal-cult. This Græcizing of Egyptian influence is not only evident in the transformation of the typical Egyptian animal-god into a man-eating monster, but also in the literary tradition. Diodorus tells us that, according to some Egyptians, Dædalus had so much admired the age-old Egyptian labyrinth — a colossal imperial palace on Lake Mœris, ruins of which still exist, with twelve courts and three thousand rooms — that he built the Knossos labyrinth on the model of it, but that of the latter there remained no trace. And Pliny remarks that even if it were not a hundredth part as big, one should not imagine it a mere maze, like those winding paths of a mile or more constructed in children's playgrounds. But most of our recent researchers are agreed that in reality the labyrinth at Knossos never existed, but was a fiction of the imagination. The Egyptian Mœris palace, described by both Herodotus and Strabo from their own sight of it, whose ground-plan (1,000 feet long and 800 wide) Flinders Petrie exposed in his excavations of 1877–88, was, according to Brugsch, called "*lepi-re-hint*" (*erpe-ro-hunt*) which means something like "temple of the canal system." Welcker and others think, on the contrary, that the numerous underground caves and grottoes in Crete were called "labyrinths," which therefore meant practically the same as the galleries of a mine. Höck, in his work on Crete (Göttingen, 1823), supposes that there was a grotto-like cult-centre to which was given the name labyrinth, but that

THE TEMPLUM OF TROY, OR THE NAVEL OF THE WORLD
(2000 B.C.)

BABYLONIAN " PALACE OF THE INTESTINES "

this was only derived from dances which wound in and out like the planets in their courses among the stars in the firmament. Ernst Krause has treated the whole subject exhaustively in his book: *Die Trojaburgen Nordeuropas* (1893) (with the sub-titles: " Their connexion with the Indo-Germanic Troy saga of the abducted captive Lady of the Sun, the Troy games, and the sword and labyrinth dances in celebration of the spring liberation "). We can only allude briefly to this interesting piece of research, which amounts to a history of the " labyrinth idea," in supplementing Krause's macrocosmical interpretation by Weidner's more recent revelation of the microcosmic significance of the labyrinth.

It should be noted that Krause included the Nordic labyrinths in his sphere of investigation, thereby giving the problem a universal significance which — as we shall show — is of great importance to the history of art also. Certain labyrinthine passages described in Icelandic saga as animal-traps are called Troy towns or Troy castles in England and Scandinavia. " The name *Trojaburg* (Scandinavian *Trojin, Trojeborg, Tröborg;* English *Troy-town* or *Walls of Troy;* Welsh, *Caer Droida*) has been given in northern Europe since ancient times to mazes (labyrinths) whose winding paths are closed with small or large stones or are cut out of the turf" (op. cit., p. 2). These antiquities, which are described as prehistoric by most researchers and have often been regarded as children's playgrounds, seem to have served for labyrinth dances similar to those reported from Crete and Delos. This labyrinth dance was called *Troa* and *Troja,* like the equestrian display dedicated to the goddess of spring. In the attempt to explain philologically the meaning of the Germanic word *Troie,* which should be read *in extenso* (pp. 10 et seq.; 37, 47), Krause arrives at some extremely suggestive conclusions, of which we adduce here only those bearing on our problem. From the general use of the word " *Troie* " for castle, jerkin, and dance, he deduces a root idea of circumvallation, wrapping round, revolving. This is the root meaning that Klausen (*Æneas und die Penaten,* II, pp. 827 et seq.) also gives to the Latin words: *Troja* (*in ludus Tròjæ*), *trua,* and *trulla* (stirring spoon and stirring pan); and even to *troia* in the sense of "sow" (Italian *troja,* French *truie*), referring in the last case to the animal's circling round and round — that is, writhing in its birth-pangs. In Greek the kindred words beginning with "tro" are still more frequent, as for instance: *trochos* (circle, race-course, wheel, ring-wall, snake-ring); *trochmalos,* the stone boundary mark of a field; *troullos,* the cupola; *Trophonios,* master of the circular buildings. Krause seems to assume "that (as has been shown to be probable in Kuhn's *Journal,* Vol. VII) all these expressions (including Scandinavian *tro,* English *true,*

TROY-TOWN FROM WISBY (GOTLAND) LABYRINTH FROM A CATHEDRAL

German *treu,* Old Prussian *druwis,* German *Glaube,* Lithuanian *drutas,* German *stark,* and others) go back to an ancient Sanskrit word still in existence: *dhruwa* (from *dhar,* to hold), which means firm, reliable, trustworthy, and generally something permanent" (op. cit., p. 12). Now, as the root *tro, troi, tru* has taken on the meaning of turning, dallying, revolving, dancing, in Germanic, Celtic, Latin, and Greek, and *Troi* and *Troyer* also mean "dance" in Old Germanic, it is easy to imagine, in view of the ground-plan and use of the Troy-towns, that the English-Scandinavian expression *Troy castle* and *Töjeborg,* might be translated as round castle or dance-castle, even perhaps as crazy castle, since the conception of turning (Old German *drajan,*

Gothic *traian,* Celtic *troian,* Middle English *throwen* — cf. modern English *throe,* German *kreisen*) melts easily into that of distorting, entangling, leading astray, and even bewitching (p. 12). Then, too, the Roman priests of Mars (the Salii) seem to have called the labyrinthine sword-dance which they executed in spring (March) *Troa* or *Troja* after the old folk-songs to which they were sung. This forms an interesting parallel to the Geranos dance in Crete and Delos which commemorated the

STONE WITH FIGURES FROM NORTHUMBERLAND

LABYRINTH FROM AN ISLAND NEAR BORGO

obscure windings of the labyrinth — and does not Homer tell of the dancing-place made by Dædalus and the choral dance of Knossos (*Iliad,* XVIII, 590 et seq.)? [1]

Putting aside for the present any discussion of the dance problem, we will return to the Nordic Troy-towns to look for the link which binds them to ancient tradition and artistic development. Krause mentions a Welsh tradition told by the shepherds, who stated that " they cut out a figure in the form of a labyrinth in the glass which they call *Caer Droia,* the walls or the citadel

[1] Creuzer mentions in his *Symbolik* some ancient traditions of religious dances, the so-called "planet-dances" which were supposed to imitate the courses of the stars. The Cretan labyrinth dance itself was similarly described as an astronomical dance, which again links the entrail cult to the heaven-ideology. Krause thinks that possibly the epic: *Les Murs de Troie ou L'origine du burlesque* (by the celebrated writer of fairy-tales Perrault, in 1650, but never printed in full) contained allusions to Troy games and Troy dances in contemporary France. Much earlier still, "la *tresque*" — the Italian *tresca,* a round dance with twisting, twining figures (from *intrezzata,* intricate) was danced in France.

of Troy." " If there were a tradition anywhere referring to the labyrinthine form of the walls of Troy, the name would appear to be an invention of pure Cymric origin, suggested by the similarity of the designations *Caer Droia* (Troy Town) and *Caer y troian,* city of windings or turnings." An interesting perspective for art-history is here opened up by the fact that these field labyrinths are found in mosaic in the naves of numerous Italian and French churches.[1] These show us, like the so-called Salzburg Mosaic of the struggle with the Minotaur,

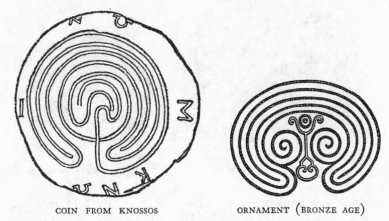

COIN FROM KNOSSOS   ORNAMENT (BRONZE AGE)

the later meander development of the labyrinth spiral, whose original significance we now propose to seek.

If, then, we follow the development of the Babylonian entrail-labyrinths through the Cretan Minotaur-saga to the Greek story, we find a progressive overcoming of the animal-chthonian element by an artistic principle of form, which we shall now follow up in some selected historical examples. In Crete we find, simultaneously with the throwing-off of the Egyptian animal-cult, an ornamental æstheticizing of the labyrinth motive, as had already been foreshadowed in Egypt. On

[1] Here the penances of the monks who hurry coughing along the windings of the crooked paths seem to have become separated from the ritual dance originally associated with it.

GRAVE STELE FROM MYCENÆ

SO-CALLED HUT-URNS FROM PHÆSTOS (GREECE)

the other hand the "palace of the entrails," which in Babylon represented a macrocosmization of the protecting womb
and was perhaps actually realized in the Egyptian Mœris palace,
is made here into a fictitious, mythological tradition; at the
same period we find the smelting-irons adorned with labyrinth spirals, while they themselves represent labyrinths or
circular dwellings, whose macrocosmic enlargement we recognize again in the subterranean vaulted tombs of Mycenæ. How
far it was a direct current of influence that flowed over Babylonia, Egypt, Crete, Mycenæ, Troy, seems to us less important

EGYPTIAN CEILING

than the possibility that it represents a genuine upspringing of
a generically human ideology in different places.[1] But also
where an influence is probable or can even be really proved,
the use of the same motive in different cultures remains a more
interesting problem. In Babylonia it is the relation to astrology,
in Egypt to architecture, in the Ægean culture-zone to art
(ornament), and in Asia Minor to national problems (Trojan
War), which emerges from the overthrow of the chthonian-
animalistic world-view.

[1] We will not discuss here the possibility of a Northern influence on southern
Europe, such as Krause upholds, because, for the moment, it seems more important
to trace the general human outline. Suffice it to say, therefore, that the Nordic Troy-
towns go back to the bronze age, according to the researchers (see particularly Aspelius
in the *Zeitschrift für Ethnologie*, Vol. IX, 1877) and that there are also found in the
North similar funeral urns in the form of Old Germanic houses, the so-called house-
urns. Scheltema has proved the spirals, which correspond to the labyrinth, to be the
essential ornament of the bronze age and has shown that their origin is probably in
the circle.

Even as late as in Homer's story of the Trojan Wars (which probably have a historical nucleus in the colonization of the shores of Asia Minor by wandering Greek emigrant tribes) we have, woven into the military history, myth-fragments, which not only embellish the historical events, but are also of high importance for an understanding of the artistic tradition. For we find, beside the relationship of the labyrinthine palace-cage of the beast-man Minotaur with the impenetrable "labyrinthine" citadel of Troy, yet another relation between Crete and the Mycenæan culture of Troy as described by Homer. A vase made after a Greek model on Italian soil in the sixth or seventh century B.C. — the curious Tragliatella vase — gives us the possibility of uniting the Cretan Minotaur saga with the famous

fable of the Wooden Horse. In the principal drawing on this vase, to which Ernst Krause has devoted a monograph,[1] the warriors, among them two mounted horsemen, are seen coming out of a labyrinth spiral which on the one hand must represent labrinthine Troy itself, but on the other hand, as I believe, may be an allusion to the interior of the horse, out of which the Greek heroes came after they had smuggled themselves into the impregnable fortress. Then, too, this carved wooden artifice of a horse — which (like Pasiphaë's bull also) was the symbol of Poseidon — was an idealized representation of the actual interior of the body, of the entrails, from which the he-

[1] *Die nordische Herkunft der Trojasage bezeugt durch den Krug von Tragliatella, eine dritthalbtausendjährige Urkunde* (with twelve illustrations; Glogau, 1893).

roes, as if rescued from the underworld, once more emerged. It only remains to add that the mythological interpretation of the Homeric tradition conceived of labyrinthine Troy itself as the underworld, and the release of Helen as that of the imprisoned moon-goddess, and we have before us, in the fable of the Wooden Horse, the mythic counterpart to the historic fortress of Troy. That is to say, the Wooden Horse with the heroes hidden in its belly represents microcosmically the same myth of the underworld as that which the Helen saga expresses macrocosmically.

I must leave for another occasion [1] the extraction of the historic kernel of the Troy saga from its mythological overgrowth and confine myself here to estimating the art-historical significance of the linkages which have been thus revealed. In these I believe myself to have discovered a principle of form which should prove to be of basic importance, especially in the development of constrained religious art into free creative art — as we see it taking its course from the old Oriental to the Greek culture. This principle is that of an *æstheticizing extroversion.* In the place of the inner entrail-spirals which were still the dominant ornament in the Cretan culture-zone, there appears not only the stylized animal body itself (the horse), but also the human being as he works himself gradually loose from his animal base, emerging eventually as the idealized figure of the Olympian who has triumphed over the chthonian-animalistic principle. This idealization-process we are able to follow step by step in the general development of Greek art, as I have indicated in the artistic portion of my *Trauma of Birth.* Compare first of all the animal figures of Greece (in particular the Sphinx and the Centaur) with their Oriental forerunners; the animal head of the Egyptian gods changes into the human upper body of the Sphinx- and Centaur-figures, whose lower parts (back portions), on the other hand, have become animal; and this is quite in keeping with the development we have described

[1] See my preliminary studies in the Psychology of the Folk-epic in *Imago*, Vol. V (1917).

from the culture of the belly to that of the head.[1] Thus the victory of the *artistic* (æsthetic) over the Dionysiac-animalistic (goat), and its advance to the divine-Apollonian, which Nietzsche so brilliantly depicts in his earliest work: *The Birth of Tragedy,* stands as the imperishable cultural achievement of the Greeks. And simultaneously with this they abstracted from their predecessors' materialistic and totemistic conception of rebirth that purely human conception of the soul, which not only was worked out in thought for the first time by their philosophers (Plato), but also lives on immortally in their works of art.

Next, the Christian ideology raised this human idea of the soul — already far removed from the soul of the dead — into a purely spiritual sphere (though without at first endowing it with divinity), and at the same time it democratized the immortal soul, which before had been the prerogative of kings, heroes, or creative people (artists). This democratization of the soul-concept had a great share in the flowering of Christian art, which expanded over more than a thousand years, and this was because it had again become essential — as in the beginnings of abstract artistic creativity — to objectify the human substrate of this abstraction for the world at large, to concretize it in figures of Christ, Mary with the Child, and so on. Everything had to have happened really and truly as it was said to have done, and what Church art put forth, therefore, was the tangible figuration of a soul-ideology which was becoming more and more cosmopolized and whose human qualities would soon have disappeared but for the saving influence of Christian art. As it was, Christian art — which, in contrast to Christian dogmatics, remained the layman's province — became permeated again by the human element, particularly in the mother-and-child relation, which was here represented spiritually by heavenly love, whereas in the be-

[1] In Rodin's "Female Centaur" the neck — the bearer of the head — struggling to free itself from the animal body, is drawn out almost into a line a sublimation which manifests itself eventually in Rodin's spiritualized portrait busts that are completely severed from the trunk.

RODIN'S FEMALE CENTAUR (*Soul and Body*)

ginning what had been symbolized was its animal underworld significance. Gradually this underworld was transferred to the Christian hell, which thereafter represented terror and the negation of all hope of rebirth. Yet even in the everlasting flames which condemn to incessant torment the sinner who clings to carnal rebirth we can recognize the yearning for immortality. In this sense hell not only is the symbol of animality, but becomes that of everything earthly and of a final forcible separation of this from the intellectual and spiritual. Those artists, however, who, like Dante or the Breughel type of hellpainters, chose to depict it in terms of an earthly life banished to the underworld were actually only giving us a copy of life on earth as this presented itself to Christianity — that is, as a preparation for the higher life in heaven.

Chapter Six

HOUSE-BUILDING AND ARCHITECTURE

❧

Know ye not that ye are the tem-
ple of God, and that the Spirit of
God dwelleth in you?
1 Corinthians iii, 16

MING GRAVES NEAR PEKING (1338–1644 A.D.)

Chapter Six

HOUSE-BUILDING AND ARCHITECTURE

꿍꿍

We have seen how the typical soul-concept of a particular cultural ideology develops from the soul of the dead, by way of the soul of the living, into the immortal soul. But the soul of the dead, in contrast to the soul of the living, does not yet stand for a part of the human being which detaches itself from the dying body in order to continue its own former existence or to incarnate itself in a new one. The soul of the dead is originally the whole man as he is after death has brought about in him transformations consisting essentially in removal to another locality. And lastly we have the immortal soul, a supernatural collective principle, independent of the individual's bodily manifestation, which is housed in super-earthly cosmic spheres high above underground death and earthly birth. The earliest conception of the soul of the dead, which presupposes a subterranean continuation of life on earth, leads inevitably to tomb-building. This is at least as old as, if not older than, house-building, for we find attempts at it as early as the palæolithic nomads. For if man continues to live as such in the soul (spirit), he needs a house with the necessary household implements, such as we find from the earliest times in grave-furnishings. In fact, from the standpoint of the living, the corpse which continues its life as a soul is more in need of a house, a safe dwelling-place, than the living man who is free to move about. In this sense the binding of corpses, which we can trace back to the stone age, may be said to be the first

Art & Artist

form of actual — not merely figurative — fettering of a man to a particular dwelling-place; and because of the grave, which he cannot leave, it becomes a house. This first house, the tomb, then becomes of its own accord a casing for the soul, a human body, in which the soul of the dead is "housed" after leaving the earth.

But we already know, from the explanations given in the previous chapter, that this house of the dead, in which man lives on as a soul, was originally regarded, not as the place of rebirth, but as a place in which to stay. It therefore represented not so much the mother's womb as one's own body. Neither has the idea of rebirth itself its origin in growth within the womb, but, as we have shown, in the idea of the soul-worm, which grows out of the corpse of the dead himself. Thus the soul-concept, even in its most primitive stages, presupposes the idea of human self-creation and represents in this sense man's earliest creative achievement, whether it be that he lives on after his earthly fashion, or that he continues his existence in another form supplied by the worm that is born of himself. But the tomb-building that arose out of this soul-concept, and the house-building into which it developed, and finally architecture proper in the form of temple-building are also developments of the self-creative principle. So also the house itself, even though it was a copy of the protective mother-sheath, was yet a substitute for this that man himself created. It was not, however, a substitute in the sense of a reconstruction of the unachievable (as I argued in my *Trauma of Birth*), but definitely in the sense of a self-contained trend towards independence of the maternal tie — a deliberate breaking-away from it, in fact. This self-creative trend, already visible in the building of a tomb, though this has merely to provide a permanent resting-place for the soul of the dead, becomes still clearer at the stage of building the house which is to provide a dwelling-place for the living soul, the human being on earth, and it finally soars above all animal and chthonian ties in the building of the temple for the shelter of the immortal, the divine,

162

soul. This gives us, at any rate for the field of architecture, a three-stage scheme of development, objectivized by the tomb (soul of the dead), the house (soul of the living), the temple (soul of God); and it may quite well be that the same scheme has a significance for art-ideology in general, corresponding, we are more than tempted to think, to the three art-ideologies that we have called religious, social, and personal. The parallel, in fact, suggested itself to me quite spontaneously, some time ago, at the mere sight of the complete output of one of the greatest of modern artists. In Rodin's complete works, to which we shall return later, we see, in the form and content of what is represented, first, man, growing out of the womb of the earth, then his emancipation from the animal (the centaur-woman, already alluded to), and finally, in the expressive portrait busts, the crystallization of the purely spiritual, released not only from the mass of earth, but from the body itself. The artist has symbolized the final result of this very development-process in his "Penseur" and in the female "Pensée," just as in "The Hand" he identified his creative organ with that of the universe's creator. Without wishing to anticipate my further investigations into the modern artist-personality, I may say here that I believe every great artist has to go through this process of development, at least potentially, within himself, even if all the stages of it do not always materialize artistically. It may be that just those sketches and lower-rated creative products of a great artist throw a keener light on the struggle of the two souls in his breast than the completed masterpieces which have entered into immortality and are explicable only as the products of the higher self's triumph over the lower.

In thus applying the self-elevating process in the human being, as disclosed by the story of architectural development, to the development of art as a whole, not only have we passed over that development altogether (an omission to be rectified in the coming chapters), but we have also left out the actual development of the art of building. To this we will now give our attention.

As a first step, let us look back at a certain burial rite, which, historically, is probably found only in connexion with tomb-building, but belongs spiritually and culturally to another stratum. We refer to the custom already noted of "animal burial": that is, the laying of the corpse inside an animal's body. We can still see evidence of this in the animal-shaped coffins in Bali and the beast-avenues of the Ming graves in China (see Fuhrmann: *Grabbau,* Plates 4, 9). At the corpse-burnings in Bali, the "animal" enters the kingdom beyond together with the man in his interior. "The animal is born again with the animal components of the man, and the human soul goes back into other members of the nation. Theoretically one may assume that the human corpse was, at some time or other, laid in the body of an actual slain animal, and that both were then burnt together. This is a link with the old myths in which the sun hero was swallowed by an animal from the underworld, but returned after he had in some way set himself free " (op. cit., p. 73). In any case, this conception of a separation of the human soul from the animal body, whether mythic or actually effected by ritual burning, corresponds to a later animistic conception (soul of the living), which postulates the pre-animistic identity of the human and the animal body as we see it in the Fanany myth. We need only recall the African chief who was burnt in a snake-skin, but whose soul reappeared in the worm. Burial *in an animal* must therefore have been preceded by burial *through an animal*. This may have taken the natural form of being devoured or have been in the nature of a rite such as was practised by Persians and other Oriental peoples, who left the disposal of their corpses to sacred dogs or vultures, the motive being to release the soul as quickly as possible from its bodily prison and everything fleshly. Our own word " coffin (*Sarg*)," to which tomb-building proper has finally shrunk, derives its name from the Greek *sarkophagos,* which literally means " flesh-eater " (Kleinpaul, op. cit., p. 70).

As a further proof of the dualism inherent in all burial customs, it may be pointed out that the animals in which man

BULL-SHAPED COFFINS FROM BALI

took the precaution to bury his dead were no flesh-eaters, but exclusively herbivorous: for example, the bull used for the burial of the African chieftain, or the elephant which predominates in Asiatic burials in animals. (The monster figures of the Bali tombs also are cattle-like.) This may, indeed, have been a determining reason for the substitution of the snake (of which even in Africa there are many non-dangerous species) for the flesh-eating worm. Be that as it may, the animal tomb certainly reappears as cosmic temple-architecture in the Egyptian sphinx-tombs of the Pyramid age, the very object of which was to preserve the corpse to the utmost. A similar meaning probably attaches to the symbolic cremation-rites in Bali, where the animal appears to be replaced by a high tower, often seven storeys high, corresponding to the seven spheres of the planets, the idea being, no doubt, to bring the soul nearer to heaven.[1] On the other hand, there exists from the first the opposite tendency, which found expression in the conception of the soul of the dead, to conserve as much as possible of the living person — whose existence is to continue as soul. This developed into the tomb-building that is known to us at its highest stage in the Egyptian sphinx-pyramids, where the animal character is combined with the cosmic.[2] Finally, in the ecclesiastical crypt or chapel we recognize the scene of the rebirth of the immortal soul, relieved from all things carnal. It is no longer the continued life or the rebirth of the individual person that is sought,

[1] I may recall here that the microcosmic foundation of the seven-storeyed towers is to be found in the seven vertebræ of the neck which support the head — i.e., the seat of the soul. The Persians, again, expose their dead to the animals, who devour them in a high building — the so-called Towers of Silence — while more primitive races used trees for the same purpose.

[2] I have made no mention here of the cosmic numbers which are alleged to underlie the construction of the Cheops pyramid. These were first pointed out by Max Eyth in his novel: *Der Kampf um die Cheopspyramide*, in which he makes the special point that the side-length of the pyramid bears a certain relation to the earth's orbital period, and the height bears a certain relation to its distance from the sun. The massive granite chests in the great pyramid are also asserted to possess their special significance. For the arithmetical aspect, see Dr. Fritz Noetling's *Die kosmische Zahlen der Cheopspyramide, der mathematische Schlüssel zu den Einheitsgesetzen im Aufbau des Weltalls* (Stuttgart, third edition, 1921).

but the rebirth of the super-individual soul from its temporary bodily prison into cosmic eternity.

In confirmation of the suggested linkage between house-building and tomb-building we do actually find that most prehistory researchers assume that men's earliest dwellings were natural caves in rock caverns or underground caves, and that it was only gradually that they rose to a place *on* the earth, to attain in the end, to the mountain tops.[1] These dwellings were purely protective in character, and the instinct which impelled them to seek them out was one allied to nest-building — the urge to re-establish the lost home in the womb. At that stage, however, man for a time remained passive, and the first house — in the true sense of the word — to which the cave-dweller aspired was the tree. This, too, had still the protective character,[2] but the fact of its elevation from the ground was already a step towards the inventiveness which presently found creative expression in the most primitive artificial house, the pile-dwelling. For this form, according to various archæologists, came into existence, not by the waterside, but on land, as an "imitation" of the protective tree-top, and whether this be the explanation or not, the pile-dwelling is undeniably found on dry land and is the first shelter which differs from the maternal cavity, in being an invention and creation of man. It seems to me that it was only later that the tree came to be worshipped as a symbol of maternity — that is, after and not before it had become a protective house. But in the tree-like, raised pile-dwelling there is — at any rate potentially — *the whole of man himself* and no longer merely the protective maternal cavity. It is, as it were, a raised, enlarged human being standing on stilts, who is already seeking protection from the dangers of the earth. The original roof of leaves, which ensures protection

[1] See Hermann Muchau: *Pfahlhausbau und Griechentempel. Kulturgeschichtliche und sprachwissenschaftliche Untersuchung* (with sixty illustrations); Jena, 1909.
[2] There is still an echo of this in the sacred groves of Classical antiquity and of the ancient German. See L. Weniger: *Altgriechischer Baumkultus* (Leipzig, 1919) and also, for the tree-symbolism, mentioned later, my *Technik*, I (chapter on the genealogical tree).

from above (rain), is later strengthened artificially, as though it stood for the roof of the old subterranean cave brought above ground. This inversion or overturning has been retained in the German name *Dachboden* (roof-floor) as applied to the *upper* part of a house, and Fuhrmann's brilliant discernment has discovered in the steep roof-form an inverted boat, which not only affords the best shelter against rain (an ark), but has apotropaic significance as a symbol of the underworld. For, according to the old ideas, the sun rides on the water by night in the underworld ship, and thus, in the boat-shaped roof (particularly of the Oriental type), we seem to have a bit of protective underworld set up as the first umbrella (*Der Sinn im Gegenstand*, p. 8).

In the year 1906 the traveller and investigator Paul Sarasin, who with his brother Fritz explored the island of Celebes, brought out his much-discussed hypothesis on the development of the Greek temple from the pile-dwelling ("*Über die Entwicklung des griechischen Tempels aus dem Pfahlhause*").[1] But, striking as are the resemblances between these two structures when we set them together, there is no explanation of the ideological hypothesis which led the one to develop on the lines of a dwelling-house, and the other to take the form of a temple to the gods. What is basically common to the two is the element of self-creative elevation above the animal-chthonian, which in the pile-dwelling resulted in a house rearing itself up high above the ground, and in the Greek temple in a god's house aspiring to heaven and situated usually on an airy hill-top. But what we know by tradition of the Greek cult of the gods allows us to follow them quite distinctly in their translation from their earth and rock caverns to the heights of Olympus. And only the overcoming of these earthy beginnings enabled the idea of the temple to develop in its purest form. For the true temple was still unknown to the Cretan-Mycenæan culture, which had no god's house, but, instead, colossal kings' palaces and monster tombs similar to

[1] *Zeitschrift für Ethnologie*, Vol. XXXIX (1907).

those of the ancient East. But the Greek culture, just as it made a sharp dividing line between those living on earth and those in the underworld, so also gradually banished the gods to the mountain heights and thus itself became the centre where culture was humanized. The Greek — whose embodiment we recognize in his heroes — thus led a purely earthly life which strove more and more to free itself from the influence of the gods and also from the power of the dead — that is, of death. In this sense the Greek temple is more like a noble tomb for the gods which has been brought from the earth's interior to its highest pinnacles, and indeed tomb-building in Greece plays no part at all in comparison with the towering architecture of the temple.

There is a tradition, equally important from the cultural and from the art-historical point of view, which bears not only on the development from pile-dwelling to Greek temple, but also on the broader development from cave-burial to sacral monument. As Muchau has pointed out, the oldest temple of the Greeks had as its most important constituent part an adytum reaching down below the ground (op. cit., p. 86). At Delphi it was on the age-old spot sacred to the earth-spirit Python — who, as a snake, was housed deep in a crevice underground — that the new cult of his heavenly conqueror, Apollo, was set up. But the Delphic sanctuary in which the earth-goddess Gæa had of old pronounced oracles was really a tomb: namely, the stone called " Omphalos " or " Navel of the earth," under which the dragon Python was supposed to be buried. The Delphic tradition, therefore, really gives us a picture of the vanquishing of the chthonian goddess of death, who in the form of a serpent delivers prophecies, by the heavenly god of light, for whom a mountain temple arose out of the tomb in the cave. The cultural and art-historical meaning of the Omphalos — which became of basic importance in respect of temple- and town-building and even of the ordering of the lands and the world — will be discussed at the end of this chapter. Our concern here is with the actual architecture of the Greek temple,

GREEK TEMPLE (PÆSTUM)

PILE DWELLING (CENTRAL CELEBES)

which, corresponding to the Hellenic ideology as set forth above, remains an unsurpassed ideal of beauty in its proportions and its structure.

As Burckhardt has pointed out, the Greek temple was the prototype of the whole of Hellenic architecture, and it can only be understood through the collective ideology of Greek culture, which was in essence human and microcosmic in contrast to the macrocosmic ideology of the East. Just as the Greeks developed the purely human soul-concept by banishing the dead to below the earth, and the gods to above it, so also did they create the first geocentric world-picture, which may have been physically incorrect but was culturally an immense advance. The proverbial saying that Socrates had fetched down philosophy from heaven so that he could philosophize from the standpoint of humanity applied equally to the whole Greek culture, which, according to another saying, made man the measure of all things. The great architectural buildings, for instance, were no longer, as in the East, macrocosmic reflections of heavenly designs, but extended microcosms: that is, not only enlarged, but elevated, human beings. But with this ideological principle there is bound up a second, of æsthetic significance, which becomes intelligible only through the investiture of man with his earthly rights. That is, inasmuch as man himself becomes a macrocosm, a standard for all things, each part of him must necessarily be a separate and complete microcosm: an idea of which the liver mantic had been a concrete, and the idea of the human soul was an abstract, expression. And so it comes about that one of the most important art-principles of the Classical style of beauty is to reproduce the whole by a miniature of its essence so that each individual part really continues, ideologically, to express the whole. In the Oriental — macrocosmic — style of architecture, on the contrary, the building is indivisible and purports to reproduce in reduced, earthly, proportions a much greater heavenly conception.

The finest example of this is found in the column, the

development of which from a mere stilting pole to a purely
decorative support goes hand in hand with an idealizing humanization. In the Greek temple, which gives us the transition
from the domestic pile-dwelling to the sacred building, the
upper portion resting on its columns — the roof, with its decorative frieze of gods — had become more important than the
interior, which thereafter appears to become a mere consequence
of the external proportions. Here, too, the function of the
columns is to raise the upper part, which represents heaven,
the divine overworld, separated from things of earth by the
human being who straightens himself out into a pillar. Every
individual column in the Greek sacred building has, like the
structure as a whole, become once more a complete human
being, whose lower body is dissolved in an æsthetic line, while
the richly decorated and individualized head crowns the whole
as its " capital." The primitive precursor of this head-gathered
pillar-man of Greece may be found in the wooden house-pillar
of art in the South Seas,[1] its artistic prototype (which, however,
does not come within the conception of the Classical ideal of
beauty), and the caryatids [2] who with their human upper body
and head support the actual templum or roof of heaven — at
this stage still a burden weighing men down, whereas the Classical column seems to swing it aloft with ease and grace.

We insert here a later tradition as to the origin of the Greek
column. Although it may appear to us today as anecdotal, a
workshop yarn, it yet conveys — as its chronicler may himself
have thought — something of the Classical spirit. Vitruvius
(30 B.C.) in his famous work: *De architectura* (*Lib*. IV, *cap*.
i, 6) tells the following story: " When Ion had founded thirteen

[1] In Emil Stephan's important work *Südseekunst* (Berlin, 1907) these simple house-
pillars are illustrated and explained. The oldest man in the village named the essential
parts of the pillar after the parts of the body, and the head played an inferior rôle in
comparison with neck, trunk, or limbs.
[2] The caryatid bearers were regarded even in Classical tradition as a primitive remnant of barbarous customs, and only a single example of this kind is in fact known to
us in Classical Greek architecture. P. Sarasin's idea that it was originally a question
of "a pictorial presentation of the men sacrificed during the building of a house or
temple" will be discussed at the end of this chapter (the "building-sacrifice").

colonies in Caria — among them Ephesus and Miletus — the immigrants began to build to the immortals temples such as they had seen in Achaia, and first of all to the Apollo Panionic. When they were about to set up the columns in this temple,

— skull
— mouth
— neck
— trunk

— mouth
— trunk
— trunk
— hand
— arm or leg

they could no longer recall the measurements. While they were considering how to make the columns at once trustworthy and graceful, it occurred to them to measure a man's foot and compare it with his height. Finding that the foot measured a sixth part of a man's height, they applied this to the column by laying off its lowest diameter six times along the length of the column (inclusive of the capital). Thus did the Doric column begin to represent the proportions and the compressed beauty of the male body in buildings." Similarly, as Vitruvius goes on to explain, female slenderness was taken as a model for the pillars of Diana's temple, the diameter of which represented one eighth of their length. "At the bottom they laid a foot, like a sole; into the capital they introduced snails, which hung down right and left like artificially curled locks; on the forehead they put rolls and bunches of fruit for hair, and down the whole shaft they made grooves to resemble the folds in female attire. Thus, in the two styles of column that they invented, the one was copied from the naked, unadorned figure of a man, the other from the dainty figure of an adorned woman. Those who came later, with a more critical and finer taste, preferred less massiveness and accordingly fixed the height of the Doric column at seven and of the Ionic at nine times the diameter." [1]

This pretty story, even if we do not regard it as authentic, but only as a late interpretation of Classical traditions, evokes nevertheless two comments of cardinal importance for the theory of artistic creation. The one concerns the question of sexual significance in artistic creation, which the "female" column again brings to the fore; the other, the sister problem of the "imitation of nature," on which Vitruvius bases his whole interpretation. It is a fact that our conception of creative dynamism in the individual leaves no room to doubt that the two problems are closely associated or that the sexual theory of artistic creation stands and falls by the conception of art as an imitation of nature. For the sexual impulse as such could not, even in its "sublimated" form, bring forth anything but

[1] According to Vitruvius, the third, so-called Corinthian column imitates the slenderness of a virgin. Whether these reputedly purely æsthetic measurements were not in reality determined, or largely so, by the significance that the spiritual culture of Greece always attached to the numbers seven and nine we shall consider later. Recently there appeared an English translation of Vitruvius's work on architecture by Frank Granger (Loeb Classical Series; New York: G. P. Putnam's Sons).

simply nature, while the urge to create, as we have tried to show, aspires from the first to be independent of nature and to reach out beyond its premises. In this sense we need hardly look for the proof of our view, beyond the single fact that, so far, in all our material we have come across no purely sexual motive.[1] Indeed, one positively has the impression that the representation of the purely sexual (the act as well as the organs) is avoided in art. Stephan, too, finds it "*most puzzling that woman herself and everything that could remind one of her sex are completely absent from art,* in all the widely dispersed regions of the Bismarck Archipelago" (op. cit., p. 121; author's italics [2]). The fact is that — as I have already indicated in my account of the soul-belief and have since demonstrated at length — mortal origin through the woman is repudiated in favour of one or another immortality-ideology, and these lead ultimately to the self-creative shaping of man that is manifest in art as in other ways. Wherever we find unequivocal sexual representations in any considerable,

[1] "In view of this fact," says Stephan, "Wörmann's saying, that 'woman stands at the beginning of art,' will not hold water as a general proposition. But even the masculine sexual organs are only twice represented in the Bismarck Archipelago — on a house-pillar taken from a bachelor's house at Lambon, and the member itself as the knob of a stick on the island of Durour. On the pillar the organs are in no wise prominent, though one might attribute a phallus-like character to the stick" (op. cit.).

[2] In his work on *Architecture*, Vitruvius, in accordance with the whole of Classical opinion, describes the navel as the central point of the human body. The argument that the genital organ, and not the navel, forms that centre I have met only once, and that in a fairly late author and in a somewhat corrupt part of his text. But Varro, the author in question, appears to use this interpretation (i, 1, 7, 17) for political reasons: namely, by way of protest against the notion that the Delphic Omphalos is the centre of the earth (see Roscher, I, p. 11, note 19).

Similarly, in the whole of the literature I have found only one single interpretation (quoted by R. Eisler, op. cit., p. 411) of the Great Goddess's meteoric stone as a *vulva* or μήτρα (see Philologus, lxviii, pp. 135 et seq.).

With this belongs also the later identification of the so-called "finger" of the liver as the phallus of the indwelling earth-god, since in fact he himself is a secondary development from the original earth-goddess (Mother) (see Carl Thulin: *Die Götter des Martinus Capella und die Bronzeleber von Piacenza;* Diessen, 1906). Moreover, in all the luxuriant traditions of body-symbolism — with its offshoot, magical anatomy — it is only here and there that we come across isolated instances of sexual indications, and many of these, again, seem to have been introduced by the interpretative skill of later traditions — the frequently coarse sexual symbolism of the Gnostics, for instance, can only be properly understood in an esoteric sense (cf. *The Trauma of Birth*).

or even excessive, quantity, we are dealing with late cultures
of what I call the "age of sexuality," which is characterized
by recognition of the patriarchal principle and in consequence
embraces the phallus cult. In this connexion we have the worship of the Lingam in the Late Indian civilization, and the over-
emphasis of the phallus in the Etruscan decadence, which
through the tradition of the hearth-phallus that appeared to
the mythical kings Jarchetus and Servius Tullius, passed on to
Rome. The Romans, in fact, used this masculine symbol as a
means of ousting the deep-rooted matriarchal principle and
establishing the father-rule which promoted the development of the state. Again, the myths in which the origin of
fire is attributed to the sexual act, which seem to have been
handed down to us from India and Africa, should be only interpreted in the sense of a first creative transmutation of that
which is given into that which is generated. By general agreement it was only a question originally of preserving (or, at
most, controlling) fire, which had appeared in a natural way,
no doubt as lightning from heaven; there is certainly no
question whatever of its being *generated* as the result of the
observation and artificial imitation of the friction-heat en-
gendered in coition. If nevertheless the generating of fire came
in fact to be connected, mythically and linguistically, with the
sexual act, the notion could only arise from a comparison of
the two acts of generation, which in turn supposes that the
sexual act was already exalted from a natural function to a
symbol of the male creative strength. One is almost tempted
to say that the sexual act was made "creative" by comparison
with the generation of fire, and not that the generation of fire
needed to be sexualized.[1]

This brings us back to the second problem presented by

[1] The apparent sexualization was much more a masculinization, seeing that heat
and fire have originally a maternal character (the heat in the whale's belly singes the
hero's hair). Frobenius thinks that it is merely from modesty that the African refrains
from calling his two fire-sticks "man" and "woman," but the words "generator"
and "maker" that he uses for them sufficiently indicate the creative transformation
of sexuality (see *Erythräa*, p. 194).

Vitruvius, that of nature-imitation, the myth of fire-generation just discussed being a case in point. According to the myth, man is supposed to have invented fire by imitating nature — that is, to have discovered the natural generation of fire in coition; whereas in reality he received it from nature, but had nevertheless to produce it self-creatively.[1] In many traditions, of which the Greek Prometheus saga is the best known, man is said to steal fire from heaven. This means that he arrogantly assumed the power of generating it, just as he finally ceased to accept sexuality as a gift of nature and took upon himself the rôle of a god who creates men. We shall return to the problem of how much denial of man's own nature was involved in this human urge to create — in any case it produced its highest achievements before man began to feel doubts about it and to be driven, by a sense of guilt at his own presumption, to return to nature and imitation of nature. So it was exactly with the Greek hybris, which soared to supreme creative power only to experience, through tragic downfall, the profound dependence of the heroic individuality. And this probably explains the contradiction that we find between the Classical tradition of the proportions of the Greek column and Vitruvius' interpretation of it. For whereas he tells the story in order to use it as proof that the principle of nature-imitation was operative in the ripest creations of the Greek spirit, our own discussion seems to justify the opposite view. We were able to see the column as, not an imitation, but actually an abstraction, of the human body; and even to detect a tendency to embody the essence of it in the head as the symbol of intellectuality. In no way does the imitation of nature appear to have played an essential part in forming the Greek column, otherwise Vitruvius' delightful interpretation would certainly have been superfluous. Even if the Greek

[1] In Africa all fires were extinguished on the death of the king, and the first act of the new king was the fresh kindling of fire, the point of this being to show his ability to do so. According to the mediæval legend of Virgil the sorcerer, the new fire was — very archaically — obtained from the genital of the woman (without the man's aid).

stone-masons had taken their measurements for the column from the human body,[1] we should still be faced with the problem — far wider than that of nature-imitation — of explaining where they got the idea of the temple that these pillars were to support. But to this larger question we have already supplied the answer and at the same time shown that the column itself is only a partial expression of the collective ideology which led to the establishment on earth of the heavenly and the divine — in other words, to sacral temple-building. But this collective ideology also explains the curious notion of taking the human foot, which touches earth, as a measure and applying it in a definite proportion (the significant one in seven) *vertically* up and away from the ground. It is the microcosmization of the cosmic and the earthly which is at the root of it, the conception first formulated by the Ionian philosophers in the psychological principle that man is the measure of all things. This does not mean a mere imitation of his proportions and forms in art, but is to be, and can only be, understood as a bold revaluation of the old Oriental world-picture, in which the sky, with its stars and the gods representing them, had stood for the measure of all terrestrial and human things.

In Classical art, as we have particularly observed in connexion with Greek temple-building, man holds a harmonious intermediate position. He has arrived at creating his own microcosmic world and also the earthly heaven — the temple — in his own image! But he still has to support the heaven above him. He is an Atlas, beginning to groan under the weight of this macrocosmic burden, as the Greek hero suffered through his godlikeness, and at the summit of his creative elevation — the Greek hybris — his consciousness of guilt throws him

[1] The earliest length measurements were, in fact (as we shall prove by linguistic examples), taken from the human body and are to a great extent still in use (ell, foot, and so on). It is important to note, however, that there was in the East, besides the natural ell (length of the fore-arm to the tip of the outstretched middle finger), an artificial ell, slightly longer, which was used exclusively for buildings and was known as the "royal" ell (see Lepsius: *Die Längenmasse der Alten;* Berlin, 1884). I imagine this royal ell must have represented the macrocosmic architecture-ideology at a time when the king was regarded as God's representative on earth.

back into the inferior human rôle. This explains the trend towards imitation which later students of æsthetic have thought to detect in the Greek art-ideology; it betokens something like a rueful return to nature after too arrogantly rising above her, a self-imposed limitation on the individual presumption of creator. The imitation theory is, therefore (like every other æsthetic, for that matter), in itself an ideology arising out of the cultural situation, and not an explanation of the artistic style. Such a conception of nature-imitation as is represented by the Classical æsthetic is, to me, the expression of an abnegation of man's own creative force, caused by a sense of guilt in creation which forces man's return to the recognition of a higher creative force of which he himself is simply a creature, and even a mere tool of reproduction. This dualism of creature and creator Christianity subsequently drove to extremes in both its aspects: on the one hand, by the completeness with which its deity " became man," and, on the other, by its sublimely spiritual conception of God.[1]

For just as the Greek temple stands for the humanization of an originally cosmic sacral structure, so the church represents its spiritualization. We cannot therefore agree with psychoanalysis in its symbolic interpretation — on biological lines — of the church as nothing but a sheltering cavity which replaces the mother's womb. Not only does church architecture rise

[1] For the detailed application of body-symbolism in mediæval church-building, both in the column and in the whole field of architecture, see Karl Borinski's well-documented work: *Die Antike in Poetik und Kunsttheorie* (Leipzig, 1924; pp. 55–70). "Augustine, with his constant reference to the profound and ordered agreement of this microcosm with the macrocosm, to those matters of proportion and relation which demand investigation (and even, as to inward structure, anatomy), and to the significance of these matters for the artist, forms the bridge between the Classical art-theory and its reawakening in the fifteenth century" (op. cit., p. 69). But Borinski also sharply defines the difference between the ideologies: "For the Classical artist-builder the temple obeys the laws of the outline and proportions of the human figure; to the Christian, on the contrary, the body is a temple" (op. cit., p. 59). This Christian conception afterwards became humanized in the Renaissance and metaphorized by the Baroque (see Maria Brzoska: *Anthropomorphische Auffassung des Gebäudes und seiner Teile. Sprachlich untersucht an Quellen aus der Zeit von 1525–1750* (published at Jena, 1931, after my book was written). In this whole mediæval anthropomorphization of the building, man is *driven back* to nature (and to himself as the centre thereof), while the original artistic creativity rises above it.

above this primitive protective character of tomb-building: it
rises also from the self-creative shaping of the human body in
domestic building to be the essential symbol of the spiritual in
religious architecture. In this sense Fuhrmann is undoubtedly
right when he interprets the church door in detail as the mouth
(with teeth, gorge, and so on) [1] and no longer as an abdominal
entrance to the underworld (*Grabbau*, p. 53). For the cathedral
represents precisely the highest architectural expression of the
transformation (already discussed) of the animal conception
of an underworld into a spiritual soul-concept localized in the
head. If, then, the church represents rather the head of a man,
with its mouth, jaws, and throat, than the whole person, Fuhrmann's ingenious idea of the bell as a "brazen mouth" should
not be taken merely as a metaphor. For this mouth (*Mund*) is
also *mundus,* the whole world — according to a further linguistic indication of the same author — and it is precisely in
Christianity that this has come to be a purely spiritual one (the
Head), in which the *Logos* has replaced the *Pneuma,* although
both originally come from the mouth. True, the church has retained much of its pre-animistic body-symbolism; but in cathedral architecture this seems to have been reworked, or at any
rate reinterpreted, in terms of the super-world. Yet we must not
on this account take the chthonian motifs that continue to recur
in the highest achievements of architecture as a proof of an
unconquered primitiveness. True, man never gets away from
his animal nature — neither desires nor should desire to do so
— but the starting-point of all the problems, whether religious,
artistic, or scientific, lies beyond this self-evident statement; it
begins with the question: what is the attitude taken by the
culture of the day or the individual vessel thereof towards this
prime phenomenon of humanness?

But if the church portal, through which the worshipper
enters into a higher world of supernatural existence, represents

[1] He refers here to corresponding examples among the natives of New Guinea,
where "the entrances of these ceremonial- or spirit-houses were themselves thought
of as faces. The gateway corresponded to the mouth and above the entrance the nose
and eyes are seen" (*Neu-Guinea*, p. 23).

CHOIR-STALL

(Valenciennes, Museum)

the mouth, the old chthonian idea of the underworld's jaws, expressed in symbols of terrifying and dangerous animals (stylized devils' grimaces and dragons' maws), comes out as mere ornamentation of the façade or, it may be, the interior (choir-stalls) and is robbed of its alarming character by the artistic form given to it. And, in general, in the architecture of the sacred buildings plastic art becomes the servant of the collective ideology of the age and robs the house of God of

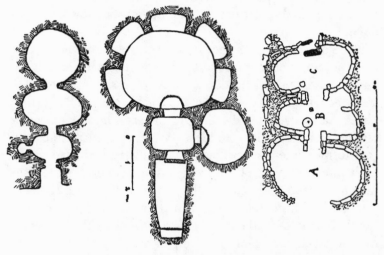

GRAVES AND HOUSES OF THE EARLY BRONZE-AGE

its ancient chthonian cave-character by a decorative ornament of spiritualized symbols. We can trace the process quite distinctly in the development from tomb-building to sacred architecture by way of house-building. The so-called atrium graves, which are found in abundance in the field of the Mediterranean culture, correspond in their lay-out (of which we give two examples)[1] to the middle part of the church and its attached side-chapels. The latter are, of course, used to this day

[1] After Carl Schuchhardt: *Alteuropa* (pp. 77 et seq. and 116 et seq.). In the same work reference is made to the original circular form of the "*con atrio*" type of tomb, which corresponds to the original circular dwelling-place (dwelling-house); see von Sydow: *Primitive Kunst und Psychoanalyse*, pp. 48 et seq.

for burials, and, indeed, the main building itself can be looked upon as the tomb of Christ. Obviously, the same basic idea is to be found here as in the ancient Oriental tombs of kings, where the lateral and exterior chambers were sought after as burial-places by ordinary mortals who wished to share the immortality of the great departed. Nevertheless, the church of today, for all those far-reaching concordances as to its having been originally a burial-place,[1] has also become the symbol of eternal life, the spiritual rebirth of which the believer can experience afresh every day by entering and leaving the house of God.

Here again we find the same creative re-formation and transformation of animal mortality into spiritual immortality operative in the genetic development of a single art-form — from the tomb as the dwelling of the body to the sacral structure (house of God) as the dwelling of the soul. During the process the biological abdomen-ideology becomes microcosmically transformed into the spiritual head-ideology, and correspondingly the reshaping of the religious underworld symbolism manifests itself macrocosmically in the artificial super-world symbolism. This development, which found its highest expression in the Gothic cathedral, seems to have been already beginning in an unimaginably remote past and to have worked up through various stages, of which we should like here to give a brief outline, at any rate so far as concerns their artistic significance. The first shadowy sign of a dualism which led later to the soul-concept and to the ideologies arising from it seems already to be discernible in the traces of a skull-cult of the later stone age; in the Upper Palæolithic Culture (particularly in South Europe) we have the so-called head burial side by side with the whole-body burial, and the discoveries in question leave no doubt that the head was severed from the trunk by force: that is, that there was intentional conservation of the

---

[1] While this work was in progress, a book appeared, entitled *The Circle and the Cross*, by A. H. Allcroft (London: Macmillan) in which ample material was produced to prove that the church was originally a round burying-place; the word "circus," with its connotation of roundness, is linguistically akin to "church," "*Kirche*."

head.[1] Opinions differ as to the meaning of this custom, but all are on the whole agreed that it was a cultural and not a practical measure (such as space-saving). Here, again, the divergence of opinion shows the inherent dualism attaching to the problem itself, for the severing of the head betokens both a tendency to conserve the essential portion of a personality and the opposed tendency to destroy the dead and render him harmless.[2] In any case, comparison with the head-cult, as it still exists among primitive races today, suggests the conclusion that the magical significance of the head as the seat of personal power may be regarded as the beginning of a belief in the soul.[3] The same high cultural estimation of the human head is seen in the equally ancient use of *head-cups,* which were originally parts of the brain-case, but are still with us as symbols in the form of artistic vases. Even in the development of vase forms the same dualism, with its creative overcoming, is to be traced. Although we have no vessels of any sort from the palæolithic age, there are various reasons for supposing that they did already exist (see, for instance, Schuchhardt, op. cit., p. 41), but it seems equally improbable that the Upper Palæolithic skull drinking-cups were used as profane objects in everyday life. The oldest known vessels, such as those which come from the Campignian, from the Litorina age of the Baltic, certainly show no head-shape.[4] If we are to seek an ideological model for such a shape, the form

[1] See R. Schmidt: *Die diluviale Vorzeit Deutschlands* (1912).

[2] See Dr. Joachim von Trauwitz-Hellwig's comprehensive theory in *Urmensch und Totenglaube* (Munich, 1929), where even the burning of corpses is shown to have its dualism: on the one hand, the most complete annihilation of the dead that is possible, and, on the other, the desire to restore the (vital) heat that he has lost, with the ultimate object of releasing his soul.

[3] M. Ebert: "*Die Anfänge des europäischen Totenkultes*" (*Prähist. Zeitschrift,* XIII–XIV, 1922) and Anckermann: "*Totenkult und Seelenglaube bei Afrikanischen Völkern*" (*Zeitschrift für Ethnologie,* 1918). Both of these authors assume the belief in the soul to have been preceded by a cult of the dead. Ebert holds, from the various kinds of burial, that the palæolithic age had no belief in the soul, and that this only came into existence with neolithic man.

[4] Occasionally there was found, besides the "breast"-form (see below), a hemispherical bowl which may very well correspond to the head-cup, although it also resembles a schematized model of the breast.

of the female breast at once suggests itself, and this would
in any case have priority as the first natural source of nourishment. This breast-shape is later found as " ornament " in the
older Lausitz pottery (bronze age) — as admitted even by
Schuchhardt (op. cit., p. 191), who in general is opposed to
such interpretations — although it can only be explained by
regarding the whole vase as standing for a female body, which
naturally possesses breasts because it serves as a drinking-
vessel.

We shall not enter here into the whole development and
significance of the vase (which will be dealt with under " Ornamentation "), but in pursuance of our train of thought I may
just refer to an opinion of Fuhrmann's, already quoted in support of my own views in *The Trauma of Birth* (p. 150). In *Der
Sinn im Gegenstand* (p. 2) Fuhrmann distinguishes two types
of vase: those that are copied from the udders of animals or,
it may be, the breasts of a woman,[1] and those which are shaped
like the guts of animals, out of which the oldest roll or tube
technique of ceramics developed. "The belly-pot, therefore,
gives a true-to-nature presentment of the human abdomen:
that is, an endless line of spirally arranged entrails which are
covered with a skin and enclose the stomach in their midst —
in other words, are made to hold the store of nourishment."
Thus in the domain of ceramic art, which is of such great
practical importance, there would appear to be a similar
development-process from the body- to the head-ideology that
we have in others. The head-cup, as used for cultural purposes,
symbolizes accordingly spiritual nourishment, and it is a fact
that the primitive, when he drinks from the enemy's skull,
is less concerned to quench his own thirst than to appropriate
his enemy's secret powers. But at the same time, the Upper
Palæolithic skull-cups show how early the human craving for
independence from transient nature and natural sustenance

[1] The very ancient custom of preserving liquids in leather bottles is, according to
Fuhrmann (op. cit.), bound up linguistically with the same basic conception (French
outre = uterus; Bocksbeutel, Beutel = French *bouteille*, English bottle), so that each
bottle is an udder standing on its base, with the nipple uppermost.

CLAY VESSELS FROM PERU

was awakened, to develop eventually into the belief in the soul and the immortality-ideology.

Another path from the primitive head-cult to that spiritual cult of the head which we observed in the building of churches was of more importance to art than the way of ceramics, which belongs more to craft-art; this is the evolution of the tomb-memorial from the primitive ancestral pole to the portrait of the dead, in the course of which the head, as the characteristic expression of the individual and personal, plays an increasingly important rôle. Whether, during this evolution from the sacred pole (replacing the sacred tree) to the plastic ancestral figure representing the dead, the skull-pole did or did not play the great part attributed to it by Frobenius, we undoubtedly seem to have before us, in the basic form of the pole, the plastic prototype of sculpture.[1] The vexed question as to whether the use of the actual skulls of the dead — the earliest portraits, so to say — was as general as Frobenius seems inclined to assume, is of less importance here than the general problem.[2] The pole (which on another line of development becomes the supporting column of the temple) is a substitute for the tree that renews itself yearly after dying down, and thus becomes the symbol of vegetable rebirth as the worm and the snake symbolize that of the animal world. In and with the ancestral pole the man accordingly becomes transformed into the tree, and the world-wide belief in the tree-origin of humanity is a natural consequence of his thus entering into the self-renewing tree.[3] The roughly carved pole, then, represents the humanized tree, which takes on more and more the likeness of a man and

[1] According to Meringer, the original meaning of the German word "*Bild*" (picture) was possibly the hewn pole (*Indogermanische Forschungen*).

[2] "Skull-sculpture"—that is, the modelling of a skeleton skull into a head—is found in New Guinea as well as in the New Hebrides, and in New Mecklenburg skulls thus modelled are used as heads on figures. See Vatter (*Religiöse Plastik der Naturvölker*, p. 62), who accounts for the strikingly exaggerated size of the head in primitive plastic as the deliberate accentuation of the "seat of the forces," in contrast to the palæolithic sculpture of the Aurignacien, where the emphasis is on the body.

[3] This like (and at bottom equivalent) spiritual importance of tree and snake (worm)—both of which appear to be endowed with chthonian powers—has led, as Küster rightly points out, to a combination of the two in the hero-cult and the

culminates in the sculptured head at the same time as, architecturally, it takes form in the column and so becomes the carrier of the immortal idea embodied in the temple.

Christ himself, in fact, is such a man-become-tree, who dies on the stake indeed, but yet lives by it for ever and, as the vanquisher of the dragon of the underworld, passes out beyond chthonian rebirth and grows up into the spiritual heights of heaven. And just as the original wooden tree-pillars lived on architectonically in the more durable stone, so does the column-borne temple reach up higher and higher, until, in the cathedral, it comes to represent only the upper portion, which has been set free from all earthliness and symbolizes macrocosmically the heaven and microcosmically the head. And yet, in spite of this, a church, with its sombre, grave-like atmosphere, still seems to be conceived of as an underground dwelling which (as Fuhrmann once remarked) is subterranean in principle even when it stands on the surface or lifts itself up above it. The architectural structure represents an underground cave brought into daylight, a combination, as it were, of cave and tree (column) — in other words, it is the expression of an ideology that is straining away from earth — skyward — and whose various stages of development have found suitable expression in the various architectural forms. To carry formulation to its limits, these two tendencies that are inherent in the art of building lead, in the one case, from the human abdomen to the spatial type in the house (palace of the entrails) or to the protective character of the fortress (the Troy); in the other, from the upper part of the body (neck, head) to the aspiring style of the temple towers or the spirituality of the cathedrals. In the first case it is the animal mother-body with its protective covering (warmth, fur),[1] and in the second the upright attitude

---

monuments corresponding thereto. The origin of the tree-cult in Greece is ascribed by Evans ("Mycenæan Tree- and Pillar-Cult," *Journal of Hellenic Studies*, 1901) to Cretan influence. Ferguson (*Tree and Serpent Worship;* London, 1872) sought to trace it to Oriental inspiration.

[1] Fuhrmann traces the linguistic connexion of *Haus* (house) with *Haut* (hide), and of *ville* (town) with *Fell, Hülle* (fur, covering) (*Peru*, I, p. 27).

proper to man himself (the tower) that forms the natural and the ideological archetype for the structure; and, correspondingly, the structure is either a utility-building or a sacral building. I say "ideological" archetype because the house is, for all its corporeal symbolism, much more than a mere copy from nature of maternal protection: it has passed far beyond that and has become the symbol of the creative ego that has freed itself from the maternal protective covering and risen to an independence of its own.

But to trace the way from the subterranean tomb and its heavenly counterpart, the sacral edifice, back to earth and earthly dwelling-places, we must again have resort to an ideological motive of microcosmization, the significance of which for the whole of cultural development has already been mentioned. This is the ancient conception of an earth-centre,[1] the figuration of which as the earth's "navel" expresses a humanization of the cosmos such as was necessary if practical-technical development was likewise to find its ideology. For it is not only religious and mythological conceptions which are linked with the idea of the Omphalos. Scientific technics (for example, geodosy and the measurement of distances), practical undertakings such as the lay-out of towns and roads, and world-moving ideologies like state and nation have issued from the macrocosmic broadening out of man to earth-scale. We cannot here explore these special domains, which are too remote from the art-problem, but the recognition of these important connexions does prove to have a bearing, if an indirect one, on the understanding of art; for it discloses the paradoxical fact that the way from the human to the earthly was not a direct one, but followed a roundabout route through heaven and the world-as-a-whole. In other words, everything that the earthly

[1] It is also found, for instance, in New Guinea or in Peru, whose capital, Cuzco (= navel), was laid out macrocosmically as a monument of the signs of the zodiac, and microcosmically in male and female halves. The body of the Inca was buried in the temple of Tampo, near Cuzco—that is, in the navel of the Peruvian world—after lungs, heart, and entrails had been removed and the body itself mummified (Fuhrmann: *Reich der Inka;* 1924; pp. 26, 35).

culture has produced in material values lies between the micro-cosm and the macrocosm, but was only enabled to come to fruition through ideological relationship between the two. How this influence may have operated we cannot therefore discover by way of ethnological or sociological study of the man-created reality, but only through the spirit which brought them forth, which is manifested most purely in religious traditions and objectified in artistic creation. It is of the specific quality of art that, even here, it adopts a middle course, or, rather, an intermediary rôle, in that it not only works out the prevailing ideology, but formally objectifies this development-process it-self. The paradox of the art-problem lies, therefore, in the fact that the nature of a particular prevailing art-style can only be detected from the other cultural achievements parallel with it and in connexion with their ideological traditions; while these, again, can only be derived from an understanding of the nature of art. This apparently insoluble dilemma we are here en-deavouring, by simultaneous and alternating treatment of all effective factors, to solve as nearly as is possible in the case of so complicated a problem as human creativity.

Before we make our brief survey of the conception of the navel as earth-centre, in its cultural function and, more es-pecially, as regards Greece, we may point out that there is also a negative proof of our view of artistic creativity as a macrocosmized self-elevation. This proof is the Jewish race, which in contrast to other culturally gifted Semites of the ancient East has produced no art and, for that matter, not even a material culture, but has exhausted itself in the forming of ethical religions. Taken in a cultural-historical sense, this fact may throw just such a light on the understanding of the creative activity of other nations as the neurotic, thwarted in production, provided for that of the psychology of the produc-tive artist. What is lacking to the Jews, besides art, seems at the first glance to be that cultural correlation of the macrocosm and the microcosm which, in its various relations and ideologies, can be traced as a culturally operative influence from the an-

SACRIFICE CUP FROM DAHOMEY, FRENCH WEST AFRICA

HEAD-SHAPED CUP FROM AFRICA

cient East, through the Classical age, till far into the Christian Middle Ages. In the Jewish "state of God" there is no room for an earthly representative of God, such as was symbolized microcosmically by Oriental rulers, let alone for an artificial symbol of him; for, as everyone knows, no representation of him was allowed. Apart from the temple, the Jews took over from the Oriental culture nothing of its earthly representation of cosmic splendour — and the temple was no house of God, but only the place in which his word could be heard by his children, assembled in synagogue for the purpose. Yet the Old Testament reads like an epitome of the whole spiritual culture of the ancient East,[1] although made over and interpreted in the sense of the specific Jewish mentality. Its ideology is a moral one which interprets "psychologically" all happenings as the outflowing of good and bad instincts in man; these can therefore be adequately expressed in terms of law and prohibition and the corresponding conceptions of reward and punishment.[2] As a typical example of the Jewish attitude to the mythic world-outlook native to the ancient Eastern macrocosmos, we may select the story of the Tower of Babel, which also will take us back to our more immediate theme. This familiar story (which, by the very choice of locality, points to the cultural centre of the East, Babylon) displays an obvious defeatist attitude towards human creative power, the presumption of which is morally condemned,[3] whereas the Greek culture reacted to its "hybris" tragically. According to the biblical tradition, the whole human race, with a single common language, is raised to a potential which presents a challenge to the gods and finds a symbol of this condition in the building of a *city* (Genesis xi,

---

[1] See especially Alfred Jeremias: *Das Alte Testament im Lichte des alten Orients*.

[2] From a religious standpoint this attitude is foreshadowed in the Egyptian Judges of the Dead, while the Zoroastrian doctrine — which also influenced Christianity — raised the dualism of good and evil to a spiritual principle of world-creation.

[3] Another example—that of the moral "making over" of the Babylonian-Sumerian account of the Flood into the biblical one—I have dealt with in *Seelenglaube und Psychologie* (pp. 110–18). Here again the Bible shows human presumption to be punished and the new creation to come from the hand of God, whereas the original account—as, for that matter, of the Tower story too—indicates a *human creation*, which it practically sets up in comparison with the divine.

4) with a tower whose top may "reach unto heaven." This grandiose plan, which placed man as the cultural creator beside God as creator of the cosmos, was, as we know, brought to naught by Jehovah, who "confounded" the language of the people and "scattered them abroad upon the face of all the earth." We shall deal with this motif of "separation of language" later. Here we are concerned with the micro-, macro-cosmic symbolism of the building of the tower, which in the Bible story is ideologically rejected.

Roscher (op. cit., III, p. 9) is convinced that in the biblical account Babylon, with its massive seven-storeyed tower, is only comprehensible as the centre of the "*orbis terrarum*" and original home of all humanity. In support of his theory he refers to a book by I. Hehn on the number seven,[1] in which the Babylonian staged towers are interpreted as symbols of the cosmos, the sovereignty over which lies with the god enthroned on the summit. Roscher adds a query as to whether the throne is possibly intended as the world's centre and thinks that the names of the towers would be in keeping with this ("House of the Seven Universes," etc.). But, as we have already seen, the seven-staged tower, an important form in ancient architecture, has been traced back by E. Hommel to the seven-tiered structure of the neck-vertebræ, with the head as dome crowning it. Now, Roscher's conception of this building as the sign of the central point of the earth or the world seems to present the macrocosmic counterpart to this. At the same time, these cosmic symbols of the spiritual elevation of man — the world-towers — were erected on precisely those spots which were regarded as the earth's navel, its centre, under the microcosmic interpretation. If the elevation of man above nature was to be justified, the architectural sign of this elevation had to be erected over the chthonian-animal symbol — as which the earth's navel originally appears.

Here, again, Greece — as the turning-point in the process of

[1] I. Hehn: *Siebenzahl und Sabbat bei den Babyloniern und im Alten Testament.* The general significance of the number seven will be discussed later.

humanizing (microcosmizing) the macrocosm — passed in the
development of its cult-centres (Delphi in particular) through
all stages of development of man from chthonian dependence
to spiritual independence. The Delphic Omphalos (navel-
stone), which we have already encountered as the gravestone
of the dragon Python, belongs, in the opinion of E. Maass,[1]
to the oldest symbols and sanctuaries of Mother Earth, for its
domed shape and the opening with which it is provided suggest
the womb (uterus). And although other authors[2] deny this
connexion of the Omphalos with the earth-mother (Ge), its
grave-like form, to which attention has already been drawn by
Rohde (*Psyche,* I, 132), remains to be explained; for the significance (presently to be demonstrated) of the earth-navel idea
cannot be disguised with this author's remark that this miniature Tholos had only come to be called the navel — that is,
the centre — of the earth as a result of misunderstanding and
fables. If we abide by tradition, we find that the old sacred
treasure of the earth-goddess, the " navel "-stone (Omphalos),
was situated in the Temple of Apollo, where the god, after
vanquishing the earth-spirit (dragon) Python, had established
his seat above the grave of the deposed demon-oracle; another
example, in short, of a building to the glory of an intellectual
god of light (god of prophecy) set on the centre of the earth
(the navel) that has the form of a grave and symbolizes the
uterus of the earth-mother. From this formulation alone it
is clear that, on the basis of what has been demonstrated, we
can explain the contradictions that are found side by side in
traditional accounts as part of the same development which
leads from the triumph over chthonian dependence to spiritual
independence.

But this development shows also why it was precisely the
conception of an earth-navel that attained such importance
among the ancient culture-nations. The answer to this question is found in considering the fact that of all the primitive

---

[1] *Österreichische Jahreshefte,* XI (1908), pp. 10 et seq.
[2] For instance, Farnell, in his *Cults of the Greek States,* IV (1907), p. 303.

biological symbols of a connexion between individual and cosmos — microcosm and macrocosm — the navel alone has that *individual* symbolic significance which (as we have seen) could, in its spiritualized form as a self-creative force, ultimately bring forth a human world-system. For the uterus, the mother-body, even the navel-cord, are all parts having continuous existence outside the ego and are, so to say, symbols of dependence; while the navel itself remains part of *the individual himself* as the sole mark of this the original connexion.[1] Symbolically interpreted, therefore, the navel stands for the visible sign of the animal origin of man, but at the same time of his selfness and independence, while, conformably to its symbolical meaning as the lost link with the universe, it is at this point that man begins to construct his world-system so as to reunite himself with, not to say to magnify himself into, the cosmos. And when further we have taken into account the fact, demonstrable by ethnological evidence (see Roscher), that the navel was equally regarded as the seat of the soul (life-force) by reason of its nearness to vitally important organs (liver, diaphragm), we have discovered also that the driving motive of the navel cult lies in the transference of the soul's immortal powers from the mother's womb (grave) to the individual.

Only through this humanization of the creative process, as it completed itself ideologically in Greece, can we understand the practical importance attaching to the idea of the earth's navel in the development of the Classical culture. If the early Eastern world-picture was oriented towards the "celestial geography,"[2] which served as model for the terrestrial, here the

[1] Rudolf Meringer alludes to the linguistic relation between *Nabel* (navel) and *Narbe* (scar) in his essay: "*Omphalos, Nabel, Nebel*" (*Wörter und Sachen*, V; 1913).

[2] See Eberhard Schrader: *Die Keilschriften und das Alte Testament*, third edition, revised by Zimmern and Winckler (Berlin, 1902–3), p. 158: "Each god had, as we see, his τεμένος, his templum, his piece of heaven; and it was therefore essential that he should have the same on earth. This piece is his *country*, the domain belonging to his temple. . . . From this view of the earth as a mirror of heaven (or, in reality, vice versa) there ensued a partition of countries, such as is met with again and again in the East, and of which the object was to represent each country as a self-contained whole. Man

ANCESTRAL FIGURES FROM NEW GUINEA
(LEFT) AND NEW ZEALAND (RIGHT) SHOW-
ING THE IMPORTANCE OF THE HEAD

earth becomes humanized by the aid of the Omphalos idea; that is to say, this heavenly geography was followed by a human geography, and it was through the latter that our earthly geography for the first time became possible. For the earth's navel counted at first only as the centre of a particular country and we need not, therefore, assume the existence of a geographical knowledge such as no primitive culture could possibly have possessed. Only at a later date, and among civilized races that had achieved power, did the country's navel become the earth's navel, and on this navel was erected the building that symbolized their cosmic ambitions; for it represented man himself built up "self-creatively" from the navel. In the "Omphalos" the navel of the individual born from the womb of the mother (Earth) grows out, as it were, in the form of a building which symbolizes his own body and no longer that of the mother. In temple form it could still be regarded as a human tribute to the higher power of a creator; but as a "skyscraper," crowning the earthly city, it was an expression of that human pride of which the biblical account of the fiasco of Babel is the moral condemnation. The confounding of tongues, which rendered the work vain, warns us that we must regard it as a symbol — if not indeed a source — of the ideology of a nation or state that races should imagine themselves to be situated at the earth's centre (China as the "Empire of the Middle," for example). There were in fact many violent disputes as to which city could pride itself on being the real centre of the empire and therefore of the world. Thus it was, too, with Delphi and Branchidæ in ancient Greece,[1] and with Jerusalem

---

is a microcosm in himself, and the land-unit must likewise be so. Like the earth itself, this particular bit of it must reflect the separate divisions of heaven. And just as the gods rule up above, so do they rule in their respective sections of country, and their doings and the ruling of the country's destiny may be observed in their celestial movements as may their workings within the smallest of microcosms — man. Hence the horoscope."

[1] Possibly the famous competition among the seven Greek cities for the honour of being Homer's birthplace is a case of this sort of rivalry between small nationalities — so also, according to the Iliad, it brought about the disaster of the Trojan war (consider its mythic prelude in the strife over the apple of Paris).

and Shechem in old Judea; and thus it is today with the various capitals of our monster states.[1]

For the further geographical-political ideologizing of the individual earth-navel, it is important that it should have a particular localization. This Roscher calls the "peak-site" (*Höchstlage*). Although the (very widespread) idea of the localization of the Omphalos at the highest point in the land may seem only an intermediate link in the development we have just traced, a knowledge of it is essential if we are to

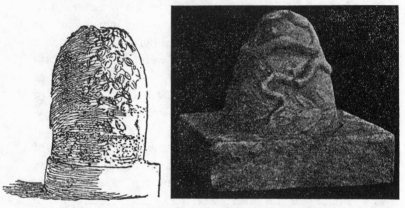

MARBLE OMPHALOI FROM DELPHI

understand what follows. For, with respect to Delphi, Roscher has arrived at the conclusion provisionally that it is not the so-called Omphalos (centre) stones that are to be regarded as the real navel, but the earth-*fissure* whence there flowed the spring-water endowed with mantic power that the prophetess drank. The conical stone set up beside it would in that case only serve to guide temple visitors to the sacred spot. Without

---

[1] As an interesting example let us take the central importance enjoyed by Paris in the French empire for many centuries past. This is to be attributed to a shifting of the ancient Celtic earth-navel from the region of the Carnutes, somewhat farther north, to Paris and Saint-Denis, which took place in the Christian Middle Ages (see L. Olschki: *Der ideale Mittelpunkt Frankreichs im Mittelalter in Wirklichkeit und Dichtung;* Heidelberg, 1913. Also, J. Loth: "*L'Omphalos chez les Celtes,*" *Revue des Études anciennes*, Vol. XVII, 1915).

entering upon the cultural and archæological problem of
Omphalos research, it will suffice for the purpose of our discussion to remember that the idea of the earth's navel was
originally a purely chthonian one, whether it was a fissure
or a grave that was in question and that, therefore, the very
use of the Omphalos stone to mark the spot signifies an ideological elevation above the navel as a natural depression —
which is as much as to say, an " artistic " representation of it.
The displacement of this conically designed navel[1] to the
highest point of the landscape is but another expression of the
same elevation-tendency which manifested itself architectonically in the temple erected over the fissure or grave.[2]

If we examine the material collected by Roscher from these
points of view, it emerges at once that the idea of the peak-
site for the earth-navel, which prevailed also among the
Semites, is connected with the erection of sacral buildings,
while the more fundamental idea of the sunk earth-navel was
the basis of earthly town- (and road-) planning. The best-
known example of the first is — after Greece — Palestine. Its
Jewish capital, Jerusalem, transcends even Delphi in its
Omphalos significance. Delphi was for about a millennium
generally acknowledged by the inhabitants of the Mediterranean countries to be the sacred navel of the earth, but the
existence of the Omphalos of Jerusalem can be proved, according to Roscher, at least two centuries earlier, and it has

[1] The effort to bring the domed shape of the Omphalos stone into harmony with its
significance as the navel has led, on the medical side, to the suggestion that the navel
of the new-born babe is actually slightly conical in form at the very first (P. Näcke:
Arch. für Krim. Anthrop.; 1912; p. 350). But this "realistic" explanation of such a
work of art will not hold water in view of the complicated traditions pointing to the
ideological interpretation. For, after all, we are dealing with a symbiotic representation of uterus, grave, navel-cord, and navel, while at the same time taking into consideration the elevation-tendency which gives the navel a conical form and sets it up
erect. What appear to be representations of the navel-cord are in fact to be seen on
many Omphalos stones; and if these might equally well be interpreted as snakes, the
same significance of rebirth is involved (see Figs.).

[2] Whether the subterranean adyton of the temple should be taken, in accordance
with Classical tradition, for a natural grotto, or, as modern archæologists think, is an
artificial cellar (of the eighth–seventh centuries) is irrelevant to its symbolic importance
as the chthonian basis of the building above ground.

been effective right through the Middle Ages and down to
the Zionism of the present day. For no fewer than three of
the most important world-religions — the Jewish, the Christian, and the Islamic — Jerusalem has ever been a holy place
of the highest order. The prophets Isaiah and Ezekiel praise
Jerusalem's position in the midst of the nations, and the
temple of Jehovah as the highest of the peaks. With this peak-
site there is linked also the idea that Jerusalem and all Palestine escaped being involved in the Flood, and consequently

TWO CELTIC OMPHALOI

not only is the rebirth of humanity after the Flood, but also
the actual birth of the first man transferred to this high-
placed navel, which finally becomes identified with Paradise
(see Roscher's dissertation on the Omphalos in the Adam
legend).

In contrast to this macrocosmic-attuned lay-out of the peak-
navel, which led to the erection of religious sacral buildings
on mountain tops, we have the rite — practised especially by
the Romance races of the Mediterranean (Etruria, Latium)

in town-building. According to this rite, the town was built round a centre previously marked out, the so-called *mundus*. This centre is a circular pit, forming the geometrical centre of the city-to-be, into which the firstlings of all fruits and other gifts of consecration were poured. After this the limits of the new city were set by a circular boundary line drawn round the *mundus* as centre in a ritual ploughing. The pit itself (*fossa*), the lower part of which was sacred "*Dis Manibus*" (to the spirits of the dead and gods of the underworld), was then filled in and closed with a round stone, the so-called *lapis manalis*. Now, Roscher regards the *mundus* as a particular form of earth-navel, which was here represented as a round pit to which the town walls and their ditches, in principle circular, conformed. He thinks it possible even to connect — as the ancients themselves did — the expressions *mundus* and *urbs;* for according to the earlier conception the world as well as the "*orbis terrarum*" and the horizon (heaven) is round, and the underworld, the lower *mundus,* must, to be in keeping, have the same form.

This interpretation of the *mundus,* which the ritual of Italian town-building discloses, completely confirms our own idea that town-building, like house-building, is based on the abdomen-symbolism (low navel) as symbolized in the earth, while the temple, symbolizing heavenly spiritualism, was erected on the high navel. Only the house, seen from this angle, retains more of the basic character of maternal protection than the temple, which strains away from earth to the representative of the upper, higher self. On the other hand, even in the architecture of the house, though its foundation and underground cellarage reach down into the earth,[1] the

[1] In a medical encyclopædia written by a West-German Jewish doctor in Hebrew five hundred years ago, there are two anatomical illustrations: the one presents a frontal cut through the human body, the other a tower-like house divided into storeys and rooms, in each of which an organ of the human body is stowed away (Max Hirsch in the *Archiv für Frauenkunde*, III, 1917, p. 129).

Abundant material on the human symbolism of the house is also found in Max Schlesinger's *Geschichte des Symbols* (Berlin, 1912).

This "relation to the basic structure of the human being" is preserved most purely

creative self-elevation of the whole ego already finds expression. Similarly the town as such, representing, as it does, a combination of houses, has retained some definitely maternal features,[1] even though here, too, the other factors of self-expansion and national rivalry gradually transform this picture into accord with the practical tendencies of commerce and communications. Perhaps the tower represents the earliest symbol of this turnover, for there we have no longer the house of God, but the insolent sky-scraper as the aim and centre of town-planning. Yet it retains a connexion — one might say, a navel-cord — with the older macrocosmic conception in that even this human city and its token the tower are erected on the navel of the earth. This humanization of the earth explains, too, the further development of the Omphaloi into the milestones that Athens and Rome have handed on to us. The altar of the twelve gods, erected by the Peisistratids towards the end of the sixth century, which stood roughly in the middle of the city, served not only as the religious centre but above all as the central milestone for the whole street and road system of Athens and Attica. Similarly, in Rome there stood in the city's midst, on the Forum Romanum, Constantine's "*Umbilicus urbis Romæ*" and the "*Milliarium aureum*" built by Augustus in 28 B.C. The first of these monuments counted as the centre of the city and the empire, the second as the basic milestone of the whole Roman road system.

These traditions of laying out town and country radially

in Chinese architecture, where, in sacral buildings, man as macrocosm is represented as almost filling the earth: the middle gate of the temple corresponds to the head; the two side-gates to the arms and legs, and so on (Fuhrmann: *China*, I, p. 23). In contrast to this, Chinese secular building appears to be the expression of a harmonious collaboration with Nature. Even in the profusely decorated pagodas we have, according to O. Sirén, the feeling of standing in front of a sort of exotic plant, just as it grows out of the ground, and not of facing a geometric abstraction straining out of the earth, as is the case with European buildings (*History of Early Chinese Art*, Vol. IV, 1930). Only Gothic unites these two inherent principles of architecture in a few of its finest cathedrals.

[1] See my *Um Städte werben*, in which the symbolical affinity between the siege of a city and the conquest of a woman is shown in mediæval folk-songs. It also plays a part in the saga of Helen of Troy.

from the centre of the city once more reflect a cultural development of the earth on the microcosmic, human basis. It
struck me, in the course of my first mythological work:
Mythus von der Geburt des Helden (1909), that most of the
heroes whose mythic birth-legends I was using as material were
also reputed to be founders of cities. The connexion between
this fact and our present theme seems to be something of this
sort: the heroic city-founder is a foundling who has been
turned adrift and is usually suckled by an animal foster-
mother (like the Roman she-wolf); thus, on the one hand
he has lost the maternal protection at too tender an age and
finds compensation in the city which he founds, while on
the other he is destined by these circumstances to a creative
self-development. The oldest literary tradition of this order is
preserved for us by King Sargon, the Semitic conqueror of the
Sumerian culture (about 2800 B.C.), who, in an inscription,
asserts himself to be the virginal son of the Sumerian mother
of the gods and therefore the legitimate saviour of the Sumerian people. The same waif-legend attaches to Moses, the
Jewish national leader, who is similarly a compound product
of two cultures, and the most famous case of all is the founding of Rome by the castaway twins Romulus and Remus.
The more abundant tradition connected with the founding of
Rome, which is said to have been established in 753 B.C. as a
frontier post against the Etruscans, enables us to reconstruct
the ideas governing the founding of cities — the ideas that came
to be concretized by the Roman nation in its earthly world-
rulership.

Legends of the founding of the capital of the Roman empire
seem to be dominated by the number seven, a number which,
as we have shown, belongs to and predicates both a projection
of the higher self and its creative representation. Thus Rome's
seven hills may, as E. Hommel suggests, rest on the conception
of seven heavens, each with its own name (*Palatium, Cælius,*
and so on), and the suggestion derives support from the con-
cordance of the Romulus saga in this respect with the seven

first patriarchs of the Bible. Romulus is the first of seven kings. Like Cain, he founds a city, calls it by his name, slays his brother (again like Cain), and like Enoch (after whom the first city was named) is taken up into heaven. This parallel, which can be still further developed, is significant as showing that the first architect and town-founder built under an urge to compensate the loss of a mother [1] and yet did so in the heavenly manner; that is, psychologically speaking, with a cosmological conception of his act of spiritually newly-creating himself, and naming the creation accordingly by his own name. From this point of view the idea of the god of heaven as architect of the universe becomes intelligible: he builds the cosmos as man builds the city. Enoch the city-builder is, according to Alexander Polyhistor (*c.* 80 B.C.), the inventor also of astrology and identical with Atlas — the uppermost, seventh, and last of a series of identically formed joints (neck-vertebræ); for (Genesis v, 21–4) he is also " the seventh from Adam " and as such brings the first world-week to a close.[2]

The Hanukkah festival, in which the seven-branched candlestick figures, is possibly, according to Hommel, the anniversary of Enoch's initiation into the heavenly mysteries and his translation to the heavenly city. But it was at about this season that the Romans celebrated in their city of the seven hills and the seven kings the feast of the seventh planet deity, the Saturnalia, and seven days previously the feast of the Septimontium — the seven hills, which correspond to the seven heavens — took place.

Side by side with these macrocosmic linkages, which affected even the daily life of the individual citizen, the city-founding

---

[1] The mother animal plays a part not only in the founding of Rome, but also, for instance, in the familiar story of the foundation of a new Troy by Æneas in Latium, on the spot indicated to him by the "Troy-sow." Similarly, in Epirus, when Hellenus built the city of Byopator (home of cattle) on the left bank of the brook Xanthos, the legend says that it was a cow that guided him by lying down on the spot (Krause: *Trojaburgen*, p. 282).

[2] Just as Enoch personifies the seventh of the neck-vertebræ, so is the first biblical father of men, Adam, localized in the neck by the popular designation of the larynx as "Adam's apple." But the uppermost of the seven neck-vertebræ corresponds cosmically to the highest of the planets, after which, later, the Jewish seventh day of the week was named (Sabbath, *Saturni dies*, Saturday).

saga also contains a human motive which proves to be of basic importance to our theory of self-creative eternalization in the work of art. The city-founders Romulus and Cain are shown to be burdened with the curse of fratricide, and it is easy to see in this an echo of the most ancient and widespread custom of a building-sacrifice.[1] This age-old custom, still practised by many primitive peoples, may be traced right into our own architectural ornamentation: it consisted in immuring living human beings — new-born children for choice — under the foundation-walls of new buildings. No clue is found to the origin of this custom in any traditions. Rudolf Kleinpaul refuses to regard these built-in persons as " sacrifices " in the true sense, on the ground that there would not at that stage be any protecting demons and gods in the new building who would require victims; the intention, he holds, was to create spirits, to make a beginning. In the deeper sense of creative force these " house-spirits " may reasonably be called victims, however, as they embody the idea that every created thing, if it is to be capable of life, owes its existence to some life destroyed. Whichever way one looks at it, the building-sacrifice affirms once more the dualistic nature of the problem of architecture, and, in principle, of all other art-creation. Above all, it throws a flood of light on the house as mother-symbol, but also as a burial-place in which the child is bedded so that it may rise to new life within the building itself. But the custom further reveals the fact that the building is not intended as a mere copy (imitation) of natural processes, but represents a spiritual re-creation, and this is made possible by the death of the walled-in person, which sets free his spirit to animate the building.

As was only to be expected, the building-sacrifice itself has likewise undergone a process of creative spiritualization, and the traces of this are to be seen to this day in architectural

[1] There is no doubt that the sacrifice of the first-fruits that were enclosed in the *mundus* also represents such a sacrifice to the building. With the primitives—in Hawaii, for instance—a man is buried near the stump of a tree which has supplied the wood for a god-image, and the mask of the Kalebue (Eastern Congo) acquires its extraordinary magical powers (in the cult of the dead) only through the sacrifice of a slave (Vatter, p. 41).

ornament. From walling up an adult or child whole in the new
building, it became the custom later in many places to use only
the head, as in the head-burial of the Upper Palæolithic. We
even have the account of one historically important case of the
kind in the old Roman legend which tells of the finding in
the reign of Tarquinius Superbus of a human head (*caput toli*)
in the foundations of the Temple of Jupiter in the Capitol
(head of the city). As Kleinpaul observes, this head was probably placed there intentionally, and was not a casual fragment.
This conception is confirmed by the animal and human head-
ornament which is preserved on sacred and profane buildings
not only on the Mediterranean, but also in the Nordic culture.[1]
We have already mentioned the artistic forerunners of these,
the caryatids, which are interpreted even by Vitruvius as models
of slaves who, instead of being killed, were exposed in their
shame to the public gaze. P. Sarasin has quite definitely described them as echoes of the building-sacrifice, on the evidence
of an old " pile-dwelling in the Minahassa in caryatid pillar
form." Almost simultaneously Otto Schell interpreted [2] a number of ornaments such as are still to be recognized in the buildings of Germanic houses as reminiscences of the building-
sacrifice. According to him, these human and animal heads
(horses, owls, bats) also serve as charms to ward off the evil
spirits which threaten the inhabitants. In the opinion of
Muchau,[3] these animal skulls were attached to the structure,
with a warding-off intention, as early as the pile-dwellings of
the bronze age. He says, further: " Greek architecture has in
numerous cases affixed to the metopes of the temple figures of
the frontal portion of the ox-skull with its pair of horns.
Although these have the appearance of forming part of
the decoration, they obviously represent the practice of some

[1] The whole of the material here discussed has been collected by Muchau in the
above-mentioned *Pfahlhaus und Griechentempel* (1909; particularly pp. 256 et seq., 290
et seq., and 296).

[2] "*Abwehrzauber am Bergischen Hause*," *Globus*, 6 June 1907, p. 335. The whole subject has recently been treated by Fr. Kohlbrugge in *Tier- und Menschen-Antlitz im
Glauben und Abwehrzauber der Welt* (Bonn, 1924). (The special problem of the Evil Eye
has been treated by Seligmann.)   [3] *Heimat der Indogermanen*, pp. 285 et seq.

ancient custom. It may be that skulls of oxen which had really been sacrificed were stuck up in this manner, or that the sacrifice of the animal's head, as the superior part, was considered as good as the whole, or, finally, that the intention was to ward off demons, as with the Germanic people."

This warding-off significance of the building-sacrifice seems to me, however, to be a later trait which probably arose from the feeling of guilt evoked by the sacrifice of real life for the creation of the building. Thus, paradoxically, the victim himself is used as protection against the vengeful spirits of the evil conscience which torments the inhabitants because of this very sacrifice. Here the deep dualism of death again emerges: on the one hand the dead is to be completely put out of the way; on the other, he is to be allowed to live on spiritually — that is, creatively. And so, in the end, under the pressure of an increasing sense of guilt, this secondary protective spirit has become transformed into the familiar ghostly terror which haunts our castles, palaces, and monasteries to this day. But this is bound up with another peculiarity of house-building, which throws more light still on the building-sacrifice. In the development of the house-idea from the chthonian labyrinth-conception (palace of the entrails), the difficulty of finding the way out of the winding maze is always the problem, whereas in the labyrinthine citadels (Troy) the difficulty naturally lies in getting in. Now, since these labyrinth-buildings have the significance not only of the womb, but of the grave also (as we have assumed for the house and particularly for the temple), it is clear that a special symbolic meaning attaches to these difficulties — a meaning which is linked with the belief in immortality and has been preserved to the present day in innumerable popular superstitions relating to the entering and leaving of a house. For if the house, under which, originally, bodies were actually buried, still retained a tomb significance after its two functions had been separated,[1] the building-

---

[1] The persistence of this grave-house parallel is proved by the so-called "house-urns," used to preserve the ashes. These are small models of the real houses inhabited

sacrifice appears to represent the dead who actually lives on in the house for ever and enables the living to leave it without risk.

But here, once more, the idea of sacrifice appears in its deepest sense: it is the dead, the decaying, that assures to the living the possibility of existence and creative fruition. And if today we speak only metaphorically of the spirit or soul that lives in a work of art, the artist is often only too well aware that in fact a life has to be sacrificed so that it may live on immortally in the work. Only, in the beginning, in the course of natural processes, this was another's life — our actual building-sacrifice — whereas the modern artist can as a rule only produce durable work at the cost of his own life. In this sense, however, the fratricide of Romulus — as that of Cain — is also to be understood as a building-sacrifice which the founder of a city was bound to offer in order to ensure to it life and (as the ideology of Rome proves) everlasting life.[1] That mythical tradition turns this building's victim into a brother — as does the biblical legend of the city-founder Cain — may be regarded as one of the doublings typical of myth-formation, and the characterization of the brothers as twins in both stories places this beyond conjecture. The idea is no doubt that the mortal "double" must be sacrificed if the immortal ego is to live on in the work. Seen in this light, Cain's fratricide, as described in the Bible, appears as the condemnation of human presumption which uses for self-glorification the life given by God. And therefore, in founding the city — which as its building-sacrifice claimed Abel in the pride of his youth — Cain does not name it after

---

by the dead in their lifetime. These house-urns are found both in the Villanovan culture and in North Germany (see Muchau, op. cit., pp. 241 et seq., and Schuchhardt, pp. 257 et seq.).

[1] In the abundant literature on the Romulus legend, only a single work—and that a recent one, by Kretschmer (*Glotta*, I, pp. 288 et seq.) — explains the death of Remus as a building-sacrifice. According to the legend (see Roscher's *Lexikon*), the twins resolved to found a city in the neighbourhood of the spot where their lives were saved. They then fell into a quarrel which ends with the slaying of Remus by the city-founder Romulus. According to the local tradition (as preserved in Livy), Remus was struck dead by his brother for having jumped over the half-finished walls.

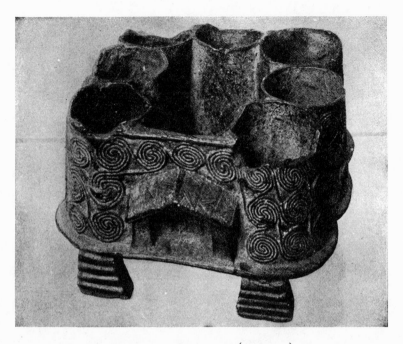

HOUSE-URN FROM MELOS (2000 B.C.)

ROMAN HOUSE-URN

himself, but after his son Enoch, in accordance with the tribal ideology of the Jewish race.[1]

Thus we find ourselves again in touch with the primary principle, already formulated, underlying all artistic creativity, and manifested ideologically in the old Oriental culture, æsthetically in Greece, and religiously in Christianity: the creation, namely, of material and spiritual values — the values of culture, art, and religion — not as an imitation of nature, but as a macrocosmization of man, pointing him towards a new spiritual reality that is created out of himself and exists only through him. The essential in this process is the roundabout path that mortal man must tread through the imperishable cosmos (the constellations) in order to create out of himself on the humanized earth immortal cultural values which survive him. To this end, however, he must sacrifice part of his actual life, his possibilities of earthly happiness, creating a spiritual cosmos analogous to the heavenly one; and thus he becomes himself a maker of worlds, but, at the same time, his own world-stuff out of which and by which he creates. This, as we shall show in the next chapter, is the meaning of all mythology — that it melts human (earthly) and heavenly (cosmic) motives into an indissoluble unity. But this betokens no more and no less than that man starts from heaven to conquer the earth — a conquest that found its most perfect expression in the Greek cultural ideology with its humanized myths. Thus, man must first be the mythic creator of the cosmos, after which he becomes the creator of everything earthly — and therefore of the human culture that finds its objective expression in art.

[1] For the interpretation of Cain, see my *Seelenglaube und Psychologie*, pp. 158 et seq.

MYTH AND METAPHOR

❧

The world is a generalized form of
the spirit, its symbolic picture.

NOVALIS

Chapter Seven

MYTH AND METAPHOR

ᔍᔪᔊ

In the last two chapters we have frequently come up against mythical traditions, which not only occupy an essential position in the general culture of peoples, but constitute an important function for the artistic productions of each period of culture. The myth lays down over earlier tradition the particular cultural stratum of the present and is thus, at least in its higher forms, the best, at times the only, source for our knowledge of that present's ideologies. The immortality-ideologies which have been discussed in previous chapters, and which lead to religious or artistic creation, find either their contemporary expression or their later interpretation in the many mythical traditions of the peoples, whether primitive or advanced to culture. These myths are all constructed on the " micro-macrocosmic " scheme, within which, however, we can establish a development from the primitive macrocosmic pattern to the more advanced, microcosmic art-forms. The peculiarity of the myth in this is that — in varying degrees, it is true — it not only presents the ideology, so to say, in theoretical form, but simultaneously interprets it, so that it appears as a forerunner of the poetic art, to which it is in any case allied by its narrative form. In the myth, however, which a people tells of its heroes or saviours the hero's creative activity appears as an activity of doing (or suffering), while the individual poet of later times finds his true creativity in the making of the story itself. But this profound difference cannot be explained only in the psychological passage from the hero to the poet, but springs from a simultaneous and parallel process which transforms the ideologically creative myth into the metaphor, and this survives into modern poetry as a decorative ornament.[1]

Let us start with a coarse macrocosmic myth of pretty high antiquity, which will lead us straight into the problem of its making. In the *Edda* we are told that the world was made from the parts of the body of the dismembered giant Ymir:

> From Ymir's flesh was the world made;
> From the legs the mountains, and the heavens from the skull
> Of the icy giant, and from his sweat the sea.
>
> VAFTHRUDISMAL

Grimm in his *Deutsche Mythologie* (IV, 464 et seq.) gives a detailed description, made up from various versions, where we have mountains as bones, rocks as teeth, heaven as skull, clouds as sweat, trees as hair, etc., and in which, side by side with the view that the gods tore the giant to pieces in order to make the world from his limbs, another account is mentioned in which the giant himself makes the world from his own limbs. This motif, which runs all through the mythology of all peoples, of doubt whether the world was created by, or out of, the gods (by men), is apparently not at all an academic question, but an essential part: in fact, as we shall see, one of the chief motifs in the construction of myths.

Another Indo-Germanic tradition of the same sort in the Vedas resolves the primary enigma by making Viraj, the first-created being, to be sacrificed by the gods, and all the parts of the world to be made from his various parts. Another Vedic tradition, preserved in a late hymn of the Rigveda, tells how the gods made the world from the dismembered body of the primitive giant Purushu: the heavens from his head, the earth from his feet, the sun from his eye, the moon from his spirit (mouth), animals and men from his fat or his legs; while the gods Indra and Agni spring from his mouth. In this story, however, as it seems to me, two different traditions are recog-

---

[1] For the relation of the poet to the hero whose heir he is, see my book: *Don Juan and the Double*, and a later chapter of this book, "The Poetic Art and its Hero."

nizable from the outset, and their separate study may perhaps carry us a first step beyond the contradictory versions. The beginning of the story — the creation of earth and heaven with its constellations — does not presuppose any dismembering, but rather represents a cosmic extension of man into the universe: the foot which touches the earth is extended to be the earth itself, the head which stretches heavenward is raised and magnified to be the heaven itself — in a term of Schopenhauer's (which incidentally contains his whole teaching), we are dealing with a " makanthropos." This interpretation, which I had deduced directly from the story, was confirmed by another version of the Creation in the Vedas themselves, in which the world grows out of the egg and the young contained within it, as a human being grows from conception till birth. When the prime being of the egg divided, the one half became the earth, the other the heavens; from that which contained the young came the mountains, from the thin membrane which held the moisture came the lightning and the clouds, from the veins the seas, from the moisture of the body the ocean. The embryo itself became the sun. This doctrine of the World-Egg, which plays so great a part [1] in the cosmology of civilized peoples, is certainly of later origin than that of violent dismemberment — which always concerns a giant, whom we have just identified as the Makanthropos. The latter therefore appears to be the original form, at least of this Indo-Germanic tradition of the Creation; and we must leave it undecided whether this breaking-up of the Makanthropos, who is already the world, into smaller microcosms reflects the fundamental growth-process of everything organic, division into smaller entities — which, for that matter, is the explanation of the creation of worlds which we ourselves adopt. A later Brahminic

---

[1] Robert Eisler's monumental work: *Weltenmantel und Himmelszelt*, treats particularly of the Orphic doctrines of the World-Egg, from which Eros also comes (pp. 416 et seq.). For the egg as cosmological idea, cf. Lukas in *Zeitschrift für Volkskunde*, IV, 227, and his *Grundbegriffe in den Kosmogonien*. Castren (*Finnische Mythen*, transl. Schiefner, p. 287) says that the myth of the egg is found not only in Finland, but in Indian, Persian, Chinese, Phœnician, and Greek myths.

doctrine, at any rate, shows this rude theory of creation transformed into a religious explanation of sacrifice, which strikes us as quite Christian. According to this, not only was the world originally created from the sacrifice of the creator, Prajapati, Lord of Creatures, but it is continually renewed to the present day by a repetition of the mystic sacrifice in the priestly ritual. Daily the body of the Creator is broken up, daily reconstituted for the renewal and maintenance of the universe, which would otherwise break up and fall in pieces. Thus the world is being ever created anew through the self-sacrifice of the God with whom the sacrificial priest identifies himself — at any rate in a symbolic ritual of animal sacrifice.

The emphasis laid in this tradition on the creative self-sacrifice of the God brings us back to the original problem. The question may remain open whether the primal creation occurred as a result of self-sacrifice or of being sacrificed and dismembered; all we need now is to emphasize that idea which is common to all these versions of creation and which we met with in the building-sacrifice — namely, that the construction of the world also, apparently, demands a living sacrifice, and later traditions, which survive right into our nursery and drawing-room games, will show that not only mythical battles and games-contests but real wars have at bottom turned on the question of who the sacrificial officiator is to be. At any rate these Indo-Germanic versions of the Creation show that we are dealing with a makanthropic phenomenon which makes man, actively or passively, into the creator of the world. These myths therefore show us not only the first, but the most gigantesque type of artist, who creates the world not so much in his own image as from out of himself. But having regard to the most primitive immortality-ideology already discussed, which makes the process of decay into one of (animal) rebirth, I should like to maintain that the sacrificing of man for the creation of the world has its origin in the same feeling of imperishableness, and that the becoming a victim, as it still survives in Christianity, is only a voluntary acceptance of this interconnexion of dying, decay, and resurrection. Naturally men try to divert this self-sacrifice on to others or to represent it as punishment; but the basic question is how men ever came to the idea, which rejects sexual generation in favour of the belief in metamorphosis and thus makes of death only a change of form. These myths too, therefore, contradict the superficial conclusion that there is immanent in man a biological creative urge that has its origin in sex. For the genital organs themselves, which are the essentials in human reproduction, have no part in the Creation; even where they are mentioned (chiefly in the cosmologies of highly developed Oriental civilizations), it is a negative happening: that is, the male reproductive organ is cut off, the god is robbed of his masculine reproductive power, he is castrated.

The relation between the mythic motive of dismemberment and the ideas of castration and rebirth I have dealt with at length in Chapter ix of my *Inzest-Motiv in Dichtung und Sage,* where I have discussed the material bearing on this and on the myth of world-parents, from the standpoint of individual psychology. In this connexion, so far as it concerns us here, it is noticeable that all myths of Creation, both individual and cosmic, show the same development which we found in the origin of house-forms. The creation is originally maternal and then gradually becomes " personal ": that is, what is first produced by the mother, whether it is an individual or a world, is later built up by the individual ego, the hero himself; only relatively late, in the period of patriarchy and patriarchal rights, is it attributed to the male reproductive principle. This process, which I have described especially in *Seelenglaube und Psychologie* and particularly in the chapter on the " Age of Sexuality," is represented to us in a decisive transitional stage in the material which I dealt with in my *Myth of the Birth of the Hero* (1909). There the hero is born of the mother, exposed by the father, and nourished and protected by the animal. These universal cultural myths thus represent the struggle of the rising father-ideology — which implies that of sexual immortality — not only with the older matrilinear organization of the family, but also with the self-creative tendencies of the individual, who, as hero, not only denies descent from the father, but attempts to make himself independent of the mother. Hence birth from the mother is replaced by birth from the water, and the mother's nurture by animal suckling — this last has probably a bearing on the significance of the animal as mother-substitute, giving nurture, warmth, and protection.

This birth of the hero from water, however, I even then was able to bring into relation with the myths which tell of the

SEPARATION OF HEAVEN FROM EARTH
(ANCIENT EGYPT)

origin of the world from water. Whether or not this macro-cosmic water-birth of the earth (Frobenius's world-pole myths of the Oceanians) can be deduced from the human fœtal condition (in water) and its birth-processes, we have certainly in the myths an identification of human and cosmic birth, a tendency to deny individual descent from parents and to associate it with the eternal birth of the cosmos. Now, there is a set of myths, assembled by Frobenius in a class as "world-parent myths,"[1] which seem to me to symbolize psychologically that stage of development in which the individual, the hero, rises

[1] *Das Zeitalter des Sonnengottes*, Vol. I (Berlin, 1904), pp. 268 et seq.

from the rôle of creature to that of creator and even self-creator. In these myths the young son forces asunder the united primal parents (not seldom when they are in sexual intercourse), so that the father moves upwards as the heavens, the mother remaining below as the earth. This conception of the heavens as father, and the earth as mother, is found all over Oceania, China, ancient India, among Semites, Greeks, and the Nordic peoples, and occurs even in America and Africa. In the last case, however, the world is represented as made not by, but out of, the parents, and as so made by the son, who thus annuls the fact of his own creation by those parents. This seems to me also to be the meaning of the incest with the mother which takes place in some of these "world-parent" myths, following on the separation of father and mother. The son thus begets himself from the mother as his own father, and he is thus assured in this rebirth of the heroic immortality.

However that may be, these parent myths can in any case have only arisen at a comparatively late stage of culture, for they presuppose not merely knowledge of the father's place in pro-creation, but the acceptance of this in the social immortality-ideology (see *Seelenglaube und Psychologie*). Consequently, too, the earliest imaginings of the world-picture, as F. Borck[1] has collected them, are free of these incestuous family compli-cations. The primal form of the world-picture is thought by Borck to be that which rises direct from the observation of the three kingdoms of earth, air, and water, as·we find them concretized in Mesopotamia in the divine Triad of the Sume-rians. The second he takes to be that of the four points of the compass, according to which earth and heaven are divided into four, an idea which, in conjunction with that of the four phases of the moon, leads to the conception of the primal god. Finally, man's earth comes more and more to take the form of a fifth part; in Borck's view the idea of a mountain of God on earth also belongs with this type. The increasing importance of the earth as the dwelling-place of man, he considers, explains the

[1] *Die Geschichte des Weltbildes* (*Ex Oriente Lux*, III, *Heft* 2–5), Leipzig, 1930.

origin of the air as sixth and that of the underworld as seventh
world, though he admits that "the formal system of the Sumerian world-picture, with its insistence on the seven — the idea
of the seven worlds — had much to do with it" (op. cit., p. 5).
On the other hand, we have seen that the sevenfold division
of the Oriental picture of the heavens is closely connected with,
if not directly dependent on, the spinal column of man (and
of the higher animals, for that matter). In any case, whatever
may have been the original picture, we are only concerned,
in this account of the genesis of human creative impulse, with
the connexion of the microcosmic and human elements that
Borck does not touch upon.

The liberation of the creative individual, of the hero, from
the paternal relation, as we saw it expressed in the myths of
the world-parents, has perhaps its original, and certainly its
clear, antithesis in a series of myths which have as their subject the liberation of the hero from his maternal origins. The
classical example of these is the "whale myths," which Frobenius collected, chiefly in Oceania, but which have also pene-
trated from the old Oriental cultures into Greek mythology,
the latter being here as in general the point of assembly and
junction of all mythological ideas, and for a good reason, since
Greek culture fulfils the process of the heroic liberation of the
individual in the climax of self-creation, from which subsequently Christianity was to be the reaction. The swallowing
myths themselves, of which we may take the biblical story of
Jonah as the type, have in outline the following form: The
hero, whether as boy or as adult, is swallowed (often along
with his mother, brothers, etc.) by a vast monster. Within its
belly he floats for some time on the sea; then (in many versions) he cuts off the heart of the fish to still his hunger, lights
a fire in its inside, until he is finally spewed up on land by
the monster or makes his own way out by ripping open its
belly. Against the solar interpretation of Frobenius — the rising
and setting of the sun — I adduced at the time the obvious
birth-symbolism, which for every impartial student is beyond

challenge.[1] But in the present connexion I wish rather to indicate the *motive* which led men to put, whether it be the birth-
process or the course of the sun, into mythical symbols. Now,
one of the motives disclosed by the tradition we recognize
clearly as the self-creative tendency of the individual, which
expresses itself in the ripping-up of the mother's womb and
the heroic form of birth. This tendency would also then explain the fusion of microcosmic and macrocosmic symbols,
whereby the individual would be raised above the ordinary
course of biological birth and assimilated to the ever-recurring
heavenly bodies. In this sense the period in the whale's belly
represents also the period in the underworld, whither the sun
descends every day, to be reborn again the next morning. Here,
then, as everywhere in the self-creative tendency of the individual, we find the immortality-ideology which appears in mythic
form as rebirth of the self (incest) and artistically as eternalization of the self (in the work).

In the "swallowing" myths of civilized peoples which have
been studied by Hans Schmidt (*Jona*, 1907) we find the victory over the monster as a typically heroic action, and the first
and essential deed of the hero is just this liberation from the
parents that constitutes the birth of the self. It is true that,
in the fashion typical of legend, the deed is set in relation with
the wooing of a maiden, which at this stage replaces the primal
wooing of the mother. Thus Heracles, according to the older
tradition in Lycophron, wins Hesione by leaping down the
throat of a shark, and remains three days in the inside of the
monster until he cuts off its liver from within.[2] Perseus also,
according to Lycophron, is swallowed by a sea-monster and
kills it by way of the liver, which is regarded as the seat of life.
A link between this tradition and the cosmic dismemberment-
myths from which we started is found in the Babylonian
Creation myth, the Story of the Seven Tablets (*Enuma elis*,

[1] *Myth of the Birth of the Hero*, English translation, New York, 1914.
[2] In the still older version of Hellanicus of Mytilene (second half of the fifth century,
B.C.) Heracles descended into the bowels of the monster and destroyed its entrails (cf.
Welcker: *Alte Denkmäler*, III, 378).

c. 2000 B.C.), which tells of the creation of the world by the youngest god, Marduk, out of Tiamat, who is conceived as the primal sea. Tiamat, who had risen against the gods, could only be overcome by the youngest god, who was to cut and destroy her inner being, the heart, with his spear — that is, he had to destroy her life, whereas her body, under the orders of the gods, he cut in two, making the one part thereof into the heavens, and the other into the ocean.

In this old tradition the universe arises from the body of the primal mother, not, as in the world-parent myths, from the primal pair, nor, as in the mutilation myths, from the parts of the body of the individual, either as giant or as god. There is a further difference in the emphasis on the preliminary death which is prerequisite for the creation of the world out of the (dead) body. Now, whether we regard Tiamat macrocosmically as primal matter (Tia-mat, primal water) or microcosmically as mother (-body), the Babylonian myth certainly tells of the conquest of this prime-symbol by the creative god, who later, in the Bible, brings the earth, and all that therein is, to being by his mere word. Perhaps the only biblical exception to this creation by the word — which appeals to us as the first poet would appeal — is the Genesis story of the creation of man by God according to his own image; but we are not at once told how, for the origin of man from the earth is only affirmed later on his expulsion from Paradise under a curse. Now, the latter has obviously a death-significance, and it is only secondarily that it seems to be transferred back to man's origin. The creation of woman from the rib of man is, however, as I have shown elsewhere,[1] so barefaced an attempt to remodel the genuine content in the sense of the masculine world-picture that it can hardly be called creative; the less so as God still appears as the creator, and man is condemned to be mortal creature. For in the making of the human being (the man) from earth there persists still, it seems, the original de-

---

[1] *Völkerpsychologische Parallelen zu den infantilen Sexualtheorien* (1912); republished in *Psychoanalytische Beiträge zur Mythenforschung*, second edition (1922).

scent from the mother;[1] only, we have before us the antithesis
to the mythic creation of the earth from man. Later traditions,
arising under Christian influence, then carried this parallelism
all through and made the first man appear as a complete inversion of the first creation of the world. In mediæval legends
Adam, the first man, is formed of seven substances: the body
from the earth, the bones of stone, the blood of water, the hair
of grass, the eyes from the sun, the breath from the wind, the
thoughts from the clouds.[2] This path which man has trodden
— passing from the world made out of the body, via man made
from the earth (Adam), to the Christ born of the spirit — includes the birth of the artist as well. He appears first as sculptor
of the world, making the universe macrocosmically from
himself; then in due course from this actual " making "
on the basis of partition and magnifying, there springs a
symbolic creation of form on the basis of the killing of what
is living (Tiamat); and this leads finally to the pure poetic
form in which a world is born from nothingness by the
Word.

But the biblical creative force of the word has its origin, as
we know today, in the magical significance of the Word, which
has preserved for us along with the creative also the dangerous
aspect of word-magic, as it survives even today in our curses.
Thus the name of God may not be taken in vain by the Jews;
in fact he has no real name at all, being called the Almighty,
the Lord. But he reveals himself to his people in a far higher
degree through the Word than ever did his Oriental predecessors, who still spoke in symbolic signs which the priest had to

[1] The creation of man is also brought into relation with the earth by many primitive
peoples, probably because of the same principle of inversion, according to which man
must rise again thence whither he goes in death. (The material is in Chantepie: *Lehr-
buch der Religions-geschichte*, I, third edition, pp. 36 et seq., and in Ehrenreich: *Mythen
und Legenden der südamerikanischen Völker*, p. 33.)

[2] See R. Köhler: *Kleine Schriften*, II, pp. 1 et seq.; also a text published by E. Barsov
(1886) of a sixteenth-century manuscript. (V. Jagić: "*Slavische Beiträge zu den biblischen
Apokryphen*, I: *Die altkirchenslavischen Texte des Adambuchs.*" *Denkschriften der kaiserlichen
Akademie der Wissenschaften*, Vienna, 1893). In Hastings's *Encyclopædia of Religion and
Ethics*, Vol. I, p. 86, there is among other things a reference to the Book of the Secrets
of Enoch (xxx, 8, et seq.), according to which Adam is made of seven substances.

interpret. The Word of the Semitic god admits of no doubt; it is revealed not as a hint from heaven which may be interpreted anyhow, but as a law, all interpretation of which was originally forbidden, and the knowledge of which was kept secret like primitive word-magic. The Jews, however, were not only forbidden to take the name of God in vain, but also to make any images of him, which explains the absence of all pictorial art as well as their unalterable faith in the spoken word of the Law. They have, moreover, no cultural material, as other peoples have, and this not so much because they had no land or home — for, after all, they had one, and lost it, in Canaan — but because the creative word is incapable of direct cultural development otherwise than in the direction of spiritualization with its climax in Christianity. If we add to the biblical significance of creative word-magic the doctrine of the Pneuma and the Logos as worked out by later Hellenistic philosophers, we obtain the spirit of Christianity; though its greatness lies not so much in this spiritualization (which really brings it back close to the animistic idea of the soul) as in its humanization, from which, indeed, even rebirth is possible for the modern individual. Only, in the struggles of the Middle Ages the Church, which had already won its temporal power, ranges itself on the side of the spiritual, while at the same time in its myth and legend it lays the emphasis on the human. If in the Old Testament it is still the breath which gives man life, in Christianity the spirit of man is already a soul; the Logos, which in the Bible only creates the rest of the world, here creates the soul also. In the Old Testament God becomes mouth — in the New, spirit.

The reason why man also is spiritualized in the New Testament lies in the fact that the Word not merely possesses a stronger creative force — the Lord makes macro- and microcosmos by it alone — but the spirit manifested in the Word makes something that is permanent, as the Word itself is permanent. The world, made of organic material, may one day die, just as its mythical creator, the hero, dies; while what the spirit

forms through the Word, or the Logos, is permanent and immortal. Hence Christianity extends the Logos-creation to man,
who in the Old Testament is the one and only created thing that
is mortal. The rude artisan's making of the world, whether from
the body of the mother or from his own body of the divinized
(magnified) ego, represents indeed only the primitive stage
preceding generation by the Word or creation from the spirit.
At the root of both, however, the fashioning out of material
and the creating from the spirit, is the primal creative urge
of the individual to raise himself from creature to creator. The
course of development from action to speech and thence to
pure thinking includes always, even though the magical character adheres still to its method, an ever-increasing emphasis
on the purely intellectual. This development is paralleled in the
bodily symbols by the rise from the inner being, the entrails,
via the neck and throat [1] — the voice — to the head, in the same
way as we have seen in the growth of architecture.[2] Hence the
inner parts, together with the sex-organs, which are internal,
at least in woman, and in any case belong to the lower body,
play no part in the creation of the world: in fact, in the Tiamat
myth and the corresponding hero-stories the inner organs, the
liver, the entrails, etc., are violently removed before the creation can begin or the hero can make the maiden his own. The
reason might be (and probably in later times the actual interpretation was) an æsthetic one; but in my belief this differentiation of kernel and envelope (which may possibly have
its influence even on fashions) is one more link with the immortality-belief. The original seat of life, and consequently that
of the later soul, was originally localized in the lower body
— the liver, the midriff, kidneys, and only later on in the heart.

[1] From the seven-graded tower of the neck, according to an old physiological Logos
doctrine (found also in the Old Testament) emerges the Pneuma of the Logos, the
voice, which, according to Hebrew and Greek ideas, is organized into the seven stages
of the vowels and the seven tones of the diatonic scale (E. Hommel).

[2] The same development is found in the vase, which is differently formed (or artistically adorned) according to the stage of culture; at first a symbol for the womb (as I
showed in *The Trauma of Birth* on the basis of the material collected by Fuhrmann), it
finally becomes a vase (the head) with neck, ears, mouth, etc.

In the creation of the world from the external parts of the body, the intention was perhaps to make it participate in the immortality of the internal by its assimilation to, or extension into, the cosmic. Here we meet with the same uncertainty as to the real seat of the immortal in man: the same underlying reason for the changes in burial customs also determines the changes in the localization of the soul. Thus, gradually, the seat of life in the lower part of the body was dissociated from the seat of the soul, which had once been united with it in a single organ of the lower body,[1] but finally became established in the head. The lower "mouth" of the woman, which "makes" man materially, becomes finally identified with the upper mouth of man from which streams his speech, the Logos, taking artistic form in the word.

The word, then, is also artistic material out of which intellectual man can create freely, and consequently the art of words is the culmination of artistic creation. The power of the Bible's language shows itself, both in point of monumental content (absorbing into itself the whole of the higher Oriental cultures) and in point of formal significance, to be its very essence. I mean, the Bible does not merely depict the creation of the world and birth of man, but, through its expressive power, actually represents it: that is to say it *is* a world-creation in words, and in this fact lies its incomparable literary glory. If we pass from this primal poetic creation to another mighty artist in language, the singer of the Homeric poems, we notice the difference at once: the Bible actually creates the world in words, Homer merely depicts that world; I say "merely" in regard to the spirit of the poetry, and not to the quality of the language, for Homer's language is in its way unique, like that of the Bible. Before commenting on Homer's language, let us note the essential character of his poetry, which finds its natural expression in its language. The Bible is wholly dominated by the creative God, who effects all doing and happening in the universe and on earth by his word, but in the Homeric

[1] *Seelenglaube und Psychologie,* last chapter, "*Natur und Geist*," p. 188.

world, which is neither created by the gods nor even really
governed by them, it is human passions which control events
on earth: the "wrath of Achilles," which the Iliad's first word
— μῆνις — sets up as its motive, and Odysseus' delight in
adventure, which keeps him all those years from home, although he must needs make the ill will of the gods responsible
for this.

It is well known that the peculiar mark of Homeric language is the simile, whose diminutive we still recognize in the
"ornamental" adjective.[1] In explaining this, even so deep a
study as that of Karl Meister[2] gets no further than showing
that these adjectives do not represent drawled phrases or poetic
padding, but are evidence of the archaistic quality of epic
poetry, which often writes itself on the poet's behalf. "Something of the splendour and glory of early days lay even in the
form of language, just as the bronze shields and chariots
were retained by the poetry of an age of iron and riding" (p.
244). But this penetration of earlier language and cultural
properties into the Homeric world, which the poet expresses
with this antiquated language, has remained characteristic of
this stage of poetry, and is thus not part of the epic form as
such. "How far," says Meister, "do the typical adjectives in
the *Mahabharata,* the Æneid, the *Nibelungenlied* fall short of
the vividness of Homer!" But the true quality of Homeric
language is to be found in the famous similes, which are not
only picturesque but at times literally plastic. I should therefore like to call them, in contrast to other forms of metaphor
to be discussed later, *spatial* metaphors, since they rise above
the merely visual to the solid. In other words, in the epic art-
language of Homer the original creative power of the word
survives not so much in the contriving of an artistic actuality
as in the *revitalization* of a lost reality, which finds expression
even in the content, in that it clings to superseded cultural

[1] For the nature of these epithets, of which the commonest (in European poetry at
any rate) is the adjective, see E. Elster: *Literaturformen,* II (Halle, 1911), pp. 160 et seq.
[2] *Die homerische Kunstsprache* (Leipzig, 1921).

forms. To make this peculiar quality of Homer's metaphor still clearer, let us mark the quality of his most direct modern antithesis, as found in the master of modern metaphor, Marcel Proust. In contrast to Homer's spatial metaphor Proust's is temporal; that is, it attempts, by the temporal association of the present with the past, to restore the latter to life, just as Homer puts it in living form before us by means of plastic presentation. The two kinds of metaphor are, however, distinct from each other in the same way as space and time are conceptually and factually distinct. Space is a concrete idea, time an abstract, and thus Homer's metaphor is plastic, Proust's intellectualist. In fact, the temporal quality of Proust's metaphor is typical not only of his famous similes but of his whole work, which one might take as a single gigantic metaphor (*Le Temps retrouvé*).[1] But in Proust the intellectualist outlook — which is almost a self-evident necessity in the modern poet — proves that at bottom it is a matter of ideas of death and the fear of death, of will to maintain the actual life-process in himself, rather than of a will to reconquer the past, which could only come out as a neurotic expression thereof.

This fact, characteristic of Proust's metaphors, that they dominate not only his language but his whole work, is probably true of Homer too, and quite emphatically so of Shakspere, whose metaphors, in contrast to those of the others, I would call *dynamic*. And this is not a consequence of his dramatic form; on the contrary, it was probably the dynamic quality of his metaphor which forced him to the drama. Shakspere's metaphors are distinguished from the other two by the fact that they do not associate the past and the present, either spatially or temporally, but pile them up, tumbling over each other, to such an extent that there is at times an impression almost of bombast. More than this, his whole work reflects a

[1] Arnaud Dandieu's admirable work, *Marcel Proust, sa révélation psychologique* (Paris, 1930), has given me valuable suggestions for this discussion of metaphor, though it had already been influenced by Heinz Werner's comprehensive study: *Ursprünge der Metapher* (Leipzig, 1919); the latter established, indeed, a change of meaning from primitive to modern metaphor, but only a change in point of content.

dynamic metaphor both in its dramatic form and even in the individual characters, which appear frequently as personified metaphors: thus Othello is unrestrainedly jealous *like* a primitive; Shylock inhumanly avaricious *like* the devil of gold himself. As I was able to show by the example of the Shylock figure alone, this simile method of representation corresponds to an original identity: Shylock really does incorporate the devil of gold as Hamlet does the old immortality-belief. And so dynamic metaphor, too, though in yet another way, achieves the representation of an old lost ideology, which survives (as it were, *incognito*) under the cover of the metaphor, but lives with its old creative vigour entire. As the Word, then, in its original magical significance (which, even in the Bible, still leads to actual creation) is capable of working miracles, so the genuine poetic art, as we find it in epic, dramatic, and lyric form, has replaced the old power of creation through its capacity to revivify in metaphor the lost past of the individual or of the people, by associating it with the present by means of the art of language and of metaphor. Thus the primal creation by the word is replaced by a re-engendering of the past not only as to content but also as to form — namely, in metaphor.

Looking at the unconscious creativity in the poet, Carl du Prel has proved this point notably for lyric poetry; and he finds under the individual unconscious a palæontological stage, of the nature-observation and nature-quickening, which he pursues to the threshold of the mythic.[1] In this process, which du Prel, particularly in lyric, follows out from primitive contemplation through Classical art to modern poetry, the chief part is played by the transference of bodily attitudes, gestures, and affections to other subjects, animate or inanimate. The poet not only may speak of the " backbone " of mountains, the " bosom " of the sea, the " tongue " of a glacier, the " head " of a rock, the " jaws " of hell, but may compare the boughs of a tree to arms, a summit to the crown of the head. All these

[1] *Psychologie der Lyrik. Beiträge zur Analyse der dichterischen Phantasie* (Leipzig, 1880).

metaphors depend on the micro- macrocosmic relation which
leads at one time to the humanizing of the world, and at another to the enlarging of man to the proportions of the world.
This process of creative heightening which underlies all metaphor we find preserved in the old anatomical terms, some of
which have survived into our own medical language. E. Hommel has devoted a very instructive article [1] to this, in which
he studies the history of anatomy as from the standpoint of
the ancient East and its premisses. He finds that our own
anatomical nomenclature is built up on the Eastern system of
anatomical cosmology or topography, which mythologically
interprets the various points or organs of man (and of animals)
as those of a microcosm. We have already mentioned Atlas,
who holds up the vault of the skull, and the gums regarded
as the roof of heaven (*palatum*), and the seven vertebræ of the
neck-column as the seven heavens. We have dealt in detail with
the navel as mid point of the earth, and with the liver as the
centre of human life and therefore as the macrocosmic mirror
of world-happenings. We will add the example, already incidentally mentioned, of the Greek meaning of "æon" as the
spinal marrow, on the silver thread of which, according to
ancient Jewish exegesis, the life of man, his æon, depends;
and we may allude also to the conception of the dark courses
of the os Petrosum as a labyrinth. The description of the external elevation of the female pudenda as "mons Veneris" is
part of the same idea, as is the name of the "Adam's apple" of
the throat.[2]

Hommel's exposition limits itself to the names of the organs
of mouth and neck and refers only incidentally to the wider
relationships which force themselves on our attention and with
which we have already dealt in relation to the artist's creative
impulse. In the anatomical section of Plato's *Timæus,* the head
with its organs is compared to a royal castle, the breast with the

[1] *Archiv für Geschichte der Medizin, Bd.* II (1919).
[2] The solar plexus, the nerve-system called the "web of the sun," to which already
Greek intuition removed the seat of the soul, has recently celebrated a resurrection in
Carl Ludwig Schleich's theory of the Sympathetic.

heart and other organs to the retainers' quarters, which are
separated by the midriff from the belly — from which, as
symbol of the earth, the water springs, as in Babylonian stories.[1]
The cabbalistic work *Zohar* carries this further and compares
parts of the temple with parts of the body — a system originating in Babylon (where it was used for augural and later for
astrological purposes); even in distant Mexico or New Zealand,
to take another example, we find the relation of the parts of
the body to the signs of the day employed for similar purposes
(Fuhrmann: *Mexiko*, I, 25).

All these originally very real and vital relations, which decisively influenced the fortunes, not only of men, but of whole
lands and peoples, we find later reduced to the level of metaphors — as, for instance, in Shakspere's famous comparisons of
the state to a human organism in *Coriolanus*, I, i, and also
Julius Cæsar, II, i. This, taken from tradition,[2] as the poet himself indicates ("it may be you have heard it"), may stand for
almost the whole development, as we have described it from the
cultural-historical point of view. In Shakspere the various parts
of the body begin to rebel against the belly, reproaching it
with its idleness, since it calmly occupies the centre of the body
and obtains plentiful nourishment. Sight and hearing, intellect
and feelings, particularly — that is, the higher faculties (of the
head) — complain of the work they have to perform for it:

> The kingly-crowned head, the vigilant eye,
> The counsellor heart, the arm our soldier,
> Our steed the leg, the tongue our trumpeter,
> With other muniments and petty helps
> In this our fabric, if that they —
>   What then? . . .
> Should by the cormorant belly be restrain'd,
> Who is the sink o' the body.

[1] Kuchler: *Beiträge zur Kenntnis der Assyrisch-Babylonischen Medizin* (Leipzig, 1904).
[2] Already in the language of Paul, early Christianity spiritualizes this old picture of
the body of the state; the saints united in the kingdom of God form a body whose
members are the individual believers and whose head is Christ.

And the answer of the belly, which asserts with emphasis its value as the centre that supplies the whole bodily economy with its nourishment — while it retains for itself only the crumbs — is here for good reasons opposed to the demands of the higher self. But the further application of the comparison introduces a further element in macrocosmically symbolizing the Roman state, the Senate being compared to the belly, and Menenius Agrippa, together with the citizens to whom he tells the story, to the mute parts of the body dependent on the belly (Menenius apostrophizes one of the citizens as the big toe).

This primeval microcosmic symbolism, sunk here to the level of a simile, was once in the ancient world-view truly alive, and it not only contributed to the forming of myths but (as we shall show in the next chapter) decisively influenced the formation of language. Between that and its highest artistic development in metaphor lies the period of the myth, which itself developed as one gigantic metaphor from language. Therefore, before we pass to speech-creation and its artistic significance, let us cast a glance at speech-formation, as we find it anthropomorphized and reflected in the myth. The tendency to transfer particular parts of the body to surrounding nature is found richly evidenced in all languages, even in those of highly civilized peoples.[1] Thus, the Assyrians spoke of the nose or crown of a tree, the mouth of a door, a tongue of fire, the rib of a ship, the arm of a river (its edge or bank) and its head — *caput aquæ* = source.[2] But the characteristic development among higher languages beyond the primitive seems to me to lie not only in the formation of independent abstract ideas out of these anthropomorphic comparisons, but also in the micro- macrocosmic world-picture which is peculiar

[1] Morel: *De vocalibus partium corporis in lingua græca metaphorice dictis* (diss., Geneva, 1875), and, generally, Knortz: *Der menschliche Körper in Sage und Sprichwort* (Würzburg, 1909).

[2] This does not apply to animals. In plants the transference of animal names seems preferred: stork's bill, dog's tongue, etc. See Hunger: *Babyl. Tieromina* (Berlin, 1909; p. 150), and Dragendorff: *Heilpflanzen* (Stuttgart, 1898; p. 1).

to them. It is only by the macrocosmization of the human body through the naming of its parts that myth came out of language. In other words, the myths which deal with the creation of the world out of the human body are really speech-myths which represent man's conquest (that is, his creation) of the world by naming the objects (that is, by metaphorically expressing them through speech). This creative power of language, which does not merely "tell" the myths, but forms them physioplastically, will be dealt with in the next chapter. Let us return now to the basis of the whole process in the formation of language.

This is the fact, established by philologists, that the "names of parts of the body are, along with the numbers, the best-preserved branch of a vocabulary."[1] The names of the most important parts of the body, inner as well as outer, go back in most cases to the oldest times; they seem, according to Dietrich,[2] to belong to the time of undifferentiation. Harri Holma in his fundamental work on the names of the parts of the body in Assyrian and Babylonian (Leipzig, 1911) explains this primeval phenomenon of language as follows: "After all, his own body is man's first field of experiment in his efforts to solve the problem of the ego and to discover its relation to the surrounding world." In any case the "anatomical" articulation of the external bodily parts occurred very early; and the Babylonian cuneiform inscriptions leave no doubt that they "were possessed of a relatively abundant though in many respects incomplete anatomical knowledge." We are astonished at the extent of their knowledge, especially when we remember that dissection was forbidden on religious grounds and was first introduced only by the Greek doctors, and that until then all knowledge of the internal organs depended on observations on the battle-field, or those made during sacrifices and over certain burial rites. Yet it is significant that there was originally no distinction between the nomenclature of the body in man and

[1] Hirt: *Indogermanen*, I, p. 304.
[2] *Abhandlungen für semit. Wortforschung* (Leipzig, 1884).

in the animals.[1] Thus the resemblance of the human and animal structures must have been noticed very early — after all, the seven vertebræ are the same in all domestic animals as in man — though, on the other hand, motives derived from the world-outlook — for example, the notion of the identity of man and animal — may have played the decisive part.[2]

Apart from this, the Assyrian language shows, according to Holma, essentially the same character of striving after concreteness as Lévy-Bruhl has established in the primitive. Most Assyrian and, in general, Semitic prepositions are really names of concrete things in the genitive case, particularly of parts of the body: for example, Assyrian for " relax " is " let (the arm) down," and " frightened " is " weak in the knee." [3] It is this tendency towards the concrete and objective, moreover, that accounts in art for the localizing of psychological emotions and feelings in various parts of the body. Thus the ear was the seat of the will and of attention (also wisdom), the heart the seat of understanding; the liver, the central organ of life, was the seat of feeling and anger, the stomach the seat of wisdom, and the nose of pride (cf. " turning up your nose ").[4] From the egocentric application of words, originally expressing parts of the body, to describe a prepositional relation, there later developed separate concepts for that purpose. Thus Assyrian *qablu,* the waist, the middle of the body, developed into a preposition " *qabal*," " in the midst of," and finally to the idea

[1] Schrader: *Reallexicon der indogermanischen Altertumskunde* (1901), p. 469.

[2] Another peculiarity — of primitive languages as well — is that originally the parts of particular animals had special names according to the context (sacrifice, hunting, domestic), and that these have survived in the anatomical language of the hunt (Hirt: *Indogermanen;* Strassburg, 1905). The same thing is to be seen at the ethical level of Persian dualism, which looks at all being and happening under the aspect of the struggle of Ormuzd and Ahriman and gives different names to the same things according as they are good or bad in a religious sense. The head and hand of the good have a different name from the skull and the claw of the bad. See E. Cassierer: *Die Begriffsform im mythischen Denken* (1922), p. 52.

[3] The still more decided tendency of the Egyptians to similar paraphrases has been emphasized by Ebers (*Die Körperteile, ihre Bedeutung und Namen in Ägypten;* Munich, 1897). Further references: Pauli: *Die Benennung der Körperteile bei den Indogermanen* (Stettin, 1867); W. D. Baskett: *Parts of the Body in Later Germanic Dialects* (Chicago University Press).

[4] We shall discuss later similar ideas in Homer.

of " middle "; " *isdu*," which is the leg, became the preposition
" *idi*," next to (the side of the body), and the notion of " basis "
is expressed in " root " (compare our " foot " of the mountain).
There is a further cultural function of language in the well-
known fact that the oldest measures which still survive are not
only named after parts of the body but taken from them.
Already in Assyrian we have the ell (*ammatu*), the hand-
breadth (*qatu*), and the inch or finger (*ubanu*).[1] Very early,
therefore, man became the measure of all things; but it was
only through the macrocosmization of the idea, which made
man a reflection of the cosmos, that the units of measure in a
man's body came to be supposed to exist in the heavens also, as
in Babylonia.[2] Counting as well as measuring originated in
the parts of the body, but since counting presupposes the notion of plurality, we must begin by familiarizing ourselves
with its expression in language.

Another peculiarity of primitive language, also due to the
urge for concrete specification, has been seen in the fact that
these languages do not possess our general plural, but always
try to express a definite plural. Hence the use of the dual and
" trial " or even " quatrial," which are less grammatical numbers than plurals with definite numbers attached to each. I
think it not improbable that this definite statement of plurality
is connected with the parts of the body, especially of the pairs,
which absolutely demand the dual. At least this is so in the
stages of more advanced differentiation, for originally similar
pairs were not distinguished, as the sole of the foot and the flat
of the hand, or the cheeks from the buttocks.[3] In any case
the dual, trial, and plural formation is closely related to nu-
merical counting, which, according to the usual idea, begins,
like measurement, with the human body. Since most primitive

[1] R. Lepsius: *Die Längenmasse der Alten* (Berlin, 1884).
[2] The measurement of time likewise arose out of counting in human terms (Fuhrmann: *New Guinea*, p. 15), and to this day we have kept to such names of clock-parts as
"face," "hands."
[3] Holma says this dates from a time when no distinction was made between four-
footed animals and men.

peoples still count with the parts of their body, it is clear that
these must first have had a name themselves. It is universally
assumed that the first system of counting was that of the five
fingers — to which the toes were later added in the case of
larger numbers; and, as a matter of fact, the five or ten or
twenty system is still widespread among old culture-peoples.
But by its side the two or four system plays an important part,
especially among the Indians; and this Lévy-Bruhl is disposed
to relate to the four directions of the wind. I myself should be
disposed to believe that here, too, the significance of the pairs
of organs — their upper and lower or front and rear duplication — was the decisive influence.[1]

In fact, I should think it possible that the whole orientation
of man in the world is connected with the two sides of the body
(front and back), which still have an important place in all
cosmologies: for instance, the earth-goddess on her back, and
the god of heaven bowed over her. My purpose here, at any
rate, is to emphasize the fact that higher cultural development
goes *pari passu* with the higher development of language, and,
more, that the self-creative development of language seems to
be a precondition of higher culture. One of the first and most
essential steps of this higher development of language is the
macrocosmization of the (already named) parts of the body
— that is, their transference not only to the surrounding objects
of nature among which man lives and with which he comes
in contact, but also to the heavens and the universe, the linguistic identification being accompanied by a psychic one,
tending to assimilate man to the cosmic immortality. Primitive
man, as totemism in particular teaches us, remained at a
materialistic level of personal immortality, which was symbolized, as our earlier study has shown, in the animal. In the higher
cultures men have to use their growing knowledge of anatomy,
etc., to get away from this now intolerable idea and seek a new,
super-terrestrial, macrocosmic immortality. But for this language was the precondition — since the names of the parts of

[1] For the meaning of the "mystic" numbers, see below.

the body were to be transferred to the world — and this macro-cosmic extension of language was subsequently justified, proved, and, so to say, made true by the creation of myths. In this sense the creation-myths we have discussed, especially the rise of the world from the members of a giant or demigod, are only grand linguistic metaphors for this projection of the parts of the body on to the whole universe.

THE FORMATION AND THE CREATION OF SPEECH

In the beginning was the word, and the word was God.

JOHN i, 3

Chapter Eight

THE FORMATION AND THE CREATION OF SPEECH

༄༅

In order to understand the essential quality of the poet and the poetic art, we have to take account of the material in which the artist works far more than we need to do in the case of the arts of plastic and picture. For this material, language, is itself a purely human creation, which had a birth and development of its own before it was used in poetry; and this we can only understand as a creative process. Although we need not enter in detail into the problem of the birth of language, to solve which attempts have been made from the most varied angles of approach,[1] we must — at least so far as lies within the framework of our investigations into the creative impulse of man — try to throw some light on this speech-creative power and on the *significance* of expression in word in the history of culture. In one point modern research is more or less unanimous: that the most vital elements in our culture — the making of fire, agriculture, domestication of animals, measurement of time, observation of the stars — originate in the satisfaction not of practical, but of religious, supersensible, and ideological needs. The same seems to be true of language, as to which recent study more and more rejects the obvious theory that it arose in the need to make oneself understood. But here, as so frequently elsewhere, the deeper understanding of cultural significance comes, not out of the narrower sphere of language-

[1] For a general survey, see Fritz Specht: *Die Sprache und ihr Ursprung* (Berlin, 1921) and the more recent *Human Speech*, by Sir R. Paget (New York, 1930).

study and from the professional philologist, but from border-lands and borderland-study: in this case from mythology and epistemology. There are two works in particular which were valuable in our discussion of metaphor and are equally so for the mythical significance of language: Fritz Mauthner's *Beiträge zu einer Kritik der Sprache*[1] and Ernst Böcklen's *Die Entstehung der Sprache im Lichte des Mythos.* A third work, by Ernst Vossler, which deals with the creation and development of speech (*Sprachschöpfung und Entwicklung;* Heidelberg, 1903), we shall return to when we have dealt adequately with its mythic character.

For what interests us most to begin with is that two works that start from such opposite standpoints as those of Mauthner and Böcklen should be in such surprising agreement in conceiving not only of the word as a mythic form, but of language itself, even the whole formation of language, as one vast metaphorical comprehension of the world. Before summarizing the views of the two authors on this, we must make it clear that we have nothing to do with the special intention and purpose of either work — the one (Mauthner's) setting out to show that language is inefficient as an epistomological instrument, since its essence is mythological and not logical, and the other (Böcklen's) to prove from language that all myth originates in the moon, which is of less importance to us than his successful proof of the mythic character of language in general, which found truly pristine expression in myth. To this mythological character of language belongs the personifying tendency, of course, but also the metaphorical. As Mauthner says (II, 450), this grew out of human thought alone and still grows only "through the transference ($\mu\epsilon\tau\alpha\phi\acute{\epsilon}\rho\epsilon\iota\nu$) of a completed word to an incomplete impression — that is, through comparison, through the eternal *à-peu-près,* the eternal paraphrasing and verbal picturing, which constitutes at once the artistic power and the logical weakness

[1] Three volumes: I, *Zur Sprache und Psychologie;* II, *Sprachwissenschaft;* III, *Zur Grammatik und Logik* (Stuttgart, 1901 onwards). Incidentally I would refer in this context to the suggestive work of R. Kleinpaul, although it has been criticized as unacademic (especially: *Volkspsychologie. Das Seelenleben im Spiegel der Sprache;* Berlin, 1914).

of language. The two or the hundred meanings of a word or a concept are so many metaphors or pictures, and since there is not a single word of which we know the original meaning, no word has any but a metaphorical meaning." Mauthner then shows how throughly we are broken in to this habit in that we never see anything wrong in " figuratively applying mutually antagonistic words, drawn from almost opposite spheres," to our most essential ideas, as, for instance, "when we describe time with spatial expressions (for example, long and short), or a musical tone by spatial or colour ideas." But he goes further and argues that metaphor, which is the means of language-growth, may perhaps have been its actual source, in the sense that metaphor may once have linked concepts of time and space on the one side to notions of sound on the other, just as nowadays it links actual experiences. " If we are in a foreign country and, not knowing its language, want to express bigness, we shall open our arm wide; if the opposite, we shall press the palms of the hands together. Now suppose the whole vocal apparatus desired to share in the gesture; suppose the glottis and the mouth pressed themselves together to articulate an ' i ' in imitation of a small space, or opened wide into an ' o ' to imitate a big one. May we not say that, even at that stage, there is metaphor? And what if, then, the sound were transferred from space to time, to colour, and so on ? "

Böcklen too, like many other investigators, believes that language was originally of gesture and therefore soundless, and further that an imitative activity led to the genesis of language; but he differs from all other students in his assumption that the object first imitated was the moon. Although he adduces a mass of material not only for the relation of moon and mouth (*Mond-Mund,* the moon-face), but for the extensive influence of moon-mythology generally, the impression we get from him is not so much that we are in the presence of inclusive and conclusive work as that these are studies preliminary to deeper research. Be that as it may, we do find, in the formation of language as hitherto in every creative act, the element of imitation being used for explanation, and certainly this fact does make some points intelligible, at least in regard to a particular stage of development. Hence, for example, the onomatopoetic theory, whose founder, Herder, tried to explain language as originally the imitation of sounds. The names of animals are usually adduced as evidence one way or the other in this connexion. Actually there are, on the whole, very few onomatopoetic animal names such as cuckoo; dogs are not named bow-wows nor sheep baa-baas; and occasional support, such as the fact that a cat in Chinese really is "*miuh,*" a goat in Greenlandic "*mek-mek,*" and a sheep in Botokudian "*mäh-mäh,*" does not validate the theory — poetic rather than scientific — of Herder. For the rest, the theory is only a special by-product of the typically Romantic attitude, which, schooled in the study of the collective creations of art (such as myth, national epic, and language-formation), assigned a more important place to the emotional than to the intellectual. And even Mauthner is deeply influenced in his critique of the intellectual values in language by Hamann, Herder, Humboldt, and Jacobi.

In opposition to this there is the philosophic conception of language-formation, which we find first in Greece and which emphasizes not so much the naturalistic imitativeness as its human creativity, which in fact is what most interests us here. According to the account of the neo-Platonist Proclus, names were for Pythagoras pictures of Being, a sort of model of the "intelligible ideas"; and Heraclitus also declared that words resembled pictures of what was intuited. Other sayings make it clear that this was not a mere onomatopœic tone-picturing. Democritus called names sounding pictures made by the gods themselves; and according to the *Cratylus* of Plato, which is a *locus classicus* for the views of antiquity on the origin of language, a name is an imitation of a thing through the medium of the voice; and, moreover, it is the "essence" of a thing that is imitated in letters and syllables. While music and painting only express the external aspect of things, language starts from the inner being of what is expressed. In the *Protagoras,* again, we see the conscious intention in the production of sounds, and the part played by lips and tongue, quite clearly emphasized. Now, while the onomatopœists believed that what was imitated was the sound heard in nature, modern theory has unanimously and entirely rejected this in favour of the mimetic explanation. This involves something more than the mere assertion that there is reproduction of gesture in sounds. The real question is why man adopted just these methods of imitation — that is, why these particular movements of articulation came to correspond with the particular sounds. Wundt says (*Sprache,* II, 635) that if there is any adaptation between language and what it expresses, it cannot lie in the speaker's adapting the sound, but can only consist in his adapting his articulation-movements to the impression or, rather, to the ideas and feelings called forth in us by that impression. The essential in original utterance is therefore not the sound but the gesture — which is itself, however, only a special form of mimic action.

Böcklen is, however, justified in asking for what reason a "sound-gesture" was added to the mimic and pantomimic motions. His book gives an answer which is of interest to us, because it emphasizes the creative or imitatively creative (*Nachschöpferisch*) element of speech-formation far more than any other theory does so. He seeks to prove that what the creators of language imitated was no sound, certainly no sound perceived by human ear, in fact nothing earthly at all, but the phases of the moon. Without subscribing to this particular assertion, it does agree in an extraordinary way with the "imitation" which we have found to exist for all creative processes, the imitation of something unearthly, heavenly, imagined, or abstracted. So here too we may take the moon to be only the symbol of man's immortality-urge, which he tries to satisfy through speech as well as in other ways. But the imitation in sound of something unheard must be regarded as a creative achievement. In so far as it is imitation of something seen or

thought, it can have only the same intent as every other kind
of imitation: namely, to identify itself with what it imitates,
but, more than that, to dominate it and make itself independent of it. This is, however, the formula for all creating, which,
fundamentally, aims, not at a duplication, but at a substitution.
By creating, man makes himself independent of that which
exists, or at least he makes a very considerable effort to do
so; so far as speech is concerned we can see it in name-magic.
Thus even the oldest form of speech is, as Böcklen says, akin
to prayer, being not merely an invocation of God or a medium
for communication with God, but an actual *being* God — " a
vehicle for the soul on which one can rise truly and actually
and unite oneself there and then with the deity — in which is
found a pledge for the eternal union which follows after death "
(op. cit., p. 80). Böcklen adduces, in support of this view, the
belief that the air extruded in speech carries upward the movements of tongue and lips which we make in honour of the
deity — a thought that was worked out by the Greek philosophers, lived on in the Pneuma-doctrine, and remains effective
to this day in our physical theories of sound-waves.

If it is hard to accustom oneself to the idea that language did
not proceed from the imitation of natural sounds or (probably)
from anything earthly at all, it is still harder to swallow the
notion that it did not originate as a means of making oneself
understood. Yet many philologists, and Mauthner most unequivocally, have come out at this view. But if this is true, then
language was not originally something collective, but a purely
expressive and individual function — in a word, an *art,* which
at first (like primitive body-ornament) helped the ego to
magnify itself and to dominate its world-around. W. von Humboldt was, I think, the first to attempt a scientific justification
for the view that language is an artistic expression, and for this
purpose he invented the now famous idea of the " inner speech-
form " — by which he understood, in contrast to the outer
sound-form of the various languages, the peculiar way in which
language does adapt itself formally to its purpose of expressing

ideas.[1] More recently Karl Vossler (op. cit.) has characterized the individually artistic aspect of language-formation in the proposition that language as such undergoes no development, but is produced anew *and in every case differently,* by everyone who gives expression in language to a mental impression. According to this view, the forms of expression in language must be studied without regard to the practical aspect, as creation or art — in a word, æsthetically. In so far as language does become a practical medium of intercourse between individuals, it is no longer an individual but a collective work, which takes empirical reality into account and is rigid or mutable according to the cultural needs of the language-community. In this second sense, which Vossler distinguishes sharply from the first, we have no longer a creation, but something that we must regard as development. This view, together with the religious origin of language, would give a good explanation of a fact which has caused the philologists much trouble: namely, the repeatedly observed fact that the meaning of words undergoes a gradual deterioration — as may, indeed, be observed right into the latest development of a language.

Böcklen explains this fact by the gradual "secularization" of language, which was at first religious and whose profanation was forbidden. We may add a further psychological motive, that language was not originally intended for understanding at all — in fact, was regarded as the peculiar property of the individual, for the attainment of personal immortality in the *unio mystica,* so that part of its magical value would be lost by communicating it to others. In every case, therefore, the profanation of language to everyday use was reflected in a profanation of the meaning of words which had once had a sacred, because creative, force. In order to understand this, we must return to the individual element in the development and use of language, which explains how the self-creative power of language continues effectual right into the most

[1] *Über die Verschiedenheit des menschlichen Sprachbaues; Gesammelte Werke, Akademie-Ausg.,* VII.

complicated forms. But there is another attempted explanation of the origin of language with which we must first deal — that which asks us to regard once more the sexual impulse as the creative principle of language. This is Hans Sperber's study " on the influence of sexual forces in the origin and development of language," [1] which brilliantly synthesizes the views of earlier theorists concerning the sex-call and the collective work-call by linking these in with the activities of tool-using, which, according to Sperber, had a sexual emphasis and was therefore accompanied by attracting sounds. He appeals, in support, to the primitive mattock-agriculture, but we know so very little of this that in the main he is forced to resort to the highly developed symbolism of ordinary agriculture,[2] which seems to me rather to be the outcome of language than to have contributed to its formation. If it comes to that, it is more likely in association with primitive methods of making fire that sex symbolism may have influenced the formation of words — the more as we find the discovery of fire associated in myths, to be mentioned later, with the discovery of language. But Sperber's theory has anyhow too narrow a basis to be admitted as a general theory of language-formation, and therefore, in the practical part, he limits himself to showing the power of expanding their meanings that is possessed by sexual words, and especially verbs with the root meaning of *"coire."*

But it seems inadmissible to use this fact (which incidentally does not need Sperber's proof) as a foundation for the *origin* of language, especially if we restrict ourselves to modern languages and dialects. There are objections not only of fact, but of method. Not only do we find in primitive languages far more words for other processes and activities than for the more or less undifferentiated sex-act;[3] but primitive implements themselves were not (or in any case not merely) sexual symbols,

[1] *Imago*, I (1912).

[2] A. Dieterich: *Mutter Erde* (1905), a work on which Sperber largely bases himself.

[3] As one example out of many: in the grammar of the Ewe language, Westermann mentions that the adverbs which qualify movement (like walking, swimming, driving) usually admit of thirty or more specifications of this one activity.

but rather projections of parts of the human body, and, above all, of the hand. Ernst Kapp — probably the first to do so — thus exposes the idea in his *Grundlinien einer Philosophie der Technik* (1877):[1] in his technical inventions, where if anywhere man nevertheless unconsciously transfers various functional relations and normal conditions of his bodily structure to the instruments of his hand, it is only after the event that he becomes conscious of the fact that his mechanisms came into being on an organic model, that his understanding of his own organism comes only by way of analogy with the mechanisms that are seemingly independent, but really free adaptations of it.[2] August Schmarsow[3] has used this idea for the understanding of primitive art-forms in order to prove the priority of body-ornament over object-ornament. " The connexion [of the tools] with the movements of man's body and the performance of his organs endows the object thus created with a permanent attitude, so that many of them, even when they lie unused, give us the impression of a dissociated member." And Scheltema sees in the transition from body-ornament to the decoration of objects nothing but the " spiritual parallel and explanatory amplification of the transition, so vastly important for human culture, from the natural organism to its self-expansion in the instrument."[4]

In addition to these considerations of cultural history there is a further linguistic argument, whether, or to what extent (especially as denoting some part of the body), the verb and not the substantive was the original form of speech. We will leave this for the moment and turn to the sex hypothesis. For the reasons already mentioned, I would rather see in Sperber's facts

---

[1] In the same year appeared Noiré's work on the origin of language, in which he emphasized the importance of primitive methods of work which are assisted by ancillary cries for the growth of language. His book on implements and their significance appeared in 1880.

[2] The way in which this primitive anthropomorphism survives into the most complicated machinery is seen in two books that are of interest for the problem of art: A. Klima: *Die Technik im Lichte der Karikatur* (Vienna, 1913), and H. Wettich: *Die Maschine in der Karikatur* (Berlin, 1916).

[3] *Grundbegriffe der Kunstwissenschaft*, p. 136; and *Zeitschrift für Aesth.*, 1910.

[4] *Die altnordische Kunst* (1923), p. 30.

the expression of an already existing speech-creative force than a root from which speech sprang. In other words, I am disposed to assume, in conformity with the general view adopted in this book, that what we have to deal with is not a growth of language out of sex-acts or sexual activity, but a comparatively late sexualization of language as a manifestation of the human creative urge which gradually usurps the parenthood of everything by bringing sexual connotations into its nomenclature. This sexualization of language is itself, then, a metaphorical way of expressing a " just-like "; that is, it gives name-forms to everything that man creates, " just as if " they were produced from him as the child is.[1]

If in what follows we develop and support this view in detail, we do so less as a matter of linguistics (which do not concern us here very much) than with a view to elucidating the human creative urge in this sphere also, the high importance of which is not confined to the cultural, but extends to artistic development in general. We have here a telling instance of the secondary rôle which sex plays in human creativity, which flows from other sources, though it may easily (for the reasons mentioned) become sexualized later on. It is very tempting, of course, to adduce the existence of genders in almost all modern languages as evidence of the sexual origin of language; but such a conclusion is so superficial that even Sperber, in his attempt to prove that sexual origin, scorns it and argues against it in the form of one of its chief exponents, Rudolf Kleinpaul.[2] This rebutting argument of his proves for our living languages what Powell had already established as a result of his thorough in-

[1] In our study of the names of parts of the body we saw that there is no preference among primitive or civilized peoples for the sex-organs over other parts of the body which seem to them more important. Rather, the universal tendency to apply euphemistically to the sex-organs the name of other parts, especially the foot, leg, hand, or even knee, seems to point to an opposite process to that of sex-emphasis; and, in my view, this is to be associated with the primitive idea of the soul and its denial of sexual immortality (see *Seelenglaube und Psychologie:* chapter on "The Age of Sex"). The sexualization which is here discussed would then belong to that particular period in the history of peoples wherein not only language but all ideologies (with the institutions based on them) take on a sex-tone.

[2] Kleinpaul: *Die Rätsel der Sprache.*

vestigation of Indian languages:[1] "The student of linguistics must get entirely out of his head the idea that gender is merely a distinction of sex. In the North American Indian languages (and probably in the Bantu and the Indo-European also) gender is usually a classification-method." We find the classification of "higher" and "lower" beings, that presently became one of "male" and "female" in the Semitic languages, which, even thus early, breathe the moral outlook of the East. Here too the primitives disclose to us the deeper sources, for (according to Powell) the main principle of their classification is to divide the animate and inanimate objects.

Thus the inclusion of primitive languages within the scope of our study has shown this phenomenon of grammatical genders to be but a part of a much wider and more complex system of classification; and this makes it all the more interesting to follow the phenomena of transition. Opposed to the two-gender system of Semitic and Hamitic languages and the three-gender system of the Indo-European, we have the Indian classification that we have just been discussing, based chiefly on the distinction of "soul" and "no-soul" (living and non-living), though, it is true, there attaches itself to this a certain valuation as "personal" and "impersonal," which reappears in the distinction of masculine and feminine. Most interesting of all are the transitional languages which show the beginning of the sexualization side by side with the old basis of classification. According to Meinhof,[2] the developed system of the Bantu languages has more than twenty classes with special prefixes; and between them and our two-gender system we have, for instance, the Hamitic Ful,[3] in which, above the old classification of nouns, we have an overlying new system with only four headings: persons, things, big, and small, whence, as the big pass into the class of persons, and the small into that of things, a twofold system is developed, corresponding to our division into masculine and feminine. This gives us a glimpse into the

[1] Powell: *The Evolution of Language*, Report, I, 9.
[2] *Grundzüge einer vergleichenden Grammatik der Bantusprachen* (1906).
[3] Idem: *Sprachen der Hamiten* (1912), pp. 22, 42.

245

valuation-principle which *eventually* identifies persons, living, big, and important things with man, and non-living, small, and unimportant things with woman.[1] This gives us an exact parallel to the totemistic system, discussed earlier, which does not stop with the prohibitions regarding certain women (exogamy) or animals (totem), but assigns values to everything in the world by division into good and bad. The only problem here is: why does woman always come into the class of the evil, the dangerous, and the less valuable? As I have explained, this arises from the individual's urge to eternalize himself personally, an urge which is threatened by sexual propagation, of which woman is the representative; and so woman passes into what I have called the Not-I class, which includes dangerous as well as unimportant (and neutral) things.

Sexuality, then, seems to have come into the formation of language comparatively late, and we can equally say that it played nothing like the part that Sperber assigns to it in its genesis. Not only in children, but also in primitive man, the *mouth,* rather than the sex-organs, plays the most important part in language-development. The mouth, as has already been mentioned, is used not only as an instrument of speech, but as a mimetic organ of gesticulation, which carries us from the movements of crying and sucking to the formation of sounds and words.[2] Sound-gesture therefore belongs to a very early stage of development, because it is already determined in part by natural life-functions and leads very soon to a general gesture-language [3] in which the individual expresses himself

[1] In Bedauye this is still quite clear. Thus, a cow is masculine because in these lands it is the chief support of ordinary existence; the flesh is, however, feminine because relatively to the whole cow it is of less importance (Reinisch: *Die Bedauyesprache*, II; Vienna, 1893; p. 59). It is a subject with which Ernst Cassierer has dealt in detail, but unfortunately only from the phenomenological standpoint. Cf. besides the short essay above mentioned: *Die Begriffsform im mythischen Denken* (Leipzig, 1922), and his large three-volume work: *Philosophie der symbolischen Formen:* I, *Die Sprache;* II, *Der Mythos;* III, *Phänomenologie der Erkenntnis.*

[2] Spielrein: "*Die Entstehung der kindlichen Worte Mama und Papa,*" Imago, VIII (1922).

[3] One stage of gesture-language in the development of the child is dealt with also by S. Ferenczi in his: "*Entwicklungsstufen des Wirklichkeitssinnes*" (*Internationale Zeitschrift für Psychoanalyse*, I (1913).

at first, physioplastically, without even wishing to be understood; here the mouth, being the most important life-sustaining
organ, functions as the organ of gestures which have the character of sounds. But we cannot follow these oral sound-gestures
to the stage of language-formation without having first referred to a second bodily organ which has played as great, in
primitive times perhaps a greater, part: namely, the hand. Even
if Sperber were right in maintaining that all implements were
sexualized, this would still presuppose a corresponding sexualization of the hand, since the hand not only controls the implement, but was the original model for it.[1] Without having
to decide here if the hand — " the human organ of culture "
— is a new acquisition of man or an original possession which
the other primates lost,[2] there can be no doubt that it was the
archetype of the implement, any more than that it is the most
important organ for the language of gesture. Both ideas have
been worked out in the wide sweep of Paul Alsberg's *Das
Menschheitsrätsel* (Dresden, 1922), in which he sees the characteristic quality of the development of man, as man, in an ever-
increasing " elimination of the body," accompanied by a
simultaneous replacement of the eliminated parts by one or
another tool. In this process of development, which affects the
spiritual as well as the technical achievement of man, the
hand, at least to start with, played the most important part.
Alsberg maintains that its development into an implement, as
in throwing stones, even precedes the upright gait and certainly the perfection of the brain. But the later appearance of
word- and idea-formation, too, Alsberg regards, like the elimination of the body, as the creation of an instrument; for the
word and the concept, which are the basic elements of language
and intelligence, are also extra-corporeal (artificial) means
towards that elimination.

[1] Even Lower Palæolithic has, as the typical form of its tools, a stone of the form
and size of the human hand. It looks as if they had wanted to translate into the more
efficient stone (the "*Faustkeil*") the hand, which is the natural and universal tool of
man. Schuchhardt, op. cit., p. 11.

[2] The view supported, as is well known, by H. Klaatsch (*Die Entstehung und Er-
werbung der Menschenmerkmale* in Abderhalden's *Fortschritten;* Berlin, 1913).

Before we proceed to deduce, if only suggestively, the language, like other developments, from manual gestures, we must return once again to this question of sexuality and the rôle which, according to Sperber, it plays in language-formation. His view depends on the psycho-analytical assumption that all pleasure has a sexual character, a thesis that we cannot here discuss. I will refer only to what has been said about æsthetic pleasure and the other well-known sources of pleasure which originate in the avoidance of tensions and the release from inner pressure. The fact, however, that sex-satisfaction has this character, of release from tension and pressure, is no justification for calling all pleasure sexual, but seems to me to point rather to the opposite view, as I explained in connexion with æsthetic pleasure. However that may be, I produced in 1925 a commentary on the problem which concerns us here — that of the relation of hand and mouth to sexuality — to which I should like to refer now,[1] since, though it still remains wholly within the cadre of the psycho-analytical mode of thought, it points to things so far outside that cadre that we can link on to it here. In the analytical study of the genesis of the purely genital libido in the individual I found that it is very little developed at first in the child and gradually increases through positive accessions in the activity and the erotic of the mouth. The intermediary between the mouth and the genitals I found, also from observations, to be the hand, which in sucking and in masturbation seems to play the same constructively important part that Alsberg (from quite other premisses) showed it to have played in the history of culture. Even if at a more advanced stage of artistic development there was an erotic emphasis placed on hand or mouth — as Hermann[2] assumes in his commentaries on the individual genesis of the artistic impulse — yet at any rate in the beginning the opposite process, the transference of

[1] "The Genesis of Genitality" (*Psychoanalytic Review*, 1925), incorporated in *Genetische Psychologie*, Part I (1927).

[2] Imre Hermann has published in *Imago*, VIII (1922) and X (1924), studies of the drawing faculty, in which he stresses the erotic significance of the hand in artistic "sublimation."

activity or energy from mouth or hand to the genitals, seems to occur. But I think it is at least doubtful if this transferred energy can be called a "libido" in the psycho-analytical sense, because the term may readily and erroneously suggest that the later process is what underlies the primary also.

We will pass over this problem here, as being one of general human energetics, and turn to the importance of the hand for human development and especially for the formation of language — which is confirmed both for the individual and for culture generally. In order to give (to what is in the first place a general investigation) a definite relation to our problem, let us remark at once that the dominant and creative function of the hand is still retained in the plastic arts — for example by the painter and sculptor — while the poet, at least in origin, derives from the speech-creative function of the mouth, though later he reverts to the hand when he writes — a process which could be followed right to the difference of written and conversational language and would throw an interesting light on the part played by hand-ideology in the development of written language. But even the spoken word seems to be influenced by the hand and the language of gesture, far more deeply than one imagines, and the study of primitive language and its social milieu in particular is convincing as to all language-formation being derived in part from the hand and its expressive movements. It would be hard to decide if this was already true of words descriptive of an object or only for the primitive sentence; but in any case the mouth in itself originally possessed only a physioplastic expressiveness, whereas probably all genuine naming and certainly all verbal description of activity derive from the sphere of the hand. Almost all observers agree about the pictorial quality of primitive language.[1] "The Klamath language, which may be taken as representative of a very widespread family of languages in North America, obeys a very definite tendency which Gatschet (*The Klamath*

---

[1] Material relating to primitive languages from Lévy-Bruhl's excellent work: *Les Fonctions mentales dans les sociétés inférieures* (Paris, 1910).

Language, p. 460) calls pictorial — that is, the need to speak concretely, in pictures, to draw or paint what one wants to express." We will leave out of account the significance of the eye, which L. Geiger [1] puts in the first place as an essential speech-forming factor, and will emphasize in this pictorial tendency — which is found in others besides primitive languages — the drawing or tracing element, which continues right into even the most abstract formation of concepts, as indeed the very name of these, including, as it does, the notion of seizing or grasping (*begreifen,* comprehend, etc.) testifies. In an important work on " Manual Concepts " F. H. Cushing [2] has pointed to the connexions of the speech expressed by movements of the hand with the oral languages. Observers of primitive man have continually emphasized the part played by signs not only as a means of understanding apart from sound-language, but as an actual part of that sound-language. Thus in the case of the Halkomele of British Columbia we may assert boldly that at least a third of the meaning of their words and sentences is expressed by this auxiliary of primitive speech, gesture, and differences of intonation. [3] This is true, however, not only of primitive peoples, but of, to a greater or less extent, our own cultural area — Semites and Southerners [4] — because the language of gesture is not merely an auxiliary of speech but a language of its own, which may have preceded the formation of syllables and certainly developed along with it.

The hand, however, not only is the organ which first grasps a thing before it can be grasped in words, but also carries the objects thus repictured, like a food, to the mouth, which then works them over verbally (we ourselves still make corresponding movements of the mouth when we write). Now, in this there is being expressed a quality of language which, so far from being the result of a desire to communicate, implies a

---

[1] Geiger (*Ursprung der Sprache*) calls man the "eye-animal."

[2] F. H. Cushing: "Manual Concepts" (*American Anthropologist*, V, pp. 291 et seq.).

[3] Hill Tout: "Ethnographical Reports. . . Halkomelan, British Columbia," *J. A. I.*, XXXIV, p. 367.

[4] Carl Sittl: *Die Gebärden der Griechen und Römer* (Leipzig, 1890).

directly opposite tendency towards incorporation, the intuition being not only to grasp the objects of the external world — that is, to dominate them — but actually to make them part of the ego. This originally possessive character of language is still very clear in the Melanesian and Micronesian group of languages. All parts of one's own body and all that concerns it, such as eating and the like, are defined by a suffix which, like our possessive pronoun, expresses the fact of " belonging " to our ego.[1] Moreover, in many of the North American languages there are no words for eye, hand, arm, and other parts or organs of the body in themselves; they are always associated with a pronoun, added to or included in them and indicating my eye, thy hand, his hand (Lévy-Bruhl, op. cit., p. 143). This peculiarity is found among many other peoples and, moreover, appears quite generally in the terminations of words describing relationship. This possessive intrusion into language, together with the strongly individual character of the language of gesture, gives, specially to primitive languages, an individualist tone which even Lévy-Bruhl has to admit, though it does not exactly support his theory of language as a social phenomenon dependent on a collective cast of mind. Dr. Peschuël-Loesche says of Loango:[2] " Everyone manipulates the language in his own way; it might be truer to say that each man's mouth utters language according to the circumstances and mood he is in. A language of this sort — I cannot find any better comparison than this rather unlovely one — is as free and natural as the utterances of animals, which are equally understood." Lévy-Bruhl says to the same effect that " words are not something rigid and fixed once for all; vocal gesture is, like that of the hand, a description, a drawing, a vivid expression of the action or object in question. In the Ronga language there is a genus of words which the writers of Bantu grammars call in general interjections or onomatopoetics. These are vocables, mostly of one syllable, by which the natives express a sudden immediate

[1] Parkinson: *Thirty Years in the South Seas*, p. 730.
[2] *Die Loango-Expedition*, III, 2, pp. 91–5.

impression that has been called forth by a play, a tone, or an idea or by which they describe a movement, an appearance, a noise. They succeed in this way in giving shades of meaning which a quieter speech could not express. In addition, these little words have given rise to numerous verbs and would deserve mention even if only on that account." That these sound-pictures (in which the language of the Ewe is also very rich) are not proper onomatopoetics follows not only from the examples adduced by Westermann (op. cit.), but also from the individual emphasis that Junod has stressed: " Yet we must admit that the use of these descriptive adverbs varies greatly with each individual, and some natives sprinkle their language to such an extent with them that they are unintelligible to anyone who is not initiated. They even invent new ones. Yet many of these words have been really incorporated in the language and are now generally intelligible." [1]

Here we have an example of a collective everyday language, which is universally understood, actually growing out of that individual " spoken gesture " of which the forceful originality still rings out in the language of high poesy (" poetic licence," as we say).

However we may picture the development of language into a collective medium of understanding, it seems at least certain that expression in language was originally, as it still is with children before they learn to talk, purely subjective and served as a discharge of inner tension. In a short but valuable essay, supplementing Sperber's theory, Adalbert Berny [2] has exhibited in some well-chosen examples the part played by physioplastic elements in early language-formation. He also starts with the mouth as the real organ for language-formation and takes as the earliest creations of language the sound-pictures which belong to the sphere of eating and breathing. If we try to evaluate psychologically these linguistic observations, the conclusions that we have already come to about the part played by mouth

[1] Junod: *Grammaire Ronga*, p. 197.
[2] " *Zur Hypothese des sexuellen Ursprungs der Sprache*," Imago, II (1913).

and hand enable us to see the basic difference between the individual expression-sound and the collective communication-speech. We mentioned above that the things which the hand grasps are also carried by it to the mouth, which takes them up and copies them. In this sense the individual sound-formation corresponds more or less to an incorporation of the indicated objects by the mouth, while the collectivizing of language to serve as a medium of understanding is more like a giving-out, or throwing-out of what has been previously taken in — as indeed the accompanying hand-gesture often shows.[1] This double character of language as a subjective means of expression and a collective medium of understanding occurs again in the highest form of language and, in fact, is the essence of art-work in general.

This basic relation of the individual to the whole we have already seen, creatively represented, in the myths of the sacrifice of man for the construction of the universe; but there is also a special group of myths in which, as it seems to me, the conflict between the individual and collective use of language is depicted. Most of these traditions, which Böcklen (op. cit.) has collected, come from primitive peoples among whom language has retained its pristine form and function. Almost all these language-myths deal less with the origin of language than with that of the difference of languages — like the story of the Tower of Babel — and in particular with the complete loss of language as the penalty of some sin of man. This sin seems to me everywhere to relate to an individualist separating-off which the myth, being a collective product, punishes by the loss of common intelligibility; on the other hand, these mythical stories show the resistance that the individual puts up against the profanation of language into a medium of communication, since here, as always, the individual, in profiting by collectivization, has to sacrifice also certain personal advantages. Among these

[1] In my latest work, on the *Technik der Psychoanalyse* (Vol. III, 1931), I was able to show the therapeutic character of the giving-out effect of this "expression," which is also the basic element of confession (p. 95).

forfeits is the magical — that is, the creative (or destructive) —
use of language, which for this reason is in later times kept
secret by its adepts so that its efficacy may not be lost to them
through profanation.

This struggle to win a language of one's own, which every
child to this day passes through, can be traced in discourse from
the peculiar elevated language of prayer and poetry, via the
secret language of sect and profession, right into the specific
language of a people or a nation.[1] The interpretation, suggested
by myths, that there had been originally only one language,
and that differentiation had come as a punishment for some
sin, is certainly of little help for the historical understanding
of language-development. It must rather be looked upon as
the tendentious invention of peoples who were trying, in pursuance of the national immortality-ideologies, to retain the
special qualities of their mother tongue and hence rejected the
general world-language. With that we come to realize that
the various languages of different people are treated by the
myth simply as an unwanted individualization, in the same
way as the language oddities of the individual are treated
within his own community. It is only when this individual is
capable of helping the community by his individual creation
of words, as the magician helps the primitive, the priest the
higher, and the poet the highest stage of culture, that his art
of speech is freed from the suspicion of personal misuse and becomes generally accessible. The myths also represent, apart
from their content, the effort to save (at least in metaphorical
form) this magical power of the individual, which has been
lost through the profanation of his language — which later was
to be taken under the fostering care of the poetic art. Berny
speaks justly of man's " exaggeration of the value of language "
in fancying that " the right name will call a thing into being."
But it is only in the case of concrete objects that this is illusory,
for, after all, it leads to the word-spell and to the effort to exercise magical influence through the word. This word-magic,

[1] See, on this, Fritz Mauthner: *Muttersprache und Vaterland* (Leipzig, 1920).

incidentally, is probably preceded by picture-magic, which we may regard as the prelude to writing.[1]

As far as ideologies are concerned, this over-valuation of language not only is justified, but leads to an intoxication of words, which is akin to that of creativity, and which is seen also in the mystic ecstasy of prayer or the pathological condition of extreme polyglot. In fact, do not the ideologies, which include at an early stage the belief in a soul and later the macrocosmic immortality-myths, owe their existence to the word and are they not made possible only by language? For language was not only the first physioplastic creation of man, but his first self-creative achievement in a truly artistic sense. All other creativity was, if not imitation in the naturalistic sense, at any rate a deliberate follow-up of something already existent for the purpose of controlling it. But in language man made something new which had creative force in itself, and it was this something that in fact transformed the world in a human sense. And not only that, but it brought forth a new world, that of ideology. Language, however, was not only the beginning of artistic creation, but has been its highest peak; for it had not during its career to pass through the stages from the belly- to the head-culture, but appeared instantaneously as one of the earliest achievements of the latter, which thereafter was enabled by it, and it alone, to become a genuinely spiritual culture.

Before we pass in the next chapter to discuss the particular effects of this process in poetry, we have still to mention a primitive motif which occurs as an essential element in language-myths. This is *eating,* which certainly represents a pre-linguistic function of the mouth and, as the only connexion

[1] Writing, in the sense of imaginative expression through an ideograph, existed of course long before men wrote in letters proper. It seems otiose to enter into any argument as to whether the so-called "Azilian signs" on the rocks of the Late Stone Age ought or ought not to be regarded as the beginning of picture-writing, since in any case they possess meaning (as is evidenced by the signs on the Australian boomerang and by tattoo-painting, which Taylor calls a "script." Painting and script are in fact difficult to separate at first, both being just ways in which man sought to express something, to "say" something (see W. Paulcke: *Die Ur-Anfänge der Bildschrift in der Alt-Steinzeit;* Stuttgart, 1923; also the more recent work of H. Wirth: *Der Aufgang der Menschheit,* I; Jena, 1928).

with the belly-culture, represents an obstacle to speech-development in the mythic sense. It seems as though this profane and extremely individual use of the mouth for eating-purposes impeded its development into a spiritual organ of expression; herein once more the difference between egoistic absorption and collective expression may have played a part. The association which the myths of the Indians and Australians (Böcklen, op. cit., pp. 136, 145 et seq.) assume between the loss of a language (or of the means of communication) and indulgence in human flesh cannot, in my opinion, be accounted for historically as a condemnation of cannibalism, but must be taken symbolically. For the consumption of human flesh was not a mode of nourishment, but rather something esoteric in the nature of *unio mystica* — that is, the appropriation of the other's soul for the strengthening of one's own ego. As against these, we have myths still surviving in our own fairy-stories in which man learns languages from animals, as Siegfried learns the language of birds through drinking dragon's blood. Whether these myths which introduce the bird as the bringer of language originally included the eating of the birds we do not know; but we have the Vedic Gandharva, the Persian Simurg, the Mexican Bird of the Flood, and the Samoan Tuli figuring as teachers of language. The last even gave designations to the parts of the human body: these the devil made from worms, but the bird named after itself, beginning with the *head*. In this part played by the bird of saviour by language we can hardly do other than see the influence of a pretty highly developed idea of the soul, which has already risen from the materialistic worm-soul state to the notion of a spirit hovering in heaven — this being at once the precondition and the consequence of language-development.

We have a further light on this motif of the confusion of tongues because of eating in certain myths of primitive peoples, in which indulgence in human flesh is punished by complete loss of speech. This certainly is connected with the silence of the dead and expresses the fear of the eater that he may have

absorbed, along with the other qualities of the dead that he
wanted, that of his "being dead" as well. But this identification with the dead is more than a punishment; it represents the
entry into immortality:[1] in death all have once more the same
language. This is probably the meaning of a myth of the
Navajos, "who had all spoken the same language under the
earth, but when they came above ground each into his own
dwelling, had soon so many dialects that hardly anyone could
understand anyone else.[2] In this case individuation is manifestly the language-separating influence; and similarly an Australian tradition shows us the growth of language in association
with the dismemberment motif. "An old woman called
Wururi, who went out in the night with a big stick and extinguished the fire, had died and the peoples were devouring
the corpse. The southern races came first and ate the flesh,
and thus obtained a clear language; the eastern races came
second and ate the upper entrails and spoke somewhat differently (presumably less clearly), and for the northern there was
nothing left but the intestines, and their talk was still more
different."[3] This myth seems to crystallize a whole linguistic
theory which connects the higher development of language
with the eating of the worthier bodily parts — another evidence
of the lesser value attributed to the lower body. More important,
however, is the fact that the eating of human flesh in this case
brings with it the discovery of language; yet we should note
that it is the corpse of a woman that *died,* while in the other
traditions of the Iroquois and Dog-rib Indians the confusion of
language follows on the eating of a man who has been *killed*
like an animal.

This draws our attention to the fact that the distinction may
really be between violent and natural death, and not between

[1] This also explains the widespread custom of imposing silence — that is, renunciation of life — on widows. We have this in a still more radical form in the Indian practice of suttee. According to Spencer and Gillen, the Australian widow is often obliged
to remain silent for twelve months, during which time she makes herself understood
by the language of gesture.

[2] Knortz: *Märchen und Sagen der nordamerikanischen Indianer* (1871), pp. 256 et seq.

[3] Steinthal: *Geschichte der Sprachwissenschaft,* p. 9.

man and animal; for in general animals are identified with or
even placed above men. Even in our own stories and fables
animals talk; and primitive man had many more scruples than
we have about killing and eating them.

It is very probable, though of course it cannot be proved,
that this religious significance of animals, which goes through
all cultural history, originated in prehistoric times. And even
if the — artistically highly developed — animal drawings of
palæolithic man had nothing to do with reincarnation ideas,
they are yet an impressive proof of the veneration of animals
which points far beyond the merely practical use of the animal
for cave-man's food and clothing. Nor is it likely that man was
originally an eater of meat; and certain traditions, especially
among primitive peoples, leave no doubt that the killing of
animals for food, "good hunting," was not so simple an
achievement as it is to the modern sportsman with his gun. I
am not referring to the fact that he had not the same weapons
or knowledge of the animal kingdom, but to the psychical difficulties in the way of his killing the animal when he felt himself one with it. Even in modern times Frobenius records the
magic ceremonies which his native carriers performed before
the killing of their prey; and these were not, as one might
suppose, charms for obtaining luck, but rather a charm for the
avoidance of the bad luck that might follow from the killing
— in fact, a sort of permission is obtained by the hunter from
his prey for killing him. This seemingly paradoxical interpretation of the magical hunting ceremonies in which the animal,
drawn in the sand, is "killed" in advance by arrows or spears
driven into it, fits the primitive mind far more closely than
any notion of ensuring luck in the chase; even in modern
hunting superstitions the purpose is much more to avoid bad
luck than to induce good. And the reason why this bad luck
may ensue is that the animal's death, if it is not permitted by
the animal itself, will be regarded as a murder to be avenged on
the murderer.

This idea, which rests on the pre-animistic belief in metamorphosis, finds a touchingly naïve expression in a myth of the Californian Indians, the Luiseno. This tribe (which incidentally lacks the usual products of Indian art) is said to have conceived the idea, on the occasion of a debate on the problem of whether men may die and live again, that stag would be good to eat — this in order to sidetrack the meeting's attention. "They talked about it with the stag, but he replied: No, he was a shaman and very powerful." The story then describes how the stag was saved from being killed by the fact that he possessed himself all the magic by which men threatened to kill him, and was therefore even in this respect identical with men.[1] It was not until he was shown a flint arrow that he gave in; here was something magic which he did not possess. In another remarkable story of the Yoghuts we are told that, after the transformation of two boys into stags, there was a stag-hunt, the killing, disembowelling, dividing, and consuming being described in such terms that Lublinski, who collected these myths, had the impression that "what was here represented was the first attempt at killing a stag for eating-purposes" (op. cit., p. 48).

The remark of the stag, that he was a mighty shaman — like the turning of the boys into stags — points already to an underlying metamorphosis idea; but, conformably to the soul-worm belief, the vehicle of the soul had to be animal and not human, and thus it came about that totemism made of this animal an ancestor. In any case, with this materialistic metamorphosis idea we have the paradox that in eating an animal man was in danger of eating his kin, which is not so in the case of a human enemy. Without entering into all the numerous and strange customs which result from this view, we will point out that this most primitive immortality-idea found expression also in the earliest form of artistic production. If the stone-age cave-paintings, as is generally assumed, served some magic purpose of the chase, there may also have been even then some such

[1] Even today with Northern hunting tribes the victim when killed receives almost divine honours before it is cut up and eaten; the skull and skin are preserved, which recalls the plastic bear-figuring discovered a few years ago by Norbert Karteret in one of the less accessible caves of the Pyrenees.

idea of a permission that forestalled the risk of evil effects on the hunter. That such "tender-hearted" thinking — produced though it was by a very egoistic motive indeed — may fairly be credited to primitive men is shown by a hunt motif which Frobenius has found in various parts of Africa. This is a line broken in many places which passes from a man, depicted in a hunting process, to the lower part of the body of a woman who is apparently praying. Frobenius gives the following interpretation to the drawing illustrated on page 23: "The beginning and the course of the long line, on the other hand, is such that, remembering the term 'uterine' (that is, descended from the same womb), is still used in the European Hamitic group, I assume that this long line is an allegorical indication of the connexion of the two figures by the umbilical cord. Thus the female figure is not the wife, but the mother of the hunter," praying for success in the chase.[1] What interests us here, in connexion with such totemistic tales, is the hunt itself, which is indicated on the drawing by three animals brought into the picture along with the weapons of man; one of the animals is an ostrich. Now if the animal was as much the bearer of a human soul for the primitive African as it was for the American Indian, then what we have here is not a mere prayer for success in the chase, but an averting of the evil consequences that may flow from killing the animal. The cord would then symbolize, at this matriarchal stage of culture, the fact that the hunter, as a human being, is, too, a vessel of immortality as the animal is, which lessens his reverential distance from it, thus justifying his killing of it.[2]

This last example reminds us once again of the opposition between the mortal dependence on the mother and the continued existence of the human soul in the animal, which had its origin in the soul-worm. And the same fundamental an-

[1] Leo Frobenius: *Das unbekannte Afrika* (Munich, 1923). The womb and navel-cord motif is also unmistakable, although already highly stylized, in a North African rock-carving (Fig. 8).

[2] I would also regard the fasts which with the Indians and other primitives usually precede the hunt as a rite of justification for the killing of animals for food.

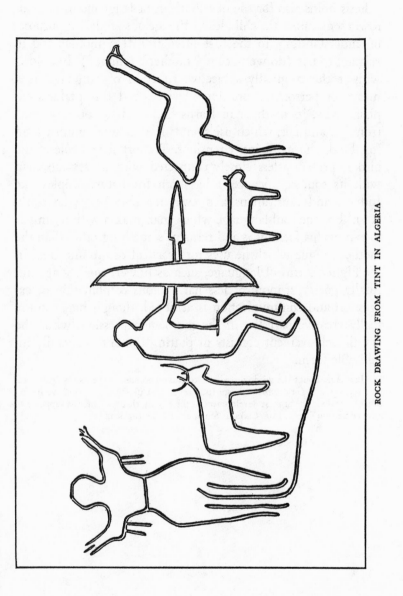

ROCK DRAWING FROM TINT IN ALGERIA

tithesis holds also for the development of language in the narrower sense, since the child learns the use of sounds, for purposes of understanding, in the first place from the mother and in relation to her (do we not say " mother " tongue?). But along with it the originally subjective function of language as a means of personal expression survives, and this perhaps explains why, in myth, man learns the language of expression from the animals, which use sounds less for intelligibility than for the discharge of inner tensions. The privileged rôle of the bird is probably less closely connected with its sex-call than with its soul-significance it has both for nature-peoples like Indians and Australians and even for ourselves (the stork, etc.).[1] For the soul-language which man makes within himself to express his feelings is and remains something other than the mother tongue which he uses for practical communication. In the higher forms of language, such as prayer, spell, song, and finally poetry, a more or less harmonious combination of expression and communication is achieved, though here too the really creative part lies in the personal expression, while the artistic achievement consists in putting this into generally intelligible form.

[1] It was no doubt the wisdom credited to birds on account of their soul-significance that suggested augury, which is a spiritual refinement of the more primitive inspection of entrails. The highest development of the augury theory, which is supposed to have come into Greece from Caria, is found among the Etruscans.

THE POETIC ART AND ITS HERO

❧

I raised myself to be a singer and made myself to be a speaker of magic.

Kalevala

Chapter Nine

THE POETIC ART AND
ITS HERO

᙭᙭᙭

The purely creative side of poetry, as we have found from our study of speech, is concerned chiefly with that subjective expressive capacity which we have called the language of the soul. By this we understood, in contrast to the mother tongue which serves as a medium of communication, the self-creative function of sound-forming which serves as an expression of inner processes, their pictorial shaping in word and sentence. Before we follow the development of this originally physioplastic faculty into the ideoplastic expression-art of the poet and its æsthetic remoulding in the generally intelligible collective language, we will illustrate the ideological character of language-creation from the example of the soul-concept itself. There is no doubt that the soul, this thing abstract in itself, was once connected with certain parts and functions of the body like the breath, which was always associated with the mouth, which is also the source of language. Berny (op. cit., p. 549) gives a short account of the linguistic development of the idea of the soul, from which for our purpose we may quote the following: " At the first stage the sound-figure *śu* denotes the wind, being an onomatopoetic copy of its soughing; a bird's feather blown in the wind and the moving air are regarded as independent phenomena. At the second stage there follows differentiation by short forms (rustling, blowing, *spirare*). The moving feather, because it moves, is regarded as animate. The feather is the god of the wind (Egyptian *św*), whose name is therefore written hieroglyphically with the sign of an ostrich feather, and the wind is his breath in nature. At the third stage the causal connexion between the waving of the feather and the wind is established. Man has learned to think sufficiently abstractly to infer a soul in other things than a body: the wind has an indwelling force which blows the feather to and fro (soul, *seele*, from *sila* = force, strength). The wind is soul, and the soul takes its name from it: *anima, θυμός, rwch*." If we complete these linguistic observations with the results of our psychological and cultural studies (and in particular those set forth in *Seelenglaube und Psychologie*), we have a typical picture of the development of ideologies that is special to the higher cultures as distinct from the primitive.

First, the assumption that the syllable "*šu*" is an onomatopoetic imitation of the wind may be countered by the physioplastic view accepted by Berny himself, which would lead us to believe that man compared the wind to the breath of his mouth rather than vice versa; in other words, that we have here a first stage of anthropomorphism, which indeed comes more and more into evidence as time goes on. In macrocosmic terms, we should say that the world breathes as man breathes — not that man rustles like the wind. For that matter, a feather is moved, and moved deliberately, by the human breath — in fact, many people use this as a test of death — and here there discloses itself another motive for the anthropomorphic identification of breath and the wind: namely, his intellectual control over the stronger powers of nature — a motive still potent at the most fully developed stages of belief in the soul, as is manifest from the idea that only the right pronunciation of a god's name can ensure the influencing of its owner. Think for instance of the intense meditation on the holy syllable *Om* which plays so great a part in Indian Yoga, or of the corresponding passages of the Upanishads, to the translation of which Deussen adds an explanation: "This Khanda places the letters of the text under the protection of certain gods, showing how they are to be pronounced in order to give proper expression to the being of the gods." [1] Similarly the cabbalist Abraham Samuel Abulafia gives hints on the pronunciation of the Old Testament name of God, the so-called Tetragrammaton, and on the mystical union with God that is to be attained in this way: "The many-lettered name of God is to be spoken not only with certain modulations of the voice by pauses, long or short, but with energetic movements and bowing of the body. This leads to an ecstasy from which one sinks exhausted into a sleep, wherein there comes over one a feeling as though the soul were separating from the body. The universal spirit then unites itself with the upward-striving soul in a kiss and streams over it. At this moment man receives his highest revelation." [2]

This ecstatic condition, which is also found in the Christian "speakers with tongues," is thus more than an expression of the divine name; it is an actual creation, through words, of the soul, which is therefore separated from the body and for a moment made independent. In these conditions all that macrocosmization is called upon to do is to make the temporary blessedness permanent. Similar temporary and momentary conditions are found also in the fast-ceremonies of primitive peoples — for example, American Indians — wherein also a union with powerful spirits is sought. [3] In these cases, though, the soul-concept, imagined abstractly as a spirit, is bound still more closely to the body — sleep, dream, fasting — a relation which, for that matter, is never wholly lost, as is shown not only by the breath-wind etymologies but by the fact (adduced by Holma) that the soul as life-giving principle has a name common with the throat (*Kehle*), both of which have the root of blowing and breathing behind them. It would take us too far afield to discuss the primitive ideas of the life-principle — how it has developed from purely corporeal speech-symbols to those of a psychic kind — for this a discussion of the whole spiritual culture of the primitive would be necessary.

---

[1] Chandoja Upanishad, I, 22, 3–5: "All vowels are embodiments of Indra, all sibilants and aspirates of Prajapati, all mutes of Mrtjus (Death)."

[2] Art. "*Kabbala*" in *Protestantischen Realenzyklopädie* (third edition, IX, 682).

[3] Material in my *Seelenglaube und Psychologie*.

We will therefore only give a characteristic example, which is taken from Lévy-Bruhl's work: *L'Ame primitive* (Paris, 1927). He is dealing with the Maori's conception of the life-principle as exemplified in his language. Elston Best (*The Maori*), on whose investigations Lévy-Bruhl bases himself, calls the Maori a people of metaphysicians and theologians, since in their language they make distinctions of the subtlest sort between the various life-principles — which Europeans find difficult to understand, and for more than linguistic reasons. Since I am presenting the material at second hand, which means in a third language, a false interpretation may easily slip in. Still I think that even a rough conception of the essentials will do for our purpose.

The Maoris have three words to describe different kinds of life-principles. The first, *wairua,* which signifies shadow or non-material copy, is not situated in the bodily organs and therefore leaves the body during sleep and, in its immaterial quality, survives the body. But though as "animating spirit" it is independent of the body, its secondary meaning as a designation for intellectual properties again relates it to the bodily organs which are conceived to be the seat of those qualities. The second word, *mauri,* denotes the physical life-principle which leaves the body at death, but, according to Lévy-Bruhl, should be translated not by "soul," but by life-energy or activity, since it corresponds to the Greek θυμός; a secondary meaning of *mauri* is that of the sacred life-principle, which is, however, material and may thus be given concrete form as a talisman. Finally, by the third word, *hau,* the living personality seems to be denoted, and in a highly concrete bodily form, since everything belonging to the body (such as the saliva, the hair, even clothes) is called *hau.* As this *hau* is often used synonymously with *mauri,* we have in essence two life-principles, of which the one is more material, the other more spiritual. This is in line with the view taken by modern ethnologists of the ideas of primitive peoples, almost all of whom distinguish two such life-principles, which we can perhaps best comprehend if we think of them as the mortal and the immortal soul, though the concepts of the primitive himself have not quite this distinct meaning.

As J. Böhme[1] has been able to show, in a work based very largely on W. Otto[2] and Arbmann,[3] it is pretty clear nowadays that the conception of an "animistic" soul, first devised by Taylor, which is the condition of life and constitutes the unity of all the spiritual faculties, is by no means the rule with primitive peoples. "Far more widespread is a dualistic or even a still further differentiated idea of the soul. Many peoples designate the soul of the living man — as the vehicle of vital and often of the conscious life — and the soul which survives, the spirit of the dead, by quite different names and regard them as two distinct entities. Sometimes the division goes even further; a number of souls are thought of as surviving, while on the other hand there are several life-souls for the vital and in the conscious life" (Böhme, op. cit., p. 115). This multiplicity of souls has, according to Böhme, to be taken in relation to the multiplicity of concrete experiences, each one of which compels an objectivization of itself in the idea of a soul, yet without correlation or unification of the ideas thus created. These originally separate and concrete localizations of the soul are connected with definite parts of the body, in which the home of the particular soul is placed — originally in the organs necessary to life, injury to which was followed by death. Böhme has established the existence of this set of ideas by a thorough investigation into the Homeric language and we cannot do better here than refer to the book itself, the conclusion of which is that the Homeric idea of the soul corresponds in essence with that of primitive peoples, there being in both a dualistic idea in which dead spirit and life-soul are separate ideas which only later came to be united in a single concept of the soul, the

[1] *Die Seele und das Ich im Homerischen Epos:* appendix: "*Vergleich mit dem Glauben der Naturvölker*" (Leipzig, 1929).

[2] *Die Manen oder von den Urformen des Totenglaubens* (Berlin, 1923).

[3] "*Zur primitiven Seelenvorstellung mit besonderer Rücksicht auf Indien*," *Le Monde oriental*, XX and XXI (1926–7).

Psyche. This word itself denoted originally only the soul which survives after death, the spirit of the dead, the duplicate soul; and it was later that it was transferred to the living — that is, to describe the spiritual faculties and emotions which had previously been called otherwise.[1]

Whether the breath-soul was the original of all these ideas or not, it certainly holds a special position among them, since it alone has led to our modern idea of the soul, which unites the soul of the living and of the dead in one — that is, has developed the spiritual significance to its utmost without wholly disregarding the bodily. This development, which is important for our whole Western culture, was accomplished in Greece and can still be traced out from the Homeric soul-concept via the popular beliefs into the purely philosophical conception of Plato. The Psyche, which thus changed from a soul of the dead to a living soul, signifies originally "breathing" (like the Latin "*anima*"), and this sensible and concrete meaning is still perceptible in certain expressions of Homer.[2] Ernst Bickel says in his afore-mentioned study of the development of the soul-idea: "The breath-soul has the advantage over other separable souls that it is capable of exhibiting the essential mark of the psychical — spontaneous movement and mutability — at any moment in apprehendable form. Further, it is felt at all times as a soul of life and vitality, and yet, in respiration, it gives us incessantly the picture of a being that vanishes into the infinite. Added to this there is the death-rattle to compel reflection and invite interpretation. . . . Historically the most important instance of the breath-soul profiting by the facility with which the image-soul combines with other forms of the separability belief is in the Greek Psyche" (p. 78). If we add that the breath proceeding from the mouth, both on account of its localization in the head and because of the relative immateriality of the invisible air, was the best possible basis for

---

[1] This rectification of Rohde's view of the Greek idea of the soul is due to W. Otto.
[2] The primitive German *saiwalô* = soul is related by Kluge (*Etymologisches Wörterbuch der deutschen Sprache*) to the Greek αἰόλος = mobile (cf. "Æolus" — wind).

the representation of the soul-concept in its sublimest form, we shall then have assembled all the elements which from the very beginning knit soul and language — and by which, in our view, the personal utterance of sound was transformed into a language of soul.

What interests us particularly in this connexion is not so much the corporeal origin of the soul (in that it was identified with a physical life-principle and placed in an organ vital to life) as the development of the purely spiritual idea which led beyond the concrete bodily nomenclature to something abstract which was to survive the body. This process too is perhaps intelligible as an anthropomorphic projection of the body-soul into the universe or at least the Beyond. Certainly it was made possible only by language and through its formation. In fact, my belief is not that the need to express the abstract idea of soul developed and enriched language, but that the self-creative tendency innate in language led to the idea of soul. Of this assumption, which all my work supports, I find an additional and supporting proof in the language of Homer, which not only displays the development of the oldest idea of the soul among the Greeks, but itself assisted the idea to develop from its original corporeality to a higher spirituality. The seat of the soul was probably at first put inside the lower body, whence man's life comes; we have seen how then the seat of the soul gradually moved upwards to upper regions of the body, which found expression macrocosmically in the inclusion of heaven and the stars within the sphere of human body-symbolism. This culture of the head found its psychical expression first in language, and it was only later that intellect and reason became the seat of the soul, which finally a materialistic science sought to localize in the brain. But even at the level of the head-culture itself the soul went through a similar dematerialization process: the sound (or a special breath-sound) continuing to be regarded materially as soul, until at last the man-made word was able not only to express the abstract idea of the soul but actually to create the spiritual through language.

Language is therefore not only an artistic creation of man that the poet only uses in order to make his feelings generally intelligible, but is itself creative. We have already indicated this in the case of the myths, in regarding the creation-legends as a macrocosmized language-process, wherein man creates himself again spiritually in the naming of his members and extends this creation to the cosmos. Hence it is, too, that creation by the Word is attributed to the God of the higher cultures of the East — as in the prayers to the Babylonian Marduk, even more in those to the Egyptian Thoth, who calls gods into existence by his words,[1] and of whom an inscription at the Chonsu-pylon in Karnak says: "What flows from his mouth happens, and what he speaks becomes." It was obvious then to assume that the god used his own name as the mightiest creative word — like the Egyptian Khepera (creator), who says: "I uttered my own name as a word of power from my own mouth, and forthwith I created myself."[2] This Logos doctrine of the East then passed by way of Judaism into the New Testament and received its purest expression in the John Gospel. Later Judaism sought to explain the word-creation of Genesis, and the Talmudists knew exactly by what letters or combinations of letters Jahwe had created the world.

Thus it is really the formation and creation of language that has produced the religions of civilized peoples, since here, even more than in myth, it is a matter of purely ideal elements, which of course only verbal expression can objectivize.[3] In this sense it might be truly said that words are gods, for gods are nothing but words. This creative power of the word has never

[1] Already in the Rig Veda we have the gods Indra and Agni springing from the mouth of the prime giant, Purusha. The above material from F. Dornseiff: *Das Alphabeth in Mystik und Magie* (Leipzig, 1922; where also, p. 54, note 1, additional references will be found) and Rob. Eisler: *Weltenmantel und Himmelzelt* (Munich, 1910).

[2] Herbert Baynes: "History of the Logos," (*J. Royal Asiatic Soc.*, 1906). See further Maspero: "*Sur la toute puissance de la parole*" (*Rec. de Travaux rel. à la phil. et archéol. égypt. et assur.*, Vol. XXIV), and A. Moret: "*Le Verbe createur et révelateur en Égypte*" (*Rev. hist. des relig.*, LX, 1909).

[3] See, for example, Konrad Schmidt: *Am Anfang war das Wort. Eine Vorstudie zur Enträtselung der griechischen Mythologie* (Gleiwitz), and L. Mackensen: *Name und Mythus. Sprachliche Untersuchungen zur Religionsgeschichte und Volkskunde* (Leipzig, 1927).

received grander expression than in the Old Testament account of the Creation, which, as we have already seen, is not a mere presentation of the story, but itself a creation through the word. This may be one of the reasons why the Jews condemned the worship of idols, dumb replicas of God (the Golden Calf, the Beast), for had they not created in Jehovah a speaking God, whose mere speech was in turn creative? The Jewish philosophy of names thus " sees in the divine name by no means a mere label of sorts, an empty sound. On the one side it stands in the closest mystical relation to the being of God, and thus shares in his might; it represents the essence of God as ' *esse* ' and ' *posse.*' On the other hand it has a sort of independent position and meaning apart from God; it is a sort of hypostasis, a shadow-figure of God. Thus to know or call his name, or to use it, means to come into the closest association with his being and power, and to make one's own his omnipotence."[1]

But in this Old Testament idea of a word-creative God, as subsequently spiritualized (by way of the Greek Pneuma-Logos doctrine) in Christianity, it is the *individual* creative power of language that is exalted: a power of new creation by speech is vouchsafed to every individual. It is only later that the poet comes to perform it for the rest, and he does so by the harmonious fusion of the individual and collective forces, for though it is a language of his own, and therewith a world of his own, that he builds, it is yet such that it conveys something to others and helps them to build a world for themselves. In the most perfect conditions poetry, which came into being in a personal language and for a personal construction, becomes as much a collective possession as the language, equally an individual creation, had already become. Language is, then, not only an individual artistic creation which copies some element of some ideology (and, by objectifying it, dominates it), but is probably the prime form of all artistic activity, which

[1] W. Heitmüller: *Im Namen Jesu* (1903; p. 154). See also Hermann Usener: *Götternamen* (1895), and the more recent book of H. Güntert: *Von der Sprache der Götter und Geister* (Halle, 1925).

urges us to speech. K. Borinski (*Der Ursprung der Sprache;*
Halle, 1911) has developed this idea and attributed to the human voice the tendency towards artistic production of sound.
He sees in the artificially systematized voice, the music of language, the purest expression of the inner form and the formation of language which as yet has nothing to do with
communication-needs but is just self-expressive. Thence he arrives at the self-relatedness of all language-formation, which
we ourselves have found to be its essence from another point of
view. Yet if language was originally not a means of communication, and if the formation of the voice and of sounds, articulation, and speech are in their truest nature individual objectifica-
tions of an artistic sort, it follows of necessity that the poet only
becomes understandable at the collective level of language-
development, even though he may have indulged in " singing
and saying " for himself alone, in prayer or song, long before
that.

Two peculiarities of the artistic creation of language, which
are particularly manifested in the poet, are thus satisfactorily
explained by the dual character of language as an individual
creation and a collective medium of communication. The one is
the much-discussed question of the relative shares of the conscious and of the unconscious in poetic creation, which has
often been dealt with by poets and æsthetic philosophers and
which psycho-analysts have tried to solve in terms of the *content* of poetry, and of course in favour of the unconscious. The
same process, however, concerns also the linguistic side of
poetry, in which language appears on the one hand as something self-creative and on the other as something created by the
poet, who is thus its master. For the self-creative urge inherent
in language is expressed for the poet himself in the feeling of
unconscious creation; but that means the tendency of language in itself, independent of his conscious will, which threatens to carry him away again and which he can only check by
linguistic means of his own, which also are special to himself.
Among these, apart from the individual word-formation

which harks back to the very creation of language, are not only the personal peculiarities of style, but also the collective forms of rhythm, rhyme, and other laws, which are received by poetry as ideologies.

So the poetic process divides more or less clearly into two separate phases, which have been called the conscious and the unconscious, but really correspond to the two processes of language-formation, the individual creative expression of an experience, and the collective communication of it. In the first phase, which might be called roughly that of conception, the poet reacts to an experience which, judged externally, may be very trivial; but his reaction is in the form and manner of language — in the widest sense — which means, and this indeed is the essence of the poet's gift, that every emotional experience forms itself for him speakably. But in this *forming* he has not yet mastered, still less finished with, the experience; on the contrary, it probably presses on him more and more, but it does so in a specific way, that of verbal expression, and thenceforward he has to shape consciously — that is, to bring into a form which is collectively intelligible. That is the second, conscious phase of poetic production, the real constructive process, and so at last he comes to the complete mastery and settlement of the experience.

These two more or less definitely separated phases of the poetic art were already observed by the Greeks, who could point to indications of it even in Homer. But the dual process, through one-sided emphasis of the conscious and the unconscious respectively, very soon led to two opposing theories, whose champions stretch in sequence from Plato and Aristotle right up to Freud and his opponents. We shall have occasion in our final chapter to discuss the various psychological attitudes of these two schools, which respectively emphasize the conscious or unconscious in poetic activity. At the moment we are concerned with the ways in which each supports its point of view and with the influence this unfruitful dispute has had on the æsthetic of poetic production. But since (as I tried to show in the *Künstler*) we have here a progressive extension of consciousness, which affects the actual process of poetic activity as well as the intuition of the process, we must first take the subject purely historically and leave the psychological penetration into the particular theories till later.

For Plato, with whom the philosophy of æsthetic, as of so much else, really begins, the poet — we should add, the Greek poet — is wholly an instrument of the divine; his faculty is purely instinctive and unconscious.[1] As Wichmann explains, Plato not only neglects the rôle of consciousness, but completely eliminates it, putting in its place mania, a being outside oneself, a divine inspiration. A view like this was, I think, inevitable in the case of the Greek poet, with his collective material and its national echo, though very probably a good deal of Plato's own artistically creative psychology has passed into his theory of genius. For in the *Phædrus* he deduces not only poetry but philosophy also, the urge to wisdom, from a condition of unconsciousness and mania — which would thus be the normal mode by which the highest gifts from the god are imparted to man.[2] The first gift of divine madness is unconscious prophecy, which is far more perfect than a calculating interpretation of signs in the light of human reason. In the *Laws* Plato says that the poet, when he seats himself on the tripod of the Muses, "is not in his senses, but, like a fountain, lets flow what comes to him, and often contradicts himself without knowing whether the one or the other thing that he says is the truth." In the *Ion,* in which philosopher and artist are contrasted, the idea developed, according to Wichmann, is that in art genius is as against technical ability all-important; and Plato expressly emphasizes here that the activity of the divine

[1] O. Wichmann: *Platos Lehre vom Instinkt und Genie* (Berlin, 1917).

[2] I take these indications from the work of Paul Plaut (*Die Psychologie der produktiven Persönlichkeit;* Stuttgart, 1929), who (p. 13) cites these views of Plato's with all respect, while (p. 157) he characterizes my own concordant views as the height of grotesque dilettantism. The reader who examines these two independent passages (when I wrote in 1905, I was unaware of Plato's view) in the originals will be convinced of the identity of the two views, both of which assume the basis of production (whether artistic or scientific) to be an illusion, a mania, or something neurotic.

power is only made effective through the elimination of the reason.

Here poet, prophet, and seer are regarded as equally the instruments of the god who reveals himself in them; but by the side of this, even if only casually indicated, we have the idea of the poets themselves that they are not mere voices of the god, but also his interpreters. In the *Timæus* there is a reference to this separation of the function of seer from that of poet and prophet, who are regarded as interpreters, orderers, and critics. This view, which admits the consciousness and the creative will of the poet, nevertheless only made its way gradually, to find its finest expression in the Pauline theory. Paul, too, was not one to underestimate the power of divine inspiration, but he said: " He that speaketh in tongues edifieth only himself, but he that prophesieth edifieth the church " (1 Corinthians xiv, 4), and it is he that makes the first sharp distinction between the Pneuma or breath from above and the Nous, which can interpret what it is given. Here the original creative power of the Word, as it triumphed in the Old Testament over all lower forms of artistic creation, becomes the conscious control of the dæmonic force of language by the Logos: in a word, the change of language from an artistic creation into a conscious medium of communication.

But before this there had already been in the development of Greek philosophy a gradual strengthening of natural science in the doctrines of the Ionian philosophers. Even Aristotle, Plato's immediate successor, no longer recognizes the primal divine force as the essence of artistic creation. In place of the dæmonic and supersensible, it is in reason that Aristotle sees the basis of all giftedness. Artistic creation is set a definite objective, as we see in paraphrase in the *Poetics,* with its laws and its rules become fossil formulæ. Aristotle does acknowledge the genius which comes through ecstasy, but for him this is rather a plastic capacity for imitation than a divine state of abnormality. As Plato's doctrine of genius in poetry underwent a resurrection in the Renaissance in the religion of genius, so did Aristotle's theory of art in the æsthetic which arose in the eighteenth century; but even in their new vigour the two streams did not manage to still the dualistic conflict, which has come to a head in modern philosophy and psychology as the problem of the respective parts played by the conscious and the unconscious in poetic productivity. For the discussion of this problem I may refer to my *Künstler* and *Inzest-Motiv,* in which, by the side of the unconscious, the increasing extension of consciousness is emphasized; and I now turn to the last stage of the problem before us, which will also link up again with our present theme.[1]

After Worringer's important pioneer work in the psychology of æsthetic it was certainly tempting to apply his point of view to a realm which he had neglected, that of poetry. The attempt was made by Albrecht Schaeffer in his *Dichter und Dichtung* (Leipzig, 1923); but this work seems to me merely to have justified Worringer's abstention from the inclusion of poetic art. For the subtle essays of Schaeffer, as he seems at times to have observed himself, make the application of the idea of this abstract art-will to poetry seem very inadequate. It is not by chance that his most successful interpretations are those relating to Greek poetry, for this is of a far more collective nature than all later poetic arts. This seems indeed to be one of the reasons why Plato regarded the poet purely as a channel for divine speech, and why Aristotle in his turn believed that from Greek poetry he could deduce laws which should be valid for all poetry. Schaeffer is certainly right in finding a good deal of " geometry " in Homer and even in Greek tragedy; he is perhaps right in thinking that this impulse to the ordering of chaos survives into modern art, since it is precisely form that has to be and will always have to be abstract. But the personal,

[1] The path from Plato and Aristotle to the present day is briefly sketched in the Introduction of my *Inzest-Motiv;* this may be supplemented by reference to the work of Professor Scott-James: *The Making of Literature* (New York, 1929). The route passes by Longinus, Dante, Ben Jonson, Boileau, Lessing, Goethe, and Coleridge, then by Sainte-Beuve, Taine, and Pater to Dilthey and the modern schools of æsthetic (see also Lange-Eichbaum, op. cit.).

individual elements, which are increasingly important in the poet of all men, cannot be neglected.

This brings us back to the problem of language, since language represents not only the material in which the poet works but also the form in which he works. In other words, the poet receives his material ready formed, at least as raw material, and has only to give it a second definitive form. But this process, as we have seen, cannot be simply split into two phases, since in each of the two phases the individual and collective elements both mingle and oppose each other. It seems to me to be one of the most complex of all psychological problems to decide in what way this reciprocal action between the individual and the collective, which is inherent in language, comes out in poetic creation; but, in conformity with our earlier discussion, we may suppose the process to be somewhat as follows: In an individual who reacts in language, a personal experience first of all finds its rough form in the traditional language-stock, which is thereby permeated by the personality and individually vitalized. On the other hand, the second stage, the verbal shaping proper, is, as it seems to me, a fresh collectivizing of what was originally expressed personally, with communication and understanding as its object. Put shortly, the first would be the expression of an individual state of feeling in the collective raw material of inherited language, the second a personal infusion into this linguistic raw material, necessitated by the social urge to communication. The two historical phases of language-creation, as we have found them in the individual copying and mastering of an ideological force and then in the surrender of this word-magic for the sake of general understanding, are thus still at work in the poet, even if no longer in their historical order. For the personal creative force, as affecting language-formation, seems only to become active in the second phase of social understanding, whereas the poet, in the first rush of feeling, gropes instinctively after the collective forms already available to him in the existing stock of language. This almost complete reversal of the historical process in the individual poet comes, however, from the fact that he has at hand a rich, perhaps even a poetically fashioned, vocabulary, and that not only has he to use it as his material and medium of communication, but it turns his creative powers from language to other elements of his productivity. In a word, the poet has no longer to create language; in fact, he can only use his creative energy within certain limits of style and occasional new coinages.

On the other hand, language itself has in the course of time gradually lost more and more of its self-creative power, as we have concluded already from a comparison of the Old Testament with the Homeric poems. Now, there is one national epic which, in contrast to the Homeric humanization, still has a clearly marked character of language-myth and whose hero is still a " speech "-hero of the type that has degenerated, with the decay of language, into what we call the bombastic fellow. This is the Finnish national epic, the *Kalevala,* which was refashioned out of a collection of old songs at the beginning of the nineteenth century by Elias Lönnrot; his work was translated into German in 1852 by Anton Schiefner and republished in 1914 by Georg Müller of Munich with notes and an epilogue by Martin Buber. In this epilogue, full of enthusiasm and understanding, a view of epic is developed from this Finnish folk-tradition which is of the utmost importance, not only for the general problem of the popular epic, but in particular for our view of the development of language.

In Finnish national poetry we can still distinguish quite clearly the magic runes and the epic runes, the latter being sung publicly everywhere, while the former were preserved as a sacred tradition and kept as a secret to be passed on from the initiate to his disciple — usually from father to son. "In Finland, almost more than among any other people, the belief is rooted in the magic power of the word, of the secret primal word; it is the belief (which lies at the base of all magic) in the power of the bound over the unbound, of rigid knowledge over swarming perils. The word is the lord of the elements;

who possesses it can create and destroy, can banish all evil and impose his will even on the gods. His song can turn his enemies to stone and chain wild beasts; he kills the frost and takes his clothes from him. Kalma — death — is his companion-in-arms. He knows the origin of all things and thus all things are subject to him; for every turbulent being is put to shame by him who has knowledge and can tell him his origin. When he begins to sing, the mountains melt like butter, the rocks like the meat of pigs, the blue woods like honey; the seas teem with mead, the deeps are raised up, the heights sink to valleys."[1]

In contrast to the magic runes — which must be used with literal exactitude (on pain of losing their force) — the Finnish folk-singer, for whom verse and measure are sacred, is much freer of the word in the epic runes: "The word is his kingdom, servant of his power; his right and calling is to change it, make it hard or soft, to raise or clarify it. Thus each Laulaja sings the song of all as well as his own, and some of them alter them many times and say different things at different times" (op. cit.).[2] Epic runes aim only at telling a story, magic runes aim at making and transforming. "Recent Finnish research has shown that epic and magic runes arose in different areas and underwent various interlinkages; in Finnish Karelia these interlinkages fused into new songs, which constitute a new kind of magical epic; in Russian Karelia the songs are grouped round a few important characters and motives and grow into cycles. Russian Karelia was the hunting-ground of Elias Lönnrot, who welded the cyclic material into epic" (op. cit., p. 476).

This fusion of the imaginative and active elements, which existed separately in the old folk-songs as the magic and the epic runes and only gradually underwent slight interlinkage,

---

[1] The same is said of the mythical singer Orpheus. The magic runes have been published by Lönnrot (Helsingfors, 1880).

[2] K. Krohne: *Wo und wann entstanden die finnischen Zauberlieder?* (Helsingfors, 1901). On the other hand, Comparetti (*Der Kalewala;* Halle, 1892) derives the epic runes from the magic.

not only seems to be characteristic of epic poetry in general, but confirms the views which we have arrived at on other grounds regarding the speech-development which forms its basis. But it seems to me that the epic or epic rune is, more than anything else, the record of the vanished power of the magic: in the same way as we showed above that Homer rather depicts a vanished world than creates one by his words in the Old Testament way. "The Finnish folk-song," says Buber, "has to be understood through its faith in the creative power of the rune. The magic song is the document containing the power, the epic poem the record and glorification of it. In it song celebrates itself by telling of its might . . . and so becomes the epic of the creative word" (op. cit.). It is typical that the Laulaja only alluded to the magic runes, whereas Lönnrot actually incorporated them in the epic runes; all the same, it is to this unpoetic confusion that we owe our deepest insight into the essence of folk-poetry and the formation of language. For although, in the epic, words can create the beasts, trees, and stones, kill men and bring them to life, expel and control the frost, just as in the magic runes above mentioned, it is only a tale recounted to a peacefully gathered assembly of things that the mighty magician who spoke and sang the runes had once accomplished — really and by means of the creation of words. When the Laulaja sometimes simply says "I," instead of naming the hero, and tells his story as if he had done the deeds, it is a naïve indication of the line of descent, magician-hero-singer; and we will devote the rest of this chapter to the deeper origins of this psychological development.

It would be a fascinating besides being in fact a very necessary task to study the whole of poetry, first from the angle of the hero and his cultural importance, secondly from the ego-centric standpoint of the poet, thirdly from that of the human need of communication.[1] We should then see that the poetry of all times gives us incidentally a history of the poet such as we

[1] Freud has some suggestions in this direction; see his essay: *Der Dichter und das Phantasieren* (1908).

should never obtain from biography alone;[1] we should also discover from the history of the hero as reflected in the poetry of
the various ages a piece of human cultural history precipitated
in hero-formation. A first outline for such a study was attempted
in two chapters of my *Seelenglaube und Psychologie*,[2] which
I should like to summarize in brief here. I showed there, substantially, that the hero of the Age of the Soul, as displayed
particularly in the folk-lore of primitive peoples, differs from
the hero of the Age of Sexuality as described in the myths
and poesy of civilized peoples. The primitive magical world-
outlook, which rests on the identity of thinking and being,
makes the hero, at this stage of development, translate his
thoughts, dreams, wishes, and desires into actual practice,
whereas the hero of the other age suffers tragic failure in the
same effort. The basis for this I felt I had found in a class of
epic traditions which portray the passage from soul-beliefs to
sex-beliefs, together with the psychical and social conflicts involved, as, for example, in the Gilgamesh epic, etc. At both
stages the problem is fundamentally similar: namely, to attain
personal immortality. Neither in primitive nor in Classical
times does he actually achieve it. But he finds it ideologically
in that his deeds, which have subserved his attempt to gain a
real immortality, have made him a hero whose fame lives on
in the song of later generations.

In that work my object was to show how the will to immortality makes the hero — whose successor is the singer —
actually and historically immortal, quite apart from the fact
whether he solves his problems with the simplicity of a fairy-
story or tragically fails in them. At present I want to emphasize
another side of the heroic character: this is the relation of word
and deed, of action and narrative, which, as we all know,
distinguishes also the two poetic forms of drama and epic. As
I showed in *Seelenglaube* (p. 113), the dream-activity, which

---

[1] This idea is put forth in the Introduction to the *Inzest-Motiv* and developed to some
extent in the course of that work.
[2] Namely those entitled "The Age of Sexuality" and "Dream and Actuality."

serves as evidence of immortality, is first described in story-form as having really happened; and in the primitive world-outlook this causes no difficulty, since its whole ideology is built up on the identity of thinking and doing. Out of this narrated dream-action (in the form of the animistic legend) the age of sexuality develops the heroic myth, in which the hero tries to transform the events into reality by accomplishing what are called heroic deeds. Now, in this process language or, better, the word performs the same magic rôle which formerly fell to the dream-thought; everything has to be carried out just as it is narrated — a principle of realization, which underlies all religious art, painting, and sculpture, but also all "illustrative," historical art as well. In short, the creative word not only brings forth the mythical or legendary story — myth means simply story — but leads also to the proper action by which what has been said is carried out in deeds.

In this sense not only the world, as we saw, but man also is created by the word; and he now seeks to do everything which he can say, as formerly he had to do all that he thought. Thus, merely to give one example for the moment, it is probable that the triple undertaking of the same deed in a story arose from a repetition of the original magical words, which were to give effect to the action in a magical way and so had to be repeated. Taking Hamlet as the type of the passive, inactive hero, whose indecisiveness has led to so many discussions and commentaries, what he really expresses is just this characteristic word-magic of the hero. Though he does occasionally despise himself for venting himself only in words, the whole play is substantially built up on a faith in words which are imagined capable of improving men and altering circumstances. Indeed, what Hamlet expected from his "play" and from his tirades against his mother or Ophelia, the poet himself also apparently hoped would be the effect of his play on the English court, whose corruptness he lashed with words. It was only when words proved ineffective that Hamlet was driven to action; since his words could not kill like daggers, he had to turn to real weapons. The demand for action in a drama is satisfied by very few plays which can lay claim to any artistic form, and finds itself fulfilled far more on the films, or in their predecessor the melodrama, than in Classical tragedy and its imitations. Even Greek tragedy was far more a matter of speaking than of doing, of philosophizing about action and its conditions than of action itself: only the actions are so vividly depicted and so well supported by the actors that we have an impression of actual events even where we are dealing with accounts of long-past incidents and reflecting thought about them. The same is still truer of the classicist drama of a Racine or a Schiller, whose qualities of language and thought we admire, as well as of Ibsen, in whom there is nothing but talk.

Shakspere, here too, holds a peculiar position. He took a number of subjects which had hitherto been treated, if at all, only novelistically in narrative, and brought them on the stage in the fullness of their action and actuality.[1] But he accompanies the action with words, and interprets it in a way which is characteristic of our view of the drama. Just as Hamlet regrets that words can no longer kill, so Macbeth is a hero *rather* of words and thoughts; he is no murderer who rushes to his aim, but a dreamer of glory and kingship, driven to action by his fancies, which the witches put into words for him. He also, like Hamlet, at first kills in words and thoughts, before he has recourse to the dagger; to which he is driven as much by the witches of his fancy as by the concrete Lady Macbeth, who rebukes him as a mere mouth-hero.

Shakspere's drama represents, then, at once the beginning and the culmination of heroic action as opposed to dramatic narrative; and we find, the further we go back in history, that the drama is proportionately less rich in action — as is shown even by Greek tragedy, which really amounts to a philosophical discussion between the hero and the chorus. But Greek tragedy itself, in this poetic form, grew from the narrative

[1] The Shaksperian drama represents the liberation of the theatre from the Classical and the religious "play" in that he humanizes and actualizes the action (see *Seelenglaube und Psychologie*, pp. 63–74).

epic, though it apparently included some elements of the cult of Dionysus (the goat-song). But between the goat-dances of the ecstatic worshipper of Dionysus and the drama of Æschylus there is a vast development, not only of Greek culture, but of that art of poetry which culminated in the Homeric epic. Tragedy takes not only its subjects, but its language as well from epic and not cult tradition; without the splendid achievement of that language in epic, tragedy would have been impossible.[1]

In the Homeric epic, however, as I already showed in my *Seelenglaube,* we have on the one hand the legendary story of a dream — in the naïve Odyssey — and on the other the first stage of its heroization — in the warlike Iliad, in which the hero is no longer content to describe his fancied adventures as actual happenings, but is compelled to transform them, at least partially, into action. In the Odyssey the plain telling of thoughts, dreams, and longings is itself a lived experience for the hero, so obviously so that we need do no more than allude to it, though the detailed expansion of this view by an analysis of the poem would give us valuable insight into the essence of the poetic art. But in the Iliad also — just as in the rhetorical drama, which is a running commentary on tragic doings — we allow ourselves to be deluded by the warlike subject and the realistic scenes into neglect of the speeches, which are the real content of the epic. This is more than merely a consequence of the fact that epic must of necessity narrate; the heroes themselves talk much more than they act — just as they are made to do so grotesquely in Offenbach's travesties. More, not only does the hero Achilles, like Hamlet, pour out his heart in words; but there is far more battling in words than in deeds in the whole poem — and the very theme of the poet's song is the anger of Achilles, together with the effects of this passion on his fellows and on the whole undertaking. The real

[1] The dramatic character of Greek epic has been brought out lately in Victor Bérard's book: *Le Drame épique* (Paris, 1930). This author's second volume, *La Résurrection d'Homère,* only came to my knowledge during the writing of this book.

theme, then, is not the fight against Troy, but only one episode, of which the subject-matter is a quarrel of the Greek leaders among themselves; a quarrel too which is carried on with words and not with weapons. It is this disunity among individuals, who represent the several Greek tribes, and peoples, that in the Homeric picture brings the undertaking to grief. But here it is no longer the languages which cause confusion among the peoples, as in the Tower of Babel, but the passions and emotions, which already the poet is treating psychologically, even though he still localizes them in particular parts of the body. But behind these individual passions there are at bottom national prejudices and motives, and these too seem in the Iliad to express themselves by way of words. At any rate I cannot regard the mixing of dialects in the artificial language of Homer as a matter of chance, for on the one hand it serves admirably to indicate the lack of national unity, and on the other it seems as though the poet wished in his collective language to symbolize the unity of the Greek race. This mingling of different dialects is in conformity with the well-known mingling of temporally separate cultures that, as we have seen, is characteristic of the metaphorical revitalizing of the past in poetry. And this latter is just as much an immortality-symbol as the mixing of the language is a collective symbol.

This brings us from the hero to the poet, who in this sense is not only a prolongation of the identity of the hero, but actually carries on his social function at a later stage of development. The original epic form of narrative poetry was probably in the first person: that is, the man who described the action or the adventure had lived it, at least in his soul; he transformed his psychical experience through the story into a true activity, he created reality by the magic of language. This word-created reality would be taken by the audience also as truth, for, after all, it rested ultimately on the same magic ideology of striving for the achievement of immortality. This was achieved first of all by the transformation of the dream-experiences which proved the immortality of the soul into real actions that we of today would call magical, but which for primitive men were perfectly harmonious with his whole outlook on the world. At a later stage it was verbal description that was transformed into deed, and those who tried or managed to achieve this were the heroes, who had preserved a bit of the magic world. Later again, someone would tell of the hero and his deeds in the past, but these he now only brings to life by the word and does not create. In this sense the poet is a mouth-hero, a liar — as he is already called in Plato — but the reproach is only fair in relation to the content and not to the form, which, as language, was still to a certain extent creative. This creative faculty shows the poet to be the successor of the hero himself, who in one sense had been socially creative and effective, in that he had changed ideas into realities, but in another was already a liar, or even a swindler, since he denied the descent of the deed from the word, while at a still later stage of poetry he refuses to translate his words into deeds (Hamlet).

Now, since the original narrator of his own experiences, and also the later hero and the still later poet, were at bottom telling of the lost magical world of the human will and of speech as its creative expression, it is not surprising that the content of their stories often betrays what it was in last analysis that man had lost with the loss of magical power. From a study of the various traditions of primitive and civilized peoples on the lines indicated in my *Seelenglaube und Psychologie,* it seems to me quite certain that the original power of this magic lay in the immortality-idea, that this faded out with the decreasing intensity of the magical belief in personal creative will-power, and that the hero had tried actively and the poet passively to make good the loss. The result of this social and artistic effort to regain the lost faith in immortality — or the symbol which represented it in the form of animal, plant (herb), or human being (woman) — is that the hero, and with him the poet, find, in lieu of the personal immortality of the magic age, an ideological immortality in the work. Ultimately this activity, whether social as with the hero, or artistic as with the poet, is a magical attempt not only to evidence but to attain to the immortality-belief by actualizing their thought, their wish, or their word. The hero and the poet do not find the way to personal immortality, but the mere effort to do so, as displayed in their work, endows them with an ideological immortality. Actually, as I showed in my *Seelenglaube,* from a study of the material, they suffer tragic collapse in this effort after personal immortality, and it is this tragic collapse which by a sort of irony of fate makes them immortal.

This is obvious in the hero and his typical destiny, and we have emphasized in various passages of this book to what extent the poet also, and the artist in general, sacrifices his life to gain immortality. How far this is a necessary precondition of artistic production, for whose purposes life must be spent, and how far it is a more or less conscious self-sacrifice of the man to his work, is one of the deepest problems in the whole psychology of productivity. And that is why we have found the problem expressed as early as the creation-myths from the double point of view — on the one hand the world made by a violent, on the other by a voluntary, sacrifice of man. The discussion of this problem from the individual psychological point of view we will postpone to our last chapter, and we shall discuss here the ways in which it is displayed in poetry itself, regarded as a revelation of collective ideologies. The belief in immortality which man seeks, first religiously, then heroically, and finally artistically, to save passes through a development in human history which I have described in my *Seelenglaube* and which is also manifested in art as a whole and in poetry especially. It is a long journey from the naïve self-assurance of the legendary hero, who suffers nothing and succeeds in everything — since, after all, he does nothing but accomplish by the magic of language all that his wishes drive him to — to the tragic hero who is destroyed by the fate he has created for himself. In tragedy man not only accepts mortality, but assists the death which is forced upon him as something that he has himself willed and for which he takes responsibility. Though the heroic

was seen at first in the birth [1] (or, better, the liberation) of man
from an established dependence through his personal heroism,
it becomes in the end the acceptance of death as a fate self-
willed and tragically accepted.

This spiritual development found its cultural expression in
Christianity, although the idea of the sacrifice or self-sacrifice
of a man or divine hero had been prepared in Classical religion
and mythology, as witness the partition of Osiris, the mangling
of Bacchus, the mutilation of Attis. The Oriental mystery-
religions which lived on in the Eleusinian and Orphic cults
of Greece all have the death and resurrection of a god as their
subject. But in the mysteries the god becomes man and suffers
the fate of mortality, while in Christianity man again becomes
god — that is, achieves psychical immortality. In the late Roman
Mithras cult, which Cumont has studied so thoroughly,[2] we
have an immediate predecessor of Christianity, with its strong
democratic cast. A close bond of intimacy united all members
of the cult into an all-embracing brotherhood in which the
lowest slave could receive the highest initiation. In the development of this democratic principle which allows every individual to become god — to attain the immortality which had
till then been reserved for the divine hero — lies the world-
historical significance of Christianity, but at the same time its
difference from the collective soul-beliefs of the primitives.
These also allow all to share in the immortality of the tribe,
as members of the whole. But thereafter man had passed
through a period of individualization which culminated in
the Greek hero and his tragic death, and so at last Christianity
came with its theory of individual immortality according to
which everyone could, by living in a certain way, become hero
and god and thus participate in resurrection after death.

This change — not produced, but only clothed in religious
symbolism by Christianity — from the active wilful man repre-

[1] See *The Myth of the Birth of the Hero*.
[2] F. Cumont: *Les Mystères de Mythra* (1899) and *Les Religions orientales dans le paga-
nisme romain* (1906).

sented in the ancient hero, to the passive sinful mankind that Christ symbolized, brought about a change also in the general ideology of art. All productivity thenceforth was consciously set to the service of religion, just as originally it had been an unconscious expression of the religious belief in the collective soul. The artist became God's servant and no longer, as he had been in Greece, his rival. And so he remained till the Renaissance, which was a rebirth, not merely of Classical art-style, but of Classical man, or, more correctly, of his heroic ideal, the strong man of will. What the Classical artist had represented in poetry and sculpture — namely, the heroic idea of the individual as such — was actually lived by *men* of the Renaissance, whereas it was only a brief life to which its *art* reawakened the Classical art-ideology and its individualism of personalities. Thus, as we have seen, the Renaissance produced the individual artist-type who sought to express in Classical form, no longer the religious content of, but the pure humanity induced by, Christianity. In this Michelangelo was the most successful, and he, too, was physically and spiritually worn down by this conflict of ideas, even though able, at that price, to harmonize them in his work.[1] He is still Christian and already pagan; but his Christianity is no longer religious, but human; that is, he crucifies himself on his human sufferings because of the inner, individualist apostasy from Christianity involved in his humanizing it. In this sense all the great artists of the Renaissance are in their lives Christian sufferers, sacrificed and crucified for their art. What Karl Scheffler [2] says of Rembrandt is true of them too: "He lived, was crucified, died, descended into hell, and rose again, this first heretic among painters." In this sense, however, Christianity was itself a vast dramatized tragedy of the heretic individual, and it not only fixed the artistic ideologies of nearly two thousand years, but was also itself an ideology, transformed into action, of the tragic man, the prototype of the drama whose weak echo is all that was

[1] See Emil Lucka: *Michelangelo; ein Buch über den Genius* (Berlin, 1930).
[2] Karl Scheffler: *Holland* (Leipzig, 1930; English translation, New York, 1932).

achieved by the religious plays, religious painting, and religious sculpture right down to the Gothic.

Only then did man rediscover his self-creative power. Though his activity was still for the honour and service of God, yet here for the first time he was able with his heavenward-striving cathedral to accomplish the bold enterprise of the Tower of Babel, and that because artists were united by a universal Christianity. But " the limitless will of Gothic humanity," which Schaeffer (op. cit., p. 35) sees in the heaven-storming cathedrals, is only intelligible as the result of the contemporary revolution in the individual, who had once more learned to will, after leaving his will to God for so long. Yet in the first instance this art was dumb, like all sculpture and plastic art, though at the same time, like all great art, it was in the highest sense dramatic or, rather, dynamic. For Gothic is nothing but " plastic art in architectural form." " When the Gothic spirit had exhausted its passion for the Beyond, it withdrew from the arts of form and poured itself forth in music, in the souls of Bach, Handel, and Mozart; what remained on this side split up into many parts and became Romantic, in the sense of the Klopstock-to-Hölderlin epoch. . . . But so far as that demand for the plastic asserted itself — unconsciously and in the depths of its essence — it entered into the poetry of language and produced the noble art of Greek corporeality in Goethe's men and Hölderlin's odes " (op. cit., p. 40).

Here we see the urge of all essentially " dramatic " art towards life and the living, which can express only in drama and culminates in the Shaksperian form. For in the drama man does not create life in language only. The actor performs it before our eyes in real, bodily, human form and so leads art back again to the life from which it had started. All that the painter wanted to copy or create in pictorial, or the sculptor in plastic form, found in the word a purely human and in the humanized drama of Shakspere a dramatic, dynamic, and vivid expression. But the prime drama of all European art was Christianity itself, at least in its significance as a new ideology of sacrifice, corresponding to the death and rebirth cycle of the ancient world. The only difference is that Christianity, out of the man sacrificed (crucified) for an idea, created the ideology of a *willing self-sacrifice* of one who dies for all others and precisely for that reason is himself immortalized. But this only represents a supreme spiritualization of the primitive myth in which the individual sacrifices (dismembers) himself so as to produce the world from his body: an ideology which we have seen to be the prototype of all impulse to artistic production. We shall return in the last chapter to this problem of artistic *renunciation;* here our interest lies in the course of the development from the primitive human sacrifice, which has always the character of a building-sacrifice, to the spiritualized renunciation of the creative artist.

The fundamental idea is that for all created things there is needed not only a creator, but a piece of life, life itself, which is somehow withdrawn from its proper destiny of death and fixed in an intransient existence. The basic question, then, is: whence is this life taken which creates and gives life to the work of art? From the creator, or from someone else, who offers himself as a sacrifice either voluntarily or by compulsion or through the lot falling upon him? The whole problem of artistic renunciation is contained in the acceptance and knowledge that the creator must give a part of life — in fact, his own life — in order to make it eternal in his work of art. The sacrifice of another life is only a sham sacrifice which does not save him from self-sacrifice, though it may be the immediate instinct of self-preservation to find a substitute.

This, too, is the whole primitive idea of a sacrifice, whether of man or of animal; in every case there is the identification of sacrificial victim and priest, and beyond this again the original identity of all living and dead things, which of course was what gave rise to the notion of a kingdom of the dead corresponding to that of the living. And on this identity of living and dead the whole world-outlook of primitive man, with its collective soul-concept, is built up. Death demands a victim; but to the collective ideologism of primitive society it is immaterial who dies; one is as good as another, in dying as in living. It is only later that each one seeks to maintain his personal individuality, and only then that the killing becomes a sacrifice; but not a sacrifice to any god (unless, indeed, the god the individual thus distinguished from the mass is himself reputed to be this god). The sacrifice itself is thus at the same time its own real object — an object negative rather than positive, and definitely not an " I." At this stage already we have the cheating of death, or of nature, out of its tribute — an idea which did not exist in the original killing of man or animal. For when a basic identity makes one as good as another, death in any case receives its tribute. It was only when it became a matter of a particular individual, and of the finding of a substitute victim for him, that the element of deceit crept in — an element which we find inseparably associated not only with sacrifice, but with games, of which, as we shall see in the next chapter, gambling with fate and competing with the rival are characteristic elements.

At this point there enters the Oracle. At first sight it appears as if its object was for destiny to settle who was to be the particular sacrifice. But already magic is inevitably in the field as a method of righting fortunes, and this shows how little serious men were in subordinating themselves to the decisions of fate. Had they done so, the whole business of oracles would have been unnecessary — it may indeed have been only an *ex post facto* justification for a sacrifice already consummated, as is suggested, for instance, by the fact that at least in the case of entrail-augury the animal had first to be killed before it could be settled whether the victim approved of the sacrifice or not.[1] Anyhow, even this inspection of entrails, that strikes us as so primitive, appears to presuppose a complicated process of justification whereby a man must excuse the deceit of vicarious sacrifice by obtaining the sanction from the victim. The fact

[1] In the primitive narrative of the Californian Indians (see p. 259) the stag is consequently asked, before he is slain, whether he consents to it.

that this justification afterwards takes on the form of a prophesying of the *future* only confirms our view, for does not the sacrifice take place in order that the sacrificer *may have a future* himself — that is, remain alive?

Such a substitution-sacrifice, however, is at bottom a drama, in looking at which we not only feel the tragedy of all human fate because of our identification with the hero, but, quite as strongly, the consolation that in this case it is not we but another that is the victim — a motive which probably guides the poet in his choice of historical material and in his poetically representing sufferings of his own in others. Here again we must recognize that Christianity represents a universal drama of world-history, which, in spite of all archaization in the Greek sense or modernization in the individualistic, still does represent the universal human quality of this ideology of sacrifice. For tragedy also, like every other art-form, has passed through an ideological development, which, in spite of all external similarity of forms, discloses varieties of spiritual and intellectual meaning.

Greek tragedy was a symptom of the collapse of Greek humanity, which the mythic hero, as prototype of the hybrid individual, interpreted with grand gesture as a fate which he could accept because he willed it. In post-Christian drama the death of the hero is merely a consolatory warning, which shows how the Greek or the Roman or the Macbeth or the Wallenstein is the victim of his own fate — which we can avoid if we would draw the right moral. The Classical drama-hero is thus different in essence from the modern, for the latter has an intrinsic individuality, whereas the Classical hero is only an individual consciously and for the occasion elevated above the people, which is represented by the chorus. The poet who sings and laments in drama the hero and his sufferings — which epic had shown as his deeds — thus becomes the heir of the hero in whose place he is put or puts himself;[1] while the sculptor or painter is in this respect the heir rather of the god

[1] See my *Don Juan. Une étude sur le Double.*

who creates men, like Prometheus, the symbol of Greek artistic creation.[1]

Modern drama, of which *Hamlet* may still be regarded as the type, thus also shows us the passive hero — which means the poet himself — who is not guilty as the Classical hero is because of his overweening actions, but because of his rejection of the heroic rôle in the fulfilment of which he is hindered by a predisposing feeling of guilt. Thus the hero, who had originally been the exemplar of the poet, gradually assumes his qualities — a process which has found so unique an expression in Shakspere's *Hamlet* because this drama shows us the heroic ideology transforming itself into the poetic. The merely biographical question, how far the passive hero shows the qualities of his particular poet, is, in my view, secondary to the far more important fact that *the hero represents the poet himself as a type;* and this at a stage of development when the magic power of the word begins to fail in face of human passions; when, therefore, the individual is already checked in his willed actions; once more the creative power of the word shines in all its poetic beauty, but it achieves nothing more than the momentary lightening of the poet's heart.

This decay of the magic power of one man's word is connected with increasing individualization, which is also reflected in the transformation of the hero and his character. In Shaksperian drama the hero no longer stands as in the Greek drama over against the chorus, which represented the whole people, nor other typical *dramatis personæ,* but a whole series of equally individual characters, of whom each one is a hero in his own way, and in this sense speaks his own language. That all the characters in modern drama also speak the language of their poet as a collective language is not irreconcilable with this; we saw it equally in Homer's epic mixture of languages which bridged the national differences of his heroes. But while, in the heroic epic which reflects the exhaustive struggles of the Migrations, we saw the poetic attempt to save the individual,

[1] See the section "*Erziehen und Beherrschen*" in *Genetische Psychologie*, II (1928).

in the form of national hero, from his submergence in the flood of the masses, we recognize in the tragedy which developed in the hour of the people's victory the ruin of a hero reborn from the mass, who perishes not because of the people's overweeningness, but his own. Tragedy shows him as freeing himself from the mass, symbolized in the chorus, only to fall a victim to the fate consequent on his own greatness. This second hero is no longer leader of the masses — their head, as it were — but he stands over against the crowd as an overdominant individual. The last modern struggle of this type we find in the already almost comic heavy tragedian, in whom the poet who would depict his own personal conflicts on the stage finds a mere megaphone.

Chapter Ten

GAME AND DESTINY

❧

> *There is no chance;*
> *And what seems hazard in our eyes*
> *Arises from the deepest source.*
> SCHILLER (Wallenstein)

Chapter Ten

GAME AND DESTINY

೫ং২

It is only after this vast detour through humanity's macro-cosmic world-picture — which has shown us art as not a copy of nature, but a replica of a cosmos created on a microcosmic scale — that we can return to the problem of play: not in order to discuss æsthetic pleasure resulting from the play-impulse, but to come nearer to the comprehension of that impulse itself. Here, too, it is not sufficient to explain matters on the basis of individual psychology without having regard to the spiritual-collective intentions which originally led to the activity of play. Already in the æsthetic discussion of the play-impulse we have had to refer to the difference, so important for art, between the psychological attitudes of the creator and the receiver, which does not exist in games — unless it is that the defeated party in games is somehow forced into the passive rôle of receptivity. The pleasure experienced by the creative artist may approach the pleasure of play to this extent, that in both cases the activity is one which in the artist is at least potentially a motor activity [1] and in play really does take effect in action. On the other hand, art as it is in the primal practice, the ritual dances and ceremonies of primitive peoples, and in the cult actions of higher cultures, [2] has, from the psychological point of view, an affinity to play in that, when the whole community participates, there is no rigid distinction between creative and receptive.

But as against this psychological resemblance between

[1] Cf. A. Winterstein: "*Motorisches Erleben im schöpferischen Vorgang*" (*Die psycho-analytische Bewegung*, I, 4; November–December 1929).
[2] Cf. Jane Harrison: *Ancient Art and Ritual.*

primitive art-activity and the play-condition we have the significant difference that the original ceremonial, even if it seems to us to be play, is for the participant something filled with the deepest and most serious meaning; in a word, that his destiny was at stake. Play has at first a very definite meaning and object, even though this is not concerned with an immediate practical purpose but (as in art) with an ideological (magical) one. When we pass from the communal customs of primitive peoples, in which every individual — at least as part of a group — has a definite rôle, to the games of higher civilizations, we find, even when they exist only for amusement and excitement, that an old idea is living on in a symbolic or metaphorical form. This is, usually, the rules of the game, which are based on tradition and which the participants no longer understand, but to which, therefore, they all the more closely conform. The macrocosmic world-pictures of the older civilizations have thrown a useful light on the original cult significance of these play-ideologies and proved their connexion with the general collective world-view.

We cannot here deal with the whole material, though in this sphere, more than in others, there is a relative dearth of literature; and, above all, the work of arriving at a comprehensive history of folk-games has not yet passed beyond the stage of fragmentary preliminaries.[1] There are, indeed, since Winckler's studies in the cosmologies of the ancient East were written, many valuable references in the literature of religious and cultural history to the macrocosmic aspect of human play, which had previously been treated from the pure point of view of individual psychology.[2] Since we are concerned here with only a single (though, in our view, an essential) character of play,

[1] Cf. Carl Hagemann: *Spiele der Völker. Eindrücke und Studien auf einer Weltfahrt nach Afrika und Ostasien* (Berlin, 1921). There is a valuable specialist study of Hans Damm: *Die Gymnastischen Spiele der Indonesier und Südseevölker* (Leipzig, 1922). And Y. Hirn's fundamental work, *Les Jeux d'enfant* (Paris, 1917), discusses folk-lore material from the collectivist standpoint of the author (cf. *Origins in Art. A psychological and sociological Inquiry* (1900). See also the splendidly illustrated book: *Kinderspielzeug aus alter Zeit* by Karl Gröber (Berlin, 1928).

[2] See references in the chapter on "The Play-impulse."

we shall have to be contented with a cursory sketch of the macrocosmic interaction, the more so as we shall construct our own view of play on the basis of what we have already arrived at concerning the significance of macrocosmic symbolism.

In the first, and still the best, summary of this sort, which Winckler gives us in the chapter " Myth, Legend, and Play " of his popular account of the intellectual culture of ancient Babylon, the fundamental fact is established that the festivals connected with various games had all a seasonal character, with a definite calendar as their basis. In these festivals and the associated games, " the events in heaven which the festival represents — for example, the death and rebirth of the deity, the victory over the powers of darkness, the dragon — are represented and played before the people " (op. cit., p. 122). Let us add, before we produce further examples, that these festivals, representing, say, the death and rebirth of a deity, are nothing else than the return to earth, after projection heavenwards, of the human immortality-ideologies which attain their true force precisely through this macrocosmization. As a matter of fact, most children's games that have survived into the present are really " seasonal " games, not only in the sense that they are favoured by the pleasant weather of spring, but in the cosmic sense, as many of their names, etc., show: for example, the game of " *Tempelhüpfen,*" where we have to hop on one foot from " heaven " to " hell." The same is seen in skittles and other ball-games.

This brings us from what is a representation, religious or profane, of the calendar myths in processions or shows, to what is a real *doing* in the competitive games alike of children and grown-ups, who — in contrast to the actor — are no longer conscious of the mythical part they are playing. The competitive character of games, too, seems to be primitive, though playing to win a prize is a very late development. The original victor in the competition, long before the days of the palm, did not content himself with honour alone: what he won was life, which the defeated rival usually forfeited. Nor is this only the case with the fighting-game; it survives into such late traditions as the legend of the " Singers' contest on the Wartburg," which according to Winckler is a typical New Year legend. "Five singers — whom he interprets as being the five planets — vie with each other, and the defeated are to fall to the executioner. Heinrich von Ofterdingen sings best, but, by a trick, is declared beaten." In the same way, in the Arabian account of the race of the five horses, the winner is cheated of the prize. This ineradicable cheating in a game, this *" corriger la fortune,"* seems deeply rooted in the instinct of self-preservation — as are all those strong feelings and emotions which games can produce in otherwise cold-blooded people. The game is originally neither a pastime nor a means of enrichment, but a matter of destiny; and that is why it is deeply rooted in cosmological and astral symbols, so that even comparatively recent inventions like card-games are entangled with them. Thus the game of tarot, a passionate favourite in many parts of Europe, is only intelligible — as a very learned work of Ernst Kurtzahn shows — from the " cabbalistic method of forecasting the future." [1] A considerable part is played, too, by magic alphabets, which originated in Egypt, but were known in Italy and Africa as well: " Magic powers are attributed to the alphabet, and it is employed to produce mystic formulæ for the curing of pains, etc." (op. cit., p. 128). The letters, generally twenty-two as in the Phœnician alphabet, " are arranged according to the phases of the moon to which they correspond and to which their names allude. So here too we have a magic which is a transferred astrology." Even this brief account, which in many cases has to omit the very convincing details, shows us the development from the real representation of death in games of fighting and sacrifice (especially among the Mexicans) to the symbolically threatened death which is still prophesied for us when we have our fortune told by cards. [2]

---

[1] Ernst Kurtzahn: *Tarot; Die Kabbalistische Methode der Zukunftserforschung als Schlüssel zum Okkultismus* (Leipzig, 1920).

[2] The much older game of dice, with its 3x6 as the highest throw, reminds Winckler

But I have succeeded, further, in finding a link in the chain
which connects even our purely intellectual games (like chess)
with that primitive symbolism of death and resurrection which,
in contrast to its more spiritual form, we have called the animal-
underworld symbolism. In a work on "The old Egyptian
Snake-game" by H. Ranke,[1] based on a publication of Quibell,[2]
there is described and discussed a favourite board-game of the

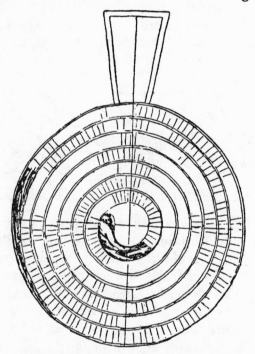

Egyptians, which is of peculiar interest for us. This is not that
chief favourite of the Egyptians, the game with the square fields
which alone outlasted the Old Kingdom, but an older vanished
form which is preserved for us in a wall-painting of a Third
Dynasty grave published by Quibell. Ranke describes it as

(p. 127) of the origin of "the number of man" ($216 = 6^3$), especially when we add
that in Pythagorean doctrine the cube is the picture of perfection.

[1] *Report* of the Sitzungsberichte der Heidelberger Akademie der Wiss., 1920–4.

[2] *Excavations at Saqqara* (1913).

follows: "The picture in Quibell shows us a board of circular form with trapezoidal, handle-like additions. The board itself has an inner drawing, representing a black and yellow spotted snake, coiled in seven leftward spirals. Near the head, in the centre of the board, a small circle is left free. The board is divided into four sectors by two red lines intersecting at right angles. The windings of the snake's body are crossed by red lines set fairly close and all radially directed to the centre. The ebony box[1] which belonged to the board contained small figures of three lions and three recumbent dogs, apparently of ivory, and six times six balls of various colours. It looks as if

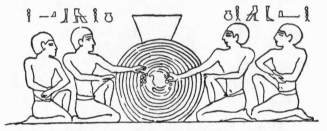

as many as six people could play the game simultaneously." A relief of the Fifth Dynasty, also from Saqqara, shows two men, one at each side of such a board, in the act of putting the animal figures on the snake, in whose coils a number of balls already lie. "Two other men with peculiar attitudes of arm and hand are sitting *apparently* inactive at the players' sides. Of how the game proceeded, what its object and the thought at the back of it were, we know nothing" (op. cit., p. 5). The idea of a symbolical representation of a lion-hunt is rejected by Ranke himself in view of the queer hunting-ground of a snake's body.[2]

[1] The handle and interior are painted bright yellow; that is, they were probably imagined as made of cedar-wood, with the exception of the snake's head and tail, which are black.

[2] A description given by Champollion of the players, whose one hand is open while the fist of the other is clenched, is referred by Ranke to the beginning of the game, not the game itself, as though a guess at the contents of the closed fist was about to settle which pair should begin.

Before we continue with Ranke's careful research into the meaning and origin of this game, we may show briefly how it interests us in connexion with our general problem. If we think away the head and tail of the snake (which are hardly recognizable on other "snake-game" boards reproduced by Ranke), we have a clear picture of one of those labyrinth spirals which we found described in Babylonian inscriptions as "palaces of the entrails," and this would also explain the animals like the Minotaur that lived there. And in fact Ranke, working from mythological considerations, which he connects with *mḥn,* the name of the game or its board, comes to the conclusion that the same name is given to a snake in "Amduat, in whose coils certain gods dwell, in one of those dark chambers which the sun-god's ship passes in the night; and also to that great snake which at the beginning of the seventh hour of the night (at midnight) appears with Isis in the ship of the sun as it passes through the underworld . . . coiling protectively round the flesh of Osiris, and rearing up threateningly against his enemies." The fact that the serpent of the Amduat — *mḥn* — which is always imagined as masculine, is written *mhn.t* in the feminine, after the Twenty-second Dynasty, seems to corroborate its obvious identification with the "simultaneously appearing Isis, since these protective entrails — the underworld — must have originally had maternal symbolism. Over and above all that, a painting on a mummiform coffin of the later New Kingdom shows a snake goddess *mhn.t* as protectress in the kingdom of the dead — parallel to the male serpent god *mḥn* who guards the sun-god on his path through the kingdom of the dead" (op. cit., p. 21). If we add that "the female termination, *mhn.t,* is handed down as one of the numerous names of the uræus snake," whose body in its many coils girds the brow-fillet of the sun-god and his earthly son, the king, the symbol of the snake confirms once more our principle of religious, cultural, and artistic development.

The development of this symbol not only runs from the

chthonian to the solar — the solar spiral arising from the picture of the entrails and being thus transferred from the lower body (the kingdom of the dead) to the brow (the heavens above) — but affords a further typical instance of the reversal of artistic symbolism, which abstracts from the ugly mortal entrails the beautiful and permanent external as its form. The encoiled serpent, which may be taken as the representation of the labyrinthine entrails, the inward parts, thus appears in the end as free of all animal significance, in its specific spiral form (biting its own tail) as a symbol of the higher resurrection-idea symbolized in the heavenly form of the sun's course. And this general ideological explanation suffices of itself to give us the meaning of the snake-game. It only remains to bring Ranke's purely Egyptological conclusions in the scope of this general explanation; but in doing this it will not suffice merely to quote his conclusion, not only because it emphasizes only one — the religious — aspect, but because it is just the detailed steps of his gradual process of thought which are of value to us.

The identification of the "sun king" with the uræus snake coiled round his brows, which we have discovered to be the cultural symbol of this process of elevation, seems to be confirmed by two passages of the pyramid texts which Ranke quotes. "In the passage," says Ranke (p. 23), "where it is said of the dead king that he 'comes forth as *mḥn* (or in the *mḥn*? or from the *mḥn*?)' we may perhaps have the identification of the king with the snake. And if in the pyramid text No. 1866 'these white teeth,' which the king is to 'receive' should be amplified: 'they are (those of?) *mḥn*,' it may well be that serpents' teeth are meant." Ranke then quotes, from amongst a number of other texts which mention a serpent *mḥn* in association with a game, the 172nd saying of the *Book of the Dead*, which is to permit to the dead the use of every one of his limbs in the Beyond. After giving a list of the parts of the head of the dead man — forehead, nose, eyes — it says: "Thy teeth are the *tpj.w* [?] of the *mḥn*, with [?] which Horus and

Seth have *played."* The word left untranslated is, according to
Ranke, a name for the teeth (of the dead), whence, by association with the "tooth" passages of the pyramid texts, we
have the conclusion that "the teeth of a coiled serpent called
mhn have significance of some sort for the dead Egyptian."
Further Ranke declares that in the Egyptian view some game
was played with (?) the teeth of the *mhn* snake, and finally
from the *Book of the Dead* argues that the divine pair of
brothers, Horus and Seth, once played together at the snake-
game; either *with* the teeth of the snake or, as Ranke interprets
it, *for* the teeth, which are a protection, as of an amulet, against
the bite of the poison teeth.

Without entering into these subtle questions of interpretation it is enough to have established that this very ancient game,
to which we have devoted so much notice as being the prototype of all games, was an actual fight for life and death, and
only later mere victory or defeat in a game. We may also pass
over the difference, important from the point of religious history, between upper and lower world, and may assume that
not only was the dead man to be protected against the bite of
poisonous snakes by magic amulets, but that it was vital for the
living to guard against the bite of poisonous snakes, even snakes
in human form. That the whole circle of ideas refers in the first
place to the living, and was only later transferred to the dead,
not only is psychologically obvious, but may also, as a matter of religious history, be deduced from the Egyptian
belief in the continued material existence of the dead, who are
threatened in the underworld by the same dangers as on earth
and who must thus have the same protection in the grave. This
is true also of the board-game, by which the dead were given
the chance to guard against the fearful serpent *mhn* in the
hereafter. "Here, it is true, the *mhn* is not only defeated, but
killed, and there is no further question of its teeth." But
Ranke himself cannot help thinking it strange that the *mhn*
is killed by drowning: since in point of fact snakes do not

drown. " Here, therefore, the basic idea is obviously that of a humanist deity, not a snake." [1] But, remembering that the two mythological opponents in the game were the enemies and brothers, Horus and Seth — of whom a bitter life-and-death duel is related, ending in the tearing-out of Horus' eye — we need have no doubt about the human character of this duel, which is emphasized in the hatred of the brothers, nor as to the meaning of the teeth or other important parts of the body, whose absence would make a continued life in the underworld impossible; and this is why the *Book of the Dead* guarantees the dead man the use of *all* his bodily parts though they gradually fall away. Whether the conjunction of the Horus eye, which dies first, with the teeth, which endure comparatively long, was meant to include the whole process of decay, I leave as an open conjecture (compare the biblical " eye for eye and tooth for tooth ").[2]

But this study, as already indicated, leads far beyond the interest of the game and even beyond the religious symbolization-process (the snake), to an insight into the deepest motives of Egyptian belief in the dead and therefore those of man's immortality-ideologies themselves. When we realize that the gift of the snake-game set, as an offering for the dead, is intended to serve the dead man in the underworld as a weapon against that death which robs him of one member after another in the process of decay,[3] such a method of protection as this which is displayed in the gifts to the dead shows us how unreliable was the foundation on which the whole grandiose edi-

[1] The assumption of Ranke that the original winning of the dangerous teeth of the snake only later changed to the killing of it (because the teeth could grow again) seems in spite of its improbability to contain a sound idea (see next note).

[2] Actually the teeth do appear in individual dreams, and their significance is confirmed by the ceremony of knocking out a tooth in puberty ceremonies among savages as a symbol of rebirth. For we know that teeth do really grow a second time and this knowledge is then applied symbolically to the whole body (man as a whole). The rebirth significance of the teeth in their transitory form is shown in the sowing of the dragon's teeth by Jason, from which armed warriors are born who themselves bring death.

[3] Ranke also concludes from his material that the *mḥn* snake itself appears as the opponent of the dead and is defeated by him after a lengthy struggle.

fice of the religious immortality-ideology of the Egyptians was built (and hence how Moses, brought up as he was in the Egyptian spirit, adopted the only concretely tenable alternative when he opposed to it the earthly immortality of sexual procreation). The Egyptian, though he had immortalized himself in a lofty sun and star religion and also clung, in his earthly animal-cult and transmigration of souls, to the pre-animistic immortality of materialism, had yet, with all this, to protect himself against decay into nothingness, against the undeniably real terror of the underworld. This is the aim of the gifts in the tombs and at the same time the reason for the material continuation of existence in the underworld — and in particular for the snake-game, by which the dead man in the last stages of decay, when he loses even his teeth, the flesh having already fallen from him, is enabled to win back this symbol of a rebirth by gambling with his teeth against death.[1] But even in life man guards himself by the symbolic game — which is in this sense really a preparation — against the dangers of the underworld, and even of his own death, since he offers in his place another, his vanquished opponent, to the hungry jaws of the underworld.

Though these perspectives of cultural history bring us to the edge of studying the great fighting- or gambling-games of the civilized peoples, which found their most brutal expression in the games of the Roman circus with their mutilation of men by wild beasts, we will turn first to those games which have intellectual victory as their object, and note how they developed out of the snake-game. But before we come to their most spiritualized representative, the royal game of chess, we will, at least briefly, recall the purely intellectual " guessing-games " which betray their originally serious nature in the games of fateful question and answer, in the Edda, the Persian Turandot

---

[1] Cf. death as the consumer of flesh, *sarkophagos*. Perhaps in this connexion we may explain the lion and dog figures in the snake game as tearers of flesh, whereas the snake, despite its dangerousness, only kills and does not destroy — in fact, leaves the body unconsumed. Then, if it is deprived also of the poison fangs, it comes to represent the ideal rebirth symbol — which again fits it to take the place of the old flesh-eating worm.

story, and many other legends. Even the common cheating of
the victor of this prize, which we have already met with in
connexion with contest-games — and which still has its reflection in legends of cheating the devil — receives a peculiar
illumination from these riddling-games. The typical triad of
questions which the hero has to answer if he would avoid
death is perhaps to be compared with this trickery, the hero
being subjected to a fresh test again and again until he has
really to die — though the fairy-story ends at the third solution
and so achieves a wish-fulfilment.[1] Besides, games may in actual
fact be continued indefinitely, since the loser always hopes
for his revenge; it was the belief of the German mercenaries
that the fallen soldier played cards in the underworld with the
"innkeeper" there, and this is perhaps no chance reminiscence
of the ancient warriors who continued their battle in the clouds.

This old Egyptian snake-game that Ranke's most valuable
investigation has reconstructed for us, vanishes with the end of
the Old Kingdom — before 2000 B.C. — but some texts of the
later New Kingdom show us a modern board-game, with
thirty squares, which the dead man plays with the *mhn* snake.
"The dead man thus succeeds in occupying one square after
another, and after making use of the opponent 'removes' one
after another of his pieces and finally casts the *mhn* himself
into the water and thus kills him. It is possible that the old
game, which was played on the round board, had the same
idea, and that a later stage transferred the game to the board
with square fields." At this point, where he comes to the verge
of hypothesis, Ranke closes his comprehensive study without
drawing the obvious analogy with chess. Chess itself we know,
not from Egypt, but from the Asiatic group of cultures.[2] In the

[1] In this context belongs the postponement of death by the prolonged stories of
Scheherazade in the *Thousand and One Nights;* and this may indicate the difference between a prose story which is ornamentally extended into infinity, and the drama which
usually represents the end of the hero in a completed action. Lyric extends the present
mood metaphorically until it becomes cosmic ("*Über allen Gipfeln ist Ruh'* . . . *Warte
nur, balde ruhest auch du*").

[2] W. Jones: "On the Indian Game of Chess" (*Asiatic Researches,* II, pp. 159 et seq.).

Bhavidja Purana King Judhishtira gives the following instructions: "Divide the board into eight squares each way. Then place the red army in the east, the yellow in the west, the green in the south, and the black in the north. To the left of the king place the elephant (that is, the bishop), then the horse (the knight), then the boat (the rook), and in front of all four of them foot-soldiers. Yet the boat must stand in the corner." F. Borck,[1] to whom we owe the latest summary of the history of chess, concludes that the colours are connected with an old world- and planet-game, and regards the original four of the chess-board as a cosmogram; this original cosmic significance he sees also in the old "boat" (which takes the place of our rook), indicating that "it is not four armies which fight, but the four worlds separated by the broad oceans, which are distinguished by the four colours and can only fight on shipboard."

Without doubting in the least the cosmic significance of the old Egyptian snake-game, we yet must inquire here into its earthly and human relations, or at least into the motives of such a world- and planet-game. It is psychologically obvious that this cannot be a mere parody of heavenly or cosmic processes — at lowest there must have been something of "fateful" application of this battle of the planets to earthly processes and to the men, who played the game so passionately. If we may, at least hypothetically, regard the newer form of the Egyptian snake-game, with its thirty squares, as a primitive (or at least a parallel) form of Asiatic chess, then the chthonian circular form (underworld, womb), with its division into four equal sectors, would not only be the original of the four-part chess, but the original form of the game would be the duel, as we have it in the mythic tradition of Horus and Seth. Borck in

---

[1] See appendix in op. cit.: *Die Geschichte des Weltbildes* (Leipzig, 1930). Other fundamental literature on the subject: H. Cox: "On the Burmah Game of Chess compared with the Indian, Chinese, and Persian Game of the same Denomination" (*Asiatic Researches*, VII, 480); A. von Oefele: *Schachspiel der Bataker* (Leipzig, 1904); H. F. Massmann: *Geschichte des mittelalterlichen, vorzugsweise des deutschen Schachspiels* (Leipzig, 1889).

fact comes to the conclusion, by the comparative method, that two-part chess is older than the four-part. While he admits the possibility of a passage from the quadruple to the dual form in Iran, which is the home of ethical dualism (good and evil = white and black), he would like to maintain the earlier origin of dual chess in the Chinese dualistic doctrine of *Yang* and *Yin*. In any case this ethical form of chess, which like the Egyptian judge of the dead assigns life to the good (the white) and death to the evil (black), hardly comes further into our consideration.

We will therefore turn to the *object* of the game, which is the same as in the newer Egyptian one: namely, to occupy one square after another and rob the opponent of all his pieces. But if these pieces originally represented, as in Egypt, amulets for various important parts of the body, the esoteric purpose of the game seems to be to rob one's opponent of his vital organs until finally with the king, who is the head, comes mate — and death. This view, apart from the evidence of the material adduced by Ranke, receives further confirmation in the fact that the snake, which is divided into fields by red cross-lines, gave him the impression of being cut in pieces; but this snake was originally the opponent, from whom the teeth, as vital "pieces," are drawn. We cannot do more than suggest an association between this and the cosmologies of dismemberment and must pass on to another and historical view of Asiatic chess, which again we can only indicate. Borck explains the chess tradition with reference to the Indian migration of the second millennium B.C., echoed in the old Indian epos of the *Mahabharata,* as the Greek colonization struggles survive in the Iliad, and the inroad of the Huns into Europe in the *Nibelungenlied*.[1] That is, in the originally dual chess, which was a fight of man against man (Horus and Seth), these folk-struggles of almost a thousand years' duration left their precipitate exactly as the Homeric battles did in our so-called Troy-games.[2] Thus the single combat, which remains

[1] Cf. my afore-mentioned study: *Zur Psychologie des Volksepos*.
[2] Krause: *Die Trojaburgen Nordeuropas*, etc. (Glogau, 1893).

characteristic for the Indian traditions of the *Mahabharata*, turned, in the chess of the transitional period, into a fight of opposing forces, whereas in the epic the leaders still fight out the battle personally in single combat before their soldiers. But in chess the king is covered by his foot-soldiers, his elephants, runners, and boats, even by the dominant queen, and only as a rule comes into action at the last crisis. We shall not try to decide whether this arrangement was a wish-fantasy of the king or an actual change in the art of war demanded by the mass-movements of the Migrations.

It is more important for us at the moment that the originally chthonian significance of the ideologies which survive representatively in the labyrinthine snake-game and the similar rôle of the boat as the vessel of the underworld (especially in Egypt) is preserved, in a religious and perhaps even a social form, in the cultural relationship that Borck assumes to have existed between eastern Asia and Elam (the home of Iranian chess). As F. W. König has shown in his brilliant study: *Mutterrecht und Thronfolge im alten Elam* (Vienna, 1926), the people of Elam were organized on a matriarchal system, and therefore familiar with the idea of a female divinity ruling over the pantheon. It was only later, after the eastward movement of south Elamite culture—put by Borck between 1250 and 1150 B.C.—that a god (Humban Jupiter) took the first place. Chess also, then—in the form in which it has survived—is the product of a transformation of the mother world-view, with its chthonian immortality-ideology, into the spiritual immortality, not of the father, but of the creative ego, of which the head (the king) became the representative. Hence in chess the king is physically almost powerless, while the domination of the mother is still retained in the dominant rôle of the queen —which she had to surrender to the king in the much later card-games.[1] This degradation of the bodily faculties, the foot-soldier, peasant, runner, in favour of the head and king, who

---

[1] The Ace which beats—i.e., kills—everything is death, and in this case, as a wish-fulfilment, is denoted by the first instead of the last letter of the alphabet.

is more spiritual, finally gave the game its wholly intellectual character; and it is probably connected, as we saw in regard to Egypt, with the decay of the body and its parts, which are now survived only by the spirit in its immortal works.

After this sweep over world-history, it remains for us to cast an eye over the primitive duel-games, before we turn finally to the higher spiritual or intellectual games. The duel-game, which we have seen to be fundamental for all play-ideology and the fateful significance of games, has been helpfully studied by Hans Damm;[1] from whom, for our own purposes, we borrow the general conclusion that the duel was probably the original form of war, and that fighting in groups or in mass was a later development, in which the intellectual leadership comes into its own. Further we will mention Damm's view that the original battle — not duel — may, because of the primitiveness of the weapons, have been carried on by ambuscade, whereas the naturally open form of battle, which is also characteristic of the war-games, depends on the invention of long-range weapons, even if these were of a more or less primitive kind. More important than these general conclusions about the primacy of the single combat, which we also have deduced from what are seemingly games of entertainment, is the conclusion of Damm that most primitive games are really questions set to fate — an idea to which Berkusky first gave expression in the case of the tug of war, a ceremonial rain-magic.[2] He assumes that the tug originally set destiny the question whether the rain-bearing monsoon would come soon or not. " But as all such questions of the future which man himself has to answer, because external factors are beyond his influence, tend to develop into a magic activity, it looks as if here also we have an attempt at forecasting the future, preceded by rain-magic." The same is true of a ceremonial wrestling-match which the Batak in Sumatra carry through each year with

[1] *Die gymnastischen Spiele der Indonesier und Südseevölker*, Part 1: "*Die Zweikampf-spiele*" (Leipzig, 1922).

[2] "*Regenzauber*" (*Mitteilungen der anthrop. Gesellschaft*; Vienna; Vol. XLIII).

reference to the sacrifice to the " common father of their race ": a bull is killed, and according to the manner of his fall, whether with the wound above or below, so will the tribe's fate be; and the wrestlers belonging to the various tribes try to influence the fall of the beast in accordance with their wishes and by their own strength — which really amounts to " correcting fortune " in connexion with the question put to destiny.

The tug of war, however, besides being used for rain-magic, has another cult meaning as an agricultural rite. In one group of islands we find it in spring at the time of seeding, the object being furthered, moreover, by obscene rites. Hoevell explains the tug in this case, in which the pull is less important than the rhythmic back and forward movement of the upper body, as an imitation of cult coitus.[1] The fact that in this case the two parties are represented by the male and female, and are not simply two groups as in the tug proper, seems an argument in his favour. But perhaps this rite will throw light on the cere- monial agricultural coitus itself, which is usually interpreted as a mimic encouragement of the vegetation processes. But the conflict in the tug of war between the masculine and femi- nine principles would seem to show that there is a deeper mean- ing underlying the sexual vegetation rite. For even in its most primitive form agriculture is a human *invention,* which presup- poses both the knowledge of the human sexual process and its exploitation in nature — for cattle-breeding as well as for agri- culture. The female may well represent spontaneous growth, the male what is consciously willed; and the question asked in the tug of war would be whether the plants are to bloom as *they* will — spontaneously, in the feminine sense — or con- sciously and in the masculine sense, as *we* will them to do. Vegetation rites are also seen in certain fighting-games which have sunk from the actual shedding of blood to a mere sham fight. Blood, too, is often made to flow, simply by beating, which would represent an earlier scourging which had itself

[1] Detailed references in Damm.

317

originally been a sacrifice. Such vegetation sacrifices, of which, however, we hear only incidentally in myths of higher cultures (for example, the sacrifice of the spring-gods), would then correspond to the type of the building-sacrifice: the field must receive a living gift.

It seems to me that the afore-mentioned superiority of the spiritual over the natural principle may also explain ritual circumcision, which, as is well known, is an essential part of puberty initiation rites. Here also blood flows (the blood-bond); and the whipping, whose purpose is similar, derives (as Preuss has shown) from purely magical motives, to give the boy, now arrived at manhood, the magical power which distinguishes men from women. If we may apply this idea to bloody mutilation also, our conclusion would be that some form of mutilation represents a real attainment of manhood in the spiritual sense, though not in the sexual. The young man who has reached manhood is symbolically deprived of his genital organs (for circumcision is equivalent to castration, as we see in the sacrificing of spring-gods like Attis, Adonis, and Osiris in the higher civilizations) and only then becomes, spiritually, man. In the case of the tug of war, which is supposed to represent an imitation of coitus, this would mean that man needs no longer to work for the fruits of the field in the " natural " way, but that he can produce them by his intelligence and thus make himself to a very considerable extent independent of nature. So far as this is *not* possible, he tries to influence sun or rain by his (magic) will. This realization by the inventive intelligence of its independence of nature may perhaps explain also why these significant and solemn ceremonies " sank," as we say, to be the mere shams which are now games. Man, who at first did not feel himself sure of his superior intellectual powers and yet tried to influence the unreliable weather for his own purposes, gradually realized by virtue of this same intelligence that the second was impossible and the first superfluous. Instead of real shedding of blood, which neither promotes growth nor causes rain, we have a sham fight as a sort of deception of

nature, which is here the real opponent and vanquished by
deceit.

This gradually achieved victory over nature has its highest
triumph among the cultured peoples in the sacrifice of the
spring-god, wherein the young god (puberty), represented in
human form or idea, symbolizes also the punishment of this human pretension. And here too we have a source, as is obvious, of
another form of play which in time has lost its serious cult-
character and has sunk to a sort of game, though it is the
sublimest form of art. I refer, of course, to tragedy, the goat-
song which developed out of Dionysiac mystery-cults and deals
with the killing of a typically sexual animal. Tragedy is thus
rightly included among the higher art-forms which have already passed so far beyond the chthonian mother-soil of art
that the overweening creative power of the self-conscious individual, as displayed in the Greek hero type, can be represented by it in its rise and fall. Originally this representation
was purely ritual, so that the part was not only played but
lived and the hero was actually killed. The festival play which
was performed by actors with a specially composed text belongs to a much later time, in which the poet, as the heir of
the hero, interprets the whole business humanly. He puts before us in metaphorical form the vanished ages of man's first
ascent above nature and reminds the present of it by admonitory
examples. The poet (especially the Greek) must not therefore
identify himself wholly with the hero and his destiny, but only
with the spirit of the old myth, regardless of the particular
hero who exemplifies it. Greek tragedy, whose heroes are types
and not individuals, deals with man's pride and its fall; a
theme which concerned not only the individual Greek or his
poetic representative, but the whole Hellenic people, which had
risen from trivial and obscure beginnings to a spiritual height
at which no pause was possible — and also no progress, but
only a tragic collapse.

Connected with this, probably, is the fact that the great
athletic festivals of the Greeks, like Greek art itself, attained

their highest significance and perfection with the rise of the city-state, the Polis, and decayed under the petty jealousies of the various cities and races and their general political collapse.[1] For the Greeks made even their games and sports a national concern in which everyone took active part, whereas the sensation-loving Romans found more pleasure in watching professional gladiators. The Greek games therefore had far more the character of sport and competition, and therefore of chance, than the Roman shows, in which the end could be foreseen and only the desperate death-struggle fascinated. This was no longer a game, nor competition, but mass-slaughtering. The circus games, on the other hand, which were to be seen in the great *ludi* (based on an Etruscan model), still give indication of old macrocosmic linkages. The wooden tower in the circus, the "*fala*," with the seven egg-shaped figures, "*ova*," is connected with the course of the planets (E. Hommel), which was symbolically copied in the circus, and which is still definitely expressed, according to Winckler (op. cit., p. 125), even in Byzantium. Further, Krause called in the *ludi* to help explain the labyrinthine Troy-game. The horse-racing in the circus (racecourse) probably conserves an earlier form, in which many traditions prove that the first arrival home meant much more than a mere sporting victory. Thus also with the Incas in Peru, where the royal dignity was raced for by a difficult course of over nine kilometres (Fuhrmann: *Peru*, I, 33); and so also the right of asylum, which survives in a degenerate form in those modern games which turn on one's timely arrival at a definite spot, meant of old the saving of a life.[2]

Just as chariot-racing appears in macrocosmic form in the chariot of Helios, so ball-games have their symbolical meaning. Danzel regards them (*Mexiko*, I, 31) as typical examples of the idea of parallelism on earth and in heaven, of the projection of human conditions, relations, and actions into the cosmic; for we shall not be far wrong in assuming that the flight of the

[1] E. N. Gardiner: *Greek Athletic Sports and Festivals* (London, 1910).
[2] E. von Kunsberg: *Rechtsbrauch und Kinderspiel* (Heidelberg, 1920).

ball symbolized for the Mexican the course of sun or moon — and, indeed, the Indians of central Brazil say the sun and moon are shuttlecocks.[1] "The ground-plan of the ball-play court (which is specific to a wide area of Central America) was that of a double T. From the side walls of the enclosure stone rings projected, through which it was one of the main objects to hurl a rubber ball. The courts were orientated exactly north-south. The game was played from one of the wider T-shaped ends to the other, and in order to count, the ball had to hit the side wall and pass the centre line. Anyone who succeeded in sending the ball through one of the two projecting stone rings was entitled to take the cloaks of all the spectators. The spectators then cried: ' He is a great adulterer,' and prophesied an early death and poured water through the ring — and this was called the spring." Danzel recognizes in this custom, besides an astronomic symbolism, some element of a sexual cult operating as fertility magic; especially since the ball-game was played at the seventh festival of the year, at which masked men in the guise of the deities of the young maize-god and the old goddess opposed each other. " But the real divinity of the ball-game is the double figure of the god Xolotl, who in his two forms represents the players who oppose each other at the festival of the eating of water cakes. Even the cult usage shows that we are concerned with a decision which of the two players is to die and which to live; and this is further supported by the general significance of the god Xolotl, who was the patron of the ball-game.

" The name of Xolotl, who is in a sense a twin brother of the in some ways cognate Quetzalcoatl, means ' he that appears in pairs, the twinned.' Hence Xolotl is also the god of twins and of the ball-game because the players are always a pair." But he is regarded also as the god who leads the sun and the dead into the underworld, though also as the leader upward — in a word, the god of life and death. He is thus also the

[1] F. Borck had already discussed ball-games and the heavens: "*Ein Himmelsbild der Pakontshi*" (*Orientalistische Literatur Zeitung*, 1915, pp. 142 et seq.).

first sacrificer of older days, who alone dared to leap into the
fire and thus became, by this self-sacrifice, the sun. This double
character he shares with almost all Mexican gods, who are
generally intermediate forms, made up apparently of two contrasting halves.[1] If the ball-game is essentially a decision of
destiny between life and death, its obvious macrocosmic char-

MEXICO: LIFE AND DEATH

acter not only indicates a surmounting of this primal conflict
by a mythological " die and become "; but also illustrates
another quality of games — the wishful conquest of the external world and especially of the cosmic influences which
ultimately decide man's destiny. In the game this wish is fulfilled by willing, whether by diverting and guiding the planets
in the racecourse or prescribing definite rules in a ball-game.
This explains also the frequent confusion of cosmic and sexual

[1] Cf. the reproduction on Plate 90 in T. Danzel: *Symbole, Dämonen und heilige Türme.
Bildtafeln zur ethnologischen Religionskunde und Mythologie* (Hamburg, 1930). This double
figure, which is typical in Mexico, gives on the one side the wind-god, on the other
the skeleton-headed death-god, thus representing "life and death." The following
plates of the bipartite and double-coloured figures from all parts of the world, including the Roman Janus, seem to show that the primal dualism was the life-and-death
principle. Here too we have a development passing from the duality of the whole man,
even of the universe, to one of the head, which may be connected with man's orientation in the universe on the basis of his sense organs. Cf. also Karutz: *Das Rätsel des
Janus. Von Wirklichkeit in Kunst und Mythus* (Basel, 1927). Danzel's illustrated work
appeared too late for me to use it in detail. I can therefore refer only summarily to the
section on sacral step-buildings (Tower of Babel, etc.), magic anatomy, world-picture
and cosmic caverns, head trophies and skull symbols.

symbolism, whether this was original or only developed later. For man, even primitive man, is, by virtue of his sex, already in a way the controller of nature-forces, as we can see, for example, by continence of Indians or Australians before important undertakings. As we have already shown with reference to various fertility rites, the immediate object is a cheating of nature of her tribute, for that is what death ultimately is; though he is manifested also sexually as partial death and thereafter transformed into sacrifice.

Though this cheating of the original opponent has left a strong tendency to "*corriger la fortune*" in games, yet in its higher development it represents a transition from deception to domination, a raising of the cosmic phenomena from the realm of necessity into that of freedom. In this sense play is no instinct, and the games of animals which are adduced as evidence (for instance by Groos) cannot, in my opinion, be compared at all with human games, because the motive of the original deception, and the later domination, of nature are entirely absent. Even children's games cannot really be brought into evidence, because the toys which children (even among primitives) receive are given by grown-ups and thus represent an early education of the impulse and capacity for control. The first step in that control seems to be the conquest of fear, for when an Indian child is given a totem-doll to play with or a Negro child some primitive demon-carving, the purpose is probably to make them familiar with the object of religious faith and lose their fear of these "black men" (see Hirn: *Kinderspielzeug*). Play is thus rather a prelude to art, as Freud regards it, than a prelude to life, as Groos thought. Only, at a primitive stage there was no difference between the two worlds of reality and super-reality, so that the control of the one in play at the same time guaranteed control of the other by magic. Both, however, primitive magic and later art, have the same impulse at bottom, the element of control which developed out of the original deception of nature.

This process of development appears in the gradual transformation of the cult or sacral festival game, with its purpose of influencing nature, into a mere sham activity with the purpose of deceiving nature. The sham manœuvre which we call play appears to us then as the survival of a once very important and serious cult-activity, which also exhibits the increasing sphere of human influence in man's passage from deception to control of nature: a process which seems to be repeated in children's games, wherein we were formerly disposed to see only an occupation imposed by grown-ups, or a means to distract children, whereas in reality play is as serious for a child as cult was for primitive man. In every case play, by diminishing fear, liberates an energy which can ultimately express itself creatively. Not every child that plays becomes an artist — a fact which makes play as useless for the explanation of creative art as the other infantile experiences which all children share in common. Through dominating his toys a child does gain confidence, and play does liberate stored energy, but whether it is to express itself in art or not depends on the particular use made of it. Domination may easily lead to destruction, as we see in the way that many children treat their toys; and whether this is followed by the creation of a new or the destruction of another seems to depend on general conditions over which we have little control. The " young scientist " who must needs examine the inside of his toy, its mechanism and its works, by " analysis " is very early differentiated from the artist who makes himself a splendid doll out of a chip of wood. In one case, clearly, the destructive, in the other the constructive, predominates; and closer study would probably show that in the artist-type the impulse to create is subjectively attached to the ego, while the other appears to exhibit a stronger objectivity of relations.

Chapter Eleven

BEAUTY AND TRUTH

❧

Thus art moves towards its own dissolution, and in doing so — most illuminatingly — it touches on all the phases, its beginnings, its childhood, its incompleteness, its earlier ventures and trespasses, and in its decay interprets its growth and becoming.

NIETZSCHE

Chapter Eleven

BEAUTY AND TRUTH

᎒᎒᎒

From this gradual conquest of nature, which is really her successful deception by the human intelligence, we can make our way back to the individual psychological interpretation of play and the personal pleasure which pertains to it — that is, to the problem of æsthetic. The exemplar from which play proceeded certainly lacks its essential characters of freedom and pleasure. Originally play was a matter of very serious and significant ceremonies which *had* to be held at definite occasions if the life and well-being of the community were not to be endangered. Therefore at these pre-religious ceremonies neither the life nor the blood of the individual was spared to compel the favour of destiny in the community. If we contrast with this the character of the games which developed out of it, we see that their freedom amounts to a liberation from the compulsion of nature, and the attainment of pleasure to the feeling of superiority that is its outcome. We have almost to invert the usual view of the " excess "-theory of play and say that instead of play originating in excess of force, it produces this force or, more exactly, sets it free. Man sees that he need not continually sacrifice life to nature; he separates the ceremony from natural process and the idea of tribute, so that he can enjoy it freely as a triumph over nature. Play is therefore not a ceremony which has sunk to a mere show, but one which has been raised to freedom — indeed, it is only as such an expression of man's increasing dominion over nature that we can explain the change of ceremony into play; so far from being meaningless or interpretable only as a survival, the activity thereby acquired a higher sense. On the other hand, our explanation also makes intelligible the pleasure which the individual gets from this sham activity, in that we regard this as a saving of vitality and, indeed, of life.

Here, obviously, lies also the origin of art, which, for all that it is supposed to be derived from an " art for art's sake " attitude, in reality, as we have seen, from the beginning subserved spiritual purposes of a magical or religious sort. Art, like play, passes from the condition of being a compulsory activity necessary for life into the realm of freedom — even if (again as in play) this liberation can never be wholly successful. Hence we have the explanation of the two types of artist: that which creates from an inner need and that which does so from an inner surplus. But in both cases the greatest part of creative force can come only from an excess that arises during and out of the actual creation, just as in play the playing itself is needed to liberate the energy in the individual. The productive process itself, combined with the incessant struggle for individual freedom against the bonds of the data (collective ideology or material), sets free excess forces with a greater accompaniment of pleasure the further its successful progress continues. This cumulative excess of force in the process we shall study separately in the next chapter, in its effect on the creative artist. At present we will begin by trying to make use of the art-ideological element in the understanding that we now have of play. For the ceremony, in rising from the compulsory sacrifice to nature into the realm of pleasure by the individual's liberation from nature, acquired not only the psychical quality of play, but its æsthetic quality also. When it is still tied to nature, the ceremony is more or less an imitation thereof, whereas the freedom of play tends rather towards stylization — the one being, even in the deeper sense, nearer to truth, and the other to beauty.

When I say " in the deeper sense," I mean that man's acceptance of his dependence on nature is more honest, while freedom-ideology, beyond a certain point, presumes the negation of that dependence and is therefore, also in a deeper sense, dishonest. This fundamental dishonesty towards nature then comes out as the consciousness of guilt, which we see active in every process of art, and which is not wholly absent from play. This feeling of guilt, of human hybris — of which the Greeks were the first to become conscious — also allows neither play nor the exercise of art to rise wholly from compulsion to freedom; nay, the more strongly man feels his freedom and his independence, the more intense on the other hand is the consciousness of guilt, which appears in the individual partly restrictive, partly creative, but in the community is accompanied by the gradual growth and formation of another ideology, that of truth, which acts paralysingly on the freedom of the ideology of beauty. This scientific ideology born of the feeling of guilt therefore appears first in Greece, where the idea of artistic beauty also attained its greatest freedom. This is the profound reason for Plato's exclusion of artists from his ideal republic; for in their extreme type, the poet, he saw the truth-falsifying element, which his scientific ideologism condemned as lying. Owing to this scientific guilt-feeling in the Greeks, the only art-ideology permitted to their philosophers was one that had to be content with the imitation of nature, whereas their *real* works represent a much higher spiritual truth. And so the Greek identification of the true with the good and the beautiful appears as the effort of a man, nervous of his likeness to god, to reconcile the freedom-ideology of art with the guilt-ideology of science.

But this latter also leads to " hybris," since its over-valuation of the intellectual faculties of knowledge in man is only possible by the denial of his animal nature. The *artistic* ideology of the " head," which, as we have seen, rose from the chthonian mother earth to the majesty of self, never in fact escaped from this mother earth entirely: the animal content was but changed into an æsthetic form. The *scientific* ideology of the " head," on the other hand, is formal and phenomenological, and the thought-processes regard it as beneath their dignity to occupy themselves with the animal content. This latter comes but

329

gradually, and it found its clearest expression in the materialistic outlook of the last century which culminated — and col-
lapsed — in psycho-analysis. In Classical Greece we can watch
this struggle of the two ideologies, on which even today every
controversy still turns, growing out of humanity's own development. The truth of the dependence of man on nature, which
play and art deny, reappears out of this guilt-feeling as the impulse to scientific knowledge; nay, more, as a compulsion not
only to admit, but to profess it. But art itself is influenced by it,
so that we find it, when at its highest point, already infected by
scientific ideas, and particularly with the laws of geometric
proportion (in architecture and sculpture) and of mathematics
(in music and metre). But far more important than these
special influences — which in fact had already begun in the
East, in Egypt and Babylon — is the general influence of the
scientific idea of truth on the æsthetic idea of beauty. For it was
not science that was born in Greece, but only the type of scientific man, just as Greece was the cradle, not of art, but of the
artistic type.

We will take two examples (which are fundamental for
the whole artistic development of Europe) to illustrate the
influence of this idea of truth on that of beauty. The one is
portraiture, the other tragedy. The problem of the beginnings
of Greek pictorial art brings us again into a regular wasps' nest
of art-history; namely, the question of when the beginning of
actual portraiture came. Ernst Pfuhl, in a recent monograph
on this subject, discusses concisely the scanty material and its
various interpretations, and we will begin by following his
rather polemical attitude, so as to get some true insight into
the actual problem itself from the contradictions involved.
There is a passage in Pliny (*Naturalis Historia,* XXXV, 153)
where he says that " Lysistratos, brother of Lysippos, was the
first to make complete likenesses of his model; till then men
had been represented as beautiful as possible." [1] This state-

---

[1] E. Pfuhl: *Die Anfänge der griechischen Bildniskunst. Ein Beitrag zur Geschichte der Indi-
vidualität* (Munich, 1927).

ment — to which the greatest importance has been attached in the history of art — is taken in conjunction with the accounts given of the technical methods that were used by Lysistratos; he is said to have made plaster casts from life, filled these with wax, and finally only "retouched" them, as we say. Pfuhl, at the beginning of his book, objects to the rash adoption of this technical statement, which would make of Lysistratos not only a realist, but a mere philistine, below the artistic level; he thinks Pliny was really talking of casts used for study.

As regards the statement itself, apart from this technical question — namely, the assertion that Lysistratos was the first to produce exact likenesses — Pfuhl thinks it must be taken *cum grano salis*. Indeed, he thinks that the idea of a likeness *in our sense* is lacking not only in archaic art but in that of the whole fifth century, and that it is only at the end of that century, and in the minor arts, that we get traces of individualization in heads which are clearly meant to be copies of real life. In monumental art there is no single real portrait throughout the fifth century. Pfuhl thinks that the common view flourishes in art-histories because of the intrusion of our own ways of thought, which have been schooled for centuries on the individual portrait and consequently are apt to take the traditional likeness of famous poets and philosophers as representing the individual personalities instead of the ideal type. For ourselves we are naturally not concerned with the conflict of opinion, which depends ultimately on a matter of dating, except in so far as it is one of the sources for studying the underlying problem. Although the fifth century was "only the necessary prelude, or at most the first uncertain step to a future portraiture, and not itself such," we can detect the truth-ideology already beginning to influence that of beauty. The likeness was no longer to be an ideal type of poet, philosopher, etc., but the particular individual, who is unique and not to be confused with others. And even if we take up no definite attitude to the purely academic question of date, it still seems very remarkable — even more so than the supposed miracle of an early portraiture —

that Pfuhl should "feel compelled to take the first individual likeness, in the purely realistic sense," to be that of Aristotle,[1] the very man, he adds, who created a literary biography out of earlier attempts; and, we may add, who is the admitted prototype of scientific ideology, which thus found pictorial expression in this individual *head*. If we add also that the first individual portrait in the general form is, according to Pfuhl, that of Plato (for the oldest Socrates portraits owe their individual character only to the fact that this philosopher happened to be cast in the Silenus type), we have a coincidence of individual portrait art with the growing type of the thinker, which, at any rate in the light of our own views, we cannot take to be a matter of chance. The very fact, too, that these individual philosopher portraits contrast with the ideal likeness of the poets whom *we* feel as individualistic heads (Homer, Sophocles, Euripides) is rather to be understood from the standpoint of cultural than from that of art history, as due to the contrast between the collective nature of the poetic material and the purely personal attitude of the philosopher. For the philosopher, who first came into existence in Greece, represents a new individual type, while the artist is as old as humanity itself and links up—in point of subject and even partly of form—to a millennial tradition.

If we now pass to our second example and inquire how the early scientific ideology springing from the guilt-sense shows its influence in poetry and, especially, tragedy, we have only to take the three great tragedians in their historical succession in order to obtain a right view.[2] The dithyrambic Æschylus is followed by the psychologizing Sophocles, and he by the moralizing Euripides. In Sophocles' *Œdipus* — which therefore psycho-analysis is quite right in taking as its

[1] In this he follows Studniczka: *Das Bildnis des Aristoteles* (Leipzig, 1908): it can hardly have been sculptured much before 325, since the philosopher died in 322, in his sixty-second year.

[2] There is no personal portrait of Æschylus; the date of the Sophocles head is disputed (Pfuhl, op. cit., p. 11); i.e., it is of the transition period; the portraits of the consciously interpreting Euripides have a strong individualistic effect.

example — we see the new truth-ideology victoriously attacking the æsthetic laws of dramatic action. The *Œdipus* gives us an action developed in reverse order, which is as much as to say that it provides a psychological genesis for the destiny theory; thus a direct path leads thence to Ibsen's *Wild Duck,* which was the product of the materialistic science of the nineteenth century. Œdipus pays for the solution of the Sphinx's riddle, if not directly with his life, at least with his happiness; but the impulse to penetrate to the truth behind appearances is stronger than any other ideology. Sophocles' Œdipus is no longer a tragic hero who, like Æschylus' Prometheus, atones for a deed of sin, but an intellectually arrogant man who crashes because of his mere striving for knowledge, so that it is unimportant *what* he wanted to discover.[1] What is not unimportant, however, is that this impulse to discover discloses itself more or less as a confession of faith; that is, that it is psychological rather than philosophical. The Œdipus of the Sophoclean age could no longer be a hero, even if he went through the same process of development as his heroic predecessor; he was so far sicklied over by the paleness of thought that he could no longer act, but only examine introspectively the psychological motives of his potential actions. He is thus not only the distant ancestor of Ibsen's Gregers Werle, who tries to cure men by showing up their life's lie, but the patron saint of psycho-analysis, which makes the same attempt in the name of a scientific ideology, but only succeeds therapeutically in so far as it is untrue.[2] Between Œdipus and Gregers stands their spiritual kinsman Hamlet, who, however, is not the pattern for the truth-seeking healer, but the godfather of the thought-obstructed neurotic.

But however far the influence of scientific ideology on art may go, art always remains interested in the representation of the type, though it has to exemplify the type individually, and if possible by something real. Science on the other hand

[1] See my remarks on this aspect of the Œdipus myth in *Modern Education.* p. 192 et seq.
[2] I have discussed these ideas in *Truth and Reality.*

is interested primarily in the study of the special case and the profound knowledge of individual variations, and only in the end may it perhaps reach its general formulations. Thus not only Œdipus, but Hamlet and Gregers too are types, as is every true poetic figure, regardless of how much or how little we know of its creator. It does not make the *Œdipus Rex* less intelligible that we know so little of Sophocles; indeed, the few facts we do know might rather mislead us than otherwise in the understanding of his work. And the type-symbolism of *The Wild Duck* gains nothing from the scanty biography of Ibsen, who all his life-time was more of a sober pharmacist than a great poet. And that we cannot even be sure in Shakspere's case of the actual author is reckoned by Hermann Bahr as an invaluable advantage which the English poet possesses over Goethe, about whom every schoolboy can quote the facts which are supposed to explain the growth and meaning of his work. In this sense the modern " psychological " biography represents the latest intrusion of the ideology of science into that of art.

This conflict between the ideologies of truth and beauty, which only worked its way into the full consciousness of mankind in Greece, is actually as old as humanity itself, because in last analysis the root of it is the dualism between mortality and immortality. For, in our view, even the most primitive art consists in the attempt to make the abstract idea of the soul " true " by making it concrete; that is, æsthetically satisfying, or, in other words, beautiful. The question whether primitive likenesses were portraits or of symbolic character could therefore become prominent in art-history only as and when truth and beauty fell apart, as they have increasingly done in the European spiritual culture from the time of the Greeks onwards. For primitive artists the question was quite meaningless, for their truth was not realistic, but spiritual. Historians of primitive art are in fact unanimous in taking the first pictures of men to be those of the dead, symbolizing their continued existence; not real portraits, but a pictorially concrete repre-

DEAD POLE FROM MELVILLE ISLAND

FLAT FIGURE OF AN
ANCESTOR, FROM NEW
GUINEA

sentation of their soul — when possible in the permanent material of stone, or at any rate in wood, which typifies resurrection.
Among those are the African poles of the dead and the totem-
poles of the American Indians, and also the schematic menhir
statues (of which about a dozen have been found in France)
of the stone age: stones of "about human size, of a rounded
shape, showing eyes, nose, necklace, and sometimes uncouth
suggestions in relief of arms and legs." Schuchhardt, who (op.

RELIEFS IN THE GRAVES OF PETIT MORIN, MARNE

cit., p. 66) gives this description, adds that " without doubt these
were the models for the similar-formed reliefs in the graves of
Petit Morin, whose outline is otherwise inexplicable (see our
illustration).

Schuchhardt has, moreover, gone the right way to explain
these primitive works of art, when he compares them with
the later grave-stelæ as the resting-place of a soul moving freely
in space: and in actual fact we find on Egyptian and Cretan
obelisks birds to represent the soul. But when he finds the
schematically indicated outline of the menhir statues coarse in
comparison with the superb observation of nature shown in the
small human figures of the palæolithic caves, he overlooks,
as his materialistic theories force him to do, the difference in the
ideological will to art in the two periods. This, on the contrary,
Herbert Kühn emphasizes: " The dead man is represented on
the menhir statues, not naturalistically, but, in accord with the
thought of the time, imaginatively. Nose and eyebrows are

335

indicated by a stroke, the eyes are usually circular chisellings; arms or fingers are often represented. Some are masculine and have weapons, but the majority are female, with breasts." These strongly stylized portraits of late neolithic times are followed by the still more schematic representations of the bronze age which have progressed into the geometric style.

SYMBOLIC REPRESENTATION OF
CHRIST'S RESURRECTION THROUGH
THE SOUL-BIRD CHARADRIUS

The reason for this no doubt lies in the increasing development of the soul-idea, which made a literal reproduction of man more and more unnecessary, while the abstract soul-idea, as the essential, received more and more expression. If we want to get back to the realistic core of the portrait, we must go right to pre-artistic times, when there were as yet no representations of man, but the embalmed corpse was the real image of the dead. This is true of the mummified forms of so-called crouched graves, of which Klaatsch gives some good illustrations, and also of the prepared skulls which many primitive peoples set on poles.

This would throw light also on the question of priority between painting and sculpture. The oldest representation of *man* that we know is the plastic figures, flat and round, of palæolithic times, which, as works of art, only reproduce the essential without being true to nature. Thus I would see in the

exaggeration of the female forms in (for instance) the Venus of Willendorf and other stone-age sculptures, not a naturalistic reproduction of a fat-bodied type of woman, but the " artistic " emphasis of the female, perhaps the maternal, principle. However that may be, plastic aims more at reality because it grows out of the desire to preserve the body as a whole; though all the same it does not reproduce an exact portrait of reality, because the belief in the soul (which is the necessary preliminary to artistic form) permits, or rather demands, an abstract representation of the essential. Painting, on the other hand, is from the first rather a subjective reproduction of what is seen, not of what is, and is therefore employed rather for the representation of animals than of men. Accordingly man is at first shown only when dead, but animals when alive; and hence the naturalism of animal pictures — which are not imitation of nature, but a representation of life — along with the stylization of human representations which are a concrete picture of the soul-idea. But it is not long, as we have shown, before the animal becomes the concrete bearer of the human soul and thence onwards the two forms mingle, because animals also can be represented as having a soul, and man also as being alive.[1]

In any case we believe we have made it clear that the truth-and-beauty ideology which corresponded to the mortal and immortal, to life and death, originally found expression in different art-forms before it split into two different spiritual attitudes in Greece. These, the scientific and the æsthetic, thereafter influence also the further development of art-ideology in Western Europe. It might be said that until the Greeks living man was never the subject of artistic, certainly not of plastic, representation, but only the dead; that is, the soul that lived on after death. What enabled the Greeks, however, to override this tabu, which is still held among savages, and to represent living men as well, was the fact that they had in the mean while achieved a philosophical notion of the soul through their ideology of scientific truth and so had disembarrassed themselves of the one great problem, which had always exercised the artist hitherto, that of the concrete representation of the soul. When the Greek idea of the soul became that of the Psyche, man acquired living that soul which earlier had been something into which death changed him, and thereafter the art of human portraiture more and more depicts the soul of the living. This artistic freedom in the representation

[1] It is generally agreed today that the animal representations of primitive times have some "religious" character. This is true both of the Pyrenees finds of French scientists and of African rock-paintings, at the base of which Frobenius found burial grounds. The problem, still unsolved in the history of art, of the relation between Bushman art and the South European cave-paintings can be left at the moment; but "even in these oldest times there is no sharp line between sculpture and painting; outline drawings probably arose out of sculpture" (Klaatsch, op. cit., p. 55).

of the living soul found its highest expression in portraiture, which does not represent the actual, but the essential, man — that is, the soul. But whereas in pre-Greek art the dead man's soul could only be represented abstractly, and not as living, the representation of the living soul, which reached its culmination in portraiture, required a living soul for its very purpose of giving the picture life. And thus finally the living soul was no longer taken from the object depicted, but " added " by the working artist himself, of whom we then say that he has " put his soul into " the work and given it both life and immortality.

The beginning of this development came in Greek portraiture of the Late Classical period, in which we admire — and for that matter the Greeks themselves admired — not the realistic likeness, even if it were photographically true, but the artistic ideology which made such work possible and, apart from the portrait-likeness, disclosed the spirit of *the* poet or *the* philosopher. Even if the artist aimed at an individual likeness or induced this effect, nevertheless the work in its spiritual expression was collective, since it showed in some indefinable way the ruling ideology of art or philosophy in the heads of the artist or philosopher. From Egypt, too, we have pictures and masks which seem to have been good likenesses, but no one will put these portraits, which served the purpose of the cult of the dead, higher than the ideal portraits of Classical Greece because the latter had less likeness and more spirit. To reproduce a likeness is not yet art — or no longer art. For the Egyptians the dead man had to live on in the Beyond just as he was, and so his portrait had to be as like as possible. But the Greek philosopher or poet was actually exchanging his material for an ideal immortality, and therefore that portrait was best which gave the purest expression of this spirituality: it was beautiful, while the other was only true.[1] In order to show how far the realistic representation in art depends on belief in the

[1] The same holds good for Roman portraiture, which was nearer an ancestral mask, however true it is that, in contrast to the Egyptian, " the self-consciousness of a people of marked force of will lies behind " (Pfuhl, op. cit., p. 17).

dead and the cult of the soul, and only in that context aimed
at the true reproduction of nature, we need only refer to
the Egyptian ka. The ka is a life-principle, different from body
and soul, which protects and blesses man and after death becomes the real representative of his personality. The body has
to be preserved out of regard for the ka, so that it may at
any time resume possession of it. "The ka has to be looked
after with food and drink, which are put on the altar-table
of the grave. If this were forgotten, the dead man might be
driven to such a pass that, tortured by hunger or thirst, he would
have to drink of his own urine and eat of his own dung —
the most awful idea which could occur to an ancient Egyptian."[1] Soon, however, it was only at the actual funeral and
on memorial days that food and drink from one's own meal
were set at the grave, and the everyday food, bread and beer,
were painted on the table (the dead also being depicted as
sitting at the entrance of the tomb), and so the nourishment
which was necessary for continued existence was made external. Moreover, a magic formula was written below, which
the ka had only to utter in order to have real nourishment.
So, in addition to the magic power of the picture, there was
the magic power of the word. Finally the dead man received
his food in the tomb, in imperishable copies, so as to guaran-
tee food and drink to the ka for ever by the magic formula;
further, besides the alabaster cakes of bread and wooden mugs
of beer there were earthenware figures of wives, servants, and
slaves. "The walls of the mastabas, the subterranean grave-
chambers of the nobility of the Old Kingdom, and the rock
tombs of the great men of the Middle Kingdom, are, moreover, covered with coloured reliefs or frescoes from the life of
the dead and the various activities of his profession. They give
a picture in colour and form of what the earthenware figures
(of which up to three hundred are found in a tomb) are meant
to imply by their mere presence — a representation of the real

[1] This and the following come from E. Huber: *Das Trinkopfer in Kulte der Völker*
(Hanover, 1929), p. 108.

340

life of the dead so that the *ka,* by virtue of the magic formulæ, may thereafter live on for ever."

In contrast to this Egyptian realism, which was part of the cult of the dead, Greek art rose higher and gave even living man a soul, a process which began with the affirmation of

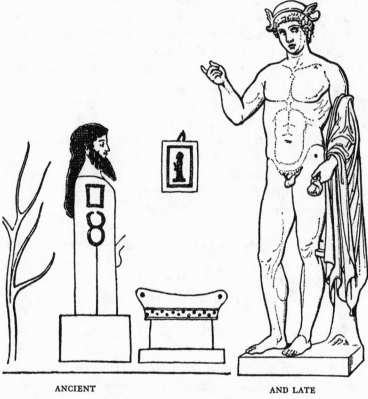

ANCIENT   AND LATE

HERMES REPRESENTATIONS

sexuality as a victory over death, and in the Classical period became the philosophical conception of the Psyche of the living. This whole process, which began with liberation from the chthonian mother-principle and leads, via the glorification of the masculine symbol of reproduction, the phallus, to the notion of the living Psyche concentrated in the head, may still be followed in detail in the development of Greek art as well as of Greek science. The god who was most frequently and at all times depicted was Hermes, whose many-sidedness in itself shows an old and long history. Perhaps the oldest form of symbolic representation is the piles of stones, named after the god, " which from the oldest time were heaped up everywhere on the roads as boundary stones and signposts and as thank-offerings from passing travellers to the god who had speeded them." [1] In these herms of the road we can easily recognize an individual development of the official Omphalos signs, whose chthonian maternal origin we have already shown. Side by side with them we have very early the ithyphallic representation of Hermes as a vegetation-god fertilizing mother earth. A third, and the really artistic form of the representation, is the anthropomorphic figure of the deity which " only gradually grew from the pillar-like stone or wood into human form, and found its expression first of all in the head, which is the noblest part of the body " (Brunn, 1884).

In this process, revealed in the herms that were everywhere to be found, and especially in Arcadia and Attica,[2] we can easily recognize the cultural movement from below upwards, from the chthonian mother-principle, via the reproductive father-principle,[3] to the head-culture of the soul, which culminates in the Classical portrait bust. The phallus on the herm represents a symbol not only of the masculine reproductive faculty, but of the human knowledge of natural processes which we may call the beginning of scientific thinking. Now, an exact knowledge of these processes presupposes speculative insight, but over and above that, has its application in agriculture

[1] All quotations relating to Hermes are taken from Roscher's *Lexikon der Mythologie*.

[2] "The peculiar mark of this art-form is the four-cornered pillar, with the head and neck of the god above; in place of arms were mere projections, on which wreaths could be hung, and on the pillar itself was the phallus as the symbol of generative power" (Roscher).

[3] For the conflict between the two principles in Greece see Bachofen's *Mutterrecht*.

and cattle-breeding. Hermes is therefore not only the god of these — with his symbol of the ram he is the patron of Arcadian shepherds — but also the representative of cleverness and inventions, even of thieves and cheats, a point not unconnected with the old deception of nature. On the other side his function as guide of the road and direction — in which the four sides of the pillar correspond to the four points of the compass and the four winds — may be regarded as a pre-scientific beginning of road-making and surveying. This significance of the god as a symbol of orientation related originally to special parts of the body (cf. the arm-stumps of the herms) and was only later concentrated in the head as the essential part of the body. The phallus is less a representation of the primitive animal principle — for that is female — than the symbol of the deliberate control of nature by man's knowledge. Since speech also is necessary for cleverness, we find Hermes figuring in Hellenistic plastic as the god of oratory, and the wings which used to be on the feet (cf. the Hermes in Naples) are transferred to the head or hat. At this later stage the original wind-god (*pneuma*) not only appears as god of speech (*logos*), but almost as such an allegorization of thought (speed) as has been given spiritual expression in modern times by Rodin.

The same artistic development towards the head-culture, which reached its final form — saturated with the scientific ideology — in post-Classical portraiture, may also be traced in Greek culture generally. We have already referred to the layout of temples, cities, and streets on the Omphalos plan, and to the egocentric outlook which produced the competitiveness and quarrelsomeness of the various Greek tribes, cities, and heroes that is evidenced even in the Trojan War stories. Greek science also, and especially its geography, mathematics (or physics), and medicine, developed out of very old traditions of folk-lore and myth. One of the most striking proofs of this is the dominance of the numbers seven and nine — obvious mythological figures, as Roscher has shown in a series of works.[1] He has also shown that, in a treatise on the number seven, ascribed to Hippocrates, we have a much older and more original document, dating from pre-Pythagorean times, which gives us a glimpse into the world of the Ionic philosophy. It is enough for our purposes to take only the main idea out of this confused and fragmentary work. We can do so the more easily since we already know its micro-macrocosmic foundation from the world-picture of the ancient East, but there is this difference, that in Greece everything seems to be subordinated to the seven. Both the world as a whole and the separate parts are under its dominion; there are seven spheres, and seven worlds within the earth, and everything, except the earth (which is imagined as the centre of the universe) is in circular motion. Further, there are seven constellations, which regulate time, seven winds, seven seasons, and seven ages. Both the universe and the single individual are constituted of seven parts — bones, flesh, marrow, blood, intestinal juices, breath, and reason. So too there are seven parts of the body — head, hands, entrails, diaphragm, veretrum, longabo, and legs; there is even a sevenfold purpose of the head. The seven vowels in speech are also included in the system. Finally there are seven parts of the soul.

Of especial interest to us here — as based upon the micro-cosm-macrocosm doctrine — is the author's sevenfold division of the known world according to the parts of the human body: the Peloponnese corresponds to the head, the Isthmus to the neck, Ionia to the diaphragm, the Hellespont to the legs, the

---

[1] W. Roscher: *Die Enneadischen und Hebdomadischen Fristen und Wochen der ältesten Griechen* (Leipzig, 1903); *Die Sieben- und Neunzahl im Kultus und Mythus der Griechen* (1904); *Die Hebdomadenlehre der griechischen Philosophen und Ärzte* (1906); *Über Alter, Ursprung und Bedeutung der hippokratischen Schrift von der Siebenzahl* (1911); *Die hippokratische Schrift von der Siebenzahl und ihr Verhältnis zum Altpythagorismus* (1919). The mythical significance of the seven and nine is affirmed also among other peoples; e.g., Germans, Mexicans, Indians, Persians, Celts, etc. Cf. F. Andrian: "*Siebenzahl im Geistesleben der Völker*" (*Mitteil. d. anthrop. Gesellschaft*, Vienna, 1901). These figures in their association of cosmic and human periodicities—phases of the moon, periods, etc.—stand not for arithmetical but for mystical values; they are, as Bergaigne (*La Religion védique*, II, 156) admirably puts it, not the expression of an undefined manifold, but of a *totality*, and are thus equivalent and may be substituted one for the other.

two Bosporoi to the feet, Egypt and the Egyptian sea to the upper trunk, the Euxine sea and Mæotic sea to the lower trunk and rectum. It is noteworthy that the author, whose home Roscher places in Miletus, identifies Ionia, in which philosophy began to flourish in his times, with the diaphragm and not with the head. He concludes that the treatise is really older because in earlier views the diaphragm and not the head was regarded as the seat of the highest function of the soul. The Hippocratean author, in making these valuations, saw no preference in the attribution of the head to the Peloponnese. This simply symbolized the undisputed fact of the hegemony of Sparta over the Greeks. The Spartans ruled by a conscious effort of will directed to the training of the body, but the true spirit, the centre of spiritual life, was Ionia, which is therefore identified with the diaphragm, as the seat of the highest spiritual faculties. We must leave it open, as an interesting problem of folk-psychology, how far this value-classification of their countries not only described but actually influenced the character of their inhabitants.[1]

We shall also have to abstain from any attempt to follow out the importance of this treatise for the development of medicine, geography, and philosophy; as to its scientific importance, we shall only remark that so far as is known, the author was first to maintain the spherical shape of the earth, the inviolability of the laws of nature, especially those that were mathematically formulable in the macrocosm and the microcosm alike, and finally the principles of the condensation and rarefaction of substances. We cannot, however, omit to point out how the ground for the later floraison of the high culture of Greece was prepared by the philosophical distinction that was established between the transitory human body and the eternal spirit by these Ionian thinkers, who yet were themselves rooted in the chthonian. Greek humanity remained fixed, with its bodily

---

[1] Similarly in Egypt the qualities of different peoples were deduced from the correspondence between their homes and the different parts of the body. Cf. Roscher: *Die hippokratische Schrift*, etc., p. 10. The peculiar position of the Jews, with their favoured land as the centre of the earth, has already been alluded to.

parts, to the earth, but the people who dwelt in the diaphragm, and therefore incorporated their spiritual psychical qualities, became the cradle of a scientific human type that as yet had nothing to do with the practical intelligence of the head. It was only at the full flower of the Greek culture that Athens became the undisputed head of Hellenism, and the head became both the seat of the soul and of the highest human faculties — and then, indeed, the culture culminated. Everything that was chthonian and animal was banished to the depths of Orcus to make way for the spiritual head-culture which appears personified in the works of Athenian poets, orators, and sculptors and later in their portrait busts.

The characteristic and peculiar quality of this flower of Greek culture seems to me to lie precisely in the reciprocal influence of the ideologies of truth and beauty. We observe in Ionia sciences like philosophy, physics, mathematics, geography, and medicine growing from a chthonian, animal ideology, which was transformed in other cultures into æsthetic art-ideologies; and on the other hand we have seen that Greek art, just at its highest point, came under the influence of an increasingly powerful scientific ideology. In other words, in Greece human dualism reached its maximum of inner intensity. With nature thus partly dominated and still more defied by negation, the resultant guilt-feeling was so strong that it impelled men not only to humanize their art and religion, but also to create for themselves in science a special ideology to justify this drive to truth. The Greek culture possesses the importance that it does, not because the beginnings of science lie in Greece, but because the scientific ideology was born there, the specific attitude to life which will always be characteristic of, and necessary to, science and the scientist. And this ideology did not restrict itself to the above-mentioned special sciences, but permeated the whole of Greek intellectual life and finally the spiritual life, which is the foundation of every ideology.

And so Greece became the home of psychology also, in that it was there that, out of the religious idea of the soul and its artistic manifestations, there developed the first scientific psychology in the sense of soul-*doctrine*. This doctrine, too, like the original idea of the soul itself, was dualistic: the spiritual side, which had been earlier expressed in religious immortality-belief, was built up by Plato ideologically into a philosophy of the soul, while the material side was reduced by Aristotle into a psycho-physiology. The development of Greek views on the soul, which was first outlined in Rohde's fundamental work, but has been corrected in many ways since,[1] is not only of basic importance for our present-day technical psychology, but had ideologically a decisive influence on the whole Christian evolution as well as on the whole art-ideology of the West. Homer, who gives us the oldest and best evidence for Greek views of the soul, has as yet no unified idea of it, any more than the primitive peoples who, both conceptually and (as a rule) verbally, distinguished the soul of the dead from the spiritual functions of the living. "Psyche" in Homer, according to the latest studies, denotes only the soul of the dead, while the various spiritual functions of the living (such as the reason, emotions, etc.) are ascribed to special important organs of the body, like the diaphragm. These qualities and functions of the soul, which were located differently according to the different experiences, were only later unified into one living soul, and this was still later identified with the "Psyche" which had hitherto indicated the soul of the dead only. The development of the idea of the soul thus leads from an original contrast between the multiplicity of living function and the unity of the soul of the dead to an explicit dualism as between the soul of the living and the dead, and thence to an ultimate unification which assumed a "psyche" (that is, a soul of the dead) to exist also in the living.

Thus the inner dualism of Greek humanity — expressed respectively in the artistic and the scientific ideologies of the

---

[1] E. Rohde: *Psyche. Seelenkult und Unsterblichkeitsglaube der Griechen* (1893). W. Otto: *Die Manen oder von den Urformen des Totenglaubens* (Berlin, 1923). J. Böhme: *Die Seele und das Ich im Homerischen Epos* (Leipzig, 1929).

beautiful (that is, the immortal) and of the true (that is, the mortal soul) — was harmoniously unified in the unitary soul of philosophy, which led thereafter in Christianity to the complete spiritualization of man. But it emerges, too, that the art-ideology is always collective and spiritual even where, as in portraiture, it uses an individual appearance for the expression of the general and typical. We can understand, therefore, how it is that the ideology of the beautiful can never be explained by individual psychology, for it is collective and its collective content is the quality of soul which is expressed artistically in beauty and religiously in faith. The concept of truth, on the other hand, in spite of its ideological elaboration in science, remains in the last resort qualitatively subjective (as I have shown in *Truth and Reality*), and consequently psychology is the most subjective of all the sciences and, basically, only the intellectual heir of the old soul-concept (*Seelenglaube und Psychologie*).

We can perhaps have no better example for the study of the mutual influence of the scientific soul-ideology on art, and of the artistic ideology on science, than Greek music — which, moreover, will serve to lead us up to the form-problem as the art-problem *par excellence*. The influence of Greek mathematics, especially of the Pythagorean theory of numbers, on the development of Greek music is of course undisputed; and there is equally little doubt as to the artistic ideologizing of the physics of the cosmos, which is expressed most distinctly in the "music of the spheres" and the revolutions of the planets. Music also was originally a pure body-art, and its essential quality of rhythm followed from the spontaneous movements of the body, long before the Greeks gave it a mathematical foundation. This mathematic itself, however, as we have seen, was not so purely scientific as it seems to us nowadays, since it rested in the main on the hebdomadal system, and the origin of the latter was undoubtedly mythic (and therefore macro-microcosmic) in kind. Not only are the seven vowels of the voice, to which later the seven notes of

the scale corresponded, pre-mathematical — and in all probability purely microcosmic (see above) — but the seven strings
of the lyre and the seven stops of the oldest syrinx, which corresponded to the seven Muses (only later increased to nine) and
the seven-membered chorus, seem to have been definitely
mythic in origin. The doctrine of the seven tones of the hepta-
chord and the associated harmony of the spheres are Pythagorean in origin [1] — indeed, the interconnexion of the ideologies
of music and physics is a characteristic of his general doctrine.

We must content ourselves here with this mere reference
to the growth of a scientifically established music from an
original rhythm of the body — not failing to note that the intermediate link is once again a macrocosmic extension: namely,
the harmony of the spheres. The driving motive seems to have
been, here too, the creative guilt-feeling which followed from
the strict application of the rule that man is the measure of all
things. The projection of this human measure on to the universe — which (as the pseudo-Hippocratean treatise on the
heptad shows us) holds for the Greek culture as for others —
gives the conscience-stricken individual a cosmic and no longer
a divine justification and so leads straight to the scientific
ideology. For man can thus again find his place in the workings
of nature, and now at a higher ideological level where the nature
is what he himself makes it, or as he himself interprets it —
subordinating himself to it at the same time, even if only in
appearance.

The fundamental problem to which this whole discussion
of the conflict of the different ideologies, the æsthetic and the
scientific — with all its effects in religion, philosophy, and art
— leads is the *problem of form*. We saw how the older art-
ideologies grew out of the religious concepts of the peoples
and their chthonian background; and the justifiable question
now presents itself: in what ways has the scientific ideology,
first appearing in Greece and culminating in modern realism

[1] See the excursus on the number of the strings on ancient instruments in Roscher:
Über Alter, Ursprung, etc., p. 129.

and verism, influenced the art-ideology of the West. As far as
we at present can see from the purely phenomenological point
of view, science manifested in the affirmative sense the same
natural and primitive content of which the denial had led to
an æsthetic creation of art-forms. In other words, the truth-
ideology of science arises from the need to rediscover that
nature which had been formally denied in the ideology of
religious art. In science, truth is a problem of content; in art
and its ideology, beauty a problem of form. But what happens
when, as in Greece, the ideology of truth intrudes on art, and
that of beauty on science?

To answer this question we have to go rather further afield
and, for a start, to link up with what we have so far been able
to say on the form-problem. The various kinds of metaphor,
which survived from mythical prehistory and its micro-
macrocosmic world-view to be the ornamental symbol of a
general identity and to figure even in our own poetry as
simile, throw back a light on to the most primitive forms of
art: ornament and music. Both of these have rhythm as principle of form, which is manifested in music as temporal and in
ornament as spatial repetition. Music we may therefore regard,
analogically, as a pure temporal metaphor, and ornament as
an extreme instance of spatial metaphor. In their developed
forms they display still more clearly than the metaphorical
speech the fundamental essence of metaphor: namely, *extension into the infinite*. For while metaphors of speech only succeed in retaining and recalling some past by association with
the present, rhythmic ornament, in drawing or music, tends
to connect the whole past as such, in abstract form, with the
future, since a rhythmic line or a tone-succession can in principle be continued to infinity. We may perhaps at this point
deal more precisely than we have done in our previous discussion with the differences in the forms of speech-metaphor,
in relation to the particular past which they revive. The space-
metaphors of Homer aim at fixing a collective pristine age of
his people, and consequently, even in form, they adhere most

closely to the strict rhythm of primitive abstract art: consider, for instance, the balance of the hexameter, which yet never becomes monotonous. The temporal metaphor of Proust tries to recall a personal past of the individual, and therefore it does not employ the ready-made language of poetry, but creates a mode of expression which is personal to the point of peculiarity and, even beyond that, arbitrariness and has been not unfairly compared to the twisted thought-paths of the victim of neurosis. Shakspere's dynamic metaphor is, in this respect too, half-way between the two others, in that the author seeks to connect his personal problems with those of his nation and of history. This explains his predilection for mythical and historical material, in which at times he is a nodding Homer and regardless of periods. But this confusion of times is not because of any negligence in the poet, but an essential quality of poetry, which enhances rather than disturbs the poetic effect — unless we insist on using the unfortunate poet as a historical source. The anachronisms of *Macbeth* or those of the Hermann battle in Kleist have hitherto not upset any spectator.[1]

Returning from this digression to the rhythmic prototype of metaphor which we find in music and ornament, we see that the potential extension to infinity which is common to these primitive art-forms expresses the eternalizing impulse *par excellence*. Ornament in line and melody in music are not only abstractions of what is seen or felt in space and time, but abbreviations of the infinite, in spatial form in the one case, in temporal in the other. The fragment of wave-line or meander represents an infinite series of the same kind, and the monotonous rhythm of primitive instruments expresses it temporally, like Wagner's "infinite melody"; such representation of an infinite totality by a partial symbol which is spatially or temporally limited corresponds to the biological distinction of individual and species and the cosmic relation of microcosm and macrocosm; and the same is true of the word also, which in

[1] Cf. my article: "*Das Volksepos*, II. *Die dichterische Phantasiebildung.*" *Psychologische Beiträge zur seiner Entstehung (Imago*, V, 1917).

point of *content* condenses the changes of meaning that have taken place in the course of many generations or ages, and in point of *form* symbolizes the primal cry of the animal as sublimated in the human voice.

Dance, again, represents a combination of the temporal and the spatial rhythms of infinity, in which the circle symbolizes the rebirth idea *par excellence* — the line in space that returns upon itself in time. Some light has already been thrown on the dance, in our discussion of play, and it is only mentioned here as a combination of space- and time-rhythms. The lineal symbol of this eternal rebirth, the circle, was of great importance in early art, and in the bronze age, especially, together with the spiral, it almost dominated all ornament; of the two, the circle, not only artistically but, in our view, ideologically also, represents a higher development of art, though perhaps the peculiarities of bronze as a material may have had something to do with this. However this may be, we must first of all obtain a clearer idea of primitive ornament itself: a subject which has been studied in a brief but valuable monograph by the ethnologist Heinrich Schurtz. He discusses " the ornament of the eye and related problems " (Leipzig, 1895), especially among the north-west American Indians, but also in Melanesia and the South Seas, and reaches a conclusion which is entirely in harmony with our view that " eye-ornament in the last resort may be traced back to totemistic figures, and thus does not owe its origin to leisurely trifling nor yet to any marvellous feeling for beauty, but is closely connected with the spiritual life of the people and springs from it." It is not only interesting but important in this connexion to follow the line of development which Schurtz has traced for eye-ornament. He shows that this developed out of head- (or face-) ornaments, and these latter he traces back to the well-known totem-poles, which consist of a set of superposed figures, crouching or sitting, and sometimes highly stylized, " of human, animal, or mythical form." This simple and obvious deduction of eye-ornament from an ever-increasing " abstraction " of the whole figure into one essential part of it — in this case the eye — not only confirms the "symbolic" character of ornament but shows with astonishing clearness the same line of development from animal (totem) via the whole man (the ancestor) to the visage (head). Finally there is left as the last and highest abstraction of man — I would almost say of his soul — the eye, which (cf. the eagle totem) is of outstanding importance to the Indians.[1]

Whether in this eye-ornamentation (which, as Schurtz shows, is common also in the South Seas) the sun plays in any way the part of the macrocosmic eye, as it does in the cosmogonies of civilized peoples, I will leave undecided. In the artistic development of higher cultures — Chinese, Persian, and German — the spiral, whose chthonian animal origin we have demonstrated, had also a solar significance.[2] But in this macrocosmic view of the spiral as the solar year which returns upon itself and yet continues, we have the same ideological elevation of animal mortality to immortal rebirth, which we have shown to be the fundamental impulse in all artistic creation. It would be particularly fascinating to expound this principle of psychic development in terms of the spiral (for which we have masses of material) because we should in this way come to a harmonious reconciliation of the various possibilities of explanation. All authorities recognize that the spiral was originally an "organic" ornament, but there is hesitation in choosing between an animal interpretation deriving from the snake and a plant-interpretation of the tendril. Our own conclusion, that it comes from the entrail-motive, makes provision for the organic meaning, though what we have in that case is not an imitation of an animal or plant body but a representation of the chthonian animal principle, into which the snake as the first immortality-symbol was artistically introduced. The plantlike stylization of the spiral, as we see it culminating on the Kamares vases of

[1] I had previously, from the pure psychological point of view, surmised that these totem-poles embodied the conflict of the maternal and the growing paternal immortality-ideologies.

[2] The phases of the moon seem also to have provided the pattern for a definite ornamentation (see Fuhrmann: *Der Sinn im Gegenstand*).

Crete, represents rather a purely æsthetic effect, though there also religious influences no doubt play some decisive part as well.

To understand this geometrization of the organic spiral motive, which we already find in the beginning of the neolithic, we must turn to the vessel which carries the meander spiral.[1] This question of ceramics, of which we have already studied the preliminaries, leads from the problem of the origin and development of ornament to the problem of its *purpose*. Most authorities agree in regarding ornament as essentially something subordinate in purpose to a greater whole (Schurtz) or indeed as deriving all its meaning from the object with which it is associated (Scheltema); but there is considerable difference of opinion as to what this purpose was. Since we first find ornament on vases after it has appeared on the body, however, we may properly inquire into the meaning of the vessel-form itself. Now, this is unquestionably modelled on the human body and, as we have shown, discloses the same principle of development as lies at the root of all human art-forms: the vase signified at first the lower body, then the whole body (the neck and shoulder of the vase), and finally the head (with mouth and ears). Indeed, for thousands of years before the wheel was invented, pots were produced by the coiling technique in which already Fuhrmann saw an imitation of the disposition of the intestines. Scheltema, too, though he did not himself put forward this human significance of the pot, nevertheless regarded the development of ceramic ornamentation as a continuation of body-ornament and worked it out by degrees to a point at which we can regain contact with our main subject. Already in his first essay ("*Zur Lehre vom Ornament*"[2]) he comes to the conclusion that ornament, which was originally an essential constituent of the vase that bore it, finally appeared independent of its vehicle, like a spirit separated from the body. But he

---

[1] Hörnes (*Urgeschichte der Kunst*, pp. 293 et seq.) puts the spiral meander ware at the beginning of all neolithic styles. The best accounts of the spiral are in Schuchhardt and Scheltema.

[2] *Zeitschrift für Aesthetik*, XV (1921). I have already mentioned the later book.

SPIRAL ORNAMENTS OF THE OLDER
(ABOVE) AND YOUNGER (BELOW)
BRONZE AGE (*The apparently
naturalistic snake ornament is
derived from the earlier spiral.*)

recognizes also the general cultural significance of the belief in the soul:[1] "The emancipation of ornament as a spiritual form from the natural body of its carrier implies a belief in the independence of spirit in relation to body, a belief, that is, in the independence of the soul."

Applied to the spiral, which is one of the earliest as it is the most widespread of ornaments, this would give a startling confirmation to our cultural-psychological view that out of the least permanent part of the body — namely, the intestines — the process of a creative transformation eventually makes an abstract picture of the immortal soul. And in this creative transformation artistic forms do not play an ancillary or merely illustrative part, but are the actual source of production, since without them the concretization of the prevailing idea of the soul would be impossible. Here, then, we have our linkage between this order of ideas and the view which we reached psychologically in our study of the modern artist-type: namely, that artistic productivity, not only in the individual, but probably in the whole development of culture, begins with one's own human body and ascends to the creation and artistic formation of a soul-endowed personality.

From the colour-painting of the body or its adornment with animal attributes — feathers, shells, etc. — a direct path leads to decoration in the narrower sense, the development of which is a very interesting part of cultural history.[2] Whereas fixed body-ornament makes its effect immediately as an emphasis of the actual body, ornaments which are hung or applied serve merely decorative purposes. Even this decoration, however, has a symbolic meaning, in which the primitive purpose survives[3] in fusion with the equally old ideology. But apart from the practical object of *body-painting,* which Scheltema has

[1] He mentions, though only incidentally, the transition from burial to cremation in the bronze age (*Altnordische Kunst*, p. 118).

[2] See E. Selenka: *Der Schmuck des Menschen* (1900).

[3] Cf. the illuminating remarks in Fuhrmann (*Neu Guinea*, pp. 15 et seq.), who puts the origin of ornament in the idea of the circle, macrocosmic ideologies (the sun's orbit, gold) appearing thus fused in one whole with microcosmic (human life, immortality).

proved so decisively, what interests us here is the ideological importance, which will no longer cause us any trouble, as far, at least, as the addition of animal ornament is concerned; for the animal dances of the Indians and the hunting ceremonies of the Bushman prove clearly enough that the object to be achieved by ornament, of frightening an enemy or of attracting friends, involves total or partial identification with the animal. But this identification, again, has not a mere external aim, to acquire strength or superiority, but depends on a pre-animistic identity with the animal which it imitated in the ceremony or the disguise. If this is certain in the case of the feathers or skins of other adornment, we are justified in asking how far the artistic painting of the body in tattooing represents the same principle at a higher level, at which man is trying to liberate himself from the animal at least to this extent, and to become independent in the self-creative adornment of his own person. If this were so, this primitive painting (of which the traces survive in the feminine world even today) would be the origin of artistic activity not only in the sense assumed by the pragmatic and mimetic theories, but also in the psychological sense of a self-creative liberation of man from his dependence on nature and her purposiveness.[1] If we add that music too, in its origins in song and dance, was a pure body-art [2] which only later and under the influence of mathematics developed into an abstract practice of art, we find here again the path leading from the rhythmically continuous repetition of the body and

[1] Clothing, which replaces tattooing in harsher climates, has obviously the aim of making man independent of nature. This is presumably the meaning of Joest when he says (op. cit., p. 56): "The less a man clothes himself, the more he tattoos, and the more he clothes himself, the less he tattoos." Tattooing as a primitive form of drawing, indeed as the essential beginning of a pictorial writing (as Taylor takes it to be), is discussed elsewhere.

[2] Robert Lach in his *Studien zur Entwicklungsgeschichte der ornamentalen Melopöie* (Leipzig, 1913) also emphasizes the primitive-ornamental origin of music in the tonalization of the primal cries. He distinguishes three stages: first, the primitive substrate; second, the original æsthetic grouping (symmetry, parallel movement); third, the architectonic influence, which leads from ornament into melody-formation. Cf. also the interesting though critical remarks of Scheltema (op. cit., p. 54, n.) on the relation of temporal rhythm (in dance and music) to ornament.

its organs to the infinite melody, elevated to cosmic immortality, of the music of the spheres.

Now, this special study of the form-problem in ornament and music opens up yet further perspectives in relation to the essential difference between the Greek art-ideology and all its predecessors. In relation to Egyptian culture particularly, which was so important for Greece, the difference is one not merely of quantity, but of fundamental quality. Egyptian culture, and especially its art, is spatial and dumb, Greek is temporal and eloquent; and in this sense not only in its religion but in its whole idea Egypt was a land of the dead, Greece a land of the living. Even Egyptian architecture, with its dark cavernous temples and vast subterranean pyramid-tombs, exhibits this chthonian "underworld style" in contrast to the high airy temples of Greeks who raised their head proudly to heaven and fought against gods by word and deed, whereas Egyptian figures of god and man, with their animal heads, are dumb. The temporal element explains the dynamic movement of Greek sculpture which Lessing in his *Laocoon* rightly takes to be the essence of Greek plastic. In myth this Greek ideology, mobile and eloquent, is characteristically expressed in an extensive victory over cosmic time (on which Oriental as well as primitive culture is wholly dependent) and in an emphasis on dynamic — that is, purely human — temporality, which is expressed practically in thought and word, theoretically in mathematical formulation, and artistically in music and sculpture. In myths the old nature-gods are killed, the compulsion of cosmic time defeated, and all that remained of chthonian and animal in the new god of heaven was violently removed. The old god of heaven, Uranus, is castrated by Kronos, the symbol of the human time-idea, and thenceforward Kronos rules.[1] This conquest of the old nature-principle is due to the

[1] This conception of Kronos as the time-god is not so self-evident as might appear, because of the similarity of sound with the Greek χρονός. The etymology of "Kronos" is one of the most disputed in language and mythical study: a Phrygian or Pelasgian origin being adduced by the opponents of the "time" interpretation. But it is certain that the Greeks themselves changed "Kronos" into "Chronos" and regarded or

357

reason; and the victory is achieved less through force than cunning—which is a common virtue in Greek heroes, such as Prometheus, Œdipus, and Odysseus, but also their ruin.

If our view is correct, there must be a connexion between the two cultural lines of development which we have found to determine that of the different art-ideologies also. First, there is the development from the chthonian underworld or belly-culture which grows essentially out of architecture, to the heavenly upper world or head-culture which produces the true arts of the Muses—speech, poetry, and music. Secondly, there is a line through the spatial and the dynamic form to the temporal. The real problem of form occurs within the first, which changes an ugly and rejected content into an admired and beautiful form, manifested spatially, dynamically, or temporally as the case may be. These last form-categories (in the Kantian sense) are, however, already given in the cultures: for example, in Egypt we have the perfection of dumb, static space and in Greece of eloquent, dynamic time. The actual artistic form, however, which arises from the spiritual victory over the (lower) content, is a psychological problem in the narrower sense. Form seems to represent the spontaneous objectification of inner processes, which make use of an external object in order to achieve material expression of that inner form. In other words, the form comes first, as an expression of a change in the inner attitude of man towards life, as for instance in the denial of nature (of the animal, for example); this denial produces (or presupposes) a new psychic dynamism which is "functionally"[1] adapted to the form in which objects are now

---

interpreted the god, whatever his original significance, as a time-god. Pherecydes the Orphic already regarded Zeus the father as Time, and the Stoics tried later to deepen the idea and to establish it physically by help of the myth (Roscher: "*Kronos,*" *Etym.*). This dispute, like some others, seems to me insoluble historically; it can only be explained on the basis of spiritual ideas; i.e., the elevating process as we have assumed it is reflected in this etymological evolution of Chronos also. Thus our view would support and explain the time significance of the god; but conversely it does not need the latter for its own support.

[1] These terms were used by H. Silberer in describing the psychological phenomenon whereby the pictorial and tangible representation of abstract thought-processes is retained.

seen and presented: thus the serpent no longer represents the intestines, but the sun-spiral. The form is thus determined by the collective will-ideology, the content by the partially independent will-psychology of the creator. Intimately as form and content may be united, especially in the finest work, this unity seems to be the result of a harmonious unification of two contraries: not merely in the sense that form is given collectively in style, while the content is in every case a matter of free selection (and therefore, amongst others, in that of the subjective choice of the artist himself), but also since a strong and powerful form often compensates a weak content and vice versa.

The view which we have reached by an analysis of the genesis of art-forms — namely, that the form is the spontaneously given expression of the particular human ideology prevailing at the moment — finds its anticipation and support in the view of certain historians of art — Grosse, Scheltema, Sydow — that body-ornament is prior to that of decorative gear, and that the latter only took over its art therefrom. The discovery of æsthetic forms by cultural ideologies, then, is the continuation and elaboration of the same subjective process at a higher objective level. In the body-art, form and content were still largely one, while at the other end, in our highly differentiated modern art, we have an unending conflict between the two: a struggle between the artist and his material to reduce it to form, or a struggle for new forms which are to dominate the material in some new way. Here we come to a point where the rôle of the individual artist again acquires significance for us; we have already analysed the psychological genesis of the human impulse to create and shown it to be common to all culture and have seen that the particular forms which grew from it and the ideologies associated with it are collective. In primitive art both the cultural urge to creation, as ideologically manifested in the form-principle, and also the content, which is a matter of religion and cult, are collective. The practice of such art is spontaneous, but it is of vital interest: a truly effective cultural factor, without which not merely further development but further life would be impossible. If we take modern art as a comparison ready to hand, we find that both, form as well as content, are becoming more and more individually subjective, and that the impulse to create, which is still fundamentally the same, is more and more a matter of consciousness in the artist. But there is a certain limit to subjectivity which the most individual of artists cannot pass; and for two reasons: because the creative impulse, which is fundamentally always the same, implies a similar principle of form, or, better, impulse to form; and secondly because, if the work is to have some general influence, it must manipulate some collective content of general human significance. Thus, subjectively, there does exist in the artist the creative impulse which in the individual, as arising from the conflict between the lower and the higher self, corresponds to what in the history of culture we have traced out as a gradual defeat of the animal by the spiritual principle. This impulse includes those elements of the conflict which strive towards the voluntary control and domination of the lower by the higher self; the actual victory comes, in art, from the will-like impulse to form, which at first aims at no more than a cessation of the conflict by delimiting and ordering it. This impulse to form seeks, and at first finds, collective traditional forms, which had been produced by similar conflicts in the course of cultural development, and which in many cases carry with them their particular content. These collectively transmitted or dominant forms constitute what in their totality we call style, by accepting which (in whatever degree) the artist does subject himself to a principle outside his individual self. And though it may be collective, it is yet a man-created collectivity, and not one prescribed by nature. Here too our earlier formulation of the imitation-ideology fits into its place, for while we allowed imitation its full importance, we showed besides that it is no matter of simply copying nature, but of representing nature as already altered or interpreted by man in his own sense (macrocosm-microcosm).

The artist, then, represents the type in which the primeval

METAL RELIEF FROM CHINA
(*Notice the sun-spirals on the animal's body.*)

conflict between the lower and higher self is still so intense that he cannot merely fall back for a solution upon the collective forms which are ready to hand, but were created by past generations in relation to their religious, artistic, and (games, sport) social institutions. He certainly uses these forms to some extent, but actively as an individual, not passively as one of the crowd. In his inner conflict, then, which corresponds potentially to that of earlier cultures, he looks instinctively — later, perhaps, consciously — for collective forms to justify and to liberate himself, but he also looks for a collective (material) content, so that he may achieve simultaneously personal freedom and collective effect. This explains the religious content of Egyptian and partly even of Greek art (though already the latter owes its significance to the humanizing tendency); it explains also the choice of biblical subjects by Christian artists, and in general the choice of historical subjects. With this view of the genetics of culture, it becomes clear not only that the individual artist, at any rate the great artist, must (at least potentially) recapitulate in himself the whole evolution from collective to individual art in its separate, though perhaps not necessarily chronological, stages, but that it is only by the subjugation in himself of these collective forms and contents that the really mature works of great masters are created. Moreover, the value set on great artists depends on the predominant ideology of their time; if it is still collective, that artist will be regarded as the greatest of his time, and the finest representative of it in the future, who has expressed the collective elements in their purest and most vigorous form. If on the other hand the general ideology is interwoven with individualistic tendencies, as at the Renaissance and in the succeeding "age of genius," the greatest artist will be he who embodies this individualized collective ideology in the purest form — which means, who has most definitely impressed on traditional forms the stamp of his personality, or (speaking in collective terms) individualism. The highest type of artist is he who can use the typical conflict of humanity within himself to produce collective values, which, though akin to the traditional in form and content — because in principle they spring from the same conflict — are yet individual, and new creations of these collective values, in that they present the personal ideology of the artist who is the representative of his age.

THE ARTIST'S FIGHT WITH ART

※

Nous sommes faits pour le dire et non pour l'avoir.

FLAUBERT

Chapter Twelve

THE ARTIST'S FIGHT
WITH ART

ᔑᓓᔓ

These last folk-psychological chapters, in which we have dealt with those cultural ideologies of the various nations and epochs that underlie artistic production, have brought us back to our initial problem — the relation of the artist to the art-ideology of his time. We began by approaching the problem from the side of the psychology of the artist and there said that the creative personality makes use of the art-ideology which his culture supplies; but the subsequent discussion of cultural questions led to another and almost contrary view. For, from that point of view, the individual, however powerfully his personality may develop, appeared more as an instrument, which the community uses for the expression of its own cultural ideology. This is not by any means a new conception, for it played the chief rôle in the so-called "environment" theories of genius; but the fresh problem that we wish to discuss here is the double attitude of the personal artist to the prevailing art-ideology, which, on the one hand, he uses for the justification of his individual creativity, but, on the other, opposes with all the vigour of his personality. This conflict between artist and art is quite as important for the understanding of the creative process as is the positive influence of the cultural art-ideology on the individual work; it has its social analogue in the defensive reaction of the individual to collective influences of every sort, and its biological basis in the conflict between individuation and generation,

365

from which the individual can only to a limited extent escape.

Thus the ideological art-will of form and the human art-willing of the artist stand in opposition, and the work of art, which results from this conflict, differs in the different epochs of cultural development according to the strength of the personal or that of the collective will. Let us take an example of a general ideology which is not only a strong one but also a pretty rigid one. The art of Egypt, as Miss Margaret Murray has well shown,[1] left almost no freedom of artistic invention. But this does not imply that an Egyptian sculptor was not an artist: he was just as much an artist as the Gothic stone-mason who could obtain the most extraordinary æsthetic effects from his single figure. Yet Egyptian art is the outstanding instance of a rigid art-ideology in which all rules of proportion and representation were fixed once and for all. As Diodorus explained, Egyptian forms were not settled, like the Greek, by external appearance, and consequently Egyptian artists are not classified according to their artistic ideas, but according to the material in which they worked. Nor indeed was the sculptor's work valued as such, but only as part of a whole building, in which it fulfilled a definite purpose. And Miss Murray regards just this external lack of freedom as the very thing that aroused an individual ambition, in creating within the limits of a rigid and obligatory framework. But this conflict between outward and inward freedom is just what we mean by the conflict between art and the artist; indeed, we have been led to conclude, from far more general considerations, that this is one of the essential dynamisms of all artistic creation.

If we take Greek art as a second example, we have here the same conflict between art and the artist — not so much individually as nationally. The classic period of Greek art, from the Persian Wars to the time of Alexander, shows us the highest and purest expression of Hellenism, freed from every cinder of Oriental influence. In other words, here it was not an individual

[1] *Egyptian Sculpture* (London, 1929).

but a whole people that in self-dependent unity completely
mastered an art-form taken from without, and impressed upon
it the stamp of their own national peculiarity. Greek art, moreover, stands so high, not only because it is so greatly art, so
beautiful, but because it is so Greek. Further, if we look at the
Renaissance, we find there, in the individualism that worked
counter to the communal ideology of Christianity, a victory
not only over the Nordic Gothic, but equally over the Classical
(that is, Greek) art-style — a victory wrested by the strong
personality of Renaissance man, who infused his individual
dynamism into both the Greek ideal of beauty and the abstract
forms of Gothic. Renaissance art does not owe its special place
to the fact that it brought back the Classical form into use.
What we admire in it is the life which was put into it by a
dynamic personality — for instance, by Michelangelo, who
represents in his work an inner conflict between pagan and
Christian tendencies, and in whom the Renaissance not only
was completed, but also finished.[1] Then comes Baroque, arising
out of the victory of a Church become worldly over the Nordic
Reformation; and in the rebuilding of Italian churches, as in
other things, the Spanish Jesuits are credited with playing the
leading part.[2] In Baroque, pagan Renaissance and Christian
Gothic are both suffocated under the dominant splendour of the
temporal Church. Rococo, finally, is the defeat of Church
Baroque by the French spirit, and so on.

Thus the great collective ideologies of art, which we call
styles, also show us the conflict between a new-born ideology
(religious, national, or individual — that is, of genius) and an
old one — ending in the defeat of the latter — as the principle
of development. This struggle of world-views, which is represented microcosmically by the conflict of the artist against art,

[1] E. Lucka describes this conflict between Renaissance and Gothic in his *Michelangelo. Ein Buch über den Genius* (Berlin, 1930).

[2] Cf. the latest account in L. Collison-Morley: *Italy after the Renaissance. Decadence
and Display in the Seventeenth Century* (London, 1930). Cf. also the earlier accounts of
this period, which is so important for the history of art, in W. Weisbach: *Der Barock
und die Kunst der Gegenreformation* (Berlin, 1921), and Wölfflin: *Renaissance und Barock.*

is undoubtedly powerfully forwarded by the strong artistic individualities and leads to the triumph of a new style. But the beginning of the movement is cultural and not individual, collective and not personal — only, through his inner conflict, the artist gains the courage, the vigour, and the foresight to grasp the impending change of attitude before others do so, to feel it more intensely, and to shape it formally. But he must do something more than gradually liberate himself from the earlier ideologies that he has hitherto taken as his pattern; in the course of his life (generally at its climax) he must undergo a much harder conflict and achieve a much more fateful emancipation: he must escape as well from the ruling ideology of the present, which he has himself strengthened by his own growth and development, if his individuality is not to be wholly smothered by it. This, however, is only so in the case of artists in individualistic ages, and even there only great artists, whose greatness consists precisely in this reaching out beyond themselves, beyond the ideology which they have themselves fostered. They must ultimately, so to say, carve their own individuality out of the collective ideology that prevails and that they themselves have accepted, like the sculptor who carves his figures out of the raw stone. In this self-representation he seeks, indeed, to make himself individually eternal, but the immediate cause is the impulse to self-preservation from complete absorption of the ego in the collective or of the individual in the genus. This battle for liberation from art, which has to be fought out again and again by every artist, received *cultural* expression in the Renaissance, in which the individualist artist-type saved himself, by the concept of genius, from threatened suffocation by Gothic and Classical. He had, indeed, to accept and employ the ideal forms which are born of the primal human conflict, if only that he might assert himself positively as artist; but the cultural significance of the much-admired Renaissance lies not in the Classical form — which was developed to a higher level in Greece — but in this individual winning through, which equally raises it above the anonymous Gothic.

368

The further this assertion of the individualist type — as man or as artist — goes, and the less capable the collective ideologies are of carrying it (especially in the case of religion), the more internal the struggle of the cultures becomes, and the great artist finally has to carry it personally, in artistic development and in human suffering. The essence of the artistic type lies therefore in this, that he can pass through his individual struggle, the conflict between individual and genus, between personal and collective. immortality, in an *ideological* form, and that the peculiar quality of this conflict compels him, or enables him, to use an *artistic* ideology for the purpose. For, as we have seen, the same fundamental conflict may, with a different attitude, lead to the individual's resolving the inner dualism by means of a scientific or a political ideology. If we ask what particular cast in the individual settles whether the personal conflict shall be fought in terms of this ideology or that, we can only find the answer by continuing to use the comparative method that we have followed hitherto. In other words, the artist, like art, is not to be comprehended through a specialized study of creative personality or of the æsthetic standards of art-ideology, but only by a combination of the two and by other comparative methods. That is, we cannot understand the artist by a purely individual psychology — without taking account of the collective art-ideology — nor the development and changes of the latter without the psychology of the artist and the primal conflict which lies at its root and which is the cause equally of art and of artists. Nor can we understand the development of this general human conflict and particularly of artistic creation without noting how, and why, the same basic struggle is passed through in other cases in terms of scientific, political, or other ideologies.

To understand this ideologizing of personal conflicts — which in a greater or lesser degree affects all choice of and all practice of a calling [1] — we must return to the most general principles of the development of personality, various other

[1] See the chapter: "Vocation and Talent," in my *Modern Education*.

aspects of which I have discussed elsewhere.[1] The human individual must have at his disposal from the start some sort of ideology, even if of the most primitive kind (such as the notion of good and evil), not only that he may find his place in the society which is built up on these ideas, but also that he may find relief from the inner conflicts which would otherwise compel him to create for himself some ideology for the objectification of his psychic tensions. This ideologization of inner conflicts manifests itself in the individual in a form which psycho-analysis has called that of " identification " — with parents, teachers, and other ideal patterns — without being able to explain the process thereby. I have shown in another place that the motive of these identifications is the individual's root fear of isolation, and that their result is that the individual masters his conflict himself, independently of the persons who mediate and represent these ideologies. But this inward independence of teachers and educators as such, which is gained in the first instance by accepting the collective ideology that they offer, turns — usually about the time of puberty — against these collective ideologies themselves, under which the growing individual feels just as dependent and as restricted as he had previously been *vis-à-vis* their individual representatives.

This liberation of the ego, as we should expect, occurs in the artist also, but with the difference that in his case no time is lost in taking up the *artistic* ideology, in preference to the general social. But this brings us back to the question: what is it that favours such a preference for the artistic ideologies in particular individuals and not in others? To make any progress on this question we must state the problem more narrowly, for we must remember that the general social ideology is made a specific in other people besides the artist, by their choice and practice of professions, so that the turn from general to special ideology is not a specifically artistic problem, but one of voca-

[1] *Gestaltung und Ausdruck der Persönlichkeit* (1928), and also the chapter on "Self and Ideal" in *Wahrheit und Wirklichkeit* (1929).

tional psychology. As to this, I will refer the reader to what I have said in other works already mentioned, and only emphasize, in the present context, the formulation there proposed, which is that, compared with the average professional man, the artist has, so to say, a hundred-per-cent vocational psychology. That is (as I have said earlier in an introductory fashion), the creative type nominates itself at once as an artist (or, in certain circumstances, as scientist or otherwise) — a periphrasis which we are now in a position to replace by the formula that in the artist-type the creative urge is constantly related, ideologically, to his own ego, or at any rate that this is so in a higher degree and fuller measure than in the average man, so that one can say of the artist that he does not practise his calling, but *is* it, himself, represents it ideologically. For whereas the average man uses his calling chiefly as a means to material existence, and psychically only so far as to enable him to feel himself a useful member of human society — more or less irrespective of what his calling is — the artist needs his calling for his spiritual existence, just as the early cultures of mankind could not have existed and developed without art.

For the artist, therefore, his calling is not a means of livelihood, but life itself; and this explains not only the difficulties of his existence, since his main object cannot be the earning of money, but his struggles in love and life, which in the productive type spring from the impulse to create, and not vice versa. This conflict arises from an intensification in him of the general human dualism, but it is soon transformed from the purely dynamic conflict between impulse and will into an ideological conflict between art and the artist. The first stage in the growth of an artist is that which we have described as his " nomination " and which marks the subordination of the individual to one of the prevailing art-ideologies, this usually showing itself in the choice of some recognized master as the ideal pattern. In doing so, he becomes the representative of an ideology, and at first his individuality vanishes, until, later, at the height of his achievement, he strives once more to liberate

371

his personality, now a mature personality, from the bonds of an ideology which he has himself accepted and helped to form. This whole process of liberation from a personal or ideal identification is so particularly intense and therefore difficult in the artist (and the productive type generally), not only because he has a stronger personality, but because this needs stronger identification for its artistic ideologizing; the process of liberation being thus particularly complex, and exposing the artist to those dangerous crises which threaten his artistic development and his whole life. These conflicts, which the " madness " theory of Lombroso and the pathological literature based on it try to explain rationalistically as neurosis, can only be understood ideologically; and when we so regard them, our insight into them is the deeper. In this creative conflict it is not only the positive tendency to individual self-liberation from ideologies once accepted and now being overcome that plays a great part. There is also the creative guilt-feeling, and this opposes their abandonment and seeks to tie down the individual in loyalty to his past. This loyalty again is itself opposed by a demand for loyalty to his own self-development, which drives him onward, even to strive beyond his own ego and artistic personality. So the struggle of the artist against art is really only an ideologized continuation of the individual struggle against the collective; and yet it is this very fact of the ideologization of purely psychical conflicts that marks the difference between the productive and the unproductive types, the artist and the neurotic; for the neurotic's creative power, like the most primitive artist's, is always tied to his own self and exhausts itself in it, whereas the productive type succeeds in changing this purely subjective creative process into an objective one, which means that through ideologizing it he transfers it from his own self to his work. The artist is helped, moreover, by another dynamic difference which not only enables him to construct a valuable ideology but to transform it into actual artistic achievement.

A deep study of neurosis has shown me that a characteristic

quality of both the productive and the thwarted, marking off these excess and deficiency types from the average, is an over-strong tendency towards totality of experience. The so-called adaptability of the average man consists in a capacity for an extensive partial experience such as is demanded by our everyday life, with its many and varied problems. The non-conforming type tends to concentrate its whole personality, its whole self, on each detail of experience, however trivial or insignificant; but as this is not only practically impossible but psychically painful (because its effect is to bring out fear), this type protects itself from a complete self-exhaustion by powerful inner restraints. Now, the neurotic stops at this point in the process, thus cutting himself off from both the world and experience, and, thus faced with the proposition " All or nothing," chooses the nothing. The artist, however, here also, in spite of many difficulties and struggles, finds a constructive, a middle way: he avoids the complete loss of himself in life, not by remaining in the negative attitude, but by living himself out entirely in creative work. This fact is so obvious that, when we intuitively admire some great work of art, we say the whole artist is in it and expresses himself in it.

This, however, holds good for different kinds of artists in different degrees — a point to which we shall return later. Some artists persistently partialize themselves and thus leave a greater complete work unaccomplished; others pour themselves out wholly in every partial work. The same seems to be true of whole periods, or rather epochs, of style, which are, after all, only the expression of psychical and spiritual ideologies. The best example of a complete style seems to me to be Gothic, not only since it strives after an all-embracing whole, but because, more perhaps than any other style-tendency, it expresses, and insists on expressing, the spiritual-in-itself. This, however, is no longer the purely abstract spirituality of primitive art, but a world-embracing " pantheistic " dynamic of the spiritual. Hence, as Worringer rightly saw, it is not merely " a phenomenon of its age, but the great irreconcilable antithesis to the Classical, which is not limited to a single period of style, but reveals itself in ever new clothing throughout the centuries." [1] Now, wherever one manages to find this opposition of Classical and Gothic, it seems to me to correspond to that eternal dualism which lies at the root of all art and all artistic creation, and precisely because it is something inherent in the individual. I believe that I have found one of the fundamental aspects of this primary individual dualism in the total-partial conflict, and in this sense Gothic would be the total and Classical the partial — a partial, it is true, which always gives the whole in the detail, the psychic dynamism expressing itself æsthetically as the beauty of proportion which was the Classical ideal. Gothic, on the other hand, does not try to symbolize the whole in a part, but rather aims at a dynamic picture of the whole in its actual totality.

In what we call Classical or Gothic, then, these two spiritual principles have been æsthetically objectified, and each presents itself to the individual artist as an external compulsion of form which he must accept as artist but fight against as individual. But we have also gained some further insight into the inner processes of the creative artist, which make it possible for him fully to express his own personality at the same time that it yields precedence to the art-ideology of the work. We must, further, return to the difference between a total and a partial experience, which is basic for the attitude of all such individuals. In the ceaseless struggle for liberation of the self from the moral, social, and æsthetic ideologies and the people who represent them, the individual goes through a disjunctive process of which I have regarded the process of birth as the prototype. But the process, though similar in principle to, is not a simple repetition of, the trauma of birth; it is, broadly, the attempt of the individual to gain a freedom from dependence of any sort upon a state from which it has grown. According to the stage of development, this separation will take

[1] *Formprobleme der Gothik*, which lays even more stress on the racial influence than Worringer's latest work, *Griechentum und Gotik* (Munich, 1928).

the most varied forms and symbols, whereas the basic conflict is always the same: the overcoming of previous supporting egos and ideologies from which the individual has to free himself according to the measure and speed of his own growth, a separation which is so hard, not only because it involves persons and ideas that one reveres, but because the victory is always, at bottom and in some form, won over a part of one's own ego. We may remark here that every production of a significant artist, in whatever form, and of whatever content, always reflects more or less clearly this process of self-liberation and reveals the battle of the artist against the art which expresses a now surmounted phase of the development of his ego. In some artists the representation of a process of personal development seems to be the chief aim of their work, by which I do not mean the accidental biographical material, though this is itself (as we said above) an objective expression of the same inner conflict. Finally, there are artists, especially among the poets, for whom not only is this self-representation the essence of their work, but who are conscious to a very considerable extent of the process and have studied it "philosophically." Goethe and Nietzsche are perhaps the most conspicuous examples of this type, which is becoming more and more common nowadays and in which we can notice an ever-increasing preponderance of the psychologically disintegrating over the artistically formative ego. This process of the increasing extension of consciousness in humanity, which psycho-analysis has fostered so enormously in the last decades — but not entirely to the advantage of mankind as a whole — was prophesied by me in my *Künstler* in 1905 (at the time of my first acquaintance with Freud) as likely to be the beginning of a decay of art. In this early work I not only foretold the collapse of art through the increasing consciousness of the artist, but observed and established the manner of it in the nascent state.

My observations of those days seem to me to have been very emphatically confirmed by the later development of the problem of art and the artist; but I can now give it a better psychological foundation, and so perhaps a more hopeful future. The question how it is that the great artist can express his whole personality in his work and yet subordinate it to his art-ideology is only to be understood, as I remarked, where the conflict of the partial and the total has come out at a particularly happy issue. I spoke of the constant detaching of the artist from earlier ideologies, which on the one side correspond to a separation of the individual from a great whole, and on the other to the extrusion of worn-out parts of the ego. This double separation of the ego from the collectivity and of part of the ego from its totality includes the two fundamental life-processes: individuation on the one hand, and procreation or generation on the other. Now, these fundamental processes, as is well known, are not sexual, but occur at a very low biological level, before the differentiation of the sexes, as cell-division. They survive, however, in rudimentary form even in the highly differentiated sex-life of humanity and thus continue to bulk large and to matter deeply in such highly complicated processes as the development of personality and the creative impulse which rises from it. At the highest level of human personality we have a process which psycho-analysis calls (without explaining its deeper biological and human aspects) identification. This identification is the echo of an original identity, not merely of child and mother, but of everything living — witness the reverence of the primitive for animals. In man, identification aims at re-establishing a lost identity: not an identity which was lost once and for all, phylogenetically through the differentiation of the sexes, or ontologically in birth, but an identity with the cosmic process, which has to be continually surrendered and continually re-established in the course of self-development. In the attempt at this re-establishment the two types with which we are dealing, the " totalist " and the " partialist," diverge fundamentally. The average type of a well-adapted " partial " being can feel himself as part of a greater

whole — in religious communion, social and vocational grouping, or family feeling — and thus find his identity with the
world. The "total" type, on the other hand, is set on maintaining himself as a whole and on absorbing the world as part
of himself. In so far the artist and the neurotic are alike, that
in contrast to the average man they have a far wider, more
"magic" feeling of the world, which is gained, however, at
the cost of an egocentric attitude towards it. The neurotic
stops at the point where he includes the world within himself
and uses this as a protection against the real claims of life,
though the price is paid for this protection in the feeling of
world-sorrow which has to be taken in with the rest. The artist,
too, has this feeling of *Weltschmerz* in common with the handi-
capped neurotic; but here the paths diverge, since the artist can
use this introverted world not only as a protection but as a
material; he is thus never wholly oppressed by it — though
often enough profoundly depressed — but can penetrate it by
and with his own personality and then again thrust it from
him and re-create it from himself. This extrusion is a process
both of begetting and of bearing, not at the level of sexual
differentiation of male and female, but at a deeper and more
fundamental level: the liberation of the individual from the
burden of generation by repulsion of part of the ego, which is
felt as a relief and not as a loss.

The primitive process of biological propagation by fission of
a part from the whole is thus ideologically macrocosmized in
the artist, and he puts forth into his work not only a personal
part of his ego but also a part that includes either the whole
world or at least an important portion of it. This representation
of a part of the world or of nature in his work is not the result
of an æsthetic impulse to imitate or of technical capacity, but
the precondition of all creation. If the artist had not already
absorbed the world within himself on account of his emotional
needs he would not have the urge to throw this cosmic self off
in creation and so save himself again as an individual. In this

super-individual, almost cosmic, creative process all the purely human factors — love, sexual relations, social duties — throng in to hinder or help, so that a psychological cast is given to the conflict (though this is by no means as important as artists themselves feel and as biographers and analytical psychographers still would have us believe).

Particularly, the relation of the creative artist to women has been, ever since Homer invoked the Greek Muse to help him, a favourite theme of rather superficial essays. For the artist to project on to the beloved woman his bisexual creative urge — of begetting and of bearing, or of self-begetting and self-rebirth, which he has fused into one — is not only his perfect right but a necessity of life for him. And that the biographer who confines himself to describing the external life-course of his hero is forced to give the Muse the position which she had in the life and consciousness of the artist is also quite natural. But for psychologists to believe that they have therefore understood anything about the creative process or even about a work of art is a presumption which has prevented a right view of very complex facts. This does not touch psycho-analysis directly, but it does so indirectly; for though it does not regard the Muse whom the poet sings of as the real source of creation, yet in the so-called " deep " psychological substitution of the mother for her it postulates an equally external and less credible motivation in place of the inner motive, which is beyond its reach. I am of course the last person to deny the influence of birth or of the mother, after my works on incest and on the trauma of birth, but the point is whether we take a concrete view as psycho-analysts still do (and many poets perhaps with them), or regard it only as typical and ideological, making the mother the symbol of the eternal separation and rebirth which is ever repeated in the development of personality.[1] When once it has become such a symbol, the idea may be easily transferred

---

[1] C. G. Jung in his *Wandlungen und Symbole der Libido* (1912) has insisted, against Freud, on the symbolic significance of the mother, though one-sidedly, with emphasis on passive rebirth and without recognition of the active self-creative force.

in the course of life to another person, especially if the latter
is identified with the ideological ego of the artist, in the same
way as the mother was identified with the biological. In this
sense the artist is both practically and theoretically justified
vis-à-vis the psychologist when he ascribes more influence on
his creativity to his master or his later Muse than to his mother
or father, to whom he owes his existence, but not his artistic
development.

For we owe our artistic development, as we do every other
form of personality-development, to none other than ourselves and the conditions of our time, though we always tend,
and sometimes are driven, to ascribe to other people not only
the development and further growth of ourselves, but of our
work and creativity. This is because of the creative guilt-feeling,
which is a problem I have dealt with elsewhere in its psychological significance.[1] At present we are more interested in the
artistic consequences and the biographical precipitates, which
are inextricably connected. One of the radical mistakes made
by most ordinary biographies and by psychography is the
notion of a parallelism between experience and creation. This
certainly exists, if not causally, at least phenomenally connected. Quite as important, however, or even more so, is the
opposition of life and creation, which has been emphasized,
but not understood, since this is impossible without taking
account of the creative feeling of guilt. It is significant that
many of the greatest artists (though by no means all) have a
strong bourgeois tinge, and Kretschmer, in his study of men
of genius, declared that genius needs a strong touch of conven-
tionality. Many whose work is of the highest value and who live
wholly in their art lead a very simple, ordinary life, and this
purely human side often comes to the surface in their work,
in contrast to the divine quality of genius. The Muse, too,
whose idealization by the poet himself and whose apotheosis
in the mother-principle by the psychographer look so fine,
often comes off badly enough in real life. Not only that she

[1] *Wahrheit und Wirklichkeit* (chapter on "Creation and Guilt").

has to endure, even enjoy, the moods of the divinely inspired master, but she very often becomes for the artist a symbol of an ideology that is no longer adequate, which she may have helped him to create, but which he has now to overcome and throw overboard. In that case we have that conflict in the artist, with which the psycho-analyst so often deals — since the artist is both unable to create without her and prevented by her presence from any further creation. His inclination may be to let her go, along with the earlier ideology, but his guilt-feeling will not allow it. This feeling is, however, not only ethical and concerned with the loved companion, but inner and psychical, since it concerns his own development and his loyalty to himself.

Not only will the artist who finds a creative issue from this conflict show its traces in his work, but his work will often enough be purely the expression of the conflict itself, whose solution has to be justified as much as the failure to reach a solution would have to be. As the artist, during this process of liberation from the ideology, has to include in what he surrenders the person or persons who were connected with it, he has to justify this action, which is usually done by magnification. That is, he will either really create something greater, in order to justify his action, or in the effort to create this greater he will be impeded by a still more enhanced feeling of guilt. In the first case he will use the guilt-feeling directly for creation; in the second even his previous creative power will be impeded. But if the artist takes the step forward in a purely ideological sense, without the need of concrete figures for the resolution of his creative conflict, his tendency will be to *lessen* his work, even if in fact it has become greater. This minimizing tendency also is due to the feeling of guilt, but, on the other hand, this has already worked itself out creatively in the artist, and it is only humbler second thoughts that are obliged to lessen the splendour of creation. A splendid instance of this is Rodin's life-work; no outsider, regarding it uncritically, would imagine that in masterpieces like the " Thinker " or even the mythological groups he sees only fragments of a never-completed work, called by Rodin himself the " Porte d' Enfer." Even though the artist was convinced and permeated by the greatness of his work, and expressed it directly in works like the " Hand of God " or the " Thinker," the aim which he set up and never attained of a vast and ideal achievement (on a par with the whole creation) represents a minimizing of the actually achieved, only intelligible by the creative feeling of guilt. This type — of which Goethe also is an instance, with his *Faust* trailing ever in his hands as his *magnum opus* by the side of which everything else was meant but as " fragments " of one great confession — has its opposite in another type of artist, who not only gives and fulfils himself in every work, but whose whole production is one vast justification of his impulse to create. Of this type Shakspere seems to me to be the best instance — and precisely because we know so little of his actual life and even doubt his authorship. Shakspere's work and the biographical material which has been gathered about the Stratford butcher's son have just as much psychological connexion as have the Homeric poems and our scanty information about the blind Ionian singer. Even if we did discover that Shakspere and Homer [1] were neither of them responsible for the work assigned to them, yet the psychological types thus designated are just as much masterpieces of a people's creation as are the poems and dramas which bear their name. I mean that Shakspere's work requires an author who because of his creative impulse would give up home and family and all the life of an ordinary citizen in order to justify a foolish and irrational migration to the metropolis by brilliant achievement there. His success is the measure of his greatness. But even if an English noble or gentleman were the author of the dramas, I am sure that folk-fantasy would have been compelled to invent such

---

[1] It is worth mentioning that a life of Shakspere by Nicholas Rowe (1709) is the first modern poet biography, and also characteristic that a life of Homer (probably the pseudo-Hesiodic life) provided the pattern. Thus fictitious biography, which essentially constructs the life from the work, is the real ancestor of all biographical literature.

antecedents for him—which means, would have invented a Shakspere who happened to exist in Stratford or was transplanted there. The same has happened with greater world-historical ideas, such as Christianity, which certainly needed a Jesus from Nazareth, and it can hardly be chance that the greatest creations of the human spirit, such as the New Testament, the Homeric poems, and Shakspere's plays, should, on the one hand, have been centres of academic disputes as to authorship and, on the other, should have inspired the imagination of whole centuries in favour of one author. Even Goethe, who could hardly dispute his own authorship, felt himself compelled to describe his whole creation as a collective work which only happened to bear his name. This feeling of the poet that he is the mouthpiece of his age or, for that matter, of all humanity, explains not only why he has to ascribe his work to a Muse and thus connect it with his personal life and give it concrete form; it also throws a light on the fact that, and the degree to which, the art-ideology affects the poet's life. There is thus an influence of personal experience on creation and a reciprocal influence of creation on experience, which not only drives the artist externally to a Bohemian existence, but makes his inner life characterologically a picture of his art-ideology and thus once more calls forth the individual self in protest against this domination by that ideology.

Let us take the case of Shakspere once more. His life may just as well have been invented to suit his work as it may have been lived by the poet in a deeper sense to suit his ideology. Paradoxical as this sounds, yet we quite habitually in simpler circumstances take this adaptation of a man to his profession as self-evident. Between a night-watchman who has to adapt his external life very differently from that of his fellows and the poet whose personal life is an ideological expression of his artistic production, there is a difference only of degree, not of quality. When modern biography and psychography attempt to explain a man's work and production from his personal experience, the effort must remain not only incomplete, but also superficial, as long as the influence of the art-ideology on life and experience is not included. But this is not as simple as it is with the night-watchman and will not fit the same stereotyped formulæ, as most even analytical psychographers try to make it do. For the impulse to create puts itself into life and into work alike, and the great artist will in himself experience his own creation at the same time as in his work he will shape what he has experienced: for here too form and content are once more one, as they were in primitive art.

This brings us to the real problem of biography. Biography is as little an objective science as history is, even when it endeavours to be so, and would never fulfil its purpose if it were. The *formative* process of the biography begins long before the actual attempt to picture the life of the artist; after all, the main purpose is the picture of the creative personality and not merely of the man of actuality, and the two portraits can naturally never be wholly identical. The effort to make them so is, however, the avowed or unavowed tendency not only of the biographer, but of the artist himself and of his public, present and future. If there is plenty of biographical material, as in the case of Goethe, we do look in his life for the experience which would explain his work. But we never find it; though masses of material are accumulated in a futile attempt to find an experience which can explain the creative work, it cannot as a matter of principle be intelligible on that basis alone. In other cases, of which we have cited Shakspere as the type, creative biography has an easier task in constructing a life to fit the work. But always the starting-point in the formation of a biography is the individual's ideologizing of himself to be an artist, because thenceforward he must live that ideology, so far as reality allows him to do so; and so far as it does not, the artist makes for himself the experiences that he needs, searches for them and gives them forms in the sense of his ideology. Nowadays we quite naturally give the lives of certain types of poet a definite dramatic and novelistic form,[1] since this is the only form adapted to the shaping of a biographical legend. That in every age the poet's life should be revalued and re-edited to suit the ideology of that age is only natural, though this does not exactly lessen the complexity of the problem.

Before we deal with this process of biographical legend-formation, which is set going by the artist's own ideologizing experience, in terms of its effect on success and permanent reputation, we must see how the process bears on our immediate question, that of the artist *versus* his art. With the partial experience of his own artistic ideology the artist is in conflict *a priori,* fighting for his life, and in the event (as we have shown) he achieves the compromise in his ideological experience which allows him to enjoy both his life and his productivity, instead of having to attain the one at the cost of the other. On the other hand, we must never forget that creation is itself an experience of the artist's, perhaps the most intense possible for him or for mankind in general. Nor is this true only of the unique instant and act of creation; for during the creation itself the work becomes experience and as such has to be surmounted by new actuality of extension and formation. This cumulative dynamic character of creativity, which marks it as an experience, can as a rule be reconstructed only genetically, since it is rarely the object of direct observation. Hence it is more easily observed in the arts of time and rhythm like poetry and music, which in their temporal succession and extension often show the development of this vehement dynamism during the process of creation, while we cannot see it in the fine arts except in sketches and studies. But it is almost typical for great artists that at the beginning of a work they are not quite clear about its formation, working-out, and completion; even in spite of a clear original concep-

---

[1] For the predecessors of this modern mania see Helene Goldschmidt: *Das deutsche Künstlerdrama von Goethe bis R. Wagner* (Weimar, 1925); Erna Levy: *Die Gestalt des Künstlers im deutschen Drama* (Berlin, 1929); Kate Laserstein: *Die Gestalt des bildenden Künstlers in der Dichtung* (Berlin, 1930). For Ibsen, who pictured the modern artist type, see later.

tion, the work turns during production into something other than the artist had originally planned. This process also is only intelligible through a realization of the specific dynamism of creativity, which must operate on the *potential* life plane if it is to liberate his energy and not consume it, as we have explained in the case of play.

We have said above that the artist-type, with his tendency to totality of experience, has an instinct to flee from life into creation, since there to a certain extent he can be sure of matters remaining under his own control; but this totality tendency itself, which is characteristic of the really productive type, in the end takes hold of his creation also, and this totality of creation then threatens to master the creative artist as effectually as the totality of experience. In short, the "totality function" of the artist-type in the end makes all productivity, whether in itself or in a particular work, as much a danger for the creative ego as was the totality of experience from which he took refuge in his art. Here the conflict of the artist *versus* art becomes a struggle of the artist against his own creation, against the vehement dynamism of this totality-tendency which forces him to complete self-surrender in his work. How the artist escapes this new danger, after he had previously avoided that of the total experience, is one of the obscurest and most interesting problems of the psychology of creative artists. There will of course be special modes of escape for each artist or artist-type, which are decided for him by his personality and circumstances. But I think that certain ways are universally accessible, of which I will mention a few that are typical. One means of salvation from this total absorption in creation is, as in ordinary life, the division of attention among two or more simultaneous activities; and it is interesting in this connexion to note that work on the second activity is begun during work on the first just at the moment when the latter threatens to become all-absorbing. The second work is then often an antithesis in style and character to the first, though it may be a continuation at another level. This can, of course, only happen with artists who have various interests and capacities; thus Goethe indulged his scientific, and Schiller his philosophical, studies at periods apparently of weakness in poetic creativity, but really, according to our view, of danger to the poet when he had to find respite from that creativity. If a second sphere of interest of this sort — which is frequently a second form of artistic achievement — is lacking, periods of disappointment, depression, and even illness are likely to occur, which are then not so much a consequence of exhaustion as a flight from it.

This brings us to a second means of escape for the artist from his own creation, which in this case is not put on to another level, but simply set aside for the time being. The creative process, with its object of totality, always contains in any case a time conflict, which expresses itself in the difficulty the artist finds both in beginning and in finishing his work. Just as he can escape from threatened domination in the midst of his creation, so he can hold back instinctively as long as possible from the beginning of it; but this so overstrains the inner dynamism that delays of various sorts must be intercalated later, so that he may not be carried off by the violence of the productive experience. The inhibitions, then, of which most artists complain, both during creation and in its intervals, are the ego's necessary protections against being swallowed by creativity, as is the case, for that matter, with the inhibitions of normal or neurotic types. This form of protection may naturally in some cases have a disturbing (pathogenic) effect. But the retardation of, or refusal to complete, some work may have another, deeper reason. The restraint which holds the totality-tendency in check is basically fear, fear of life and of death, for it is precisely this that determines the urge to eternalize oneself in one's work. Not only, however, has the completed work the value of an eternity symbol, but the particular creative process, if it involves an exhaustive output, is by the same token a symbol of death, so that the artist is both driven on by the impulse to eternalization and checked by the fear of death. I have elsewhere shown that this restriction between the two poles of fear

—fear of life and fear of death—is one of the fundamental processes of life; the artist seems to experience it in a similar intensified fashion to the neurotic, but with the difference that in the neurotic the fear of life predominates and so checks all expression in life, while the artist-type *can* overcome this fear in his creation and is driven by the fear of death to immortalize himself.

This conflict of the artist, first against his art and then against the dynamism of his own work and finally against its actual accomplishment, finds a peculiar expression in modern artists —clearest perhaps in the poets, but unmistakable also in plastic and pictorial artists. This is the diversion of creation into knowledge, of shaping of art into science and, above all, psychology. Naturally, spiritual self-representation in the work is always one essential element in artistic creativity and in art, but it is only in modern artists that it becomes a conscious, introspective, psychological self-analysis. But we are not concerned with those artists of the day whose work claims to represent a psychological confession as such and no more— though in point of fact it *is* something more. Here we are discussing the far more interesting half-way type, which, whether in the course of an ensemble of creation or even within the compass of a single work, passes suddenly from the formative artist into the scientist, who wishes—really he cannot help himself —to establish, or, rather, cannot help trying to establish, psychological laws of creation or æsthetic effect. This diversion of artistic creation from a formative into a cognitive process seems to me to be another of the artist's protections against his complete exhaustion in the creative process. We have here the ideological conflict of beauty and truth, which we have already studied from the general cultural point of view, reappearing as a personal conflict in the creative artist. But we also better understand how far the artistic form is in itself a necessary protection of the artist against the dynamism of a conflict which would destroy him if he failed to put it into form. In this sense, in the need, that is forced on him by that dynamism, for putting order, meaning, and control into the psychic chaos into which his totality-urge drives him, the artist, even if he is never conscious of the fact, is always a bit of a scientist. Conscious reflection about creativity and its conditions and about all the æsthetic laws of artistic effect is only a continuation of the process at a fully conscious level which ensues whenever the artistic formative power is inadequate to control the chaos — that is, when, instead of being a protection, it becomes a danger to the survival of the ego.

Seen thus, the development of modern art and the modern artist is a manifestation of the same general development of Western art-ideology, as this resulted from the Greek conflict between the notions of beauty and truth. There is a rescue of the immortal soul by the æsthetic idea of beauty, and a controlling of the psychic chaos by the artistic form, with its eternal material. This was followed by the disruption of the form by individuality in the modern genius-art, the overflow of the ego beyond the form in a romantic " *Sturm und Drang,*" and finally the flight from that loss of the ego which would be involved in a total creation or a total experience, into psychology. This cultural development-struggle between art and the ideologies of art has to be gone through by modern artists — burdened as they are with the whole weight of Western culture, both in their personal development and in their individual growth as artists — in themselves and with themselves. And if one of the leading art-historians of the day, Worringer, some ten years ago delivered before the Munich Goethe Society a funeral oration over modern Expressionism, contrasting our generation's will-to-art with its formative capacity, we must balance this view with some understanding of the artists' struggle if we are to avoid passing prematurely from the establishment of a fact to its valuation. Worringer is certainly right [1] in his warning to modern artists to be satisfied with the last flicker and echo on the fringes of our culture and to avoid the great mistake of promising us, because we possess an in-

[1] *Künstlerische Zeitfragen* (Munich, 1921).

creased insight into the essence of what art was at creative periods, an equal increase in the decaying vigour of our own uncreative epoch. That is easier said than done; not because real resignation is always harder than a struggle, but because the problem that is touched is the deepest problem of artistic creation, and it can never be solved by conscious deliberation and decision, however correct and sincere. As long as there is in man an impulse to create, he seeks and finds artistic expression in the most varied ideologies, and yet these have always been in some way traditional and collective. Nietzsche was therefore quite right when, long ago, in *Human All-too-human* he warned us against " revolution " in art and saw in its break with tradition its end. For unless it has some collective or social basis — for instance, in religion or, later, the " genius-religion " — artistic creation is impossible, and the last hopeless effort to base it on a psychological ideology not only leads away from art into science, but, even so, fails on points of principle. Education or art can no more be supported on psychological ideologies than religion can be replaced by psychology. For psychology is the individual ideology *par excellence* and cannot become collective, even if it is generally accepted or recognized. But modern humanity, through its increasing individuation, has fallen ever deeper into psychology and the ideologies thereof, precisely because they justify its individuality and its consciousness of it. But this individual ideology — as I declared in my first book in 1905 and have since sought to prove from the examination of world-outlooks [1] — is an impossibility for art and has brought us to our present pass, which we may regret, but cannot alter by comparative studies of culture. So that Worringer's " funeral oration " really applies to art as a whole and not its present form of expressionism.

If, however, we regard the whole culture of a people or of an age as being not merely a means for the production of art, but as the expression of a particular form of life, within which a particular art-form plays a part, great or small, we may reach a

[1] *Seelenglaube und Psychologie* (1930); *Modern Education.*

less pessimistic position. As I have already hinted in my *Künstler,* we shall perhaps have to be content with cutting down the claims made for art and, further, shall have to sacrifice the artist-type as it has hitherto existed. Modern art, as Worringer complained, does suffer from the claims of modern artists to be put on a level with creative artists of other ages, and the artist-type suffers also, since he has to put this modern ideology of art for art's sake in the place of every other. The modern artist attempted to maintain the vanished art-ideologies of earlier ages at least in his personal ideologies, even if he could not transform them into productivity. But this draping of the modern individual in the ideologies of earlier ages was bound to lead, in such individuals, to a conflict between their real selves and the self adopted as an ideal — like the fundamental struggle of the neurotic. The conflict between the idealistic and realistic aspects of all art, which we have described as the struggle of the notion of beauty against that of truth, is duplicated in the modern artist as a conflict between his true self and an ideal self, in which he tries to conserve the art-ideologies of past ages. But it is not only modern art that (as opposed to Classical) is realistic, but the modern artist also, which means that he is oriented towards truth and not beauty, and this not only in his pseudo-naturalistic art-ideology, but in his whole psychological attitude towards himself and his art. His aim is not to express himself in his work, but to get to know himself by it; in fact, by reason of his purely individualistic ideology, he cannot express himself without confessing, and therefore knowing, himself, because he simply lacks the collective or social ideology which might make the expression of his personality artistic in the sense of earlier epochs. This individual realism, however, which reveals itself as a search for truth in art and life, only intensifies the conflict in the person of the artist. The more successful his discovery of truth about himself, the less can he create or even live, since illusions are necessary for both. The clearest representative of the modern artist-type seems to me to be Ibsen, who was still just capable of an artistic elaboration of this destructive problem — and he too sometimes came suspiciously near didactic, doctrinaire psychologism.

Thenceforward nothing was possible but a frank breach of all artistic forms and restraints, and the door was opened to a purely personal psychology of self-confessing and self-knowing in art, especially in poetry. Poets at first seemed to find some support in psycho-analysis, which they hoped to be able to transform into a new artistic ideology. But, for the reasons mentioned, this proved impossible, and, further, psycho-analysis has rather used the modern artist as an object of study than helped him to a psychological ideology of art. Thus from both alike, from the side of art and that of science, the way seems to be prepared for the decisive crisis, in the midst of which we stand — but also for its solution, which I foresee in a new structure of personality. This will be able to use in a constructive form the psychological insight which is so destructive when it exists as introspection, and the individual impulse to creation will turn positively towards the formation of its own personality, as indeed it did, and actively, in the earliest phases of primitive art. This is the goal which has hitherto been vainly sought by the so-called neurotic; in earlier ages he was occasionally able to achieve creatively, thanks to some collective art-ideology, but today all collective means fail and the artist is thrown back on to an individual psycho-therapy. But this can only be successful if it sees its individual problem as one conditioned both by time and by culture, whereas the modern artist is driven by the unattainability of his ideology into that neurosis out of which the neurotic vainly seeks a creative escape — vainly, because the social ideologies are lacking which could fulfil and justify his personal conflict. Both will be achieved in a new formation of personality, which can, however, be neither a therapy of neuroses nor a new psychological art-ideology, but must be a constructive process of acceptance and development of one's individual personality as a new type of humanity, and in order to create the new it will have to give up much that has been received from tradition and become dear to it. This new must first of all be a new personality-type, which may thereafter perhaps find a new art-form suited to it, but in any case will not feel any compulsion to justify its personal impulse to create by starting from the ideology of long-surmounted art-forms.

Chapter Thirteen

SUCCESS AND FAME

Not in that he leaves something behind him, but in that he works and enjoys and stirs others to work and enjoyment, does man's importance lie.

GOETHE

Chapter Thirteen

SUCCESS AND FAME

ᘐᙇ

The struggle of the artist against the art-ideology, against the creative impulse, and even against his own work shows itself also in his attitude towards success and fame; indeed, these two phenomena are but an extension, socially, of the process which we saw beginning in subjective form with the vocation and creation of the personal ego to be an artist. In this entire creative process, which begins with this self-nomination to be an artist and concludes in the fame of posterity, two fundamental tendencies — one might almost say, two personalities of the individual — are throughout in continual conflict: the one which wishes to eternalize itself in artistic creation, the other which wants to spend itself in ordinary life — in a word, the mortal man and the immortal soul of man. This universal human conflict, which was resolved through many thousands of years by religion and the art which rested upon its ideology, has become more and more acute and difficult with the growth of individual art, until with modern artists it has taken on a form very like that of a neurosis. The conflict was always particularly intense in the artist, and this of course is one of the reasons why he was obliged to seize hold of ideological means for its settlement. For because of its "totality-tendency" the creative type is inclined, in this struggle between life and creation, to give up the one wholly in favour of the other, and this naturally intensifies the conflict rather than solves it.

We have already discussed in detail how this conflict spreads itself over experience and production. I should like to add, in outline at least, how the same fundamental conflict is reflected in that most remarkable relation between achievement and success, which are often indeed in the harshest opposition. This problem falls within the bounds of our present investigation in point of subject — seeing that it concerns the artist and his creativity — but even in method it does not go *beyond* them, since we are once again concerned with interaction of individual and society. Nevertheless, I can only deal with it in outline because, whereas the history of religion and art provided a basis for the arguments in our earlier chapters, in this case the collective phenomenon which stands opposed to the individual — namely, the group or community — has been very inadequately studied hitherto. There is in fact no really useful social psychology which deals with the relation of the individual to the group, and vice versa, in a way which we could draw upon for the study of the special relation of the artist to his public and of the attitude of posterity to his work. We should therefore have ourselves to lay the foundations of a social psychology before we could apply it to our special problem; and this is obviously far beyond the scope of this investigation, which is, indeed, only a preliminary towards a social psychology.

The problems of a group, of the crowd and its leader, with which we are here concerned, have been so inadequately treated hitherto that even Lange-Eichbaum, who, so far as I know, has provided the best collection of material, complains equally that he can find no basis of social psychology for his chapters on the effect of works of art and on the fame of the artist. Independently, in my book *Modern Education,* I had found myself compelled to give a sketch of a psychology of leadership, because in the very little literature existing I found nothing of use. In fact, there is a complete lack of a fundamental study of social psychology, which has always been one-sidedly treated as art has, either by the psychologists in terms of the individual or by the ethnologists and sociologists in terms of the group; and there is no real common ground. Even these one-sided studies are of course useful as preliminaries, but they cannot be turned to account here, since they are merely peripheral and we have to study the particular relation of the artist to the world around and after him — though this study itself may of course provide another stone for the edifice of a future social psychology, which will have to take the relation of the individual to the group as its basic principle.

We shall therefore begin by trying to show, in the light of our own study and without any regard for the ordinary views of social psychology, what seems to be the relation of the artist to his public and to posterity, and their attitude to him and his work. It seems to be quite certain that primitive art, in contrast to modern, was collectivist — though doubt begins immediately with the conclusion that Hirn draws, that the driving power of primitive artistic creation was not individual but social: namely, the imparting of pleasure. We are the less in a position to say this in that we know nothing of the individuality of primitive artists; while it does appear on the contrary that primitive body-ornament, which is the preliminary to art and artistic creation, indicates strong subjective motives and forces. Probably both tendencies, the individual and the social, have always been at work, though naturally in different measure and with different emphasis. For just as primitive body-ornament indicates subjective tendencies in the otherwise collective view of primitive man, so also we find in the most subjective and egocentric modern artist a need to communicate himself, to rouse applause or at least to make an impression on others — in a word, to win success. This very rough schematization of the development-history has further to be toned down by the fact that artists emphasize the one or the other aspect, according to the times, from personal motives; and we must not be misled by the fashionable generalizations and slogans of the day concerning the artist's exhibitionism and the like into forgetting that almost every productive type is also possessed of an opposite tendency to secrecy, which can in some cases be just as pathological a tendency as exhibitionism is in others. Even in judging this exhibitionism we must be careful not to take it at its face value, for what the artist exhibits in this apparently frank way is not his real, certainly not his whole, self, of which he only gives away part that he may keep the rest the more secretly for himself. Nor is it even simply that the artist always shows us his best side, in order to conceal his weakness and deficiencies. Experience has shown that man often has the opposite tendency to show his worst side and keep the best for himself.

Without going here into the deeper individual-psychological reason for this attitude (for it is far from being explained by the concept of " self-punishment " [1]) I should like to show here how this parsimony of oneself may affect actual creation and influence both success and fame. We can naturally study only the one side, that tendency in the artist which we have called the struggle of the artist against art, his work and success, and must ignore for the present the opposite tendency to want effect and success. From this one-sided standpoint the artist obviously creates for himself; we do not mean this in a narrow egoistic sense, but as primitive art was part of collective life, so modern artistic creation is an expression of individual life. The artist creates in the same way as he eats and breathes; that is one of his forms of life-expression, which — by chance, one might almost say — results in a work which happens to be of significance for others. But here begins in the history of the work a sort of second chapter, which we might call the discovery of the work of art: not by patrons or dealers, but by the artist himself, who discovers to his surprise that what he is producing has æsthetic qualities and artistic value. The attitude of the artist towards this discovery is of course determined by his personality, but in its turn it decides, to a considerable extent, the destiny of the work and therefore that of its creator also. For the creation was a liberating process of life, a bringing to light — a birth if one likes — which, though of great, is not of final significance for the future of the child. The next problem which confronts the artist is that of giving on his part, and of accepting on that

[1] See my latest technical work: *Die Analyse des Analytikers* (1931).

of the public. Obviously I do not mean supply and demand in the market, but a purely spiritual problem, which is one of the deepest there is: the problem, that is, how far the artist is willing and capable of "weaning" this work which he created by and for himself, and how far he tends to keep it for himself, or at least refuse to impart it to others.

We must leave aside here the important economic and practical motives which force the artist to overcome his opposition to public demand, though they may often be so strong or so emphasized that they overshadow all others. Indeed, many artists feel in this regard that they only produce for the public. This of course is true in part of successful artists; but psychologically what they do is to use the fact to justify their own need to create. But however the artist may settle this problem of publishing his work, the decision, coupled with other motives, affects his future creation. Whatever the admitted or hidden incentive, one motive for further creation is certainly the need to keep something for himself which others do not yet possess. That this work is meant to be something better is due not only to obvious artistic ambition, but to the already mentioned egoistic tendency to keep something better for oneself alone, to keep it away from others. For from the moment when the work is taken over and recognized by the public, or even merely offered to the public, it ceases to be the possession of the artist, not only economically but spiritually. Just as the artist created it from his own needs, the public accepts it to alleviate its own wants, and, whatever they may make of it, it never remains what it was originally; it ceases to be the personal achievement of the individual and becomes a symbol for others and *their* spiritual demands. This "misunderstanding," which the artist *feels,* is inevitable and the price at which fame is bought.

While we have here an important motive of the struggle against fame, which is to him almost a depersonalization, we can trace in the artist an opposition to success which is perhaps still stranger. The artist or his circle may complain unceasingly of lack of success and yet they will often reveal motives which impede or delay that success. We have already mentioned one such in what we said above about fame: the retention of individuality, which is meant here not only ideologically, but personally. Achievement and success are seen to be psychologically representative of the two basic tendencies that struggle against one another in the artist, the individual and the social. Achievement is ideological, success is personal; and the more the artist achieves in idea, the less disposed will he be to follow this up by personal success; we might say, indeed, the less need also, since the great achievement finally transforms itself into success without the help of the artist. Our interest here is in the psychological attitude of the artist-type which has diverted the creative impulse away from its own person into art and its ideology. Here we come upon the same antagonism which lies at the root of life and creativity; for success, even when it is won by artistic means, implies a personal success in life and is thus that very life from which the artist had originally fled to art as a refuge. Gustav Ichheiser therefore is quite right to distinguish, in his subtle study: *Kritik des Erfolges* (Leipzig, 1930), between "achievement-competence" and "success-competence," though he does not go far enough beyond the social phenomena. He comments tellingly on the fact that with many individuals social success is automatically ascribed to personal achievement, whereas it implies rather that a man is skilful at "putting a thing across" than a really productive activity.[1]

In artistic success or fame the process at work is indeed usually the reverse; for the artist's competence is credited with,

[1] Of the earlier literature on this subject I would mention here: Norbert Einstein *Der Erfolg. Ein Beitrag zur Frage der Vergesellschaftung* (1919); Julian Hirsch: *Die Genesis des Ruhmes* (Leipzig, 1914); and the literary essays of Remy de Gourmont: "*La Gloire et l'idée d'immortalité*" and "*Le Succès et l'idée de beauté*" (1901), both in *Le Chemin de velours*; the last work particularly has a very modern analysis of the social rôle of art. Philosophic thoughts on the greatness of historical persons, as well as of artists, in Burckhardt's *Weltgeschichtliche Betrachtungen* (see the special edition under the title *Grösse, Glück und Unglück in der Weltgeschichte* (Insel-Bücherei, No. 126). I would mention also that Max Dessoir's *Ästhetik und Allgemeine Kunstwissenschaft* differentiates the type of man who accomplishes and the type who creates.

or directly associated with, his "deserved" success. In other words, the gaining of fame does for the artist what he cannot or will not do for himself: it hands back creative power from the ideological work to the individual, who can indeed nominate himself to be an artist, and even ideologically make himself one, but whose power of achievement does not include that of imposing himself. In this the artist, with all his opposition to pushing and publicity, is dependent on critics and dealers, who usually represent the complementary type of success-competence without exhibiting any particular achievement-competence. This successful type, which is usually centred on personal effectiveness, is in other ways too the psychological counterpart to the artist, whose only desire, indeed, is to achieve indirectly through his work. It differs from the artist particularly in the fact that his "identification" faculty remains concentrated on persons and does not extend to ideologies as it does with the creative type; it is thus from this point of view much more personal than the artist-type, just as it is more personal, direct, and immediate in the assertion of its own ego.

This brings us, however, to an essential quality of the public in general, which is also decisive for its attitude to the creative type and his work. The average man has great difficulty in dealing with ideologies; he needs concrete personifications — in religion, for instance, or myths or leadership — and his preference for a definite concrete person is something that even such spiritual movements as Christianity cannot evade. It is here, and not merely in a curiosity and sensationalism, that the origin of the public's interest in the person of the artist lies. This interest, moreover, cannot be satisfied with the usually dull facts of the artist's external life, for his personality is inquired into, not for human or psychological reasons, but in order that he may be made the concrete representation of his work. In this also the public completes the process of artistic self-creation which the artist alone cannot achieve and would not if he could. For the residue of human nature which lies between his person and his work is his life in actuality, and it disturbs the harmonious unitary picture of work and creator which the hero-worshipping public demands. And we see at once the similarity between this and the creation of a god, a process which has been so magnificently successful because the god could be abstracted from the creation without even a cinder being left.

But though the artist, at least at the summit of his ideological development, is far less dependent on concrete personalities than the masses, yet he cannot wholly dispense with them and is therefore dependent on men for a link between his artistic creations, however vital, and real life. In this need to make real and actual, humanly and through the public, the unreality of his creation and of the immortality impulse which is its symbol lies the deepest root of his striving after success and fame — since it is they that give his individual and ideal creation a completion in accord with reality and the truth of life — and it is this necessity that enables him to overcome the individual resistances, of which we have spoken, to the fame which collectivizes him. Here again we have the two root tendencies, individual and collective immortality, of which the second is seen to be the only permanent form and to which the first must be surrendered. But such a collective immortality is no longer religious, but social, however many religious elements may infiltrate into the psychology of fame and success.

We must now deal with the relation of achievement and success, but particularly that of success and fame. Without committing ourselves to definitions of these very vague terms, I should like to refer success to the living and fame to the dead, or, more loosely, to understand by success something which means something actual to the creative artist (I do not mean merely material gain) — whereas fame, like work itself, has a more ideological significance and concerns the work rather than the artist. No matter how far this distinction is justified, it at least opens up the possibility of approach to the actual psychological problem, which is what chiefly interests us here. Fame, which we have taken as a collective continuation of the artistic

creative process, is not always, certainly not necessarily, connected with the greatness of a work; it often attaches to an
achievement whose chief merit is not its high quality but some
imposing characteristic, sensational either in itself or in its topical circumstances. Putting it roughly, we might say that an
achievement marked by supreme quality tends to bring success,
and one marked by something other than this quality to bring
rather fame, both then and thereafter; not only because the
masses are probably inaccessible to the supreme quality and
can only be gradually educated up to it, but because the qualitatively supreme achievement leaves nothing for the public to
do — at most, to imagine another equally perfect creator. The
one-sided or (psychologically speaking) compensatory work
is more amenable to the catch-phrases of a fashion or movement, but to attain to such importance it needs certain favourable circumstances, whereas the supreme work can wait in
peace, since the valuation it awaits will always supervene. In
the other case, what the work lacks to make it complete is
added to it by the social acquisition of fame. After all, society
and posterity are far more concerned in this than in the original
creator and his work, which is only more or less annexed by
some collective need, as a means of giving concrete expression
to some general trend, and at the same time to invest it with
the sanction of genius.

Seen thus, fame not only is a hollow thing, because it is almost a depersonalization, but is transitory, since it is dependent
on definite circumstances which give it birth and with which it
often perishes, even though later ages may give it a new life
for other purposes.[1] Fame seems to attach itself to men and

[1] Well-known instances are the revival of Aristotle in the Middle Ages and of Plato
in the present as the expression and justification of similar ideologies. Shakspere was
unheeded for nearly a century and a half after his death, till the Romantics made him
their ideal of the poetic genius. Goethe's influence originally, in *Götz* and *Werther*,
worked over wide areas quite anonymously; later in Weimar he was only admired as a
poet by a small group of friends. It was only later still that he became the national
hero of Germany, symbolized especially in *Faust*. Lange-Eichbaum has referred (op.
cit., p. 195 et seq.) to the transformation in the poet in the growth of his fame. Luther,
being pathological, becomes a hero type, the melancholy Mozart a lively contemporary
of Rococo. One of the most interesting examples of this kind in the history of art is

achievements which we call "epoch-making," but when a creation of the moment is recognized and rewarded with fame, it is really conditioned by an epoch already in course of growth. Again, fame seems to come to men and achievements which do in some sense make history, or help to make it, exercise (or are subject to) some practical influence; in a word, act on life immediately and more directly than the higher artist-type who creates purely ideologically, whereas the epoch-making artist is something that the masses can develop further themselves, since this type stands nearer to life and practical success. I do not mean necessarily actual practical success, but the ultimately practical success of a whole movement, to represent which he has been summoned by the masses. For there would appear to be another contradiction here, between actual personal success and the renown attaching to epoch-making, just as a man who is personally very successful is often ideologically higher and draws no practical advantage from being recognized. Men whose work has been epoch-making and who have later become famous, whose work has had great practical influence, have often been dreamers and phantasts — and all the better material for the formation of legends (Columbus). It almost seems as though there were an economic law that only *one* party can extract something from a great achievement, either the man himself or others, either his contemporaries or posterity. From this it is clear that the chances for the creator to get something for his work are one against three, and that even the first possibility is never perfectly fulfilled, because he must in any case share his success and fame with others, and thus has to give up a share not only in his work but of his own self, for collective valuation in terms of success and fame.

These last remarks lead us once more to the actual problem of *artistic* success, which we have unwillingly lost sight of in this discussion of success and fame as social phenomena. Artis-

---

Virgil, who appears in the Middle Ages as a magician, a true predecessor of the black magician Doctor Faustus, whom Goethe again transformed into the type of the struggling poet's soul.

tic success, concerned with essentially ideal values — which
indeed are ultimately the only epoch-making values, or at least
used to be — is less disputed than success in other social spheres,
and the person of the artist, in spite of all the public interest,
vanishes to a very large extent behind his work. The building
up of fame is a collective creation of the community, and thus
the artist, with his work, becomes the material for a new creative achievement of the community. In the course of this process
the individual work is incorporated socially in a particular
community-group, which may in some cases extend to the
whole of humanity, and in any case is oriented towards a common assertion of the immortality of the individual artist. When
contemporaries or posterity grant an artist immortality, they
participate in that immortality, just as burial in a royal tomb
or a similar-intentioned burial in the church (as the grave of
Christ) gives the ordinary mortal a share in divine immortality.

The artist, therefore, not merely creates collective values
from his individual need, but is himself finally collectivized,
since out of the totality of his existence the community makes a
new collective work, which survives as posthumous fame.
From this point of view art is unintelligible without a consideration of its effect on its contemporaries and posterity —
meaning thereby not its æsthetic but its social and cultural
effect.[1] The continued existence of art through successive
generations shows that the individual creative process, even its
actual product in work, is no more than the precondition of
collective creation, which selects and transforms whatever in
individual work can maintain itself as an expression of the
contemporary general ideology. The artist in himself provides
in his work the raw material which the community uses in the
creation of biographies and fame as an expression of its own
eternalization. This partially explains the mysterious agreement between the great achievement and the prevailing general ideology — especially when we consider that this process

[1] As du Prel effectively remarks, the co-operation of the recipient begins even with
the æsthetic pleasure, in which the individual annexes the work just as the community
does in the creation of fame.

always begins in the lifetime of the artist, who often anticipates this collective transformation by adapting his creation to a great extent to the needs of the community. This obviously does not mean in the case of great artists a concession to the masses, but something of a deeper kind, a strong sympathy with the spiritual ideals of his public.

On the other hand there is always a distinct reaction of the artist not only against every kind of collectivization, but against the changing of his own person, his work, and his ideology into an eternalization-symbol for a particular epoch. This resistance of the artist to his absorption into the community will show itself in more than his objection to success and fame; it will also influence his further activity so far as the assertion of his own individuality is concerned, and become a strong stimulus to further creativity in general. Certainly this will be the case with the great artist, who always tries to escape this collectivizing influence by deliberate new creations, whereas the weaker talent succumbs to a conscious concession to the masses or becomes mere raw material for the collective perpetuation instinct. These diverse outcomes of the struggle of the artist against success and fame explain, too, why many of the greatest geniuses only attained fame after their own time, and, on the other hand, why mediocre gifts enjoy a seemingly undeserved success. A strong-willed creator lends himself far less to collective influence than a merely talented artist, whose work may easily be made the material for a mass creation that genius opposes.

But we see too in this matter of success and fame that the struggle of the artist against the art-ideology and his own creative dynamism is objectified and becomes a struggle of the artist against the community of living men and against posterity. The struggle is carried on on both sides and is so obstinate because it is at bottom again that opposition of individual and community which was the original source of all artistic productivity. The individual artist wants to free himself by his own creativity from the spiritual immortality-idea of the community, while the recognition of his achievement, manifested as fame, amounts to an incorporation of his own personality in that of the community. Thus general recognition of the artist and his work is the spiritual counterpart to his own asserted claim to be an artist; the latter is a gesture of independence, whereas fame, which is something granted to him, again makes him dependent.

Success stands, in a sense, half-way, since it is both deserved and won by the self, but leads easily to the fame which must be bestowed by others. This brings us also to the positive side of the whole problem, which we have hitherto kept in the background, because it could only be understood after considering the artist's disinclination to fame. The assumption that the artist seeks only success and fame originates with the unproductive type, who may not only be eager for it himself, but also be actuated by a belief that the artist wants to become famous, whereas really he himself wants to make him famous so as to participate in his immortality. It would be an exaggeration, of course, to deny that the artist is attracted by success and fame, but his motives are other than the motives of those who grant it to him. For the artist, success is a way of returning to life when the work is completed, and fame is a sort of collective after-existence which even the greatest cannot dispense with, since there is no more individual after-existence. The tragedy lies in the fact that the collective continuation of existence which every individual aims at extends in the artist's case to a complete depersonalization in his work, or at least to its radical transformation into a collective product: in any case, leads far beyond the goal that the artist himself aimed at. Success gives him both, the individual justification of his work and its collective recognition, whereas fame stamps both himself and his work as a creature of the community.

These observations indicate that the desire for success and fame may at first act as a stimulus to the creative impulse, but that later, when the artist approaches success or has attained it, other social ideologies must take its place. In any case this

change in the social relation of the artist decisively affects his
art-ideology, and the success-fame motif turns from a stimulus
to creation into the material of creation and may thereafter as
such determine the artist's life as well. It would be fascinating to
follow out in art — and especially in literary history — the relations between the personal success of the artist and the representation of success as a theme in his work, as well as the effect
which the success attained has, not only on his creation, but on
his life. The successful artist will evolve a quite different personal and artistic ideology from that of those who are not a
success during their own lives. Many artists return, artistically
or at least spiritually, to an earlier period of their struggle for
success, as we can see from the well-known dreams of great
poets and other successful artists, in which they seem to be set
back in their modest beginnings. Here there is obviously a
rejuvenation-wish,[1] for fame has a flavour of death, and immortality is only distinguished by two small letters from the
arch-evil they dread.

But fame not only threatens the personal immortality of the
artist by making it collective; it is moreover directly hostile to
life, since it forces the artist to stay officially in the groove that
he has chosen for himself. This is seen in success, of which we
said above that it was a sort of " return of the artist to life." It
is a return which disappoints the artist because it does not give
him freedom of experience, but compels him to further *artistic
creation*. Success is therefore a stimulus to creativity only so
long as it is not attained — which means, as long as the artist
believes he can regain life by his success and so free himself
from the bondage of creating. Bitterly, then, he finds out that
success only strengthens the need for creating, and that fame,
which is the end of it, leads to depersonalization during his lifetime and is of no use for life if it comes after death. The artist
does not create, in the first place, for fame or immortality; his
production is to be a means to achieve actual life, since it helps

[1] In this context belongs Goethe's well-known remark about his repeated adoles-
cences.

him to overcome fear. But he cannot get out of the bypath he has once trodden, which was to lead him back by means of his work to life. He is thus more and more deeply entangled in his creative dynamism, which receives its seal in success and fame.

But along with all these expressions of the opposition of the artist to art-ideology, to the dynamism of creation and the final absorption of his individual immortality by the community, there must exist other, and even stronger, tendencies of surrender, self-renunciation, and self-sacrifice. These seem to be just as necessary for the artist as the tendencies of self-assertion and self-eternalization; and, indeed, we have had to assume that what is perhaps the most decisive part of creative dynamism originates in this conflict of opposing tendencies and their settlement in the harmony of the work. This conflict between self-assertion and self-surrender is a normal phenomenon in human psychical life, which in the artist is extraordinarily intensified and reaches gigantic, one might say macrocosmic heights. As the strong creative personality is driven to destroy a pre-existing ideology, instead of a mere individual, as his " building-sacrifice " before he may eternalize himself in a new one, the conflict between surrender and assertion, which otherwise takes place in relation to a person, is here manifested with society and its whole order as the player on the other side.

The individual may, by his nomination to be an artist, have asserted his independence of the human community and rooted himself in self-sufficient isolation; but ultimately he is driven by the work he has autonomously produced to surrender again to that community. This creative self-sufficingness which generates the work out of oneself alone has misled us into thinking of the artist, at least spiritually, as a bisexual combination of the male and female principles, which create the work as it were hermaphroditically. But this view, which the artist himself often shares, is contradicted not only by the existence of definitely masculine or feminine types among artists, but by the complete lack of creative power in many hermaphroditic or homosexual types. In any case this explanation seems to me to be rather a metaphorical illustration of a much more complicated fact. I believe that we have here a deliberate denial of all dependence — in other words, a primary expression of an antisexual creative impulse which seeks to bring forth the world and itself from itself and without help. This tendency towards a self-sufficing independence brings the individual into conflict with sexual life, of which the very essence is creation or generation by the help of another. But even the autonomously functioning artist, who may produce his work himself, is ultimately dependent on others for recognition, success, and fame, and even more so than the average man is dependent on his sexual partner. The artist therefore has to give himself the more and the more intensively and exhaustively in his work because he has created it the more independently of others.

This seems almost a compensative justice, but is really only the result of a violent dynamism which wilfully alters a natural dependence of the individual into an apparent freedom in creation. Success and fame then supervene to assure the artist that for all his lordliness he is still dependent on the collective forces that he seeks to escape by autonomous creation. From our point of view, according to which an artist is made by the individual's raising himself above nature and making himself eternal in his work, we might put it in this way: that success and fame make him once more a collective being, take him from his divine creative rôle and make him human again; in a word, make him mortal. However much he may like to return to earth and become human, he cannot do it at the price of his own immortality; and the paradox of the thing consists in the fact that success and fame, which make him collectively immortal, make him personally human once more and restore him to mortality. His work is taken from him by the community, as the child is taken from its parents, and in place of it he receives his title to fame, rewarded like a mother by a state hungry for soldiers. The artist, too, looks for this reward, but he hopes to return by his success to life, whereas fame condemns him often enough to spiritual death.

If success is the result of an irresistible dynamism which gives success to that artist who achieves it, fame is in the same way the result of an irresistible dynamism in a community which is always hungry for material for its own eternalization. Every group, however small or great, has, as such, an "individual" impulse for eternalization, which manifests itself in the creation of and care for national, religious, and artistic heroes. Yet this is impossible without the productive achievement of outstanding individuals, who then become the pioneers and victims of this collective immortality, whether they will it or not. In this sense success is a measure of the extent to which the individual paves the way for this collective eternity impulse; and fame might then be taken as an expression of regret on the part of the community which has annexed this man and his work as its own.[1] In spite of this guilt-feeling, however, the community really only takes back what genius, by using collective ideology, had previously taken from it — magnified, it is true, by the personal achievement of the creator. And this is the more important since the community annexes the man and his work, depersonalizes him, and thus really robs him of the fruit of his work — in return for which he is offered the distinction of fame. Success and fame thus complete not only the work of the artist, but, far more than that, a vast circle in the eternal conflict between individual and group. The individual tries, by taking over a collective ideology which he creates anew in the personal sense, to assure his own immortality, and this is manifested in success; but the community, by the bestowing of fame, annexes for itself the immortality which had really been won by an individual, makes itself eternal in the work, and offers the artist in return its collective glory.

[1] Cf. a similar idea in Lange-Eichbaum, op. cit., p. 181.

Chapter Fourteen

DEPRIVATION AND
RENUNCIATION

> *The individual becomes conscious
> of himself as being this particular
> individual with particular gifts,
> tendencies, impulses, passions, under
> the influence of a particular en-
> vironment, as a particular product
> of his milieu. He who becomes thus
> conscious of himself assumes all this
> as part of his own responsibility. At
> the moment of choice he is thus in
> complete isolation, for he withdraws
> from his surroundings; and yet he
> is in complete continuity, for he
> chooses himself as product; and this
> choice is a free choice, so that we
> might even say, when he chooses
> himself as product, that he is pro-
> ducing himself.*
>
> KIERKEGAARD

Chapter Fourteen

DEPRIVATION AND RENUNCIATION

❧

The last chapters have brought us back to the narrower problem with which we started, the relation of the artist to art; but permit us now to formulate it from the standpoint of the artist, whereas at first we had to do so from that of art. We started with the primitive art-forms of ornament and noted that their abstractness yet contained an element of the concrete which alone really made them works of art. For if they were nothing but abstraction, we should value philosophical ideas more highly than art and so return to the position of Greek thinkers, who identified beauty and truth and saw their ideal in the wise man and not in the inspired artist. The essence of art, however, lies precisely in the concrete representation of the abstract; and we tried to show why such a representation was thought beautiful and roused æsthetic pleasure. In order to understand primitive ornament we adduced, in addition to the personal and social motives of the " artist," the general ideology within which these forms were necessary or possible, and thence we found the first deduction of the concept of beauty from the concept of the soul. The primitive world-outlook rests on a collective ideology of the soul, which must in its nature be abstract to attain its object of supporting the belief in immortality. Primitive art is abstract, because it wants to, or must, represent this abstract idea of the soul as like as possible, in order that its actual existence may be proved by concretization. Whereas, then, primitive (and even later) religion supports the belief in immortality by a collective soul-ideology, art proves the existence of this abstract conception of the soul by its concretization in symbolical form.

We traced the development of art from its primitive beginnings to the personal masterpieces of Classical, Renaissance, and modern times, until we finally found in the individual artist himself a representative of the same ideology of immortality. Not only does his work become the most concrete proof that the individual can live on in spirit for centuries; but the last chapters have shown us how the artist is under a sort of organic compulsion to transform his art-ideology into experience. In this he makes reality of the unreal to just the extent that it represents the concretization of the soul-concept in the work. In other words, the artist must live his ideology so that he, as well as others, may believe in it as true; on the other hand, this ideological experience acts both as a means to make artistic productivity possible and as a means to live a real life. For we have seen that the basic conflict of the creative personality is that between his desire to live a natural life in an ordinary sense and the need to produce ideologically — which corresponds socially to that between individuality and collectivity and biologically to that between the ego and the genus. Whereas the average man largely subordinates himself, both socially and biologically, to the collective, and the neurotic shuts himself deliberately off from both, the productive type finds a middle way, which is expressed in ideological experience and personal creativity. But since the artist must live as a human being and yet feels compelled to make this transitory life eternal in an intransient work, a compromise is set up between ideologized life and an individualized creativity — a balance which is difficult, impermanent, and in all circumstances painful, since creation tends to experience, and experience again cries out for artistic form.

In this sense the general problem of the artist — not only in its psychological, but in its human aspect — is contained in the two notions of deprivation and renunciation. The psychological point of view, as it culminates in psycho-analysis, always emphasizes only the deprivation, from which artists seem to suffer most in themselves; the philosophical view, to which a few artists like Goethe or Ibsen attained at the height of their achievement, emphasizes renunciation. But the two aspects are complementary, like outer and inner, society and ego, collectivity and individuality. The great artist and great work are only born from the reconciliation of the two — the victory of a philosophy of renunciation over an ideology of deprivation.

From this point of view discussions about life and creativity, the conflict of various modes of life and ideas of creativity, seem superficial. An artist who feels that he is driven into creating by an external deprivation and who is then again obstructed by a longing for life can rise above these conflicts to a renunciant view of life which recognizes that it is not only impossible but perilous to live out life to the full and can, willingly and affirmatively, accept the limitations that appear in the form of moral conventions and artistic standards, not merely as such, but as protective measures against a premature and complete exhaustion of the individual. This means the end of all doubt as to whether he is to dedicate his whole life to art or send art to perdition and simply live; also of the question whether he is to live a Bohemian life in accordance with his ideology or live an ordinary life in despite of his art; and in the end his creativity is not only made richer and deeper by this renunciatory attitude, but is freed from the need to justify one or the other mode of life — in other words, from the need for compensation.

But this justifies a question as to whether such a human solution of the creative conflict may not have an unfavourable influence either on the urge to create or at least on the quality of the work. A study, psychological and ideological, of the artist and the history of art certainly gives the impression that, as we said above, the great artist and his work are due to a forced justification or a strained over-compensation; but also that only the greatest artists at the end of this struggle reach a renunciatory philosophy. The "at the end" is important, for it would indicate that their chief work dated from the period before this achievement and therefore came into being out of the still unresolved conflict of life and creation. It is certainly clear that a thoroughly satisfied bourgeois existence would give no stimulus for creation; it is equally clear on the other hand that the creative genius must approximate to such a life if he is not to sacrifice the one to the other and so possibly land himself again in sterility. We often see the artist, and the neurotic, who vacillates in a similar conflict, manufacturing the conflict (or intensifying it if it already exists) just so that he may resolve it. For the neurotic this is a test which he fails; he remains neurotic and proves to himself that he must do so. For the artist these self-created conflicts are also ultimately tests, but, in contradiction to the neurotic, they prove his capacity to create, since he masters the conflict, in form and content, by giving it æsthetic shape. This tendency, which is especially marked in the Romantic, to dramatize this experience does not, then, come from a mere wish to make oneself interesting, but is deeply connected with the general problem of artistry. On the whole we may say that the great artist — and most admirably in the Classical type — can free himself from the parallelism between his life and work, while the Romantic is more dependent on the dramatization of his experience on the lines of his ideology, since his creativity has definitely a compensatory character.

Here too we must pass, in the case of the individual artist and his work, if we are to judge it rightly, beyond this classification, since the same artist may in the course of his life develop from Romantic to Classic. It seems, indeed, from our previous observations, that the mature artist can only be born from victory over the Romantic in himself, irrespective of whether this Romanticism has come out in actual work at an early period, as with Goethe, or whether the artist only emerges at the fullness of life, as a complete Classic, as did K. F. Meyer. Here, too, as in an ordinary professional career, the spade-work will find its reward in magnificent masterpieces. This view of the development of the artistic personality and his work is only now beginning to appear in the study of art and has so far no solid principles on which to build. I will mention as characteristic, and as far as I know as the best, examples two works which deal respectively with the work of maturity and of youth. The one is A. E. Brinckmann's lucid work on the *Spätwerke grosser Meister* (Frankfurt, 1925), the ripe humanity of which work is manifestly and admittedly conditioned by the author's entry into his fifth decade; the other is the contrary: *Die Frühvollendeten; ein Beitrag zur Literaturgeschichte* — a study of artists who reached maturity young, in which the author, Guido Brand, puts before us a series of poets of the seventeenth to twentieth centuries who died prematurely, so that he may find the typical connexion between early maturity and early death. He can naturally not avoid touching, at least in an introductory way, on the borderland problem between masterpieces produced in youth and mature works of age; and rightly feels that " works of youth and of age should be regarded as a new theme which should explain to us by the help of psychology and phenomenology the psycho-spiritual attitude of youthful and the older creative types and thus describe the spheres within which the one grows up through the intuition of origin, the other from the experience of long life. Critique of language and philosophy of style would reveal the hall-marks of a creativity which is, inwardly, fundamentally different in the two cases."

In my book on incest (1912), which was conceived essentially as a basis for the psychology of poetic creation, I included, together with some remarks on the decisive periods of change in great poets (for example, Schiller; op. cit., second edition, p. 106, n. 49), a chapter on the psychology of youthful poetry and attempted a psychological valuation of the " fragments and outlines " (chapter vii) of greater and uncompleted works. In many cases the youth has nothing in common with the old man except the name; sometimes also, though not always, he has a favourite theme, which he uses at various periods in such different ways that it might be the work of more than one artist with more than one ideological attitude. In the sphere of this study come the works of pupils, which — especially in painting — are hardly to be distinguished from the masters', and the whole problem of schools of art, both plastic and poetic. Schiller's *Räuber* is as much a poem of the "*Sturm und Drang*" as it is an individual work, and several of its motifs can only be grasped ideologically and not psychologically. I had once intended to deal with this problem under the title of " Schiller's Brother " and to point out, in connexion with the ideas already treated in relation to the incest theme, that the motif of fraternal hate which in Schiller lasts right up to the *Braut von Messina,* might lead a biographer — supposing he had to construct the picture of his author from the pattern of his work and had lived in a less exact philological age — to assume a quarrel between brothers in Schiller's family, which, as is well known, contained no brother. But I did show, in my incest book, how Schiller, thanks to his "*Sturm und Drang*" ideology, made a brother out of his brother-in-law, called him so, and used him so. This same motif of fraternal hatred, which is one of the typical requisites of dramatic poetry from the time of Greek tragedy (see chapter xv in that book), is to be found very often in Shakspere, of whose family life we are less well informed, but of whom we do know that he, or the author of his plays, lived during the reign of Queen Elizabeth; and she was regarded on many sides as a usurper of the English throne, which she ruthlessly withheld from the rightful heir, her " sister " Mary Stuart. If an English court-poet wanted for some reason or other to refer to this idea, which was afloat among the people, he would not only have to use a historical or mythological dress,[1] but would be well-advised, in view of the

[1] Similar ideas, though carried to excess in their application to detail, I saw later in Lilian Winstanley: *Hamlet and the Scottish Succession. Being an Examination of the Relations of the Play of Hamlet to the Scottish Succession and the Essex Conspiracy* (Cambridge, 1921). Miss Winstanley identifies Claudius and Gertrude with Bothwell and Mary, who also occur later as Lord and Lady Macbeth (cf. her book: *Macbeth, King Lear and*

proximity of the Tower, to make the feminine rivals into masculine rivals of two royal families — which indeed is the case
in the main plot of *Hamlet* and is the chief motif in many
other plays. Whether he had really quarrelled in childhood
with a brother about his toys or for his mother's love or a
father's notice is of very little importance when we remember
how common such things are and how often they are absent
in the childhood of other poets. Indeed, the facts which are
so well known in Schiller's case, and may be assumed with
probability in Shakspere's, should warn us against drawing
over-hasty conclusions on the strength of some superficial relation in the biographical material. For the artist is either born
as such, in which case his attitude to his family involves almost
a priori a sort of Hamlet tragedy, or else his experiences make
him an artist, in which case again we cannot be concerned
with those universal childhood impressions which are in no
way different in his case from those of others.

This does not mean, of course, that such childhood influences
are not among the important ones in the work of great artists,
nor that psycho-analysis has not done a service in definitely
emphasizing them; the question is simply that of the value to
be ascribed to them, and their importance for the understanding of the artist and particularly of his work. The undoubted
over-emphasis which psycho-analysis lays on this fact of artistic
biographical method has various reasons, and these will lead
us in their discussion back to our proper theme. First there is
a confusion, or at least a certain want of distinction, between
the development of personality in general and that of the artist
in particular; but even in the former case, in which infantile
influences are undeniable, psycho-analysis over-estimated their
effect and neglected the individual will, which interprets these
influences in its own way. This is still more the case if the personality is one in which the will is strong and shows itself not

Contemporary History), Polonius as Lord Burleigh, etc. Cf. also Percy Allen: *Shakespeare and Chapman as Topical Dramatists*, and E. Stucken's novel: *Im Schatten Shakespeares* (Berlin, 1929).

only as dominant but as creative. Childhood influences therefore do not build up the personality by themselves, and decidedly not the artistic type, which, after all, distinguishes itself very largely by its surmounting of everything traditional. A second reason takes us deeper into the psychology of the development of personality in general and of that of the artist in particular. The aim of psycho-analysis, indeed, in its interpretation of childhood influences was to emphasize, not the rôle of these as such, but that of the unconscious in general in artistic creativity. This was not new — what analysis did contribute to the subject was the scientific proof of this influence in some particular childhood impressions which the individual had repressed, yet which forced their way upward and manifested themselves later in his work.

On the other hand, there are two points to be taken into consideration. Firstly, childhood impressions are not so unconscious, in either the artist or the neurotic, as is so eagerly assumed. Indeed, most neurotics suffer from conscious recollections of their childhood — of which, try as they may, they cannot rid themselves — and we have very complete childhood memories in the case of poets particularly, who provide more, and more interesting, material than we can ever get from the analysis of neuroses (Goethe, Rousseau, Tolstoy, etc.).[1] Secondly, exacter observation has shown us that artistic creation is far less unconscious than the psycho-analyst, or even the artist himself, believes. From Schiller, who was both artistically productive and psychologically interested, down to the modern æsthetics, such as Oscar Wilde, there is a long series of facts which prove the part played by consciousness in artistic and especially in poetical creation, which I traced in its main stages in my incest book, though I then put the unconscious too much in the foreground. The part played by the latter is undeniable; but ever since the time of the Greek poets it has been so much emphasized, especially by the productive artist, that it was

[1] See the comprehensive study of H. Reichardt: *Die Früherinnerung als Trägerin kindlicher Selbstbeobachtungen in den ersten Lebensjahren* (Halle, 1926).

necessary to give its due to the consciousness or, as I prefer to say, to the conscious artistic will. The question, too, of the greater or lesser part played by the unconscious or conscious cannot be taken as a problem only of the individual artist, though there are certainly types in which one or the other predominates. How could it be possible otherwise that, in spite of all individual differences, two poets like Goethe and Schiller, subject to the same contemporary ideology, could express such contrary views on this question? We can understand, too, that the difference of ideologies would account for the fact that the æsthetic philosopher, who is somewhat akin to the scientist, would as a rule agree with the poet here, but — from Aristotle to Baumgarten — regards the poetic art as teachable and learnable. But how can we understand that the singer of the Homeric poems calls to the Muse for inspiration and then produces a masterpiece of political history, in the logical development of which his memory failed him far less than it did in his incidental digressions — which also were perhaps intentional?

This example, which is possibly too far away from our theme, is meant to show that the invocation of the Muse, the demand by the poet himself for unconscious inspiration, is perhaps not infrequently a pretext — a poetic licence even — for a more unrestrained expression of himself. If he is inspired by poetic frenzy, he is less responsible for what he says; and, remembering our previous remarks about Shakspere, it seems to me not improbable that the inspired poet portrayed himself in the Danish prince, so that he might with impunity utter high treason. It does not seem to me improbable, for example, that the participation of Hamlet in his entrapping play might be explained from the fact that powerful opponents of Elizabeth did really use the poet as a means to attack her and stir her conscience. In this case we should have a reflection, in Hamlet's editing of the "play," of the part which important friends of the poet actually had in his work. Anyhow the invocation of the Muse, which we have seen to be the effect of the guilt-feeling, and the emphasis by the poet himself on the unconscious impulse to create must not blind us to the part played by the conscious in creation; the reference of creation to the unconscious, if nothing else, is a conscious act. If, then, for example, Goethe and Schiller were different artist-types, it might well be that for that very reason the one worked more unconsciously than the other, but also that one exaggerated the part played by the conscious, and the other that played by the unconscious, in his own observation of himself. The over-valuation of the unconscious would then be explained by a more or less strong feeling of guilt, such as is felt by every productive type; and the over-valuation of the conscious would be due to a desire to magnify and exalt oneself — as the other is due to the already mentioned tendency to minimize.

From these observations we arrive at a similar view of the value of artistic psychology as we did previously in the case of æsthetic as a science. We came to regard æsthetic as a scientific ideology which changes with the contemporary art-ideology so that it justifies, positively or negatively, the dominant art-ideology, as we explained in the illustrative instance of the nature-imitation. Similarly the psychology of the artist that is fashionable at the moment, though naturally more individually conditioned, represents an ideological justification of the creative artist. In our account, which penetrates to the roots, in cultural history and in individual psychology, of the creative feeling of guilt, there was no room for an æsthetic which laid down laws for art, nor for an artist's psychology in the ordinary sense, which would always have to resort to values, whether like Lombroso's mania theory or the psycho-analytical justification of creative lordliness in the unconscious. We tried to understand all these phenomena, included under the label of " art," in their psychical and historical genesis, as the expression of the individual's impulse to create, and to understand this in turn from the ineradicable belief of man in immortality. This impulse, however, produces both the work and the artist, and ultimately the ideologies necessary for artistic creation and for the artist's psychology — which are neither true nor false —

that is, have no eternal validity — but change with the development of collective and individual ideas and thus fulfil their real purpose, their extension to infinity.

But the more conscious the creative process becomes in the artist, the more the creative tendency is imperceptibly and unnoticed being pushed back from the work to the artist himself from whom it originated. Only, primitively this self-creative tendency showed itself, as we saw, corporeally in *body-ornament,* whereas in the modern artist it ends with the psychical will-to-experience, his own art-ideology in full. This is, of course, impossible and brings the artist into all the conflicts — which we may describe as neurotic, but which are not any the more intelligible for being so called. For these difficulties of the creative type show also that his true tendency is always towards actual life; as is shown also in the so-called realism or verism of modern art. This, therefore, discloses itself as the counterpart to the tendency, which has been mentioned earlier, to mould life in accordance with an artistic ideology, since the idea is now that art is to be made wholly true to life. But in this wise the boundaries between art and life are obliterated; each is to replace the other, whereas formerly each complemented the other. In both spheres the movement from art to life is clear; but the creative men of our time are not capable of going the whole way and accepting the development of their personality as the truly creative problem. What hinders them is the same individual feeling of guilt which in earlier times was able, owing to the counter-force of religious submissiveness, to work itself out creatively, but nowadays limits both complete artistic creation and complete personality-development.

For artistic creation has, in the course of its development, changed from a means for the furtherance of the culture of the community into a means for the construction of personality. But the more successful this is, the greater is the urge of this personality away from art towards life, which yet cannot be fully grasped. Our Western art has thus lost its old function in proportion as this movement (beginning perhaps with the

Renaissance) from the collective to the individual increased. But similarly it has had to give up its new function as soon as its purpose of personality-development was attained. This historical process, which we can trace from the Renaissance through the *"Sturm und Drang"* into Romanticism, has become an individual process which runs its course in the modern artist's life. The productive individual of today tackles artistic production under the influence, which still operates, of the original art-ideology, which promised immortality to the individual in the form of success and fame, but he does not possess, socially or spiritually, the attitude inherent in that old ideology. In this sense the "art for art's sake" movement was justified at least psychologically, for art had lost its old collective function and had not yet discovered the new one of personality-development.

Now, however, this last function of art having worked itself out as far as is psychologically possible, the problem of the individual is to put his creative force directly into the service of this formation of personality, without the assistance of art. The more an individual is driven towards real life, the less will traditional art-forms help him — indeed, they have for the most part already been shattered individualistically. Especially in poetry, which of course represents in general this conscious level of artistic creation, this permeation by the personal psychology of the poet and the psychological ideology of our age is almost completed. Even the last element of art which poetry retains, language, is becoming more and more an echo of realistic talk or a psychological expression of intellectual thought, instead of being a creative expression of the spiritual. But the reality which modern art seeks to reproduce cannot be represented in language, and other traditional forms are suited only to the creative form of the spiritual and not to a realistic expression of the actual. That is why the film and talking film have become the most popular art, because this art reproduces the real faithfully, and the more so, the more it progresses.

I would not deny, however, that there are still great artists in all spheres of artistic activity, who have succeeded either in preserving the old art tradition and ideology a while longer into our times or have breathed a new spirit into old forms. But in both cases I feel that the modern artist has to buy his success too dearly, since he feels either like a believer among unbelievers or like the founder of a new religion who is persecuted and scorned by the members of the old religion. This comparison with religious conflicts comes naturally to us; for just as there is a continuous increase in the number of the irreligious and at the same time an enhanced need for substitutes for the old belief in the gods, so the art-manias of modern society, with their over-valuing of the artist, indicate a decline of real artistic vigour, which is only speciously covered over by the last flicker of a snobbish enthusiasm. It is certain that artists nowadays do not create for the people, but for a few exclusive groups, particularly of intellectuals who feel themselves artists. With an increasing individualization art-forms also must become more individual so that they suit the ideology of a few small groups, and no attempt to exalt artists into national heroes can conceal the fact that there are ever fewer artists of really national importance and still fewer of international.

On the other hand, this individualization of art-forms and art-creation leads not only to the break-up of the collective function of art, but to its democratization, which is the direct opposite of the aristocratic religion of genius that constituted the last effective art-ideology. From the Renaissance on, a man felt himself driven to, but also chosen for, artistic expression; nowadays, with individualism so common, art is looked upon as a means to develop personality. Every strong individuality feels nowadays that a potential artist lies somewhere within him, which is prevented from growth and expression only by the external decay of a materialistic and mechanistic environment. And though it is true that a strong personality is necessary for the creative artist, it is a fatal confusion to assume that every strong personality must express itself artistically if it is to develop. Furthermore, as we have seen, artistic creativity does not, after a point, favour the personality, but impedes it, since it forces on the artist a professional ideology which more and more penetrates the human self and finally absorbs it.

It is certainly not, however, merely the outward deprivation (that is, the pressure of a mechanical age) that obstructs the artistic development of modern individuals, but the strong impulse towards life which goes hand in hand with personality-development and makes the creative will of the individual feel that artistic creation is an *unsatisfactory substitute* for real life. In other words, the conflict between life and creation, the basic problem of all productive work, has nowadays become a social instead of a psychic conflict. A harmonious reconciliation of an art-ideology with an ideology of practical life is more and more difficult as life becomes more technical and the members of a community become separate individuals. The two masters whom the artist has to serve at the same time, a self-confident productivity and a life of sacrifice, are less and less reconcilable, so that art and life are both dissatisfying, or, rather, the individual attains neither, because he is not satisfied with one and cannot attain both. This is characteristic of the so-called neurotic type, in which I had long ago seen an *"artiste manqué"* rather than an undeveloped normal type. The neurotic is himself a symptom of the modern conflict between the individual and society, a conflict which might in other ages have been productively surmounted in artistic creation. Nowadays the old art-ideology is no longer, and the new personality-idea not yet, strong enough to admit of either solution for the individual impulse to create. Everyone suffers — individual, community, and, not least, art as an ideological expression of their interrelation.

Everything seems to drive us to the conclusion that we are at one of those crises in human history in which once again we must sacrifice one thing if we want the full enjoyment of another. If we look back at the modern artist-type as we know it, even in biographical form, since Renaissance days, there can be no doubt that the great works of art were bought at the cost of ordinary living. Whatever our attitude towards this fact and interpretation of this fact, it is at least certain that the modern individualist must give up this kind of artistic creation if he is to live as vigorously as is apparently necessary. Not only are the two things incompatible, in terms of soul and of energy, but there seems to be a spiritual law whereby nothing can be wholly won or enjoyed without something being given up or sacrificed for it. From the fabulous ring of Polycrates, who tried to buy his good fortune from heaven, down to the neurotic feeling of guilt, with its apparent self-punishment, we see this compensatory principle operating in the relation of individual to society. The individual, it seems, cannot permanently endure one sort of condition — even if it be happiness — because he immediately loses a part of the full humanity which is needed for his real personality. Where happiness and misery are concerned the individual is clearly controlling his own destiny by meeting good and ill fortune half-way ere it can surprise him.

If there are really these two incommensurable magnitudes, such as supreme art and full experience seem to be, the conflict can only end with the surrender of the one to the other. But as long as this involves a feeling of sacrifice, there is no real solution, rather an intensification of the conflict, for the responsibility is always laid on an external deprivation which is to be fought against. Only a full renunciation, such as a few great artists have achieved despite their natural inclinations, can overcome this feeling of sacrifice so that surrender means, not an imposed necessity, but a freely chosen decision. This turning-point in the life of the individual artist has also become a secular crisis of our age, in which we have to see that the surrender of traditional forms no longer means a loss to us, but a liberation of creative force from the chains of old ideologies. Now, our previous conclusions show that this creative impulse can be set free from artistic ideologies, because it is not irrevocably bound

thereto as an art-ideology is obliged to assume. We have seen
that the impulse was originally directed towards the body and
only gradually was objectified in collective art-forms. On the
other hand we see modern individuals, particularly the neurotic,
striving once more to direct this creative instinct towards the
ego in order to make it more useful and efficient for life. The
fact that the neurotic at present fails in face of his problem
cannot diminish his pioneer achievement — if he seeks his salvation in artistic creation instead of in the development of
his own personality, it is because he is still in the toils of old
art-ideologies. The many forms of psycho-therapy, psycho-
analysis included, cannot free him from the dilemma, since
they either try to restore him to the normal or force him to
a false artistry instead of allowing to develop a true form of
himself.

The new type of humanity will only become possible when
we have passed beyond this psycho-therapeutic transitional
stage, and must grow out of those artists themselves who have
achieved a renunciant attitude towards artistic production. A
man with creative power who can give up artistic expression in
favour of the formation of personality — since he can no longer
use art as an expression of an already developed personality —
will remould the self-creative type and will be able to put his
creative impulse *directly* in the service of his own personality.
In him the wheel will have turned full circle, from primitive
art, which sought to raise the physical ego out of nature, to the
voluntaristic art of life, which can accept the psychical ego as
a part of the universe. But the condition of this is the conquest
of the fear of life, for that fear has led to the substitution of artistic production for life, and to the eternalization of the all-too-
mortal ego in a work of art. For the artistic individual has lived
in art-creation instead of actual life, letting his work live or die
on its own account, and has never wholly surrendered himself
to life. In place of his own self the artist puts his objectified
ego into his work, but though he does not save his subjective
mortal ego from death, he yet withdraws himself from real

life. And the creative type who can renounce this protection by art and can devote his whole creative force to life and the formation of life will be the first representative of the new human type, and in return for this renunciation will enjoy, in personality-creation and expression, a greater happiness.

INDEX

ℜ Index ℜ

Index